THE THINGS THAT MATTER

Essays Inspired by the Later Work of Jacques Maritain

THE AMERICAN MARITAIN ASSOCIATION
BOOK SERIES • VOLUME 28

AMERICAN MARITAIN ASSOCIATION BOOK SERIES

Since 1988, when the American Maritain Association Book Series was founded by Anthony O. Simon, the American Maritain Association has annually published a collection of essays based largely (although not exclusively) on papers presented at its international meetings. The many volumes of the series range over the entire span of themes and problems found not only in Maritain's writings but also in those of St. Thomas Aquinas, and are intended for specialists and non-specialists, alike. In Maritain we find a Thomist who is fully engaged with his times and an encouragement to do the same with our own. So encouraged, these volumes are offered in the same spirit of friendship for which Jacques and his wife, Raïssa, had so notable a genius.

THE THINGS THAT MATTER

Essays Inspired by the Later Work of Jacques Maritain

EDITED BY HEIDI M. GIEBEL

AMERICAN MARITAIN ASSOCIATION

Distributed by

THE CATHOLIC UNIVERSITY OF AMERICA PRESS

Washington, D.C.

Manufactured in the United States of America

Distributed by the Catholic Univesity of America Press
620 Michigan Avenue, N.E., 240 Leahy Hall
Washington, D.C. 20064

Library of Congress Cataloging-in-Publication Data
Names: Giebel, Heidi Marie, editor.
Title: The things that matter : essays inspired by the
later work of Jacques Maritain / edited by Heidi M. Giebel.
Description: Washington, D.C. : American Maritain Association, [2018] |
Series: The American Maritain Association book series ; volume 28 |
Includes bibliographical references and index.
Identifiers: LCCN 2018033774 | ISBN 9780997220506 (alk. paper)
Subjects: LCSH: Maritain, Jacques, 1882–1973.
Classification: LCC B2430.M34 T485 2018 | DDC 194—dc23
LC record available at https://lccn.loc.gov/2018033774

Dedicated to my son James:
May your own untrammeled approach to life
bring lasting joy.

Contents

Acknowledgments

My heartfelt thanks are due to many: first and most obviously, to each of the contributors for an outstanding essay. I am deeply grateful to several anonymous reviewers for their comments on dozens of submissions, which helped me to make some difficult decisions, and to series editor Giuseppe Butera and previous volume editor Travis Dumsday for their helpful guidance. Many thanks are also due to my graduate assistant Angela Drennen for her efficient and skillful copy editing work (and to my department chair Matthews Grant for supplying the funds to hire her). I thank Anne Kachergis of Kachergis Book Design for the beautiful cover design and typesetting. And I am most grateful to my husband Jerry for patiently supporting yet another project for which I didn't really have the extra time but which I thought—correctly this time!—would be really fun. Above all, and as always, *Deo gratias.*

HEIDI M. GIEBEL

Introduction

The Things that Matter

IN THE LAST YEAR OF HIS LONG LIFE, eminent Thomist philosopher Jacques Maritain prepared a final book for publication: a collection of previously unpublished writings entitled *Approaches sans entraves,* later translated into English as *Untrammeled Approaches.* That collection, both in its conversational yet reverent tone and in its weighty topics—faith, love, truth, beauty—gives the reader the sense that she is receiving from a great teacher and friend the most important nuggets of wisdom for the next generation. Throughout the book, Maritain shares with his readers, from his heart as well as his intellect, regarding the things that really matter; that book—and those things—are the primary inspiration for the present volume.

This volume, comprised of original essays by twenty English-speaking Thomists on the occasion of the twentieth anniversary of *Untrammeled Approaches'* first English appearance, explores several of Maritain's still-untrammeled (or at least less-trammeled) themes. While following his unbeaten paths, the contributing authors find and refine hidden treasures at every turn. They develop some of his more speculative ideas regarding the spiritual world—including the last things, the fate of the fallen angels, and a possible angelic role in evolution. They reflect deeply on a few of Maritain's recurring themes: for example, the nature of beauty and intuition. They analyze the implications—positive and negative—of Maritain's philosophy of love, marriage, and sexuality. And they consider and apply his arguments regarding appropriate roles and interactions of Church and state. Finally, they step back for a big-picture view of Maritain, his thought, and his enduring relevance.

We begin, as Maritain did, with the ending: his reflections on the last things, the topic of this volume's first part. In the opening essay, "Maritain's Eschatological Reverie," Lawrence Feingold discusses the essay with which Maritain began *Untrammeled Approaches*. In particular, he considers Maritain's arguments—among the last of their kind—for the fittingness of a permanent state of limbo for unbaptized infants. As Feingold notes, Maritain supposes that those in limbo love God and have their wills permanently conformed to His, and thus seem to have supernatural faith via instruction in salvation history by the angels. Thus, his position already implies that they should have an unconditional desire for the beatific vision, and they have no obstacle to receiving God's grace. Further, since Maritain imagined (or "dreamed") in the same essay that the damned would though God's mercy be released from the lower regions of hell into limbo, Feingold suggests that it would have been quite fitting for Maritain to suppose—though he did not—that the unbaptized infants, through a seemingly less-radical act of mercy, are granted the grace necessary to enter heaven.

Also taking his inspiration from Maritain's "Beginning with a Reverie," Travis Dumsday focuses in his essay "Maritain on Limbo and Demonic Beatitude" on the fate of the damned: Maritain imagines that even the fallen angels will eventually be liberated to the natural beatitude of limbo. This position, as Dumsday points out, has its difficulties: for example, how can one enjoy natural beatitude while acknowledging that she has culpably missed out on its higher, supernatural version? Maritain's speculations are also in some tension with a Thomistic argument for the existence of purgatory—i.e., that since those in hell cannot be helped by our prayers, purgatory is necessary to explain Scriptural references to prayers for the dead—and with Aquinas's angelology, according to which angelic wills are not mutable. However, Dumsday also highlights some intriguing parallels between Maritain's ideas regarding limbo and those of several Orthodox theologians—parallels that certainly seem to merit further exploration.

The second part of the volume engages with Maritain's thought on intuition and aesthetics. Incoming American Maritain Association president James Hanink leads off with "Being, Beauty, and Converging Intuition," which focuses on Maritain's position regarding the pivotal role an intuition of being plays in metaphysical thought. After defending Maritain's view from recent objections, Hanink offers a new argument for the importance of an intuition of being, based on Maritain's (and Aquinas's) theory of beauty—which theory he also defends against objections. Because beauty is (along with goodness and truth) a transcendental, Hanink argues, it is convertible with being itself; thus, by having an intuition of beauty, we also have an intuition of being.

Taking "Eschatological Ideas," Maritain's foreword to *Untrammeled Approaches,* as her starting point and drawing from several of his writings on the topic, Megan Furman's essay, "The Place of Poetry in Human Blessedness," distills an understanding of "poetry" from Maritain's work in aesthetics and epistemology and then considers it within the context of his moral philosophy. Based on intuitive reason working "in vital connection with imagination and emotion," poetic knowledge in Maritain's sense is "the intellectual activity proper to artistic creativity in the realm of the fine arts." Furman argues that, as Maritain understands it, poetic knowledge has a special role to play in human blessedness: through its cognitive aspect, it participates in God's knowledge; while in its creative aspect, it participates in His governance.

Gregory Kerr explores Maritain's theory of intuitivity and its influence on American novelist Flannery O'Connor in his essay "The Centrality of Intuition: Jacques Maritain and Flannery O'Connor." For both writers, as Kerr explains, intuition allows us to expand our knowledge of reality beyond the limits of discursive reasoning. After presenting Maritain's emphasis on intuitivity for gaining a fuller picture of reality, and contrasting that approach with the more linear and limited method of philosophers like Descartes, Kerr discusses Flannery O'Connor's exemplification of Maritain's aesthetic ideas. In particular, he notes her use of distortion or transfiguration of appearances to show a hidden truth, the penetration of her vision beyond the surface of reality, and her intuitive insight into the "texture of existence." This insight, as O'Connor herself recognized, confronts the reader with the mysteries of humanity—mysteries often obscured by a merely scientific point of view.

The book's third part focuses on the topic of biological evolution, its causes, and its spiritual effects. First, Marie George explores Maritain's suggestion of a possible angelic role in species differentiation in her essay entitled "What Are We to Make of Maritain's View that Angels are Intermediary Causes in Evolution?" In considering whether, for example, beneficial "chance" mutations may be a result of angelic activity, George addresses arguments for and against intelligent design; finding that such arguments on both sides are inconclusive, leaving room for angelic activity but not necessitating it, she turns to fittingness-based arguments for and against the angels' involvement in producing new species. Drawing primarily from the work of Aquinas, George finds that such involvement is indeed fitting for two reasons: first, it is fitting that God impart intelligent causation to some of His creatures; and second, angelic contributions to evolution make the universe more interactive and thus more perfect.

In his essay entitled "Maritain, Mascall, Pendergast, and Ashley: Untrammeled Approaches to the Doctrine of Original Sin from an Evolutionary Perspective," Mark Moes also takes Maritain's ideas regarding the role of angels in evolution as his starting point. He then turns to speculations by Eric Mascall, Richard Pendergast, and Benedict Ashley on that topic and its implications for our understanding of the doctrine of original sin: Mascall suggests that pain and disorder in nature may be attributable to the angelic Fall rather than entirely to the Fall of humans; Pendergast speculates that the human condition of original sin consists not just of absence of grace but also of susceptibility to evils predating humans in the natural order; and Ashley provides several arguments—from both theology and science—for the existence of intelligent, conflicting spiritual beings. Finally, Moes considers Maritain's discussion of the doctrine of original sin, also in *Untrammeled Approaches*; utilizing the work of Anthony Zimmerman, he proposes an interpretation of original sin and concupiscence that harmonizes the thought of Maritain and the other three thinkers: due to the angelic Fall, our animal (biological) inheritance includes psychic disorder; due to the human Fall, such disorder cannot be overcome except by grace.

In the fourth section of the volume, we turn to the nature and meaning of love, marriage, and sexuality. First, in "The Meaning of Sex Differences and Marriage in Maritain," Michael Pakaluk considers Maritain's view of human sexuality and marriage, contrasting it with the classical Aristotelian-Thomistic view. In his analysis, Pakaluk differentiates three main questions: sex *determination* (What causes a developing human being to become male or female?); sex *difference* (What is the distinction between male and female, and what does it mean?); and *procreation* (How is sex difference connected with procreation?). Pakaluk argues that Maritain misunderstands the classical answers to these questions, which are significantly less "sexist" than is often supposed. Further, he contends that Maritain's own alternative response—which includes claims that the sexes share differently in the qualities of human nature and that the highest sort of marital love transmutes and transcends romance and sexuality—is not an improvement upon the classical one.

Matthew Minerd proposes a more favorable interpretation of Maritain's view in "Maritain and the Metaphysics of Sexual Differentiation": Although he notes that Maritain sometimes seems to speak of matter as though it were in opposition to personality, he suggests we view Maritain's words through the lens of his remarks on the historical destiny of human beings. "In order to be truly human," Minerd summarizes, "sexual differentiation must bear the mark of the intentional/moral existence that we exhibit in our activity as historical and cultural beings"; thus men and women are complementary not merely for purposes of reproduction but "at the very root of our individual immaterial natures." He concludes his essay with reflections on the role of precreation and the family for preserving, stewarding, and extending humanity's moral and cultural life.

In his essay "Matter, Spirit, and Teleology in Human Generation," Nikolaj Zunic takes inspiration from "Towards a Thomist Idea of Evolution," developing Maritain's ideas regarding human generation to form an argument against the use of *in vitro* fertilization. After critiquing common arguments in the procedure's favor, which assume a materialist account of human beings, Zunic presents the classical case for a hylomorphic understanding of human nature before turning to Maritain's work. Maritain defends the Aristotelian-Thomistic account, whereby rational ensoulment takes place not at fertilization but late in pregnancy. Finding arguments against this view unpersuasive despite their proponents' admirable motivation to safeguard the dignity of fetal human beings, Zunic agrees with Maritain that to attribute a rational soul to an early human embryo would violate the Aristotelian (and commonsense) principle of fittingness. He finds promise in Maritain's distinction between formal and *virtual* (i.e., "in power") possession of human nature, arguing that the latter is sufficient to establish the early human's dignity—and thus the wrongness of treating it as a product rather than as a person, as occurs in technological reproduction. Zunic concludes by reflecting on the teleological nature of human generation—which, he argues, is also violated by *in vitro* fertilization.

In the fifth section of this book, we turn to matters of faith and the

Church, including the priesthood, the spiritual life, and the work of two recent popes. Romanus Cessario, O.P. begins our reflections on these weighty topics with his essay entitled "Sacrifice and Priesthood: Maritain's Still *Untrammeled Approaches*." He begins by noting the prescience of Maritain's critique of directions that Catholic theology took after the Second Vatican Council: downplaying the sacrifice of the Mass and overemphasizing the priesthood of the laity; he then points to parallels—recognized by Maritain himself—between Maritain's work and discussions that took place in the Church after the Council of Trent. Cessario provides an overview of post-Tridentine debates regarding the precise nature of the Eucharistic sacrifice before turning to Maritain's own explanation, according to which at the Mass we are "present at the sacrifice of the cross as it is eternally preserved in heaven." Finally, he turns to Maritain's theology of the priesthood as having grandeur in its ministerial function—particularly enactment of Christ's sacrifice—rather than in its being a more perfect state of life than that of the laity. Although Maritain's ideas regarding these topics raise questions of their own, Cessario concludes that they deserve our attention—and that they rightly direct us to affirm the dignity of the priesthood.

In "Towards an Aristotelian Prologue to the Spiritual Life: Ecclesial Themes in Maritain and Aquinas," Heather M. Erb focuses on three themes in Jacques Maritain's writings: the Church as (1) a transcendent, eternal Person, (2) the life of the blessed, and (3) the spotless Bride of Christ. These themes, she argues, give insight into the final causes of the spiritual life—drawing us to greater holiness, participation in the life of the Church, and, ultimately, beatitude. Noting that Aquinas's Aristotelian prologues tend to organize the subject matter around the four causes of being, Erb also finds among the Aristotelian elements in Aquinas's mystical theology insights regarding the remaining three causes of spiritual growth, human nature and its powers being the material cause, the supernatural virtues and Gifts along with the grace that sustains them being the formal causes, and God Himself being the principal efficient cause.

In "Ratzinger on Faith, Philosophy, and Trust," Alice Ramos takes Joseph Cardinal Ratizinger's work *Faith and the Future* as a starting point, arguing that his perspective on faith as existential trust—trust in a Person, rather than merely a system of belief—is vital for understanding the meaning of faith in the contemporary world. After considering Ratzinger's view and its implications, Ramos turns to Aquinas's work on faith and hope, and to the reasons for unbelief (distrust) in today's world—including moral failures such as pride and covetousness—before presenting the lives of Jacques and Raïssa Maritain as examples of faith as existential trust. Their sincere quest for truth and meaning led them to realize, through the influence of Bergson, that it could be found and that it could include the supernatural. Through the influence of Bloy and other believers, they also immersed themselves in Christian experience, which ignited their minds and imaginations and ultimately led them to trust God with their lives. Ramos concludes with a brief reflection on the implications of Ratzinger's account—and the Maritains' exemplification of it—for the role of beauty and narrative in contemporary Christian philosophy and apologetics.

The final essay in this section on matters of faith is "Canticle: Maritain, John Paul II, Benedict XVI" by John J. Conley, S.J. Noting the twentieth-century surge in popularity of writings on the *Song of Songs* despite its relative neglect by theologians in preceding centuries, Conley explores the uses of this biblical book by Maritain, John Paul II, and Benedict XVI. Maritain insists on a purely supernatural interpretation of the text, using it to support his doctrinal arguments regarding the infallibility and moral impeccability of the Church. In striking contrast to Maritain's interpretation, John Paul II uses the *Song of Songs* in a much more literal way: to explain legitimate and illegitimate expressions of human sexuality. And Benedict XVI's analysis of the book shows the parallel between the erotic desire of spouses and the desire of the believing soul for union with God. What unites their divergent interpretations, Conley argues, is an "ecclesial hermeneutical perspective." Despite their differences, all three authors effectively use their interpretations of *Song of Songs* to address crises of faith and morals.

Next we turn to Maritain's thought on politics and society. In the first essay of this section, "Toward a Grammar of Liberation: Exploring the Contours of Salvation in the Twenty-First Century," Canadian Maritain Association president Walter Schultz explores connections and contrasts between Maritain's writings on salvation history—and its relation to the concrete historical ideals of various epochs—and those of liberation theologian Gustavo Gutiérrez. He notes Maritain's observation of a concrete historical ideal in modern times: holy freedom, which succeeded the medieval notion of a holy empire and placed more emphasis on personal dignity. On Maritain's account, freedom is fulfilled through giving of the self—the unique, indispensable person—through love in family and community. Thus, Schultz suggests, Maritain may have been prescient in detecting a corresponding new historical ideal beginning to take shape at the end of the twentieth century: that of "the holy community united in peace through the grace of God"—an ideal of inclusive, voluntary cooperation opposed to "bourgeois liberalism." Schultz finds in several recent developments, organizations, and movements the seeds of this new ideal of global community; he notes, however, that Maritain would resist the common tendency to overemphasize class struggle but would instead return to Christian emphasis on love and forgiveness.

Michael D. Breidenbach considers two of Maritain's political works, *Man and the State* and *The Things that are Not Caesar's*, in "Jacques Maritain and Leo XIII on the Problem of Church-State Relations." Breidenbach clarifies Maritain's position on relations between Church and state, defending its compatibility with the teaching of Leo XIII against recent criticisms by Thomas Pink, who has taken exception to Maritain's claim that contemporary separation of the religious and political spheres exemplifies the Gospel standard of distinction between God's and Caesar's domains. Although Pink fails to take account of context and of other statements of Maritain's position, Breidenbach argues, he does raise important questions regarding the relationship between principles and practical realities in Church-state relations. As Breidenbach interprets him, Maritain saw the Leonine teaching, in which the Church-state relation is analogous to the body-soul relation, as expressive of a more perfect realization of absolute principles regarding Church and state—and the modern democratic separation of powers as an application of those principles in a more difficult context.

In "'All the Articulations of the Real': Jacques Maritain on Catholic Social Teaching," William McCormick, S.J., explores the relationship between Catholic social teaching as taught by the Church's Magisterium and as studied academically. He finds in Maritain's "The Spiritual Conditions for Progress and Peace"—a speech he gave to UNESCO in 1966 and included in *Untrammeled Approaches*—the resources to sketch an answer to that question. Drawing from Maritain's claim that the temporal task of the spiritual is inspiration, education, and cultural renewal, McCormick sees the role of both Magisterial and academic Catholic social teaching as seeking "to inspire in the temporal an awareness of the dignity and primacy of the human." He finds helpful guidance in Maritain's work, including emphasis on prayer and spiritual depth as a foundation for Catholic social teaching—and exhortation to scholars of Catholic social teaching to live out what they teach and to found political efforts in love.

In this volume's final section, we step back a bit to look at the big picture of Maritain's life and work: its unity, influences, and significance. The authors' style in these last three essays is reminiscent of Maritain's own in many of the essays collected in *Untrammeled Approaches*, interspersing personal reflections with philosophical insights and observations. Mario D'Souza leads this section with "The Unity of Thought in Jacques Maritain," in which he finds in the impressive edifice of Maritain's work the unifying themes of contemplation and the dignity of the human person. In Maritain's thought on education, we also find (some) philosophical unity among the various branches of knowledge. D'Souza concludes with reflections on the significance of Maritain's educational philosophy, its relation to unity of knowledge and of the person, and its enduring implications.

Michael Novak explores Maritain's spiritual and intellectual influences in his essay "The Crucial Role of Léon Bloy in the Maritains' Catholicism." In this short essay, Novak briefly recounts Jacques and Raïssa Maritain's early existential despair and suicide pact and their disenchantment with both skeptical science and bourgeoisie religion before turning to their initial meeting with Bloy, which they experienced as an encounter with pure spirit. His spiritual vigor—and his disdain for bourgeois religion—helped them to see Catholicism as a live option. Although the Maritains were quite at home with rationality and argumentation, Novak points out, it was not these that ultimately won their conversion; it was rather the living witness of Bloy, their godfather, whose love for God and thirst for holiness was an inspiration to them—and, through their lives and work, including their own accounts of his influence, he continues to be an inspiration for all of us.

Finally, the volume ends on a fitting note with "'*Un Bras d'Athlète et Une Haute Voix de Lamentateur*': Why I Love Jacques Maritain," in which then out-going American Maritain Association president Michael Torre offers a reflection on how Jacques Maritain has been an inspiration in his own life and work. He begins by telling the story of his own conversion from agnosticism to Catholicism—like Maritain's journey, Torre's required the removal of intellectual obstacles but was primarily fueled by living examples of Christian love. In his life and work as a Catholic philosopher, Torre—no doubt also speaking on this point for his fellow AMA members and contributors to this volume—continues in many ways to find Maritain worthy of emulation. In particular, Torre highlights Maritain's adherence to holy tradition, his practice of Christian philosophy with a genuinely philosophical method, his engagement with science and culture, his thoughtful treatment of controversial topics and, ultimately, his love for Christ and the Church—and his care, via accessible philosophical arguments, for all those still outside Christ's fold.

I

LAST THINGS FIRST

LAWRENCE FEINGOLD

Maritain's Eschatological Reverie and the Fittingness of Limbo

I. Introduction

JACQUES MARITAIN explores the question of limbo—the ultimate fate of those who die before the age of reason without Baptism—briefly and in imaginative form in the eschatological reverie that opens *Untrammeled Approaches*.[1] This reverie is quite interesting for two reasons. First, it is one of the last defenses, together with that of his close friend Charles Journet,[2] of the fittingness of the traditional doctrine of limbo. Secondly and far less traditionally, he dreams that the hell of the damned will eventually be emptied into limbo. I will focus here principally on his presentation of the fittingness of the state of unbaptized infants in limbo, and conclude by briefly examining his proposal for the conversion of the damned. I will suggest that it would be more fitting to reverse Maritain's reverie, hoping for a miraculous intervention of God not on behalf of the damned, but rather on behalf of those who die unbaptized before the age of reason.

The reader should remember that Maritain himself considered his thought here to be tentative, especially with regard to his speculations on hell. At first he only distributed a few copies of this essay,[3] and he chose the literary form of a dream rather than a more sober style of argumentation.

1. Jacques Maritain, *Untrammeled Approaches*, translated by Bernard Doering (Notre Dame, Indiana: University of Notre Dame Press, 1997).

2. Charles Journet, *La volonté divine salvifique sur les petits enfants* (Bruges: Desclée de Brouwer, 1958).

3. See Maritain, *Untrammeled Approaches*, 3, which states that thirty copies of this essay were

Maritain warns the reader that he is not offering a theological hypothesis, supported by argumentation, with regard to the Last Things, but rather a conjectural and imaginative reverie to explore hopes and possibilities.[4] Someone might object that this is not the proper way to do theology. I would agree in general, but nevertheless an imaginative reverie like this has value for two reasons. First, in order for the doctrine of the Last Things to be the catalyst for the Christian life, these realities have to be presented in a way that imprints itself on the imagination so as to attract the heart. Every Christian culture has to produce imaginative representations of the Last Things. Dante's *Inferno* and Michelangelo's "Last Judgment" are great examples. Secondly, the format of the reverie gives Maritain the freedom to play with the question of fittingness with regard to Last Things, and express ideas that are more tentative and adventurous.

II. Maritain's Presentation of Limbo

Maritain pictures the world of the Last Things as a planet divided into two hemispheres: one receives endless sunlight, while the other is in endless night. He discusses the freedom of the blessed to glorify God through the celebration of His creation. Maritain imagines this way of giving glory to God as a kind of artistic enterprise of narrating the *magnalia Dei*, reciting and celebrating the great epic of God's work in salvation history: "They communicate with the angels in endless revelations; they and the angels tell one another the history of this poor world and of all the fragile deeds immortalized in their holy memories. Of all that has been done, nothing is lost; all is poetry and song."[5] This is a beautiful idea, illustrating the axiom that grace does not destroy nature but elevates and perfects it. Eternity does not destroy history but elevates it to an eternal contemplation.

Limbo is in the hemisphere of night but is illuminated by brilliant constellations and the reflected light of a moon. This alludes to contemplation of God through the mirror of creation. Maritain begins his reverie on the hemisphere of night with the limbo of the just, the place where the souls that died in a state of grace before Good Friday awaited their redemption.

---

distributed in 1939 and again in 1961, before finally being published in 1973, the year of Maritain's death.

4. Ibid.

5. In *Untrammeled Approaches*, 14, Maritain speaks of limbo as "the state of pure nature raised to its highest degree."

This limbo came to an end on Holy Saturday when Christ "harrowed" hell and gave the vision of God to all those who dwelt there.[6] Maritain's concern, however, is not with the limbo of the just, which ended long ago, but with the limbo of the children, who died with original sin but no personal sins. They alone are left in limbo after the harrowing of hell. Maritain, with the common tradition of the preceding centuries, thinks of this limbo as a state without end, and it is the main focus of his reflection.

This limbo is populated by those who died without Baptism (or its Old Testament type, which is circumcision) before reaching the age of reason. Maritain imagines that they sleep until the Resurrection of the body, and then they awaken to a natural happiness, in which the only penalty of original sin is the privation of the beatific vision, so that they eternally remain in the order of nature alone, "of a nature now preserved from all fault."[7] Their resurrection is seen to be a kind of "repercussion" from Christ's Resurrection:

> At that moment they will awaken, not to the Beatific Vision, but to the life of nature and natural happiness. As soon as they are again united with their now incorruptible flesh—risen, not in the virtue of the resurrection of the Savior, but through a kind of over-splash or repercussion from it, setting in motion the miracle of the natural order (supernatural *quoad modum*) called for by the natural incompleteness of the separated soul—then, these human persons now and forever fixed in the right direction will produce, in the discontinuous time proper to spirits, their first deliberate act; and this act will bear on their last end, it will—in the natural order—constitute God as the end of all their action; they will love God more than themselves, with a natural love that is perfect in its kind, incapable of attaining to community of life with God, but which will nevertheless cherish more than all else the All itself.[8]

This natural happiness, although it belongs to the natural order, is different from any happiness we experience on earth because it occurs in a terminal rather than in a pilgrim state, and thus involves the security and tranquility of knowing that it can never be lost. The terminal state involves the will being fixed in its final end. Here the final end is a natural contemplation

6. See Maritain, *Untrammeled Approaches*, 12: "One day eternity was shaken, the soul of their Savior comes like a May breeze to set them free; ... and rushing into the blessed vision, they leave behind in the land of Limbo the souls of those little children who died without the sacraments."

7. Maritain, *Untrammeled Approaches*, 14.

8. Ibid., 13–14.

of God, known by analogy through creatures, together with a natural love for Him above all things.[9] In this terminal state the will never chooses anything incompatible with this end.

III. St. Thomas's Two Hypotheses Concerning the Knowledge of the Souls in Limbo

Maritain's presentation of limbo attempts to be faithful to the teaching of St. Thomas on this subject, combining elements from Aquinas's two articles on limbo, one written at the beginning of his career (*In II Sent.*, d. 33, q. 2, a. 2) and the other from his maturity (*De malo*, q. 5, a. 3).[10] In both cases, St. Thomas vigorously defends the thesis that there is no interior suffering or sorrow in this state. The reason for this is that a terminal suffering, no matter how light, is a fitting penalty only for unrepented and grave personal sin, and those in limbo are there only because they died with original sin, which is the pure privation of sanctifying grace. Thus, it is fitting that those who die with only original sin should suffer a penalty that is the privation of the vision of God due to their lack of sanctifying grace but nothing more. Since there was no personal sin, there should be no personal suffering as a penalty, no matter how light.[11] This generates a very difficult theological problem. How could those in limbo not suffer an interior sorrow on account of the loss of the beatific vision?

There are two possible avenues to tackle the question. Either those in limbo know what they have lost, or they do not. Depending on how one answers this initial question, the explanation of the lack of interior sorrow will take two different forms. Interestingly, St. Thomas tried both possibili-

9. For the notion of a natural love of God above all things in Aquinas, see *In III Sent.*, d. 27, q. 2, a. 2, ad 4; ST I, q. 60, a. 5, ad 4; q. 62, a. 2, ad 1; q. 63, a. 1, ad 3; I-II, q. 62, a. 1, ad 3; q. 109, a. 3, ad 1. See also Lawrence Feingold, *The Natural Desire to See God According to St. Thomas and His Interpreters*, 2nd ed. (Naples, Florida: Sapientia Press of Ave Maria University, 2010), 416–21.

10. On St. Thomas's theory of limbo, its sources, context, and influence, see Serge-Thomas Bonino, "The Theory of Limbo and the Mystery of the Supernatural in St. Thomas Aquinas," in *Surnaturel: A Controversy at the Heart of Twentieth-Century Thomistic Thought* edited by Bonino, translated by Robert Williams (Ave Maria, Florida: Sapientia Press of Ave Maria University, 2009), 117–54.

11. See St. Thomas, *In II Sent.*, d. 33, q. 2, a. 1 (my translation): "As the sin was not through their own operation, it follows that the penalty should not be through their own suffering, but only through the lack of that for which nature itself was insufficient. In other perfections and goods that follow on the principles of human nature, those damned on account of original sin will suffer no loss."

ties.[12] His earlier treatment supposes that they would know the fundamental outline of salvation history, and that they would thus know what they lost, but they do not grieve over it because their wills are permanently constituted in conformity with the divine will.[13] Thus there is no possibility for sin in this state, nor any possibility to rebel against the divine plan or grieve over it on account of its resulting in their deprivation of the beatific vision, because they will recognize that the vision is immeasurably above their own proportionality:

> It should be realized that if someone lacks that which exceeds his proportionality, he will not be afflicted, if he follows right reason. He will only be afflicted if he lacks that to which in some way he was proportioned. No wise man is afflicted that he cannot fly like a bird, or that he is not king or emperor, since such things are not due to him. He would be afflicted, however, if he were deprived of something which in some way he had an aptitude to possess. Therefore I say that every man having the use of free will was proportioned to achieving eternal life, because he could prepare himself for grace, by which he would be able to merit eternal life. Therefore, if he fails to achieve this he will have a maximum sorrow for having lost something that could have been his. However, the children [who died before the age of reason without baptism] were never proportioned to having eternal life, because this was not due them from the principles of their nature since it exceeds all the powers of nature, nor could they accomplish personal acts by which they could have attained so great a good. Therefore, they will not sorrow at all because they lack the vision of God; rather, they will rejoice in the fact that they participate greatly in the divine goodness in their natural perfections.[14]

In his response to the fifth objection, St. Thomas says that the souls in limbo should not be considered to be deprived of beatitude in that they are perpetually separated from God,[15] for he indicates that there are two grades

12. Scotus, in his treatment of limbo, *Ordinatio* II, d. 33, q. un., n. 4 [13], also presents both of these alternative explanations.

13. This type of solution, using the notion of wise resignation, was defended by St. Bonaventure in *In II Sent.*, d. 33, q. 3, a. 2, ad 2 (797b), and by St. Albert in *Quaestio de poena parvulorum sine baptismo decedentium*, a. 1, in *Opera omnia*, vol. 25/2 (Aschendorff, 1993), 141, lines 10–19 (my translation): "Since these children have the rectitude of reason, they are not afflicted by the fact that they lack the vision of God, since they know they could not have had it and that they lack it not because of their own fault, but justly."

14. *In II Sent.*, d. 33, q. 2, a. 2 (my translation).

15. *In II Sent.*, d. 33, q. 2, a. 2, ad 5: "Although the unbaptized children are separated from God with regard to that union which is through glory, they are nevertheless not wholly separated from Him. On the contrary, they are united to Him through a participation in natural goods, and thus they will also be able to rejoice in Him through natural knowledge and love."

of union with God: through natural goods and through glory. The souls in limbo are deprived of the union with God through glory, but they are still united with Him through a "participation in natural goods," in which they will rejoice in a natural knowledge and love of God.

In the later work, *De malo*, q. 5, a. 3, St. Thomas explains the lack of sorrow by another path, which is their lack of knowledge of the supernatural order:

> We say that the souls of children are not without natural knowledge proper to a separated soul according to its nature, but are without supernatural knowledge.... Now it pertains to natural knowledge that the soul knows it was created for happiness and that happiness consists in the attainment of the perfect good. But that that perfect good for which man was made is that glory which the saints possess is beyond natural knowledge. Hence the Apostle says in 1 Cor 2:9 that "Eye has not seen.... But to us God has revealed them through His Spirit," which revelation pertains to faith. And therefore the souls of children do not know that they are deprived of such a good, and do not grieve on this account; but this knowledge which they have by nature, they possess without sorrow.[16]

IV. Difficulties in Both Hypotheses

Both solutions involve grave difficulties. The second solution, to my mind, is clearly more consistent, but that consistency creates its own difficulty. The consistency lies in picturing the state of limbo as a purely natural state in which all knowledge of the supernatural order is absent—and thus they have no supernatural faith, hope, or charity—whereas they have a perfect knowledge of natural theology and a natural love of God above all things.

Although this solution is elegant and clear, it is problematic because it presupposes that the souls in limbo will be entirely ignorant of the true shape of human history, which in fact is salvation history. It seems that a key element of natural happiness for a rational being is a true understanding of one's own identity, origin, and place in human society and history, and in God's plan. We know that orphans suffer from a lack of knowledge of their biological parents. We all have a proportionate natural desire to understand our place in the world and in society and history. This later solution of St. Thomas does not provide for such knowledge to be possessed

16. *De malo*, q. 5, a. 3 (my translation).

by these children, for human history and destiny cannot be understood without knowledge of the supernatural order. It seems that such a proportionate natural desire to know one's true origins, family history, and proper destiny, could not remain unfulfilled in a true state of natural happiness. Parents of children who died before Baptism (as in a miscarriage), for example, are distressed by the thought those children may never be united to them, through no fault of their own.

In other words, the purely natural state that St. Thomas is suggesting as the state of souls in limbo is not at all equivalent to the well-known hypothesis of a "state of pure nature."[17] For in a "state of pure nature" human beings would rightly understand themselves as living in a purely natural order with its own proper history and development, in which their family history would be situated. Here the inhabitants of limbo are actually living in a supernatural economy with a supernatural history of salvation, of which they would be entirely ignorant, and thus they would be mistaken about who they are and unable to understand their own history. That would not be the case at all in a hypothetical "state of pure nature." Thus, one could without inconsistency maintain that God could have made human beings without elevating them to the supernatural order,[18] and yet maintain that a purely natural state for human beings in this concrete order (limbo) would not be fitting.

I am presupposing here that the notion of natural happiness implies the fulfillment of all natural desire that is *proportionate* to the principles of human nature and its natural powers. Not all natural desires are proportionate to human nature. There is also a natural desire that is *disproportionate* to human nature, which is the natural desire to see God. Supernatural beatitude includes the fulfillment of *all* natural desire, even that which is disproportionate to human nature.[19] The fulfillment of the natural desire to see God thus belongs to supernatural beatitude, because intuitive knowledge of God is infinitely disproportionate to human nature. Knowledge of one's own identity and place in the divine plan, however, would seem

17. See Bonino, "The Theory of Limbo," in *Surnaturel: A Controversy*, 118–19.

18. See Pius XII's encyclical *Humani generis* (1950): no. 26: "Others destroy the gratuity of the supernatural order, since God, they say, cannot create intellectual beings without ordering and calling them to the beatific vision." In Denzinger, *Enchiridion Symbolorum definitionum et declarationum de rebus fidei et morum*, 43rd edition, edited by Peter Hünermann, Robert Fastiggi, and Anne Englund Nash (San Francisco: Ignatius Press, 2012), no. 3891 (hereafter cited as *DS*).

19. See Feingold, *The Natural Desire to See God*, xxxvi–xxxvii, 75, 236, 239, 253, 326, 341–43, 437, 441, 445.

to be proportionate to a rational being who poses the question: "Who am I?" and "What is the meaning of history?" Therefore, the fulfillment of that proportionate natural desire ought to be fulfilled for natural happiness to exist as a terminal state.

Christ truly became man and died for the unbaptized children, as for everyone else.[20] It seems that it would be unfitting for them never to know this fact essential to who they really are in the divine plan. They are beings destined for a supernatural end and persons for whom Christ died. The earlier solution of St. Thomas is better in this regard, I think, because it supposes that the unbaptized children would come to know the true shape of human history, their place in it, and why they are not united with the blessed in seeing God.

It is interesting that Maritain seems to follow the logic of the earlier treatment of St. Thomas,[21] even though he leaves open the possibility of the later solution. Maritain imagines that the children in limbo know what they have lost through Adam but are not envious of their blessed brothers and sisters. Furthermore, he thinks that they *know and love Jesus with a natural love* and are taught by the angels about salvation history:

> They are not envious, and having themselves everything to which their nature as such can lay claim, they rejoice rather in the happiness of the elect, supposing that they are aware of the existence of these elect.... For if not they, at least their happier, blessed, sisters have profited from the redemption which this fall brought about. And they are happy that their sisters are blessed, and they admire and love Jesus, with a natural love—just as they love Beauty and Goodness. And the holy angels—who can cross the chaos, and who like stars illumine the night of Limbo—tell them the stories of Paradise.[22]

Why do they not suffer from knowing what they have lost? This is a crucial question if one accepts St. Thomas's earlier position. Maritain offers three points. First, they know that they are at the summit of the natural order and they enjoy a real natural happiness, which means that their proportionate natural desires are fulfilled. Secondly, although they would have a desire to surpass nature so as to see God, if such a thing were possible, Maritain

20. See the condemnation of the fifth proposition of Cornelius Jansenius, *DS*, 2005: "It is Semipelagian to say that Christ died or shed His blood for all men without exception."

21. Maritain acknowledges the position of *De malo* in *Untrammeled Approaches*, 16n16, and presents it as a positive rethinking, but nevertheless Maritain follows Aquinas's earlier treatment for the most part.

22. Maritain, *Untrammeled Approaches*, 16–17.

sees this to be a conditional desire whose lack of fulfillment would not destroy their happiness.[23] Maritain thus sees an essential difference between the souls in purgatory who, being in a state of grace, have an unconditional desire to see God, and those in limbo who never received grace or faith and thus never desire the vision of God as something proportionate to themselves to which they unconditionally aspire.[24] For, unlike the damned, they know they never were proportioned to the vision of God and did not lose it through their own fault. Third, they are not envious because their wills are permanently conformed with God's will. Neither St. Thomas nor Maritain explain by what means God brings about this perpetual conformity with His will. In the case of the blessed this conformity is caused by the beatific vision, for all who see God face to face can never prefer some other finite good to Him and His plan. But in limbo it is not clear how free will is made perpetually indefectible in the absence of the vision of God.[25]

Furthermore, how could there be a purely natural love of Jesus? Even though he conceives of limbo as a state pertaining entirely to the natural order, Maritain (following St. Thomas's commentary on the *Sentences*) seems to be admitting supernatural knowledge, but not supernatural love. If the souls in limbo know (by faith?) that Jesus died for them on the Cross and has loved them in a mad and superabundant way, how could their love for Him fittingly remain on the purely natural level? In order for them to love Him with a supernatural love, God would have to elevate their wills to a supernatural love by grace, and why would God not want to do that when they are incapable of posing any obstacle to such elevation and are aware that they have been loved above the proportionality of nature?

Furthermore, if they are aware of the outline of salvation history and know Jesus, this must involve supernatural faith, because they do not see God. They would be believing what they cannot see. It is certainly odd that souls in limbo would have faith but without any hope of ever having vision of what they believe.

In other words, if one assumes that the children in limbo have knowl-

23. See Feingold, *The Natural Desire to See God*, 261–76.

24. Maritain, *Untrammeled Approaches*, 16. One difficulty with Maritain's account, however, is that it seems that the persons in limbo would actually have faith, for they receive supernatural knowledge. If they have faith, would this change their natural desire to see God to an unconditional one?

25. The same question can be posed about the souls in purgatory, whose wills are also confirmed in good, but in that case they are confirmed through the power of grace.

edge of what they have lost, there follows not only the problem of how they are not envious, which St. Thomas and Maritain solve by supposing that their wills are perpetually conformed to that of God. A no less difficult problem, to my mind, not addressed either by St. Thomas or Maritain, is why God could fittingly will to give them some supernatural knowledge without giving them supernatural grace, charity, or the beatific vision. He would be giving them the power to know *truths worthy of the deepest adoration, but without giving them the power to love them accordingly*. How would this be for God's greater glory? This hypothesis admits some elements of the supernatural order—such as supernatural knowledge and the perpetual conformity of the will with that of God—into the natural happiness of the persons in limbo, while at the same time denying the most essential elements of the supernatural order, which are sanctifying grace, charity, glory, and ultimately the vision of God.

V. Maritain's Vision of Limbo and the *Catechism of the Catholic Church*

What should we think of Maritain's vision here? The doctrine of limbo as pictured by Maritain brings out well not only the hierarchy of creation, but also the gratuitousness of the supernatural order, the necessity of Baptism as the ordinary means of entrance into the supernatural order, and the fact that the natural desire to see God is not incompatible with the possibility of a proportionate natural happiness, even though that happiness would certainly be *imperfect* in failing to satisfy the natural desire to see God, as I argued in the book, *The Natural Desire to See God.*[26]

It can be regretted, however, that Maritain did not have the benefit of the teaching of the *Catechism of the Catholic Church*. Despite the merits of his position, I prefer the brief words on this subject in no. 1261 of the *Catechism*:

> As regards *children who have died without Baptism*, the Church can only entrust them to the mercy of God, as she does in her funeral rites for them. Indeed, the great mercy of God who desires that all men should be saved, and Jesus' tenderness toward children which caused him to say: "Let the children come to me, do not hinder them," allow us to hope that there is a way of salvation for children who

26. See Feingold, *The Natural Desire to See God*, 266–67, 432.

have died without Baptism. All the more urgent is the Church's call not to prevent little children coming to Christ through the gift of holy Baptism.[27]

It is important to separate distinct questions with regard to limbo. The doctrine of limbo, as understood, for example, by St. Thomas Aquinas and the Thomistic school, is based on five presuppositions. Three points are common to Catholic theology: (1) It is a doctrine of faith that those who die with original sin (alone) cannot attain to the beatific vision. (2) In this economy of salvation, the only ordinary means to obtain forgiveness of original sin is through sacramental Baptism. (3) It is not always necessary to actually receive the sacrament. The forgiveness of original sin is also given by a sincere desire for Baptism (explicit or implicit), or by the Baptism of blood (being killed for Christ). Nevertheless, a desire for Baptism is a personal act, and thus presupposes the use of reason.

St. Thomas also defended two more points. As we have seen, he argued (4) that there will be no penalty of suffering after this life, whether spiritual or sensible, for those who died with no personal sin. (5) Finally, he also held that a purely natural happiness is possible for man (after this life), proportionate to his nature, consisting in the loving contemplation of God, known through His creation.[28] St. Thomas and Maritain think this will be the lot of the infants who die before the age of reason without Baptism.

The *Catechism of the Catholic Church*, no. 1261, is adding a sixth point. We can hope that God, by extra-sacramental means, will give sanctifying grace to infants who die without Baptism, such that they will not die with original sin, and thus will not be deprived of the vision of God for eternity.[29]

27. *Catechism of the Catholic Church*, 2nd ed. (Washington, D.C.: United States Catholic Conference, 2000); emphasis in original. Hereafter cited as *CCC*. The text of *CCC*, no. 1261, is based on the Congregation for the Doctrine of the Faith, Instruction on Infant Baptism *Pastoralis actio* (1980): no. 13: "The Church has thus shown by her teaching and practice that she knows no other way apart from Baptism for ensuring children's entry into eternal happiness. Accordingly, she takes care not to neglect the mission that the Lord has given her of providing rebirth 'of water and the Spirit' for all those who can be baptized. As for children who die without Baptism, the Church can only entrust them to God's mercy, as she does in the funeral rite provided for them."

28. See ST I, q. 62. a. 1; I-II, q. 62, a. 1. See also Feingold, *The Natural Desire to See God*, 231–47.

29. See the International Theological Commission, *The Hope of Salvation for Infants Who Die without Being Baptised* (2007): no. 37, which states that the magisterial statements from the Middle Ages concerning the punishment of those who die with original but without personal sin (such as *DS*, 780, 858, 926, 1349) "do not oblige us to think that these infants necessarily die with original sin, so that there would be no way of salvation for them." In *International Theological*

Even if this does not occur through Baptism of blood because they were not killed for Christ, or through Baptism of desire because they cannot yet make a personal act of desire, it is reasonable to think that it could be granted through the desire of the Church, expressing the desire of Christ who died for those children.

VI. Limbo in the Hierarchy of Creation

One of the most interesting aspects of this reverie is Maritain's reverential presentation of limbo, despite its difficulties, as occupying a key place in the hierarchy of creation, at the summit of the natural order. Without limbo, an important potential degree in the hierarchy of being would never be realized. There would be no actual purely natural happiness as the terminal state in which the natural order in its pure state would be brought to the highest point that it is capable of. He writes:

> What is more exciting for a philosopher, and more instructive, than this fact that the state of pure nature at the best of its own order is the same as that in which, when the flesh has risen … the souls of the children who have died without baptism will be found! It is doubtless for this reason and because in this way *all the degrees of being* will find their fulfillment, that I feel so attached to the notion of Limbo.[30]

He ends his reflection with a similar thought:

> Oh, little children who have died without baptism, rejected though you have never done evil, you are not an accident in the divine economy, a peculiar case from which the theologians, pressed on all sides, extricate themselves as they can, an insignificant parenthesis. Your role is great, and your destiny well determined and very significant. You are the first fruits of natural felicity, of nature divinely restored.[31]

Maritain's position is based on the idea that God maximizes the manifestation of His goodness in creation by realizing many hierarchical and complementary levels of being, rather than limiting Himself just to the higher forms, such as angels. Given this principle of hierarchy, wouldn't it be more

---

Commission: Volume 2: Texts and Documents, 1986–2007, edited by Michael Sharkey and Thomas Weinandy (San Francisco: Ignatius Press, 2009), 374.

30. Maritain, *Untrammeled Approaches*, 16; emphasis added.

31. Ibid., 17. Maritain calls them the "first fruits" because he imagines that they will eventually be joined by the damned who he dares to hope will repent through a divine miracle.

fitting for God to create a world in which there exists not only supernatural beatitude, but also a purely natural terminal state? In other words, wouldn't a world order that includes limbo be more complete?

Some years ago I was defending a position similar to Maritain's concerning the place of limbo in the hierarchy of creation, and a student challenged it by asking me if I would be willing to volunteer to make the sacrifice to occupy that position. Of course no one would or should volunteer for such a destiny.[32] When put in those existential terms, I think it becomes clear that the divine glory is not more magnified by having many souls occupy the terminal position of natural rather than supernatural beatitude.

I would argue that the hierarchy of creation manifested in distinct levels of being is not lost even if no soul is left in limbo. Natural happiness is *included* within supernatural happiness, and thus it will be present for eternity glorifying God by representing a certain form of participation of the divine goodness. The fact that it does not exist in a pure state, but only as a part of supernatural beatitude, does not take away from its ability to glorify God by filling out a level of being at the midpoint of the created order.

Other forms of complementarity do not work in this way. It is good that there are males as well as females, because each represents a complementary way of being human, and they cannot be fittingly combined in one person. It is good that people have different abilities and belong to different cultures, for this causes mutual enrichment. Natural and supernatural beatitude, however, are both immensely perfected when they exist together in the same subject. It is not necessary for this particular kind of complementarity to exist in distinct subjects. On the contrary, supernatural beatitude presupposes the possession of natural happiness as grace presupposes nature and perfects it.

VII. Ordinary and Extraordinary Means of Salvation

The most important argument in favor of limbo is that if God were to mercifully grant salvation to all the unbaptized who die before the age of reason, leaving limbo empty, it would seem that the necessity of Baptism as the ordinary means of salvation would be undermined. This objection can

32. One could, on the other hand, volunteer to have natural misfortunes, such as persecutions, short life, physical handicaps, etc. (as St. Ignatius teaches in his Principle and Foundation), because, as Jesus tells us, all of these could lead to a more perfect supernatural life of grace.

be answered, I think, by considering the distinction between covenantal justice and extra-covenantal mercy. Baptism gives a certainty of salvation through the title of justice, on the basis of God's own fidelity to His covenantal obligations. Those who die before the age of reason without Baptism do not have this title. It is certainly better for the infant to be baptized and thus inserted into the New Covenant with its immense privileges; he is made a son of God and heir of heaven, whom God has obligated Himself to save. In other words, even though salvation is always supremely gratuitous, it is due, in virtue of God's own utterly gratuitous covenant, to those received into the covenant who place no obstacle of mortal sin. Salvation is not *due* in that sense to infants who die without being inserted by Baptism into the New Covenant. That, however, does not mean that we cannot hope that they receive the grace of salvation through God's mercy, for mercy is the foundation of all of God's works.[33]

A similar objection is that if all the unbaptized who die before the age of reason are indeed saved in an extraordinary way through God's mercy, this would confuse the ordinary and extraordinary means, making the extraordinary ordinary. That would be the case if one thought that God was obligated in justice to give supernatural grace and glory to all. Ordinary and extraordinary means of salvation are not confused, however, as long as God's mercy and covenantal justice are clearly distinguished. The extraordinary path is the fruit of mercy alone, whereas the ordinary path is better, because it manifests both mercy and justice.[34]

What would seem more fitting to our limited theological imagination: a creation in which some rational creatures enjoy only natural happiness, because they died without Baptism before the age of reason and thus lacked a title of justice to receive salvation, or one in which the mercy of God supplies what His justice is not obligated to give?

Another related argument in favor of Maritain's view of limbo is that it better demonstrates the gratuitousness of our supernatural end. I would answer that the gratuitousness of grace is not endangered by the lack of a terminal state of purely natural happiness. What guarantees the double gra-

33. See ST I, q. 21, a. 4: "Now the work of divine justice always presupposes the work of mercy; and is founded thereupon."

34. Furthermore, even if God grants supernatural salvation to unbaptized babies, as the *Catechism* invites us to hope, baptized babies who die before the age of reason will have an added glory given by the indelible mark of baptismal character by which they have been sacramentally configured with Christ.

tuitousness of the supernatural order is solely the fact that God *could* have created us in a purely natural state without elevation to the supernatural order.[35] The actual realization of such a state is not necessary for supernatural beatitude to be doubly gratuitous.

VIII. God's Universal Salvific Will

The position of the *Catechism of the Catholic Church*, no. 1261, is favored by the development of the Church's understanding of the full import of God's universal salvific will. God "desires all men to be saved and come to the knowledge of the truth," according to 1 Timothy 2:4. God's universal salvific will is not a mere metaphor, but implies action on God's part to make the means of salvation, merited for all men by Christ, actually available to all.

The universal salvific will was affirmed numerous times by the Second Vatican Council. Perhaps the clearest statement is in *Gaudium et spes*, no. 22. After speaking about how Christ reveals man to himself and has united Himself in a certain manner with every human being, it says, "For, since Christ died for all men, and since the ultimate vocation of man is in fact one, and divine, we ought to believe that the Holy Spirit in a manner known only to God offers to every man the possibility of being associated with this paschal mystery."[36]

The ordinary means by which salvation is made available to all is Baptism. Baptism of blood is available to those who are killed out of hatred of Christ and thus are conformed to His death; baptism of desire is available to all who get to the age of reason through the prevenient action of God's actual grace, calling men to acts of faith, hope, and charity. However, what about people who die before the age of reason and without Baptism? How has God's universal salvific will made possible their salvation, offering them sufficient grace? And if it is made open to them and they can pose no ob-

35. See Pius XII, encyclical *Humani generis*, no. 26. The supernatural is doubly gratuitous because God did not have to create us, but having freely decided to create us, He could have made us for a purely natural end. See ST I–II, q. 111, a. 1, ad 2. See also Feingold, *The Natural Desire to See God*, 384–85, 391, 424.

36. Vatican II, Pastoral Constitution on the Church in the Modern World *Gaudium et spes*, no. 22, in *The Sixteen Documents of Vatican II* (Boston: Pauline Books and Media, 1999), 645. Other relevant conciliar texts are *Gaudium et spes*, no. 19; *Lumen gentium*, nos. 15–16; *Nostra aetate*, no. 1; *Dignitatis humanae*, no. 11; *Ad gentes*, no. 7.

stacle through a contrary and rebellious will (as in the case of the damned), then why should one doubt that God's mercy, under that glorious title, will bring them to salvation by infusing sanctifying grace?

The *Catechism of the Catholic Church* speaks of the necessity of the sacrament of Baptism for those "who have had the possibility of asking for this sacrament."[37] These infants, for whatever reason, have not had that possibility. The *Catechism* also says that "the Church does not know of any means other than Baptism that assures entry into eternal beatitude." However, "*God has bound salvation to the sacrament of Baptism, but he himself is not bound by his sacraments.*"[38]

Baptism is the ordinary means established by God for the forgiveness of original sin, to which He has "bound salvation." Adults can attain the effect of the sacrament through an upright desire for it, but this would not naturally be available to infants. Nevertheless, this text emphasizes that God "is not bound by His sacraments," implying that He can cause the infusion of grace in an infant outside of the sacrament of Baptism.

Let us take an analogy of the apostolic blessing given at the point of death. The Church, from her treasury of merits, offers a plenary indulgence to all the faithful who are properly disposed—that is, if they are in a state of grace and have contrition for their sins—and have prayed during their life. This is given even if no priest is available to impart the apostolic blessing.[39]

If the Church takes care that nothing is left undone for those duly disposed at the point of death, is it not reasonable to hope that God would not fail to withhold what He alone can give, imparting sanctifying grace at the point of death, through the merits of Christ and out of His love for those who are conformed to Him by their innocence, their littleness, and their suffering?

St. Thomas was very concerned to defend the universal salvific will of God with respect to children who died before the promulgation of the Gospel. He argues that the children of Israel received sanctifying grace on

37. CCC, no. 1257; see Mark 16:16.

38. CCC, no. 1257; emphasis in original.

39. Apostolic Penitentiary, *Manual of Indulgences: Norms and Grants* (Washington, D.C.: United States Conference of Catholic Bishops, 2006), 54: "If a priest is unavailable, Holy Mother Church benevolently grants to the Christian faithful, who are duly disposed, a plenary indulgence to be acquired at the point of death, provided they have been in the habit of reciting some prayers during their lifetime; in such a case, the Church supplies for the three conditions ordinarily required for a plenary indulgence."

the eighth day when the boys were circumcised.[40] It seems that the best way to explain how the giving of grace in the Old Testament is tied to circumcision is that circumcision is the visible sign by which males became members of the people of Israel, and salvation was given by God to the members of Israel on the occasion of their incorporation into the People of God.[41] We can suppose therefore that girls were made participants of this grace when they were incorporated into the People of Israel on the celebration of their naming.

But what about the Gentile babies? St. Thomas holds that the grace of God to remit original sin would likely have been given to the children of believers prior to the institution of circumcision. He hypothesizes that this gift would have been given on the occasion of the prayers of parents for the sanctification of their children, according to whatever rite was traditional in their culture:

Just as before the institution of circumcision, faith in Christ to come justified both children and adults, so, too, after its institution. But before, there was no need of a sign expressive of this faith; because as yet believers had not begun to be united together apart from unbelievers for the worship of one God. It is probable, however, that parents who were believers offered up some prayers to God for their children, especially if these were in any danger; or bestowed some blessing on them, as a "seal of faith"; just as the adults offered prayers and sacrifices for themselves.[42]

40. The salvation of the circumcised infants of Israel is maintained by Innocent III, Letter "Maiores Ecclesiae causas" to Archbishop Humbert of Arles, 1201 (*DS*, 780); St. Thomas, ST III, q. 62, a. 6, ad 3: "Grace was conferred in circumcision in so far as it was a sign of Christ's future Passion"; q. 70, a. 4.

41. See Christianus Pesch, *De Sacramentis*, pars 1: *De Sacramentis in genere. De Baptismo. De Confirmatione. De Eucharistia* (Friburgi Brisgoviae: B. Herder, 1914), 76 (my translation): "Being incorporated into the People of God was the condition of sanctification for Israelites. Circumcision was the instrument of incorporation into the People of God. Thus man attained to justification by way of circumcision."

42. St. Thomas, ST III, q. 70, a. 4, ad 2. See also ST III, q. 61, a. 3: "The state of the human race after sin and before Christ can be considered from two points of view. First, from that of faith: and thus it was always one and the same: since men were made righteous, through faith in the future coming of Christ. Secondly, according as sin was more or less intense, and knowledge concerning Christ more or less explicit. For as time went on sin gained a greater hold on man, so much so that it clouded man's reason, the consequence being that the precepts of the natural law were insufficient to make man live aright, and it became necessary to have a written code of fixed laws, and together with these certain sacraments of faith. For it was necessary, as time went on, that the knowledge of faith should be more and more unfolded, since, as Gregory says (Hom. vi in Ezech.): 'With the advance of time there was an advance in the knowledge of Divine things.' Consequently in the old Law there was also a need for certain fixed sacraments significative of man's faith in the future coming of Christ: *which sacraments are compared to those that preceded*

If the grace of justification was given gratuitously and liberally even to pagan infants before the promulgation of the Gospel, it seems reasonable to think that God would still will to give it gratuitously to those not able to receive Baptism. The promulgation of the Gospel should not limit the availability of the infusion of sanctifying grace, but, if anything, enlarge it.

IX. Maritain's Hope for the Conversion of the Damned

Part of Maritain's interest in limbo is his hope that the damned be converted so as to enter there. He begins his vision of hell with the traditional understanding of the damned being fixed in their final will before the moment of death. He sees their state, however, not as inactivity, but precisely as a kind of feverish activity: "They have the religion of work. They build, they organize, and what they build crumbles because of their division and their hatred. But they continue to build and to work without ceasing. They engage incessantly in politics. Their life should not be imagined as very different from our own."[43]

Maritain does not leave the dream there, however. He imagines the blessed appealing from God's justice to His mercy, asking for the damned the grace of repentance. "And why could their prayer not be granted?"[44] He goes on:

> Why could not the excess of their love be the excess of a miracle.... God can make a man out of a stone; He can change bread into the Body of Jesus Christ. It is no more difficult by a miracle to change the will of a man or an angel, to raise up and rectify in its inmost being a will that is dead and confirmed in evil.[45] It is by virtue of the order of nature that the will of the damned is fixed in evil in an absolute and

---

the Law, as something determinate to that which is indeterminate: inasmuch as *before the Law it was not laid down precisely of what sacraments men were to make use: whereas this was prescribed by the Law; and this was necessary both on account of the overclouding of the natural law, and for the clearer signification of faith*." (Emphasis added.)

43. Maritain, *Untrammeled Approaches*, 20. Maritain's vision here is similar to C. S. Lewis's treatment of hell in *The Great Divorce*.

44. Ibid., 21.

45. This assertion seems very problematic, for the conversion of an adult depends not only on an operative grace given, but on our free cooperation with that grace (continuing in the form of cooperative grace). God does not treat our free will like a rock or piece of bread. See Lawrence Feingold, "God's Movement of the Soul through Operative and Cooperative Grace," in *Thomism and Predestination: Principles and Disputations*, edited by Steven A. Long, Roger W. Nutt, and Thomas Joseph White (Ave Maria, Florida: Sapientia Press of Ave Maria University, 2016), 166–91.

> immutable manner. A miracle, and a miracle alone, can change this. I mean leaving them in Hades, and simply transferring them from the abyss to the summits of an eternal Hell.[46]

The most interesting and novel feature of Maritain's *Reverie* is his idea that the inhabitants of hell will be given the grace of conversion so that they will eventually repent and cease rebelling. He does not thereby repeat the position of Origen, who suggests that such a conversion would entail their eventual arrival in heaven, a position condemned in the Fifth Ecumenical Council.[47] Maritain proposes something more modest, dreaming that they would be transferred from the pains of hell into the regions of limbo, conceived as a kind of natural beatitude which is technically still part of hell, because of the eternal deprivation of the vision of God: "No one leaves Hell; ... we are concerned here with no more than a transfer within the infernal regions ... from the abyss to Limbo."

Maritain also clarifies that this cannot be asserted as certain, but can be dreamed: "Who can know this? It depends on the pure divine will. I ask simply: Is it not possible that it take place.... And are we not permitted to hope for this?"[48]

There are various great difficulties with Maritain's proposal concerning the conversion of the damned who are to join the ranks of limbo. The most important problem is that this question, as Maritain emphasizes, depends solely on the divine will, and we know His will only if He reveals it to us.[49] Revelation does not seem to offer any support to this position but rather indicates the contrary, as when Jesus speaks of "hell, where their worm does not die, and the fire is not quenched."[50]

A second problem with Maritain's reverie on the conversion of the damned is that it would imply that the time of trial in which we currently find ourselves is not limited by this life, but has a potentially indefinite extension. Not only does this seem to be contrary to Revelation in Scripture and Tradition, but it also does not seem fitting, for the very notion of a trial in a state of pilgrimage implies that the length of the trial be something determinate, and it is reasonable that this entire earthly life be the

46. Maritain, *Untrammeled Approaches*, 21.
47. See *DS*, 411.
48. Maritain, *Untrammeled Approaches*, 221–22.
49. See ST III, q. 1, a. 3.
50. Mk 9:48. See also Is 66:24 and Luke 16:26.

length of the trial. This trial is given according to the mode of the nature of the rational being, whether angel or human being. The angels were given a trial to merit heaven or hell which lasted one angelic instant. Their trial was based on one initial choice, made in the fullness of angelic knowledge, after which they were either granted the beatific vision or fell into hell. It is fitting for human nature that the trial extend exactly to the whole course of our earthly life in which there is the use of free will. The greatest problem in understanding our earthly life as the time of trial does not concern the damned, but those who never attained the age of reason. In their case, they are spared a personal trial because they were never able to freely cooperate with grace during their earthly life, and thus are entrusted to the prayers of the Church and the mercy of God.[51]

A third problem is that Maritain's proposal relies on a miraculous conversion in which all the damned are eventually converted by an intrinsically efficacious and irresistible grace with which they are necessarily moved and do not freely cooperate. God's action in the damned would be imperiously reversing the fixed order of their wills and changing their final end from self to God. This seems contrary to the great respect God shows for angelic and human free will and for the free determination of our final end that we make in our deliberate choices during this state of trial. In the case of those who die before the age of reason without Baptism, on the contrary, God's salvific action, if He chooses to do it, would not involve changing the free determination their will that has not chosen anything contrary to His grace, but simply *elevating* their innate natural love to a supernatural one by the infusion of sanctifying grace and charity.

Fourth, the grace of conversion given to the damned souls would seem to be something supernatural that would have to include charity, by which they repent for their sins for love of God. But this would make their condition supernatural, and not natural, whereas the claim is that they would receive *natural* happiness. Thus, there is a strange mixture of the unnatural (in their previous unrepented sin in which their trial ended), the supernatural in their miraculous conversion from supreme love of self to love of God, and the natural happiness in which they would remain for eternity.

51. See the prayer in the funeral rite for unbaptized babies in *The Roman Ritual: Order of Christian Funerals* (New Jersey: Catholic Book Publishing Co., 1998), 154: "My brothers and sisters, the Lord is a faithful God who created us all after his own image. All things are of his making, all creation awaits the day of salvation. We now must entrust the soul of N. to the abundant mercy of God, that our beloved child may find a home in his kingdom."

These problems are similar to those involved in the way Maritain depicts the condition of the souls in limbo, but greatly magnified.

In conclusion, it would be much more coherent to reverse Maritain's reverie, and hope that the terminal state of a purely natural happiness is a level in the hierarchy of creation that God has chosen not to fill, so that natural happiness only occurs together with supernatural beatitude as an integral part of it. It is reasonable to hope, following the *Catechism of the Catholic Church,* that God grants to the infants who die without Baptism the infusion of sanctifying grace before their death, not through their personal desire, since it is proper to their natural condition to be entrusted to others, but through the desire of the Church who prays for all. It is not reasonable to hope for the miraculous repentance of the damned after death, when Jesus speaks of the worm that does not die and the fire that is not quenched (Mk 9:48). But it is a very different and more fitting thing to hope that limbo is empty through the merciful action of God infusing grace into those who never posed any obstacle to it.

TRAVIS DUMSDAY

Maritain on Limbo and Demonic Beatitude

I. Introduction

THE FIRST CHAPTER of Maritain's *Untrammeled Approaches* is an essay titled "Beginning with a Reverie."[1] Originally composed in 1939, the essay deals in part with limbo. That afterlife state, never firmly ensconced as Roman Catholic dogma, has today fallen on hard times; it does not receive so much as a mention in the new *Catechism of the Catholic Church*,[2] and the 2007 report of the International Theological Commission favored dropping it altogether (at least conceived as an afterlife state for unbaptized infants).[3] Maritain, by contrast, defends the traditional Thomistic conception of limbo. In fact, he not only *defends* that traditional conception, he also *extends* it, putting it to some novel theological uses. Specifically, Maritain tentatively suggests that all of the damned in the various lower regions of hell (those who have committed one or another of the mortal sins) will one day be freed from those lower regions by the grace of God working through the prayers of the Church. That is, they will be liberated into the uppermost "layer" of hell, namely limbo, the inhabitants of which enjoy natural beatitude while yet lacking supernatural beatitude. They will remain damned, in a sense, insofar as they forever miss

1. Jacques Maritain, *Untrammeled Approaches*, translated by Bernard Doering (Notre Dame: University of Notre Dame Press, 1997), 3–25.

2. Holy See, *Catechism of the Catholic Church* (New York: Image/Doubleday, 1995).

3. Holy See, *The Hope of Salvation for Infants Who Die Without Being Baptized* (Rome, 2007), available at http://www.vatican.va/roman_curia/congregations/cfaith/cti_documents /rc_con_cfaith_doc_20070419_un-baptised-infants_en.html.

out on the beatific vision. Yet they will not experience any actual suffering beyond regret over having missed out on their divinely ordained supernatural end—and even that, Maritain suggests, will be overtaken by their love of God and free acceptance of His justice. Eventually all the damned in the lower regions will be thus liberated to enjoy natural beatitude, even the demons.

Given the provocative nature of Maritain's suggestions, it is surprising that this essay has received so little attention from theologians working on eschatology and from Maritain scholars.[4] I hope the present essay will begin to redress this. More specifically, my principal aims are twofold. First, I wish to draw out certain implications of Maritain's unique understanding of limbo, and to raise some critical questions: (a) if Maritain's conception of limbo is true, then one of Aquinas's core arguments for the reality of purgatory is rendered unsound; (b) if Maritain's conception of limbo is true, then a significant aspect of Aquinas's angelology will need revision; and (c) is it really possible for a rational being to experience natural beatitude while cognizant of having *culpably* missed out on supernatural beatitude? This is a special worry for Maritain's proposal, one that does not arise for the Thomistic conception of natural beatitude in unbaptized infants (who *inculpably* miss out on supernatural beatitude). Second, I wish to draw out some parallels between Maritain's understanding of limbo and certain strands of thought in Eastern Orthodox eschatology.

The remainder of the essay is divided as follows: in the next section I lay out Maritain's conception of limbo in greater detail, emphasizing the new uses to which he puts it. In the succeeding two sections I engage in the two tasks just described. The concluding section consists of a brief recap and a suggestion for further exploration of Maritain's thought.

II. Maritain's Conception of Limbo

As noted above, the doctrine of limbo, while possessed of a long history,[5] has today become the object of increasing skepticism among Roman

4. For a notable exception to this general neglect see James V. Schall, "The Natural Restoration of Fallen Angels in the Depths of Evil: Concerning the Obscure Origins of Absolute Human Autonomy in Political Philosophy," in *Faith, Scholarship, and Culture in the 21st Century*, edited by Alice Ramos and Marie George (Washington, D.C.: American Jacques Maritain Association, distributed by The Catholic University of America Press, 2002), 251–68.

5. Concise summations of this history may be found in the previously cited 2007 report by

Catholic theologians. More and more today affirm the likelihood that unbaptized infants will somehow have the opportunity to enjoy the beatific vision, and in consequence, interest in limbo is waning. Still, even if that aspect of the doctrine is frequently rejected, it is important to recall that limbo has historically functioned as more than just a proposed location or state of being for unbaptized infants.[6] It has also been posited as a temporary dwelling place for the Old Testament-era saints and righteous pagans prior to Christ's crucifixion and descent into hell, which event freed them to enter heaven.[7] So the theological utility of limbo is not automatically to be dismissed, even if one thinks it unnecessary *qua* explanation for the status of unbaptized infants. This is important for purposes of engaging with Maritain, insofar as he ascribes still further theological roles to the doctrine.

Maritain begins his discussion of limbo by affirming the traditional Thomistic conception of this post-mortem state, namely that it is the uppermost region of hell, yet a region whose inhabitants are wholly free of suffering (whether punitive or penitential). Prior to Christ's atoning death, limbo was the temporary dwelling place of all those who died in a state of grace and without a debt of penance, whether faithful Jewish believers or righteous pagans, and whether adult or infant. All in limbo at that time had the hope and expectation of leaving it for heaven once their atonement had been accomplished by the Messiah, provided they had received the sacraments of the Old Law (i.e., circumcision) or the Natural Law (i.e., the pagan substitutes for baptism), which removed the stain of original sin.[8] Maritain describes the situation as follows:

> In Limbo there were not only the souls of the little children who had died without having received the sacraments of the Law of Nature or of the Old Law, because

---

the International Theological Commission. See also the entry on "Limbo" in the *Catholic Encyclopedia* (New York: Robert Appleton Company, 1910), accessed via www.newadvent.org; and Francis A. Sullivan, S.J., "The Development of Doctrine about Infants who Die Unbaptized," *Theological Studies* 72 (2011): 3–14. For more in-depth treatments of the relevant history, see for instance Christopher Beiting, "The Idea of Limbo in Alexander of Hales and Bonaventure," *Franciscan Studies* 57 (1999): 3–56; George Dyer, "Limbo: A Theological Evaluation," *Theological Studies* 19 (1958): 32–49; and George Dyer, *Limbo: Unsettled Question* (New York: Sheed and Ward, 1964).

6. I will not here delve into the difficult metaphysics of the afterlife, for instance the debates over the "location" vs. "state" models of heaven, hell, and purgatory.

7. See for instance Aquinas's ST Suppl. III, q. 69, a. 6.

8. On the latter see ST III, q. 70, a. 4, ad 2.

> of which in former times, *in fide ecclesiae,* God remitted original sin, as He does now ... through the efficacy of baptism.... There was that immense multitude of all the souls of those men and women who had died in the state of grace, and who with an actual expectation awaited the coming of their Redeemer in order to enter heaven and who had been waiting there in pressing throngs for centuries. And not only four thousand years, but hundreds of thousands of years, as many as paleontology requires.... But one day eternity was shaken, the soul of their Saviour comes like a May breeze to set them free.[9]

So even before Christ's atoning death there was already a split between two groups in limbo: those who were there *temporarily* (i.e., those adults and infants who died in a state of grace), and those who were there *permanently* (i.e., those who died as infants without having been cleansed of original sin). The former class exited limbo upon the harrowing of hell during the interim between Christ's death on the cross and his resurrection. The latter class remained in limbo, and will forever remain there. Indeed, after the harrowing of hell the permanent population of limbo continued to grow as it became the location for all those infants who died without baptism, which sacrament replaced the previous methods (again, circumcision and its pagan substitutes) of wiping out infantile original sin. Those permanent denizens will forever be deprived of the beatific vision, yet will not experience any suffering in consequence of this deprivation. In short, they will lack *supernatural* beatitude, but will possess *natural* beatitude, that highest level of happiness possible to man's natural state. Maritain puts it as follows:

> What can be said of the condition in which they will live? They still carry the blemish of Adam's sin, with which they came into the world here on earth, and which has not been effaced in them.... The sole sanction to which they remain subject—and which is in itself the greatest—is to be eternally enclosed in the order of nature alone—but of a nature henceforth preserved from all fault. In short they find themselves in an absolutely new condition, which exists only there, the state of *pure nature raised to its highest degree.* For these creature there will be realized what is very improperly called philosophic or natural "beatitude."[10]

This state of natural beatitude will involve a certain natural knowledge of God, great and ever-increasing joy, and a total absence of suffering. Still, those in limbo will never know the face-to-face vision of God. How will

9. Maritain, *Untrammeled Approaches,* 12.
10. Ibid., 14–15; emphasis in original.

that deprivation be compatible with any form of beatitude? Aquinas struggled with this question, and held different views at different stages of his career.[11]

Maritain himself seems uncertain as to how this compatibility will be effected, and he reviews three relevant considerations:

> They experience no affliction whatsoever, because (1) at the summits of the state of pure nature where they find themselves, they possess such a happiness that it eclipses for them the desire, natural in us, to surpass nature, and in them, as in the souls of Purgatory, there are not found the unconditioned aspirations of grace; (2) it is not through their fault that they are deprived of the vision of God, and they have God in a certain way, in the way of pure nature in the mirror of creation; (3) they are not envious, and having themselves everything to which their nature as such can lay claim, they rejoice rather in the happiness of the elect, supposing that they are aware of the existence of these elect. But although they do not feel its effects, it is a punishment nevertheless with regard to the destination of the human race, and the fall of Adam. *Felix culpa* nevertheless: for if not they, at least their happier, blessed, sisters have profited from the redemption which this fall brought about. And they are happy that their sisters are blessed, and they admire and love Jesus, with a natural love—just as they love Beauty and Goodness. And the holy angels—who can cross the chaos and who like stars illumine the night of Limbo—tell them stories of Paradise.[12]

Maritain apparently does not see these three points as exhaustive; perhaps there are still further explanations for the compatibility of genuine natural beatitude and the blameless deprivation of supernatural beatitude.

So far Maritain's discussion of limbo adheres pretty closely to the traditional Thomistic conception. However, in the remainder of the essay Maritain moves into new theological territory, assigning limbo some novel explanatory roles that should remain of interest to contemporary theologians (even those who reject limbo as a dwelling for infants). Specifically, Maritain goes on to suggest that limbo could be put to work reconciling the *prima facie* incompatible doctrines of eternal punishment of the justly damned (i.e., the punishment of those who died in a state of mortal sin) with a fittingly robust view of divine mercy according to which all the damned will one day escape positive punishments (i.e., punishments over and above the loss of supernatural beatitude). Maritain boldly extends this suggestion even to the demons, such that the devil himself will one day

11. For discussion see Dyer, *Limbo: Unsettled Question*, 44–52.

12. Maritain, *Untrammeled Approaches*, 16–17.

ascend from the lowest depths of hell into limbo, enjoying there a natural beatitude appropriate to angels.

How does that come about? It is effected by the grace of God working through the prayers of the Church. The elect continually intercede on behalf of those in the lower regions of hell: "How could our love, this love which He has given us, be content to see God hated endlessly, and endlessly blasphemed by beings who have issued from His hands, to see crime endlessly added to crime? And among these damned there are some whom we have loved, there are some whom we still love, as much as St. Paul loved his race, for which he wished to be anathema. No, we shall not cease, we shall continue to pray and to cry out through the Blood of the Savior."[13] Maritain proceeds to argue that it is not outside the realm of possibility that God could grant such a prayer, miraculously moving the wills of the damned, wills otherwise confirmed in hate. Those wills are, in the post-mortem state, naturally fixed in orientation, but that natural state is still subject to God's supernatural, miraculous intervention:

> He can change bread into the Body of Jesus Christ. It is no more difficult *by a miracle* to change the will of a man or an angel, to raise up and rectify in its inmost being a will that is dead and confirmed in evil. It is by virtue of the order of nature that the will of the damned is fixed in evil in an absolute and immutable manner. A miracle, and a miracle alone, can change this. I mean leaving them in Hades, and simply transferring them from the abyss to the summits of an eternal Hell.... It seems that the possibility of such a miracle is conceivable in accord with the revealed formulas and sacred writ concerning the state of the damned.[14]

Maritain goes on to emphasize further that this is not a case of post-mortem salvation; it is rather a miraculous lifting of the damned from a worse to a better state of damnation, indeed to a state of damnation devoid of any positive punishment and consistent with natural beatitude. Yet it will be a natural beatitude enjoyed with an accompanying awareness not only that the individual is missing out on the beatific vision, but that he or she (or it) is missing out on the beatific vision *culpably*. In that latter respect, these transplanted occupants of limbo differ importantly from the unbaptized infants whose company they join. Still, their knowledge of culpable exclusion will be compatible with natural beatitude, insofar as the justly damned-but-transplanted will so exult in their miraculous delivery from

13. Ibid., 20.

14. Ibid., 21; emphasis in original.

the lower depths of hell, and so love divine justice, that they will freely consent to their exclusion from the beatific vision.[15]

Maritain further emphasizes that this miraculous transfer is not a necessary one that can be seized upon with any firm confidence. Still, we may rationally hope: "And I do not say that this transfer *must take place*—who can know this? It depends on the pure divine will. I ask simply: Is it not *possible* that it take place—*if God wills it* (and who would dare to impose limits on Him)? And are we not permitted to hope for this?"[16]

Maritain does not expand much on the mechanics of this transfer process; still, he seems to think that what the prayers of the Church accomplish for those in the lower regions of hell specifically is the deliverance of their wills from the naturally settled state of confirmed hatred of God. That is, those in hell (like those in any other post-mortem state) naturally have fixed wills. What the grace of God effects is the miraculous alteration of that state, such that their wills are once again mutable. Thus, God does not directly and immediately override the wills of the damned, switching them in a single step from hatred of God to love of God. Rather, God miraculously renders the wills of the damned mutable, whereas they were previously, and naturally, fixed—and fixed in hatred. Maritain does not state this explicitly, but something like it seems implied by his conception of the *gradual* manner in which the lower regions of hell are emptied out:

> And so, through the prayers of the saints (and not only of the saints, but of their head, Jesus in His glory, and of His Mother) a damned soul is drawn from the fire, but not from Hell. It is restored to the norm of nature, not of grace or of glory. Those who remain in the fire only rage and blaspheme and despair all the more at the departure of their companion. For they do not believe in divine mercy, which for them is nothing but hypocrisy. And they do not want to be made good by a miracle, such an idea exasperates them. And now, let this miracle be renewed at intervals of time as great as one would wish; since eternity exhausts all time, it will inevitably come about that at a certain moment the lower regions of Hades will be completely emptied. If such is the case, Lucifer doubtless will be the last one changed. For a time he will be alone in the abyss and will think himself the only one condemned to endless torments, and his pride will know no bounds. But for him also there will be prayers, there will be cries. And in the end he too will be restored to good, in the order of pure nature, brought back in spite of himself to the natural love of God, borne miraculously into that Limbo whose night glitters with stars.[17]

15. Ibid., 24.
16. Ibid., 21–22; emphasis in original.
17. Ibid., 22–23.

Maritain does not take up the potential criticism that the radical nature of freedom might allow some of the damned (whether demonic or human) to forever resist the prayers of the Church. Presumably, he would admit that as a theoretical possibility yet one unlikely to be realized. Rational beings are ordered to natural beatitude. As such, given sufficient time and opportunity they will turn, *inevitably yet freely*, towards Him who is the ultimate source of it, once their post-mortem wills have been miraculously rendered mutable once again.

This picture is one suggested only *tentatively* by Maritain; he emphasizes that he presents it only as an object of hope not explicitly ruled out by Roman Catholic dogma. In the work's very first paragraph he states that "it is a conjectural essay destined to remain conjectural."[18] He also makes it clear that he places it under the dogmatic authority of the Magisterium: "Need I add that my reveries, as is the case with everything I write, were conceived and brought to light in a spirit of faithful submission to the judgment of the Church, a judgment to which I adhere in advance, if it should ever happen that the Church should consider worthy of its attention so modest and completely conjectural an imaginative essay."[19]

However one assesses the ultimate dogmatic fate of Maritain's picture of the complete emptying of the lower depths of hell, one must admire both its theological daring and its underlying motive: love of all, even the justly damned. In what follows I will explore briefly some of the potential theological implications of his model, some of the difficult questions raised by it, and some of the connections which might be drawn between it and aspects of Eastern Orthodox eschatology.

I should emphasize again that my concern is principally with the novel aspects of Maritain's conception of limbo. Obviously a great many questions and concerns can be (and of course have been) raised about the tra-

18. Ibid., 3.

19. Ibid., 4. Maritain was likely aware of the difficulties Mivart had encountered in the previous century when the latter floated a comparable conception. Of that episode Dulles writes: "The anatomist St. George Mivart (1827–1900), who had been converted to Catholicism in 1844, made a contribution to apologetics by his efforts to reconcile evolutionism with the faith.... Mivart also felt impelled to answer the objection that the standard teaching on hell was a 'horrible doctrine, worse than atheism.' He speculated in 1892 that the sufferings of the damned would be progressively reduced until these souls achieved a certain relative felicity. After the Holy Office had placed his essays on this subject on the Index, he published another article expressing his total and faithful submission to the judgment of the Holy See." Avery Dulles, *A History of Apologetics* (San Francisco: Ignatius Press, 2005), 251.

ditional Thomistic aspects, including the very idea of unbaptized infants being damned in any way—I leave these to one side here.

III. Implications and Queries

First, if Maritain is right about limbo, then one of Aquinas's central arguments for the reality of purgatory is rendered unsound. Consider the following:

> It is said (2 Maccabees 12:46): 'It is a holy and wholesome thought to pray for the dead, that they may be loosed from sins.' Now there is no need to pray for the dead who are in heaven, for they are in no need; nor again for those who are in hell, because they cannot be loosed from sins. Therefore after this life, there are some not yet loosed from sins, who can be loosed therefrom; and the like have charity, without which sins cannot be loosed, for "charity covereth all sins" [Proverbs 10:12]. Hence they will not be consigned to everlasting death, since "he that liveth and believeth in Me, shall not die for ever" [John 11:26]: nor will they obtain glory without being cleansed, because nothing unclean shall obtain it, as stated in the last chapter of the Apocalypse (verse 14). Therefore some kind of cleansing remains after this life.[20]

The idea is that there must be some reason why the Church mandates prayers for the dead. Since prayers for those already in heaven would be superfluous and prayers for those already in hell would be useless (the damned being *irrevocably* damned), the only remaining theological justification for the practice is a third afterlife state in which such supplications could be useful to the dead. Now, if Maritain's view of limbo is correct, this argument obviously fails, since there *is* a way that prayers for those in hell can benefit them: namely, such prayers are the very instruments by which the damned are relocated from lower regions of hell up to limbo. The damned can in fact benefit from the prayers of the Church.

Now, there are certainly other philosophical and theological arguments for purgatory that would remain unaffected by Maritain's treatment of limbo.[21] Moreover, this argument is vulnerable to some significant objec-

20. ST Suppl. III, Appendix 2, a. 1, c.

21. Consider for instance the very next argument presented by Aquinas in that same article of the *Summa*: "I answer that from the conclusions we have drawn above ... it is sufficiently clear that there is a Purgatory after this life. For if the debt of punishment is not paid in full after the stain of sin has been washed away by contrition, nor again are venial sins always removed when mortal sins are remitted, and if justice demands that sin be set in order by due punishment, it

tions,[22] so its sacrifice may be no great loss. Still, from the perspective of the apologist for purgatory it is a loss nevertheless, and one worth noting in the present context.

Second, Maritain's conception of limbo may conflict with some commitments of Thomistic angelology. Recall that for Aquinas, angels find their supernatural beatitude in the beatific vision, just as we do. Their natural beatitude is also similar to ours, though not quite equivalent. For while the natural beatitude of both angels and humans chiefly consists in knowing and loving God (to the extent possible to unfallen humans and angels absent special grace), a *human's* natural knowledge of creation and of God via creation is mediated through the bodily senses (and, for those dwelling in limbo prior to the general resurrection, mediated through whatever temporary substitutes God puts in place of the bodily senses). For *angels,* by contrast, natural knowledge of God is clearly not mediated through bodily senses, as they are incorporeal. Rather, angelic knowledge of God's creation, and of God through and in His creation, comes about by way of direct intellectual apprehension of the species of things (including the angel's own essence), which direct apprehension is itself the product ultimately of divine action, insofar as those species are granted the angelic intellect by God.[23] Moreover, the human intellect is mutable, with objects of knowledge passing in and out of the human mind, both in the sense that we learn new things and forget things, and in the sense that we regularly change our goals and beliefs (even goals and beliefs we had previously deliberated upon with care). By contrast, the angelic intellect is higher and immutable. It never acquires new concepts and never forgets. And since the angelic intellect functions non-discursively (the angel does not reason out a conclusion from premises in a temporally extended process, but simply draws implications instantaneously), whatever beliefs and intentions an angel has, it will always have.

That significant difference in human vs. angelic modes of knowledge raises a potential complication for Maritain's account of demonic restoration and subsequent beatitude. On my reading of Maritain, we should see him as suggesting that God miraculously renders mutable the wills of the damned,

---

follows that one who after contrition for his fault and after being absolved, dies before making due satisfaction, is punished after this life."

22. One longstanding Orthodox reply to that line of reasoning consists basically of a direct reversal: the Church mandates prayers for the dead, and since there is no such thing as purgatory such prayers must benefit those in hades.

23. ST I, q. 55, a. 2; see also ST I, q. 56, a. 3.

such that the damned are enabled *gradually and freely* (though inevitably) to turn back to Him. God does this instead of instantaneously overriding their wills by His absolute power, switching them from hatred to love. It is relatively easy to understand how damned *humans* could turn in repentance to God, if such a renewed post-mortem mutability of will were indeed possible (itself a debatable claim). After all, humans on earth have mutable wills and turn towards God or away from Him all the time. In this miraculous act they are simply restored to that sort of condition—one they previously enjoyed and one with which we are all experientially familiar. But the Thomistic conception of angelic will is quite different: for Aquinas, the wills of the angels, both fallen and unfallen, are fixed and have been fixed since their very first free act of moral choice, forming an intention for or against God. Why? In large part it is because of their unique mode of knowledge. Having their intellectual species directly from God right from the first moment of their creation, angels' knowledge was complete from their beginning. For Aquinas, angels were created in a state of complete knowledge and natural perfection, such that their primordial choice for or against God was utterly clear-eyed and, correspondingly, utterly irrevocable:

> Now the angel's apprehension differs from man's in this respect, that the angel by his intellect apprehends immovably, as we apprehend immovably first principles which are the object of the habit of "intelligence"; whereas man by his reason apprehends movably, passing from one consideration to another; and having the way open by which he may proceed to either of two opposites. Consequently man's will adheres to a thing movably, and with the power of forsaking it and of clinging to the opposite; whereas the angel's will adheres fixedly and immovably. Therefore, if his will be considered before its adhesion, it can freely adhere either to this or to its opposite (namely, in such things as he does not will naturally); but after he has once adhered, he clings immovably. So it is customary to say that man's free-will is flexible to the opposite both before and after choice; but the angel's free-will is flexible toward either opposite before the choice, but not after. Therefore the good angels who adhered to justice, were confirmed therein; whereas the wicked ones, sinning, are obstinate in sin. Later on we shall treat of the obstinacy of men who are damned.[24]

If Aquinas's account of demonic obstinacy is correct,[25] it would be much more difficult to see how even a miracle could restore mutability to the de-

24. ST I, q. 64, a. 2, resp.

25. Note that there are some interpretive complications surrounding this text (and related texts), and a thorough account of Aquinas on demons' obstinacy would require a much more

monic will, allowing for a gradual and free turn back to God. The reason is that the source of its fixity is not some (arguably) accidental feature of a contingent post-mortem state (as is the case for humans) but the very essence of the angelic will and intellect. If Maritain's account of demonic restoration is correct, then it seems Thomistic angelology will need some significant revisions.

Alternatively, it might be suggested that Maritain adjust his specific model of demonic restoration, shifting from the gradualism and freedom of his own account to one in which God by His absolute power directly changes demonic will from hatred to love. Aquinas grants that God could do so.[26] But Maritain's intuition regarding God's respect for His creatures' freedom is plausible, so that would not be a good corrective.

Obviously this worry may not be a deal-breaker; perhaps Aquinas's account of the angelic constitution is actually in need of revision, and its incompatibility with demonic restoration to natural beatitude is simply a new line of evidence for this fact. Still, for Thomists at least, it is a further complication to be taken into account when assessing Maritain's view of limbo.

Third, Maritain's claim that natural beatitude will be enjoyed by culpably damned humans and demons after their transfer to limbo faces a worry not faced by the claim that inculpable unbaptized infants in limbo enjoy natural beatitude. As we saw in the previous section, it is already a difficult task to explain how exactly unbaptized infants can enjoy genuine natural beatitude while cognizant of missing out on the beatific vision. One possibility is that they are unaware of what they are missing out on—an explanation Aquinas first rejected and then later came to view more favorably.[27] However that issue is to be addressed in the case of inculpably damned infants, for present purposes the key point is that it is still *more* difficult to explain how the culpably damned adult humans and demons could possibly enjoy natural beatitude—for they are clearly aware of what they are miss-

---

extensive treatment than I can provide here. The key point for present purposes (and one on which most interpreters would agree) is that their obstinacy is for Aquinas a fact following from certain essential elements of angelic constitution. For a useful overview, consult Joseph Suk-Hwan Dowd, "Aquinas on Demonic Obstinacy," *American Catholic Philosophical Quarterly* 89 (2015): 699–718.

26. See *De Malo* q. 16, a. 5, ad 13.

27. Contrast ST Suppl. III, Appendix 1, q. 1, a. 2, resp. (which material is, recall, simply a reprint of material from his early *Commentary on the Sentences* posthumously appended to the *Summa*), with his later treatment of the issue in *De Malo* q. 5, a. 3.

ing out on, and they are aware further that they are to blame for their own deprivation. As noted in the previous section, Maritain's suggestion seems to be that their proper and just regret over their culpable deprivation will somehow be overtaken by their new natural beatitude—that the regret felt by adults and demons in limbo will still be compatible with blessedness in limbo. He puts it as follows:

> There will be Milky Ways of regret and of sadness in the natural felicity of the pardoned. True beatitude, beside which everything else is as nothing, they must never look to have, they will never see the divine essence; and this is an eternal privation—a painfully felt privation because, unlike the children who died without baptism, they were called personally to the glory in which the three Divine Persons give themselves to the blessed.... Nevertheless, it is this very sorrow which crowns, without diminishing it, their happiness at seeing the order of nature fully accomplished in them, and they give their full consent; they know it is just, it dignifies them, and they thank God for it.... The risen Redeemer keeps His wounds for divine glory; the pardoned of Hades keep the scars of their wounds for divine justice. But now they love this justice, according to the wisdom of right reason. Exulting in their pardon and giving thanks for this supreme miracle of love, they know themselves unworthy of beatitude. Too happy, if I may put it this way, at having been restored to natural felicity, by their own initiative they exclude themselves voluntarily—this time not because they are confirmed in evil but because they are confirmed in natural justice—from that divine vision to which they aspire with an inefficacious natural desire but of which their rational will wants them to remain deprived.[28]

Maritain is obviously trying very hard to keep these two pieces of data (awareness of culpable exclusion from supernatural beatitude + genuine natural beatitude) together despite their tension. I think it is apparent he has not quite succeeded, something Maritain himself would, I suspect, readily grant. This is certainly an area of his theology of limbo that needs further development. My concern is simply that this tension may not in the end admit of resolution, such that one will be driven in one of two directions: either (1) abandon the idea that the culpably damned enjoy natural beatitude, which would entail that they cannot in fact be transplanted into limbo (though they may perhaps be restored to some other upper level of hell, one still devoid of positive punishments beyond deprivation of the beatific vision); or, (2) affirm that the culpably damned somehow get a second chance at supernatural beatitude. In fact, one might use the tension

28. Maritain, *Untrammeled Approaches*, 23–24.

just identified as a positive argument in favor of considering one of these options, though the second option is heretical within Roman Catholicism.

On that note, I would like now to bring into play some interesting parallel speculations in Eastern Orthodox theology, speculations that might help resolve (or sidestep altogether) some of the worries facing Maritain's conception of the restoration of the damned, while yet satisfying the intuitions motivating it (especially the undying love of God for all His creatures, even those in hades).

IV. Some Relevant Strands of Eastern Orthodox Tradition

It should be observed at the outset that the Orthodox Church has left a great deal of eschatology undefined; that is, the Church has formulated relatively little in the way of eschatological *dogma* (doctrines which all Orthodox are obliged to affirm). In this, Orthodoxy differs importantly from Roman Catholicism, insofar as the latter has a great deal of defined doctrine concerning the afterlife.

Turincev for example writes: "The Orthodox Church does not possess dogmatic formulations about these 'last things' ... except for the articles of the Nicene Creed. She has no eschatological doctrine. So we will just try to highlight some characteristic features of Orthodox eschatology based on the written tradition, and drawing inspiration from various literary sources —the liturgical texts in particular."[29] Or consider Andrew Louth:

> "He is coming in glory to judge the living and the dead, and his kingdom will have no end"; "I await the resurrection of the dead, and the life of the age to come." Despite the fact that, in the doctrine of "the last things," *ta eschata*, the whole of Christian doctrine—Creation, Incarnation, redemption and deification—finds its fulfilment, there is little explicitly defined in the formularies of the Orthodox Church, hardly anything more than these two phrases of the Nicene Creed. Nevertheless, there is nothing bleakly agnostic about Orthodox beliefs concerning the afterlife, nor is awareness of an eschatological dimension absent. Rather these beliefs are expressed primarily in the rich liturgical life of the Orthodox Church.[30]

29. Alexandre Turincev, "An Approach to Orthodox Eschatology," *Canadian Journal of Orthodox Christianity* 9 (2014): 8. Originally published as "Une approche de l'eschatologie orthodoxe," *Contacts* 18 (1966). Translated from the French by Brad Jersak, Michael Gillis, and the monks of the Holy Transfiguration Hermitage in British Columbia.

30. Andrew Louth, *Introducing Eastern Orthodox Theology* (Downers Grove, Illinois: IVP Academic), 141.

As such, both historically and in recent Orthodox theology there has been a great deal of speculation concerning the possible restoration of the damned, either to a comparatively pleasant level of hell (though not one involving natural beatitude—Orthodox theologians reject the Thomistic distinction between natural and supernatural beatitude), or even to the kingdom of God. The following distinct positions have been taken up by Orthodox theologians:

(1) For those who are sent to hades at the *particular* judgement (i.e., one's own death, in contrast with the *universal* judgement to take place at the apocalypse and general resurrection), there is no hope of escape, but there is hope of having one's sufferings eased by the grace of God working through the prayers of the Church. Just how much they might be eased is a matter up for discussion, and may depend on the damned individual and his or her degree of sin and consequent placement in hades.[31]

(2) For those who are sent to hades at the particular judgement, there is hope of escape by means of the grace of God working through the prayers of the Church. Those damned at the particular judgement thus still have hope of entering heaven. However, such escape is possible only in the time between the particular judgement and the universal judgement. After that final judgement, one's post-mortem state is irrevocable.[32]

31. Vassiliadis is a representative of this first position: "Our holy Church prays to Christ the Bridegroom both for those who have departed 'in repentance' and for those who have departed 'in sin.' The Church prays out of love for all.... While the Mother Church prays also for sinners, it does not teach nor promise that those who departed unrepentant will receive forgiveness of sins. Also, the Fathers, who are made wise by God and who advise us to pray for the sinners, do not support the view that these prayers and Memorials will absolve them from the sufferings of Hades or remove them from the place of punishment to Paradise. They only note that those who depart from this life with their sins receive through all of these prayers a certain consolation; that their punishment becomes somewhat lighter." Nikolaos Vassiliadis, *The Mystery of Death*, translated by Peter Chamberas (Athens: The Orthodox Brotherhood of Theologians, 1993), 434.

32. Cavarnos writes: "In regard to the possibility of a change in the soul's condition during the interval between the Particular and General Judgements, the Orthodox Church teaches that it is possible for it to change for the better.... In this Middle State, says the blessed Nectarios, 'some of the sinners will be relieved of the burden of the penalty and will be completely delivered from sufferings of Hades, not through their own action,' not through some Purgatorial Fire as Roman Catholicism teaches 'but through the prayers of the Church.'" Constantine Cavarnos, *The Future Life According to Orthodox Teaching*, translated by Hieromonk Auxentios and Archimandrite Chrysostomos (Etna, California: Center for Traditionalist Orthodox Studies, 1985), 35–36. This is a relatively common position amongst Orthodox theologians; for another example consider Alfeyev: "According to the Orthodox teaching, it is possible to be freed from the torments of hell: the practice of praying for the departed and even for 'those in hell' at Pentecost vespers is based on this. However, this liberation occurs not because of some automatic necessity and not because the sinner serves a kind of 'prison term' established for those who

(3) For those who are sent to hades at the particular judgement, there is hope of escape into heaven by means of the grace of God working through the prayers of the Church. Such escape is possible in the interim state. One may hope that it is also possible after the final judgement, though this cannot confidently be affirmed.[33]

(4) For those who are sent to hades at the particular judgement and/or the final judgement, eventual salvation is guaranteed.[34]

Of these positions, (2) seems particularly prominent within Orthodox tradition, though (1) and (3) are also widely defended; (4) has had very few takers and is regarded by most Orthodox theologians as heretical on grounds of its apparent conflict with the standard Orthodox conception of God's respect for human freedom. Note too that these thinkers are generally worried about the status of damned humans; there has not been as much explicit speculation about the possible restoration of the demons, though that idea has been held out as a permissible hope by certain theologians.

Having briefly laid out some of these options, I can now say a bit about their relationship to Maritain's conception of limbo. Clearly the closest parallel in Orthodox tradition is option (1), according to which the damned can have their condition improved while yet remaining damned. Again, Orthodoxy would deny Maritain's notion of *natural* beatitude, and hence would have no room for his precise conception of limbo as a state of natural beatitude for damned humans and demons.[35] Still, Orthodox tradition

commit certain sins, but through the prayers of the Church and God's ineffable love for man.... The Orthodox belief is based on the idea that, until the Last Judgement, changes for the better are possible in the fate of any sinner." Metropolitan Hilarion Alfeyev, "Eschatology," in *The Cambridge Companion to Orthodox Christian Theology,* edited by Mary Cunningham and Elizabeth Theokritoff (Cambridge: Cambridge University Press, 2008), 107–20, at 115.

33. For defenders of this third position see for instance David Bentley Hart, "Saint Origen," *First Things* 256 (2015): 71–72, and Andrew Louth, *Introducing Eastern Orthodox Theology,* 157–59.

34. Sergius Bulgakov leans toward this idea; see *The Bride of the Lamb,* translated by Boris Jakim (Grand Rapids, Michigan: Eerdmans, 1945/2002), 482–500 and 505–17. Turincev goes further, affirming it unambiguously: "Let us state frankly—the idea of eternal hell and eternal suffering for some and eternal bliss (indifferent to suffering) for others, can no longer remain in the living and renewed Christian conscience as it was formerly presented in our catechisms and our official theology courses. This archaic conception which claims to be based on the Gospel texts, understands them in a literal, coarse and material sense, without penetrating the hidden spiritual meaning of the images and symbols. This conception is increasingly showing itself to be an intolerable violation of Christian conscience, thought and faith. We cannot accept that the sacrifice of Golgotha has revealed itself to be powerless to redeem the world and conquer hell. Otherwise we should say: creation is a failure, and Redemption is also a failure." Alexandre Turincev, "An Approach to Orthodox Eschatology," 17.

35. And the Orthodox Church has always firmly rejected the notion that unbaptized infants

would allow for something very similar, namely a notion of an "uppermost" region of hell whose denizens suffer comparatively little positive penalties (penalties over and above their exclusion from the Kingdom). This partial parallel in another ancient ecclesial tradition (one well-respected by the Roman Catholic Church—indeed regarded as a "second lung") arguably lends some theological support to Maritain's general project. Note too the important parallel in the understanding of the *instrument* of restoration: both Maritain's conception of limbo and all four strands of Orthodox tradition regarding post-mortem restoration identify the grace of God working through the prayers of the Church as the means.

So the closest parallel is to be seen in model (1). Still, were it not for the fact that options (2) and (3) are heretical in Roman Catholicism, one suspects that Maritain's real preference would be for one of those. (One advantage of doing Maritain scholarship as a non-Catholic is that one can point to and actively encourage such heretical tendencies!)

V. Conclusion

To sum up: after introducing the topic, I proceeded to review in some detail Maritain's unusual conception of limbo. I then laid out some implications of that conception, and some arguably troubling questions facing it. Finally, I briefly laid out relevant strands of Orthodox eschatological tradition, noting both some interesting parallels with Maritain, and the fact that one or more of those strands might have served more effectively to satisfy the underlying theological motivations prompting his novel treatment of limbo.

As I conclude, it is perhaps worth drawing attention to the fact that the congruence between Maritain's speculations on limbo and certain ideas within Orthodox eschatology may not be entirely coincidental. Maritain of course had some personal connections with the exiled Russian Orthodox intellectual community active in Paris in the 1920s and 1930s. So far as I can tell, these connections have not received much attention from Maritain scholars. If this essay could spark some interest on that front, that would be a very welcome side effect.

---

are damned, in part because of its different understanding of original sin (one that involves no notion of inherited guilt).

II

INTUITION AND AESTHETICS

JAMES HANINK

Being, Beauty, and Converging Intuition

> Like the one, the true and the good, the beautiful is *being* itself considered from a certain aspect; it is a property of being: it is not an accident superadded to being, it adds to being merely a relation of reason, it is being considered as delighting, by the mere intuition of it, an intellectual nature. So everything is beautiful just as everything is good, at least in a certain relation.
>
> —Jacques Maritain, *Art and Scholasticism*[1]

> If each one of the diverse existents is good in its own way or one in its own way, it is *because* each one *exists,* or is posited for its own sake and in its own way, outside the mind, and after all is said and done, precisely because there is a self-subsistent *Esse*—known to us analogically even though infinitely above our grasp—in which and with which all the other transcendentals, also raised to pure act, must be absolutely identified.
>
> —Jacques Maritain, *Untrammeled Approaches*[2]

A QUARTER CENTURY AGO, John F. X. Knasas painstakingly assessed the debate between Jacques Maritain and Étienne Gilson on the place of an intuition of being in philosophy. "The thunderclaps in

1. Jacques Maritain, *Art and Scholasticism with Other Essays,* Cluny Media Edition. Introduction by Brian Barbour, translated by J. F. Scanlan (New York: Sheed and Ward, 1933), 31.

2. Jacques Maritain, *Untrammeled Approaches,* translated by Bernard Doering (Notre Dame, Indiana: University of Notre Dame Press, 1997), 226.

the exchange," Knasas wrote, "should not be allowed to grow silent."[3] For Thomists, the role of an intuition of being at the beginning of metaphysics is a pressing *questio disputata*.[4] Maritain's signature thesis, long held and provocatively reaffirmed in *Untrammeled Approaches*, is that there is such an intuition and that its place is pivotal. In this essay, I begin with a sketch of Maritain's thesis. Then I defend it against one of John F. Wippel's recent criticisms. In the interest of advancing a wider debate, I next offer a fresh argument for such an intuition that draws on Maritain's theory of beauty. To defend that argument, I address in turn Umberto Eco's dismissal of Maritain's account of aesthetic intuition. Lastly, I note the personalist exemplar of the convergence of being and beauty.

I. Elements of the Intuition of Being

Maritain begins with the apprehension of the sensible. Early on, in *Existence and the Existent*, he writes that intuition comes into play in the first operation of the intellect: "Existence—the existence of material realities—is given us at first by sense; sense attains the object as existing," and thus, "the pattern of all true knowledge is the intuition of the thing that I see."[5]

Next comes judgment, the second operation of the intellect; its role is critical. The intellectual intuition of being, we read in *Untrammeled Approaches*, "is produced *in and by an affirmative judgment* of existence."[6] With it, one is able to "*to see*, the being, the existence, the extra-mental *esse* of that subject [of judgment]."[7] One grasps the "to be," or *esse*, of sensible things, as well as the being, or *ens*, of things not limited to sensibles. (Here I have in mind the deliberate and free acts of the human person. Such acts, each with its *habens esse*, are not reducible to the empirical.) Given this intuition of being, we can form a concept of a trans-physical and supra-sensible *esse*. Thus,

3. John F. X. Knasas, "Gilson vs. Maritain: The Start of Thomistic Metaphysics," *Doctor Communis* 43, no. 3 (1990): 265.

4. Three recent and important contributions to the debate appear in *The Wisdom of Youth: Essays Inspired by the Early Work of Jacques and Raïssa Maritain*, edited by Travis Dumsday (Washington, D.C.: American Maritain Association, distributed by The Catholic University of America Press, 2016). See therein Matthew S. Pugh, "Maritain, Critical Realism, and the Intuition of Being," 101–19; John F. Wippel, "Maritain and Aquinas on Our Discovery of Being," 120–46; and Jason West, "Maritain and Dewan on the Intuition of Being and the Birth of Metaphysics," 147–59.

5. Maritain, *Existence and the Existent: An Essay on Christian Existentialism*, translated by Lewis Galantiere and Gerald B. Phelan (Garden City, New York: Image Books, 1956), 21.

6. Maritain, *Untrammeled Approaches*, 219.

7. Ibid., 220; emphasis in original.

one "can plunge into the world of existence and escape from the world of essences."[8] In virtue of the basic unity of the intellect, apprehension and judgment are simultaneous.[9] "The intellect," Maritain writes, "is wholly present in each of its operations."[10] It is very easy to lose sight of this unity in an attempt to assign—neatly—the tasks of conceptually distinct operations of the intellect.

How are we to understand the world of existence? We best do so in terms of act. The intuition of being, for Maritain, is "of that act of existing which is the act of every act," and "in which all the intelligible structures of reality have their definitive actuation."[11] To be sure, act depends on substance; but substance exists only in act. Moreover, since the *esse* of knowing is formally identical with the *esse* of the known, Thomism, *pace* Heidegger, is hardly "forgetful" of being. In exculpating Thomas from such a charge, Christopher S. Morrissey highlights the act of cognition: "What is first known of the *ens* (i.e., as it first appears to cognition as 'an essence existing') is the identity of knowing thought with known Be-ing," which indicates that, "act is prior to subsistence, not temporally, but as the condition for the possibility of knowing thought becoming identical with actual, known Be-ing."[12] Our focus is on the dynamism of act and subsistence rather than on the world of essences.

As Morrissey suggests, even in a sketch of Maritain's intuition of being, we need to recognize that this intuition shapes the whole of a truly existential metaphysics. In his *Preface to Metaphysics*, for example, Maritain argues that even the principle of identity, if we understand it as expressing the intuition of being, is a revelatory principle of reality. As such, it serves being's "intelligible nature" by securing its analogical "multiplicity."[13] Insofar as

8. Ibid.

9. John Wippel notes that the simultaneity of apprehension and judgment accords with Thomas's view. See his "Maritain and Aquinas on Our Discovery of Being" in *Studia Gilsonia* 3 (2014): 415–43. This essay was later published in *The Wisdom of Youth: Essays Inspired by the Early Work of Jacques and Raïssa Maritain.*

10. Maritain, *Existence and the Existent,* 32.

11. Jacques Maritain, *Approaches to God,* translated by Peter O'Reilly (New York: Macmillan, 1954), 18.

12. Christopher S. Morrissey, "The Intuition of Being: Guardian of Metaphysics in a Time of Unbelief," in *Love and Friendship: Maritain and the Tradition,* edited by Montague Brown (Washington, D.C.: American Maritain Association, distributed by The Catholic University of America Press, 2013), 160–61. Here "Be-ing" underscores the *act* of being.

13. Jacques Maritain, *A Preface to Metaphysics: Seven Lectures on Being* (New York: New American Library, 1962), 60.

each being is what it is, each honors the irreducibility of every being.[14] It is noteworthy that with regard to Maritain's critical realism, Matthew Pugh has ably argued that knowing the unity of the intellect and the intelligible calls upon an intuition of the principle of identity. Judgment, for Pugh, "is resolved in the principle of identity, the grounding principle or condition for the intelligibility of being."[15]

II. An Objection from Neglected Imagination

To be sure, Maritain's intuition of being faces many and sharp objections. Here I will chiefly focus on just one of them: John Wippel's charge that it neglects the internal senses and imagination in particular. We cannot grasp being if we slight either. He tells us that Maritain cannot put aside, even for the sake of simplicity, the necessary "role of phantasms produced by the imagination."[16] It will not do to suppose that the intelligence can directly access sensory perception. Imagination offers a *thesaurus* of phantasms from which the intellect must abstract intelligible content. Yet Maritain seems to allow the intellect to bypass them. Consider the act of conjoining the idea of *x* with *x*'s existing. Already in *Existence and the Existent*, he claims, "it is not by reflection upon phantasms that the intellect proffers the affirmation, but by and in this 'judgment' itself, and in this intuition of sense which it grasps by immaterializing it, in order to express it to itself."[17] In *Untrammeled Approaches* he tells us that an intellectual intuition of being might well come to us "on the occasion of some individual reality grasped in its pure singularity," and recalls Raïssa's sudden intuition of her very being as a hint of a metaphysical absolute.[18]

Nonetheless, however one might sympathize with Wippel's concern, Maritain does give great weight to the interplay of imagination and intelligence. But he insists on doing so in light of the Fall. Because of the first sin, the intellect struggles with an impediment that hampers its operation. Yes, imagination has an "essential role in the first operation of the mind, which is simple apprehension, and the abstraction of the form or idea, drawn from the phantasms with the light of the agent intellect," and, yes, "there

14. Ibid., 61.

15. Pugh, "Maritain, Critical Reason, and the Intuition of Being," in *The Wisdom of Youth*, 110.

16. Wippel, "Maritain and Aquinas on Our Discovery of Being," in *The Wisdom of Youth*, 438.

17. Maritain, *Existence and the Existent*, 37n13. This long footnote begins on p. 35.

18. Maritain, *Untrammeled Approaches*, 225.

is no intellection without 'conversion toward images.'"[19] We cannot overlook, however, the compromised context in which this takes place.

Indeed, now comes Maritain's more specific consideration:

> Let us recall that the disordering or loss of control due to the first sin gave to the "lower powers of the soul," as St. Thomas said, a certain independence or autonomy freeing them from control of that reason which was proper to the state of original justice, and at the same time had a certain impact on reason itself. Well, from our speculative perspective, the same seems to be the case with that internal sense which we call the imagination in regard to the intellect which makes use of it.[20]

The Common Doctor himself presents the "wound of ignorance" as an effect of the primal sin, one that weakens reason's "order[ing] to the true."[21] Sin puts reason at risk. Noting this disorder, what are we to make of Maritain's supposed "shortchanging" of the imagination? Or, for that matter, Wippel's perhaps uncritical reliance on it?

Because of the Fall, Maritain writes, "reason cannot attain that natural wisdom fully and without some defect."[22] Of critical note is that sin disorders the interaction of intelligence and imagination. The immaterial intellect abstracts intelligible content from the material phantasms of the imagination.[23] These phantasms or images, nonetheless, retain "an independent vital energy in the process in question, by reason of which the imagination attaches them to the *intentio intellecta*, to the idea which has been abstracted from them, like a lining or a doubling which reinforces and hardens it from below, a kind of screen on which the intelligible as perceived by the intelligence takes shape."[24] How, though, does this happen?

The intelligence, while ordered to the intelligible, "remains turned toward the phantasm, and hence unconsciously subject to the vital pressure of the imagination."[25] Even our experience of intellectual clumsiness seems to confirm this claim. Because of what Maritain calls the "*notionalizing*" of intellective acts, we lapse into a confused conceptualism. This "notionalism" impedes "the intellectual intuition of being."[26] It seems, perplexingly, that

19. Ibid., 215.
20. Ibid.
21. ST I-II, q. 85, a. 3.
22. Maritain, *Untrammeled Approaches*, 213.
23. Thomas notes that the phantasms "exist in corporeal organs." ST I, q. 85, a. 1, ad 3.
24. Maritain, *Untrammeled Approaches*, 215–16.
25. Ibid., 216.
26. Ibid.

the phantasms necessary for intellection can compromise its work.[27] This occlusion by the phantasms damages our intuitivity. Reason struggles to treat this wound; in contrast, a blind and disordered romanticism denies that it exists.[28] Maritain, I submit, does not "shortchange" the imagination. His verdict, however, is sober: "In the state of fallen nature the philosophical intelligence ... has a natural inclination to a notionalism that admits of the most varied degrees but by its very nature acts as an obstacle to the intellectual intuition of being."[29] Even so, we can benefit from Thomas's intuition of being, given "in a climate of grace," and its trajectory toward *Ipsum esse subsistens*.[30] Wippel, for his part, does not examine the phantasms in light of the Fall, and he mentions the wounds of the intellect only in a footnote.[31]

Maritain, in any case, has something more to say about imagination that we should note here. He asks that we consider the scientist working with an appropriately distinct *habitus*; for such a scientist a perceptive intelligence and intuitivity come into play. So, too, does an "intelligentiated sense," a sensory ability that intelligence already shapes.[32] We are to consider, as well, the natural philosopher. With intelligence and intuitivity "turned to reality," the natural philosopher employs a creative imagination that makes it possible to see reality in a way that the eye alone cannot. Going beyond already formed images, this creative imagination offers fresh images that help the intellect to redirect itself. (Maritain offers the analogy of scouts who begin by following a rough map but after a time can help the mapmaker improve it.) Here we can say that an "intelligentiated imagination" comes into play. Indeed, on occasion and "in confrontation with these images ... the intellect perceives intuitively that rational discourse has wandered astray into a false theory, or risks doing so, and must be put

27. In fact, John Wippel, citing SCG I, chap. 4, no. 5, notes that a "mixing of phantasms" can impede our reasoning to the existence of God. See his *The Metaphysical Thought of Thomas Aquinas: From Finite Being to Uncreated Being*, Monographs of the Society for Medieval and Renaissance Philosophy, vol. 1 (Washington, D.C.: The Catholic University of America Press, 2000), 383.

28. See Michael Raiger, "Cocteau, Opium, and Art: A Coleridgean Account of the Imagination as a Cognitive Power," in *A Piercing Light: Beauty, Faith and Human Transcendence*, edited by James M. Jacobs (Washington, D.C.: American Maritain Society, distributed by The Catholic University of America Press, 2015), 125–28.

29. Maritain, *Untrammeled Approaches*, 216.

30. Ibid., 217.

31. Wippel, "Maritain and Aquinas on Our Discovery of Being," in *The Wisdom of Youth*, 235n56.

32. Maritain, *Untrammeled Approaches*, 337.

back on track."[33] Reason, in such cases, relies on intuitivity. Maritain lauds such imagination as a "noble and marvelously precious 'internal sense.'"[34] Reason and imagination, rightly seen, are complementary. He decries those who invoke imagination to dismiss reason when it is the intellect's task to guide imagination.[35] Nonetheless, a friend of Maritain might well pause to ask how the phantasms of creative imagination avoid their own disordering. Nobility, it seems, needs ongoing conversion.

John Wippel, however, also raises a different objection. I would like to note it only briefly for two reasons. First, the objection leads me to revisit Maritain's Thomist credentials. Second, once I have done so, I can develop a fresh way to extend his distinctive Thomism. Wippel objects to Maritain's distinction among, and use of, three concepts of existence. His first concept is reached at the first level of abstraction. This concept is "formed in the mind *before* the intuition of being has welled up within it."[36] The second concept is judicative in origin and reached at the level of metaphysical intellection. This concept emerges "*after* that intuition [of being] by a turning back of simple apprehension, or of intelligence as formative of ideas, onto that intuition."[37] His third concept, like the first, is abstractive rather than judicative, but is reached at the third level of abstraction.[38] Wippel, however, rejects both Maritain's intellectual intuition of being and any concept of being it might suggest. He reminds us, instead, of Gilson's claim that Thomas does not discuss any specific concept of *esse* and does not treat of an intellectual intuition of being, because he does not think that there is one.[39] This return to Gilson, who thought it a scandal that Thomists sharply disagree about being, sets the stage for the question of whether Maritain's existential Thomism together with its intuition of being puts him at odds with his master.

33. Ibid., 341.
34. Ibid.
35. Ibid., 420.
36. Ibid., 221.
37. Ibid.
38. Ibid., 221n29.
39. Wippel, "Maritain and Aquinas on Our Discovery of Being," in *The Wisdom of Youth*, 441–43.

III. On Being a Good Thomist

Real Thomists do not put words in the mouth of the Common Doctor. Neither Maritain nor Wippel do so. What, then, of the spirit of St. Thomas? On Maritain's behalf, we can draw on the testimony of Joseph Owens. No doubt, he observes, Thomas and Maritain have different starting points with regard to our grasp of being.[40] We see that Maritain's allow him both to locate the intuition of being in judgment and to place metaphysics at the third degree of abstraction. Owens writes, "This metaphysics of Maritain is authentic and penetrating. It throws extremely desirable light upon the key tenets of Aquinas such as the intuition of existence through judgment, and should continue to serve as the best means of bringing readers to appreciate them. But one-to-one correspondence should not be expected. Maritain was too original a thinker for that."[41] In my view, Maritain's epistemology coherently develops Thomist metaphysics, and his emphasis on intuitivity shows intellectual boldness.

Wippel is decidedly skeptical about Maritain's development, and there is a truth in the idea that everything is what it is and not another thing. Yet each thing is in relation to every other thing—as well as in relation to students of *that which is*. We can affirm that Thomists can have different metaphysical starting points and do so without forfeiting our realism. By looking to the fruit of one line of metaphysical inquiry in comparison with the fruit of complementary lines of inquiry, we can advance to a fuller truth.

IV. Intuition and the Metaphysics of Beauty

In this vein, a metaphysics that accounts for beauty shows promise, and Maritain's Thomism does so. We can now propose a fresh way to extend its

40. In like vein, Thomas Joseph White, O.P. writes that for Aquinas the first principles of metaphysics are the causes of being, while for Maritain the first principles come with the discovery of transcendentals, through the intuition of being. See his *Wisdom in the Face of Modernity*, 2nd ed. (Ave Maria, Florida: Sapientia Press, distributed by The Catholic University of America Press, 2016), 145. Maritain, nonetheless, held that while "metaphysical intuition is formally independent of the philosophy of nature," yet "materially and as to us, it presupposes the philosophy of nature: not in its completed state, no doubt, but at least in its first positions." See his *The Philosophy of Nature* (New York: Philosophical Library, 1951), 3–4.

41. Joseph Owens, "Maritain's Three Concepts of Existence," *The New Scholasticism* 49, no. 3 (summer 1975): 309. For Owens, Maritain was unsurpassed in making Thomism a live option for his contemporaries.

range. For Thomas, beauty has three essential conditions: *integrity* or *perfection*, due *proportion* or *harmony*, and lastly, *brightness* or *clarity*.[42] Given these marks, he defines beauty in terms of its effect: "beautiful things are those which please when seen."[43] His definition reflects that we ordinarily come to understand a cause through its effects. Thus, Aristotle defines the good as "that at which all things aim."[44] In like manner, St. Hilary defines the true as "that which manifests and proclaims existence."[45]

The beautiful, the good, and the true reflect the intelligibility of nature that the scientist and the mathematician acknowledge in practice. For Maritain, the mathematician and the artist both rely on intuitivity—an intuitivity of the beautiful. Does not, he asks, the mathematician "who suddenly sees a principle of intelligible fecundity and intelligible organizing power open up to his particular science new horizons and new avenues of approach to a higher synthesis?"[46] Like all who appreciate beauty, the mathematician and the scientist draw on both intelligentiated sense and intelligentiated imagination. The artist attuned to the true finds a beauty that transcends the disordered. In keeping with this theme, The Pontifical Council for Culture's helpful document *Via Pulchritudinis* connects the integrity of a culture with its ability to join beauty and truth. To reduce beauty to mere sense pleasure is to deny the transcendent: "Perception requires an education, for beauty is only authentic in its link to truth."[47] This same document also reaffirms St. John Paul II's view that beauty is "*the visible form of the good*, just as the good is *the metaphysical expression of beauty*."[48]

Indeed, we can see beauty—like the true and the good—as a transcendental, predicable of every being and of the whole of being. In his commentary on *De Veritate*, Thomas derives a range of transcendentals. Some predicates, he explains, express a mode of being that the term *being* does not express. Thus, *substance* expresses "a special manner of existing, name-

42. ST I, q. 39, a. 8.

43. "Pulchra enim dicuntur quae visa placent." ST I, q. 5, a. 4, ad 1. *Summa Theologica*, translated by the Fathers of the English Dominican Province, 2nd ed. (New York: Benziger Brothers, 1947). All translations from the *Summa Theologica* are from this source.

44. Aristotle, *Ethica Nicomachea (Nicomachean Ethics)*, translated by W. D. Ross, in *The Basic Works of Aristotle*, edited by Richard McKeon (New York: Random House, 1941), 1.1, 1094a3.

45. St. Hilary, *De Trinitate*, V (PL 10:131).

46. Maritain, *Untrammeled Approaches*, 347.

47. "*Via Pulchritudinis*, Privileged Pathway for Evangelisation and Dialogue," The Pontifical Council for Culture (2009): no. 4.

48. St. John Paul II, *Letter to Artists* (April 4, 1999): no. 3; emphasis in original.

ly, as a being in itself."[49] Others, like *one,* express a mode of being "common and consequent upon every being."[50] In addition to transcendentals applicable to every being as such, there are the relational predicates. They are based "on the correspondence one being has with another,"[51] and such relational transcendentals are of particular interest here. These depend on the soul in that it can be in accord with every being, for the soul is "in a way all existing things."[52] The soul, moreover, has both an intellective power and an appetitive power. So it is that *good* expresses being as it corresponds to the appetitive power and *true* expresses being as it corresponds to the intellective power.

Although Thomas does not in like manner derive beauty as a transcendental, nothing stops him.[53] Consider beauty as *id quod visum placet.* Here "visum" reaches beyond the visual; it indicates an intuitive knowledge coming from the intellective power of the soul. Similarly, "placet" reaches well beyond sensation; it indicates joy.[54] If sought for itself, beauty corresponds to the appetitive power of the soul, and this beauty is a path to the soul.[55] There is, as well, a link to the good. "If a thing exalts and delights the soul," writes Maritain, "by the very fact that it is given to the intuition of the soul, it is good to apprehend, it is beautiful."[56] Because of this double relation to the soul, beauty is a unique transcendental.

Here, to be sure, we are speaking of metaphysics or, better, of the ontol-

49. Aquinas, *De Veritate,* q. 1, a. 1, in *Truth,* translated by Robert W. Mulligan (Chicago: Henry Regnery, 1952), 5.

50. Ibid.

51. Ibid.

52. Aristotle, *De Anima,* 3.8, 431b21, translated by J. A. Smith in *The Basic Works of Aristotle,* 595.

53. Thomas does not discuss beauty as a transcendental in the *Summa Theologica.* But neither does he there discuss other transcendentals that he considers elsewhere. See Kevin E. O'Reilly, *Aesthetic Perception: A Thomistic Perspective* (Dublin: Four Courts Press, 2007), 106n19.

54. Empirical correlates are intriguing. Anjan Chatterjee reports: "The pleasure that people derive from viewing objects they find beautiful taps into our brain's reward circuity." He adds, though, that often "knowledge, more than the hedonic qualities of the visual image, modulates these neural activation patterns," and comments that works of art "are often vehicles for ideas embedded in specific contexts." See his "Neuroaesthetics," *The Scientist* (May 1, 2014): 5.

55. Neuroscience, indeed, finds that works of art that an individual ranks as especially beautiful seem "so well-matched to an individual's unique makeup that they obtain access to the neural substrates concerned with the self." The everyday stimuli of task-oriented activity have no such access. See Edward A. Vesel, G. Gabrielle Starr, and Nava Rubin, "Art Reaches Within: Aesthetic Experience, the Self and the Default Mode Network," in *Frontiers in Neuroscience* 7 (2013): 258. Published online 2013 Dec 30 doi: 10.3389/fnins.2013.00258.

56. Maritain, *Art and Scholasticism,* 23.

ogy of beauty that grounds aesthetics. With this in mind, W. Norris Clarke highlights beauty as an object of both the intellect and the will. Since beauty "gives delight to our wills precisely as intuitively contemplated by our cognitive faculties," it is an avenue to "the full splendor of being."[57] For Maritain, reasoning in like manner, beauty is "the splendor of all the transcendentals."[58]

We can now turn to the convertibility of transcendentals in light of Maritain's intuition of being. "It is *the real itself*," Norris Clarke observes, "that is one, true, good and beautiful, but seen according to different perspectives."[59] Thus, each transcendental leads us to every other transcendental. Maritain's metaphysics of intuitivity suggests "a convertibility argument" for the intuition of being. Consider the following:

1. Transcendentals, though conceptually distinct from each other and from being, are by nature convertible with each other and with being.
2. Beauty is a transcendental.
3. Therefore, beauty is convertible with being. (1, 2)
4. We have an intuition of beauty.
5. Therefore, we have an intuition of being. (1, 4)

(For an expanded version of this argument, see the Appendix.)

An initial question is in order. Is the "intuition" of beauty different in kind from the "intuition" of being? It seems not. John Trapani refers to the former as divinatory and the latter as philosophical. Nonetheless, as he acknowledges, in both cases intuition is direct and intellectual in character; in both cases, it admits of subsequent reflection.[60]

Because this argument, as clarified, offers significant and fresh support for Maritain's disputed signature thesis, I will explore a pair of its premises more closely. Umberto Eco is an influential and historically informed critic of Maritain's theory of beauty. For this reason, I will address Eco's hesitancy about premise (2) and his rejection of premise (4).

Consider premise (2), "beauty is a transcendental." Eco admits that Thomas takes beauty to be a transcendental. He does so, Eco suggests,

57. W. Norris Clarke, *The One and the Many: A Contemporary Thomistic Metaphysics* (Notre Dame, Indiana: The University of Notre Dame Press, 2001), 299.

58. Maritain, *Art and Scholasticism*, 132.

59. Clarke, *The One and the Many*, 291.

60. John G. Trapani Jr., *Poetry, Beauty, and Contemplation: The Complete Aesthetics of Jacques Maritain* (Washington, D.C.: The Catholic University of America Press, 2011), 50, 166.

on the strength of Albert the Great's reading of Dionysius's *On the Divine Names*. For Dionysius, God, the ultimate cause of beauty in things, is beyond being—and so, too, is beauty.[61] Yet for Thomas God is *Ipsum esse subsistens*. He writes: "Everything that exists comes from beauty and goodness, that is from God, as from an effective principle that preserves and maintains," quickly adding that "all things are and all things become because of beauty and goodness, and all things look to them, as to an exemplar cause."[62] Nevertheless, Eco claims that Thomas borrows beauty, as a participation in the Divine, from a source that he simply misreads.[63] While both Dionysius and Thomas see the beauty of all things, for Dionysius *pankalia* evokes poetry while for Thomas it summons a hierarchy of existents. "Beauty," he teaches, "adds something to the good, namely an order which enables cognition to know that a thing is of such a kind."[64] He coordinates the beautiful with the good, and as an object of knowledge, with the true. For Eco—contrary to Clarke—this treatment of the beautiful is "anodyne" and "ambiguous."[65]

To be sure, Eco thinks that in the *Summa Theologica* Thomas clarifies the relation between the good and the beautiful. While we seek each as an end, beauty has to do both with appetite and with knowledge, the second of these because "beautiful things are those which please when seen."[66] Later Thomas adds: "The beautiful is the same as the good, and they differ in aspect only," and this because "the notion of good is that which calms the desire; while the notion of the beautiful is that which calms the desire, by being seen or known."[67] Furthermore, just as God is goodness itself, God, too, is beauty itself.

Yet Eco also worries that Thomas's definition of beauty in terms of its effects introduces a subjective and even sociological note and thereby under-

61. Umberto Eco, *The Aesthetics of Thomas Aquinas*, translated by Hugh Bredin (Cambridge: Harvard University Press, 1988), 24.

62. Aquinas, *In De Div. Nom.*, c. 4, 8. Here and throughout the translation is that of Hugh Bredin in Umberto Eco, *The Aesthetics of Thomas Aquinas*.

63. Aquinas, in any case, rightly reads Dionysius to reject a polytheistic Platonism. Rudi A. te Velde writes that for Dionysius there is not a plurality of ideal forms but that "they are all one and identical with the first cause of all things." See his "Aquinas's Aristotelian Science of Metaphysics," *Nova et Vetera* 13, no. 3 (Summer 2015): 761.

64. Aquinas, *In De Div. Nom.*, c. 4, 5.

65. Eco, *The Aesthetics of Thomas Aquinas*, 33.

66. ST I, q. 5, a. 4.

67. ST I-II, q. 27, a. 1, ad 3.

cuts the objectivity of beauty. But if beauty is not objective, how can it be a transcendental? To his credit, Eco recognizes that the intrinsic structure of the good and the true is prior to our seeking them, and such could also be the case for beauty. "It then seems natural," he supposes, "that beauty is formally constituted in relation between a subject and a thing, but that the thing has an objective structure [that] offers itself for contemplation."[68] So understood, this relational dimension supports beauty as a transcendental.

How, then, should we evaluate Eco's worry about premise (2), *Beauty is a transcendental*? Tracking the worry does lead to a useful consideration of Thomas's sources. It leads, as well, to a clarification of the structure of beauty. Nevertheless, I submit, Eco's hesitancy does not raise any serious doubt about the transcendental character of beauty.[69]

Let us turn then to premise (4), *We have an intuition of beauty*. Eco argues that Thomas could not accept such an intuition because of "the central *aporia*" of his account of beauty.[70] For Thomas, beauty is grounded in form, and form is the object of aesthetic experience. It is form that causes a thing to be in act. We must distinguish, though, between the form of a natural thing and that of an artifact. As the work of the Creator, the form of a natural thing is vastly richer than that of an artificial thing. The latter is accidental; it gives the artifact its specific order but does not confer its being. We can grasp the accidental form of an artifact, but we cannot, in practice, grasp the substantial form of a natural thing. "It is God," contends Eco, "who 'informs' matter and guides the intimate coalescence of form and matter into a substantial reality; and it is God who measures the created object against his own eternal idea of it."[71] For these reasons, "only God has the kind of knowledge of the formal structure of being which permits the perception of it *sub specie pulchri*."[72]

Eco's conclusion is hasty. Why can we not intuitively know the beauty of a natural thing even if we cannot know it with anything like the completeness with which God knows it? Why must our grasp of beauty be as acute as God's grasp of it? In addition, might we not suppose that

68. Eco, *The Aesthetics of Thomas Aquinas*, 59.

69. Nor, I think, does the claim that beauty is only a derivative transcendental, since it is consequent on the good. Were the good *not* beautiful, it would not be good. For an opposing view, see Kevin E. O'Reilly, *Aesthetic Perception: A Thomistic Perspective*, 108.

70. Eco, *The Aesthetics of Thomas Aquinas*, 202.

71. Ibid., 203.

72. Ibid.

a connaturality touched by grace would bring us some share in God's vision of beauty?[73] Moreover, intuition need not be exhaustive; indeed, we commonly enough speak of "probing our intuitions." Finally, we first grasp something's transcendental beauty, though not aesthetic beauty, simply in its existing.[74] Eco, though, draws a second hasty conclusion. He contends that beauty requires *claritas*, but in comparison to created forms, artificial forms are sadly deficient in this regard. Hence, for Aquinas, strictly speaking, there is so little beauty in artifacts that one could scarcely intuit it. Here again Eco ignores the analogical character of beauty. Why, might we not ask, does Thomas emphasize beauty as an artist's goal if the beauty of an artifact is so deficient?[75]

Nonetheless, Eco also contends that Thomas's theory of cognition precludes the intuition of beauty. For Thomas the first "moment" of simple apprehension is an intellectual abstraction. However, we need to attend to the order of the elements of cognition. How, Eco asks, could Thomas allow for "an intuitive act *of the intellect*" to occur either immediately before or after this initial abstraction? Since in any case, "the human intellect, for Aquinas, is compelled to engage in discourse," Eco argues, "the 'lightning' of intuition in the strict sense is denied to it."[76] So much for Maritain's view of beauty as the "lightning of mind on a matter intelligently arranged."[77] So much, then, for "breathtaking" or "stunning" beauty. In simple apprehension, moreover, direct contact with particulars always needs context: "there is an infinity of concomitant circumstances connected with particulars—existence, place, time, to name but a few—which are not perceived intuitively [but rather] are brought together with things, in our minds, through a complex discursive act, the act of judgment."[78] Thus, aesthetic vision can only follow the act of judgment that is subsequent to simple apprehension. How, then, could Thomas recognize Maritain's intuition of beauty? Eco's question is a worthy one, but there are resources for answering it.

Thomas holds that "sense is a sort of reason, just as is every cognitive faculty."[79] He singles out sight and hearing as serving reason and enabling

73. See Kevin E. O'Reilly, *Aesthetic Perception: A Thomistic Perspective*, 120.

74. See Armand Maurer, *About Beauty: A Thomistic Interpretation* (Houston: The Center for Thomistic Studies, 1983), 115.

75. *In De Div. Nom.*, c. 4, lect. 5.

76. Eco, *The Aesthetics of Thomas Aquinas*, 62; emphasis in original.

77. Maritain, *Art and Scholasticism*, 26.

78. Eco, *The Aesthetics of Thomas Aquinas*, 62.

79. ST I, q. 5, a. 4, ad 1.

us to appreciate the beautiful.[80] Based on this understanding, Maritain's view of how we grasp beauty emphasizes, in a new context, the role of intelligentiated sense. The senses, with which knowledge begins, already provide us with something of the intelligible. Perception, too, might come with some inchoate concept. Connaturality also comes into play. Our intelligent sharing in the natural world enables us to experience its beauty. The more receptive we become to beauty, the less labored is our recognition of it. There is no judgment without apprehension, and yet prior judgments tutor apprehension. Mediation gives way to intuition. Maritain distinguishes, as well, between the intuition of beauty and the abstraction of truth: "We must conceive that it is mind and sense combined, or, to use such an expression, the *intellectualised sense* which gives rise to aesthetic joy in the heart. It is thereby clear that the mind has no thought—unless secondarily and reflexively—of abstracting from the sensible particular, in the contemplation of which it is fixed, the intelligible reasons for its joy."[81] Does Maritain meet Eco's objection? Could Thomas accept an intuition of beauty?

Eco thinks not. In simple apprehension, he argues, the intellect does not know sensible particulars. Such knowledge requires a return to the phantasms elicited in sensation; only then can judgment occur. Thus, Eco explains, "the senses then give us an intuitive knowledge of the sensible," while "the intellect gives us knowledge of the universal."[82] Joining the two operations yields "a direct and immediate seeing of the species or nature of an object," but this falls short of "knowledge in which the intellect is in direct contact with the sensible."[83] Only God and angels have such knowledge. (In a way, his complaint calls to mind Étienne Gilson's claim that an intuition of being would be an intuition of God.) Maritain, however, is steadfast: the beauty which art expresses "is apprehended *in the sensible and through the sensible*, and not separably from it."[84]

Eco's line of criticism, it seems, returns us to our earlier remarks on Maritain's account of the intuition of being in relation to the act of judgment. I propose that Maritain would integrate the intuition of being with the intu-

80. ST I, q. 91, a. 3, ad 3 and I-II, q. 27, a. 1.

81. Maritain, *Art and Scholasticism*, 172n55; emphasis in original.

82. Eco, *The Aesthetics of Thomas Aquinas*, 62.

83. Ibid. On this point, Kevin E. O'Reilly agrees. See his *Aesthetic Perception: a Thomistic Perspective*, 37.

84. Maritain, *Art and Scholasticism*, 27; emphasis in original.

ition of beauty, and in doing so, he would similarly locate both with regard to the interplay of simple apprehension and judgment. (A full discussion of this interplay would require another essay.) As Eco himself notes, cognition "has no chronological structure."[85] For his part, Maritain insists, as noted above, that intellect "is wholly present in each of its operations."[86] In like manner, at the conceptual level, Maritain would subsequently develop his philosophy of beauty, together with that of being, at the metaphysical level of abstraction.[87]

The unfolding of the objection that Eco raises to premise (4), *We have an intuition of beauty,* does lead to a useful consideration of the interplay of the senses and the intellect as well as the relation between intuition and judgment. Nonetheless, since Maritain's treatment of both considerations is tenable, I find Eco's criticism less than compelling.

V. Envoi

However we analyze beauty, the Christian first experiences it in the human person, the work of the Divine artist. Only then can we experience the Beauty of the Lord. "Late have I loved you," Augustine writes, "beauty so old and so new: late have I loved you!"[88] Many are the ways of participating in this beauty. Maritain's affirmation is striking: "As being is everywhere present and everywhere various, the beautiful likewise is scattered everywhere and everywhere various."[89] *Pankalia,* in the beginning and in the end.[90]

85. Eco, *The Aesthetics of Thomas Aquinas,* 193.

86. Maritain, *Existence and the Existent,* 32.

87. Research suggests a neurological correlation. The activation of the medial prefrontal cortex in the presence of beauty "occurs subsequent to an initial perceptual and semantic analysis, and early enough to be a potential basis for response selection [yet] leaves open the question of how, in time, explicit evaluation relates to these dynamics." See Edward A. Vesel, G. Gabrielle Starr, and Nava Rubin, "Art Reaches Within: Aesthetic Experience, the Self and the Default Mode Network," in *Frontiers in Neuroscience* 7 (2013): 258. Published online 2013 Dec 30 doi: 10.3389/fnins.2013.00258.

88. "Sero te amavi! Pulchritudo tam antiqua et tam nova, sero te amavi!" See Augustine, *Confessions,* 10, 27: CCL, 27, 251.

89. Maritain, *Art and Scholasticism,* 31.

90. Thanks are due to John C. Cahalan, John F. X. Knasas, Michael D. Torre, and especially David R. Arias and Christopher Gilbert for their comments on earlier versions of this essay.

Appendix

An Expanded Convertibility Argument

1. Transcendentals are by nature convertible with each other and with being.
2. Transcendental predication is analogous.
3. Transcendentals share the same primary and infinite analogate.
4. The finite subject of a transcendental participates in its primary analogate.
5. The nature of a transcendental and the nature of being, though not their respective concepts, are necessarily the same.
6. If we have an intuition of a transcendental, then we have knowledge of its nature in keeping with our receptivity.
7. Beauty is a transcendental.
8. Therefore, beauty is
   a. by nature convertible with other transcendentals and with being,
   b. predicated analogously,
   c. such that each of its finite subjects participates in its primary and infinite analogate,
   d. one in nature with being though conceptually distinct.
   (7, 1, 2, 3, 4, 5)
9. We have an intuition of beauty.
10. Therefore, we have an intuition of being. (7, 8 (a), 9).
11. The nature of beauty and the nature of being, though not their respective concepts, are necessarily the same. (5, 7)
12. Therefore, we have knowledge of the nature of beauty and of being, though the concepts of them are not equivalent, in keeping with our receptivity. (6, 9, 10)

MEGAN FURMAN

The Place of Poetry in Human Blessedness

An Epistemological Expansion

I. Introduction

UPON LIFTING THE COVER of *Untrammeled Approaches,* one is confronted with a foreword, written by Maritain himself, self-consciously describing the nature of what is to follow: "The kind of essay, or rather poem, which this foreword precedes is not even an hypothesis which one would wish might some day become an accepted theory. It is a conjectural essay destined to remain conjectural."[1] Building upon this injunction, the piece that indeed follows offers to its own interpretation an additional preemptive word. Labelling it a "reverie," Maritain qualifies the essay, or rather poem, as a certain *kind* of poem, or rather, a "poetic form of expression naturally suited to those things which cannot be attained by the ordinary ways of knowing." Thus the reader enters into the introductory essay, or poem, or reverie, with an explicit word of caution: "We must never confuse poetic assertions with doctrinal affirmations."[2]

As others in this volume have more fully elaborated the content of and theological issues at stake in "Eschatological Ideas," the opening text of *Untrammeled Approaches,* such topics shall not receive primary attention in this essay. Instead, they will give way to certain meta-questions: What is Maritain *doing* here? With what implications? *Untrammeled Approaches*

1. Jacques Maritain, *Untrammeled Approaches,* vol. 20 of *The Collected Works of Jacques Maritain,* edited and translated by Bernard Doering (Notre Dame, Indiana: University of Notre Dame Press, 1996), 1.

2. Ibid., 4.

presents an ideal situation in which to examine Maritain's appropriations of Thomistic epistemology, most especially the peculiar expansion he calls "poetry" or "poetic knowledge." By distilling a fair understanding of "poetry" from Maritain's work in aesthetics and epistemology before considering it within the context of his moral philosophy, I hope to show how poetry, as Maritain understands it, assumes a special role in human blessedness.

On what basis does Maritain claim to legitimate his extensions? In *Creative Intuition in Art and Poetry,* he points to an understudied passage of the *Nicomachean Ethics* in which Aristotle identifies a certain power of human intelligence—which has been neglected, according to Maritain, by traditional epistemology. This is the fundamental power of "intuitive reason":

> If, then, the states of mind by which we have truth and are never deceived about things ... are scientific knowledge, practical wisdom, and intuitive reason, and [as concerns the perception of the first principles] it cannot be any of the three, the remaining alternative is that it is *intuitive reason* that grasps the first principles.[3]

While a lack of familiarity with its terminology may lead someone to think that, in emphasizing intuitive reason, Maritain has begun to lead him down a path toward a mystical or supernatural kind of knowledge, Maritain's point, in fact, is quite the opposite. The intuitive reason, Maritain underscores, is perhaps the most natural power of the mind. To prove its existence, one needs no special recourse to notions of mysticism, grace, or "the supernatural"; it is enough, he says, merely to reflect upon the nature of conceptual knowledge: "Any demonstration finally resolves into first principles which are not demonstrated, but seen; and any discovery which really reveals a new aspect of being is born in a flash of intuitivity before being discursively tested and justified."[4]

What is the philosopher's purpose in reclaiming this neglected power of human reason? Actually, Maritain has several objectives, all of which hinge upon not only the recognition, but the significant estimation, of intuitive reason. Included among Maritain's career-long projects, for example, is the attempt to recover "connatural knowledge," a Scholastic notion "thrown into oblivion" by modern philosophers, with devastating effects for, among other things, ethics. Enter moral philosophy. For Maritain, the restoration of happiness, both conceptually and in practice, requires the

3. Aristotle *Nicomachean Ethics* 6.6, 1141a2–8, translated by W. D. Ross. Quoted in Maritain, *Creative Intuition in Art* and *Poetry* (New York: Pantheon Books, 1953), 76.

4. Maritain, *Creative Intuition,* 76.

reclamation of connatural knowledge—not only, however, in its Scholastic iteration. Going beyond his forebears, Maritain calls for something more robust: "We have to ... recognize its basic role and importance in such domains as moral practical knowledge and natural or supernatural mystical experience—and"—here Maritain will make his most significant contribution—"in the domain of art and poetry."[5] Importantly, the principle undergirding Maritain's elaborations upon connatural knowledge is precisely "intuitive reason."

What do intuitive reason, art, and poetry have to do with happiness? As usual, Maritain's preoccupations are, even in aesthetics, to establish the proper order of things and to identify the pitfalls and perversions at risk in their disorder. Navigating a positive position in part by critiquing alternative theories, Maritain discloses two primary aims: first, to vouch for the intellectual (or rational) nature of the activity of "poetry," and second, to defend it from the incursion of conceptual, logical, discursive reason.

II. The Preconscious Life of the Intellect

As employed by Maritain, "poetry" is "first of all an intellective act which by its essence is creative, and forms something into being instead of being formed by things."[6] Derived from the Greek word *poièsis*, "poetry" for Maritain refers to the intellectual activity proper to artistic creativity in the realm of the fine arts. As we see in *Creative Intuition in Art and Poetry*, if Maritain is going to argue that poetry involves *a real kind of knowledge*, then he must show how poetry is essentially and undeniably intellectual. Prompting us to expand our understandings of "reason" and "intellect," Maritain writes: "I use ... reason and intellect as synonymous insofar as they designate a single power or faculty in the human soul. But I want to emphasize ... when they are related to the spiritual energy which is poetry, [they] must be understood in a much deeper and larger sense than is usual."[7] Reason, he adds, "does not only articulate, connect, and infer, it also *sees*." Moreover, "Reason's intuitive grasping" is not merely *one* function of the intellect, it is more fundamentally "the *primary* act and function of that one and single power which is called intellect or reason."[8]

5. Ibid., 118.
6. Ibid., 114.
7. Ibid., 4.
8. Ibid., 75; emphasis added.

At the core of Maritain's expanded epistemology lies an anthropological tenet that cuts across the dualism of his contemporary context. Every activity of the soul is, he insists, the operation of a single soul which is, in turn, one co-principle of the composite soul–body unity: the human person. The unity of the human person entails that every human activity is permeated by spirituality, even if its "mark" is "imprinted on only some part, either on this or that aspect of our being or our life." If such is the case, "It is then spirituality *of a kind* . . . under a certain aspect."[9]

Invoking Aristotle and Thomas Aquinas, Maritain identifies spirituality with intelligence and claims that the active intellect, or the "illuminating intellect," is the activator not only of conceptual thought, but of intelligence in all its operations, speculative and practical.[10] After all, he writes, "the will, like the intellect, is a spiritual faculty," and "there is no liberty or virtue without some spirituality." Thus, he asserts, intelligence "is there secretly animating the humblest efforts of the peasant or artist to impose the form of reason on earthly things."[11]

These premises bear significant epistemological import: for Maritain, human knowledge is much broader than conceptual knowledge. Upon this foundation, Maritain posits the existence of the "spiritual unconscious, or rather, preconscious," the "common root" of the soul's powers, upon which, he says, "everything depends."[12] The spiritual preconscious (which is also, at times, called the "musical unconscious") is that from which *all* "the acts and fruits of human consciousness and the clear perceptions of the mind emerge."[13] Thus the spiritual preconscious grounds every human intellectual activity, whether they involve concepts, judgments, actions, or "poetry."

1. *The Intellectual Nature of Poetry*

Maritain's remarks on poetry generally can be categorized in either of two ways: as (1) descriptive insights into the poetic process, or (2) philosophical statements classifying the kind of knowledge proper to poetry in relation to other kinds of knowledge. Insofar as the aim at hand is to as-

9. Jacques Maritain, *Distinguish to Unite or The Degrees of Knowledge,* vol. 7 of *The Collected Works of Jacques Maritain,* edited and translated by Bernard Doering (Notre Dame, Indiana: University of Notre Dame Press, 1995), 283.

10. Thomas Aquinas, *Q. disp. de anima,* a. 15, ad 9; SCG III, chap. 45.

11. Maritain, *Degrees of Knowledge,* 283.

12. Maritain, *Creative Intuition,* 92.

13. Ibid., 94.

semble a taxonomic understanding of poetry's distinctive nature, we shall focus on the latter category. Maritain must begin by establishing that poetry is intellectual in nature, which he does by situating it within a larger knowledge-schema and drawing a first divide between knowledge of two kinds: conceptual and nonconceptual. Distinguished by its term, conceptual knowledge is scientific; it is the kind whereby, through the abstracting activity of the agent intellect, a concept is produced in the passive intellect. Nonconceptual knowledge, by contrast, does not arrive by way of a concept; instead, it proceeds by way of "union or inclination, connaturality or congeniality."[14] One example of such knowledge is that involved in moral virtue, a kind of connatural knowledge that attracts Maritain's attention more keenly than it might have his predecessors'. Penetrating its nature, Maritain demonstratively shows how in connatural knowledge the intellect is still at play, "not alone, but together with affective inclinations and dispositions of the will, and is guided and shaped by them."[15]

According to Maritain, *poetic* knowledge is a particular kind of connatural knowledge distinguished by its origin in a certain kind of "affective resonance," which is to say, emotional experience of the world. Its emotional aspect, however, is no "brute feeling," nor anything detached from the full intellectual life of the human person.[16] To the contrary: the emotion involved in affective, connatural knowledge "imbues the soul"; it resounds in the "nocturnal empire of a primeval activity of the intellect which, far beyond concept and logic, exercises itself in vital connection with imagination and emotion."[17] What accounts for poetry, therefore, is not emotion *per se*, but intelligent emotional experience.

The principle grounding these extensions to a more traditional Thomistic epistemology is quintessentially Maritainian: one can logically distinguish what is, in reality, united. In this instance, Maritain emphasizes the underlying unity of the soul whose activities can be separated philosophically, but which are integrated in reality. The principle itself offers nothing new, but what Maritain may suggest uniquely is the constancy and omnipresence of the agent intellect. In other words, Maritain claims that the agent intellect is constantly in act, abstracting not only from sense-information, but also

14. Ibid., 117.
15. Ibid.
16. Ibid., 8.
17. Ibid., 76.

from emotion-information (which likewise arrives by way of the senses). His vision of the mind is therefore one in which the agent intellect operates upon, and in relation to, the *totality* of experience.

2. *The Situation of Poetic Knowledge*

Using conventional epistemology as his paradigm, Maritain shows how affective knowledge runs in parallel with conceptual knowledge. Whereas, in conceptual knowledge, the agent intellect abstracts from sense-data to produce a (spiritual) concept, in affective knowledge, the agent intellect abstracts from one's emotional experience of the world to produce a "spiritualized emotion." Spiritualized emotion, also described as "intelligentiated sense," therefore serves as the nonconceptual analogue to the concept;[18] importantly, it is by its means that one may attain to poetic knowledge. Thus we can say that spiritualized emotion serves as *the formal principle of poetic knowledge.*

What, though, is poetic knowledge? Maritain describes it in *experience* as the "moment" of intuition or "flash" of insight into reality that contains—virtually—the germ of all creative activity that will fructify in a work. But to penetrate its distinctive content, one will need to analyze it philosophically within the greater scheme of Maritain's epistemology. While the terminology begs elaboration, poetic knowledge is said to be connatural, non-conceptual, and existential.

Whereas the addition of any new knowledge involves the acquisition of being, the mode by which being is obtained, along with the aspects obtained, differ among the various kinds of knowledge. In its mode, writes Maritain, poetry is "that intercommunication between the inner being of things and the inner being of the self which is a kind of divination."[19] Why does he choose divination? Like poetic knowledge, divination proceeds by connatural resonance, rather than conceptual abstraction. Its non-conceptual mode accounts for the seeming "darkness" or "hiddenness" of its sources, which, as in poetic knowledge, lend an air of mystery.

18. See Maritain, *Creative Intuition,* especially 113–16. Noting statements such as those made by Maritain in *Creative Intuition,* 118, critics John W. Hanke and John Trapani claim that it is not the spiritualized emotion, but rather the work itself, that is analogous to the concept. I would suggest that further work is needed on this point. As indicated above, I would propose a revised epistemology in which the "spiritualized emotion" serves as the proper analogue to the concept (the "mental word"), and the work serves as analogue to the spoken word.

19. Maritain, *Creative Intuition,* 3.

By "existential," Maritain appropriates a contemporary term and uses it in a peculiar, provocative, and potentially groundbreaking way. Essentially, he claims that certain kinds of knowledge do not pertain *directly* to the essence of a thing, but to "concrete existence." The assertion requires significant nuance in order to retain its Thomistic roots. According to Maritain, "concrete existence" refers to "the secret properties of being involved in its identity and in its essential relations with other things."[20] The description remains ambiguous, and a number of scholars have attempted to elucidate it further. One of these is John Trapani, who suggests that these "secret properties" refer to the relation among things due to their causal dependence on the divine *Esse*.[21] John W. Hanke, in turn, associates them with "a thing's way of *existing*, vs. *way* of existing," which is not expressible in a concept, but only in the act of affirming or denying.[22] Put most simply, it seems as if the "secret properties" relate to the transcendental properties of being tied up in any particular thing.

Notably, in describing poetic knowledge as existential and "free from the concept,"[23] Maritain does not mean that poetry is *anti*-conceptual or *merely* particular. As Hanke clarifies:

> Since the intellect is at play in aesthetic experience, there may be concepts present—having to do with the subject or other material elements and relationships; but the presence of a concept is not what formally constitutes the aesthetic experience or serves as the means of appropriating the aesthetic object.[24]

Hanke's explication would seem to agree with Maritain's holism, which distinguishes to unite: "Caught up in the intuition of sense, [the intellect] is irradiated by an intelligible light that is suddenly given to it, in the very sensible in which it glitters, and which it does not seize *sub ratione veri*, but rather *sub ratione delectabilis*."[25]

20. Ibid., 126. To illustrate the "contents" of knowledge that is of an existential character, Maritain identifies three facets: (1) what a thing is existentially, in its full context, here and now (2) all manner of similarities and correspondences to the thing in reality, including by analogy and metaphor; and (3) all manner of similarities and correspondences to the thing in "ideality," which is to say, by virtue of its being known by a subject. See John W. Hanke, *Maritain's Ontology of the Work of Art* (The Hague: Martinus Nijhoff, 1973), 89–90.

21. John Trapani Jr., *Poetry, Beauty, and Contemplation: The Complete Aesthetics of Jacques Maritain* (Washington, D.C.: The Catholic University of America Press, 2011), 85.

22. Hanke, *Maritain's Ontology*, 26.

23. Maritain, *Creative Intuition*, 126.

24. Hanke, *Maritain's Ontology*, 28.

25. Jacques Maritain, *Art and Scholasticism and the Frontiers of Poetry*, translated by Joseph W. Evans (New York: Charles Scribner's Sons, 1962), 23–26.

While poetic intuition can result from the perception of any aesthetic object, in a work of *fine* art, one encounters something more profound. Its connatural character implies, upon reflection, that poetic knowledge discloses proportion, or "consonance," between an apprehending power and its object. As in all apprehensions of beauty, there is a recognition of order, the chief beauty in things. Moreover, since order implies one-who-ordered, the work implies an efficient cause endowed with intelligence, capable of "making" according to a *ratio*. Thus, at a single glance, the work manifests the human's unique position in the universe, the only creature capable of making art, the sole creature made in the image and likeness of the "first poet."[26] "The work," writes Maritain, "breaks out of the confines of its status as an artifact ... it will swarm with meanings, and will say more than it is, and will deliver to the mind, at one stroke, the universe in a human countenance."[27] Signifying a reality far beyond itself, the work also points within, making present a transcendent reality only through its very concrete existence.[28]

III. The Place of Poetry in Human Blessedness

Having analyzed the peculiar kind of knowledge Maritain calls "poetic," the question remains: why is it important? Here one must enter the moral realm. From the Thomistic tradition, Maritain has inherited a twofold notion of happiness corresponding to the perfection of the two distinctive human powers, intellect and will, a twofold notion sometimes articulated as "knowledge" and "governance." The way in which poetry—in its fullest sense—contributes distinctively to these two tasks, and so to human perfection, can be seen by examining its two essential aspects, which is to say, the "cognitive" and the "creative," respectively. Poetic knowledge, which represents poetry's cognitive aspect, participates in a special way in the knowing activity of God, while the creative aspect participates in governance. Maritain writes:

If in the natural order anyone has entered into a sort of agreement and, if one may dare to say so, a kind of metaphysical conspiracy with God as cause of beings, it is

26. See Jacques Maritain, "The Frontiers of Poetry," in *Art and Scholasticism and the Frontiers of Poetry*, 121–22, 126–28; see also Hanke, *Maritain's Ontology*, 43–44.

27. Maritain, *Creative Intuition*, 93.

28. On Maritain's ontology of signs, see Hanke, *Maritain's Ontology*, 43–67.

not the philosopher but the poet. He is the one who, after the manner of a man, also creates; his art is the grandson of God.... The poet is ... much better prepared than anyone else to understand things that are from on high. ... His proper task is to create an object that brings joy to the spirit in which the brilliance of form shines forth.[29]

In both its cognitive and creative aspects, poetry partakes in the activity of the divine artist. By its very nature, as both affective and connatural, poetic knowledge inclines the will, and thus it leaves its mark upon the soul, igniting a thirst for beauty. It may also incite a poet *to order* things beautifully. For Maritain, the desire "to create in beauty" is poetry's most proper "effect" whereby the poet imitates—and participates in—the activity of the "first artist." "The poet," he asserts, "completes the work of creation, he co-operates in divine balancing, he moves mysteries about."[30] But must this act of governance occur only in art?

In most cases, Maritain treats poetry as oriented solely to the production of a work. Not always, however, is this the case; as John Trapani argues, poetry "transcends art." Trapani points out that "the creativity of the spirit is a *free* creativity that inclines toward creation, though it *may not* actually bear fruit in a work."[31] Trapani's purpose is to attempt "the final reconstruction of a notion of poetic contemplation," or what Trapani calls "the path undeveloped" by Maritain, implicit yet underdeveloped in his thought. He demonstrates where, according to Maritain, poetic intuition bears fruit *virtually*, if not actually. Quoting Maritain, Trapani writes: "Now it is quite true that one may be a poet without producing—without having yet produced—any work of art, but if one is a poet, one is virtually turned towards operation."[32] And further:

As soon as [poetic intuition] exists ... it is, in the depth of the nonconceptual life of the intellect, an incitation to create. This incitation can remain virtual ... Nay more, a poetic intuition can be kept in the soul a long time, latent (though never forgotten), till some day it will come out of sleep.[33]

29. Maritain, *Degrees of Knowledge*, 299–300.

30. Jacques Maritain, "Answer to Jean Cocteau," in *Art and Faith: Letters Between Jacques Maritain and Jean Cocteau*, translated by John Coleman (New York: Philosophical Library, 1948), 90.

31. Trapani, *Poetry, Beauty, and Contemplation*, 158–59.

32. Jacques and Raïssa Maritain, *The Situation of Poetry*, translated by Marshall Suther (New York: Philosophical Library, 1955), 52.

33. Maritain, *Creative Intuition*, 134. The implication here is that "poetry" applies more broadly than to that intuition of beauty that results in a work of art. One way to account for

Even if poetic intuition produces fruits which remain immanent, never coming to transitive expression, the contemplation of beauty has nevertheless had an effect, or rather, an *affect,* upon the soul. Therefore, while poetry is always found in the artist, it "can also be found in a boy who knows only how to look and to say ah, ah, ah, like Jeremiah."[34] The consequence is that poetry has moral significance not only for the artist, but for every person. Even a brief look across Maritain's corpus ratifies this claim. In *Approaches to God,* Maritain goes so far as to suggest that poetry can in fact be natural proof of God's existence. In *Creative Intuition,* he expounds upon the mechanics of this claim: "Poetry is an absolute ... it tends of itself to make man more thirsty for *the* Absolute—the first Poet, the creator of the universe."[35]

This discussion began with poetry. I could not have planned for it to end as tidily as Maritain himself concludes it with the final essay of *Untrammeled Approaches.* As John Dunaway points out, the closing piece, in which Maritain gives his rendering of the Biblical enigma *Song of Songs,* cannot be mere happenstance. Thomas Aquinas was reported on his deathbed to have given a teaching on the Canticle; Maritain follows suit. Here again, it is not the content but the form of the work that most solicits our attention. According to Dunaway, Maritain insists that his account represents neither a formal theological exegesis, nor any matter of conceptual thought, but rather, the simple act "of obeying, in order to give it a voice, an entirely intuitive and supra-conceptual élan of the soul in which the resonances of language reverberate *ad infinitum.*" In a way that could be articulated by one alone who is truly both philosopher and lover, Maritain continues: "It goes straight to its object, which is absolute love. It sings of love in its pure essence as its immediate signified."[36]

It is one thing to claim a place for "poetry" in human blessedness; it is another to consider what sort of place it occupies. In the case of Jacques Maritain, as of St. Thomas before him, a life drawing near to its earthly

---

this is by underscoring the fact that Maritain first coined the term within the context of artistic creation.

34. Maritain, *Situation of Poetry,* 44.

35. Maritain, *Creative Intuition,* 82.

36. Jacques Maritain, "Le Cantique des cantiques," in *Approches sans entraves* (Paris: Fayard, 1973), 533; quoted in John M. Dunaway, "Maritain on the *Song of Songs,*" in *Jacques Maritain and the Many Ways of Knowing,* edited by Douglas A. Ollivant (Washington, D.C.: The Catholic University of America Press, 2002), 316.

summit turns in its last days to a particular kind of connatural knowledge, giving reason to consider the possibility that poetry may yield knowledge of a kind higher than conceptual thought. Whether or not this is the case, what Maritain uniquely demonstrates, philosophically and in practice, is that poetry may deserve greater attention in the human pursuit of blessedness.

GREGORY KERR

The Centrality of Intuition

Jacques Maritain and Flannery O'Connor

> Every work of art reaches man in his inner powers. It reaches him more profoundly and insidiously than any rational proposition, either cogent demonstration or sophistry. For it strikes him with two terrible weapons, Intuition and Beauty, and at the single root in him of all his energies, Intellect and Will, Imagination, Emotion, Passions, Instincts and obscure tendencies. Art and Poetry awaken the dreams of man, and his longings, and reveal to him some of the abysses he has in himself.[1]
>
> —Jacques Maritain, *The Responsibility of the Artist*

> Modern art "transforms nature, not only by carrying to extremes the law of deformation of natural appearances which painting has always brought into play, but also by causing another universe of forms and relations between forms—disclosing a deeper reality, more akin to our dreams, angers, anguish, or melancholy.[2]
>
> —Jacques Maritain, *Creative Intuition in Art and Poetry*

1. Jacques Maritain, *The Responsibility of the Artist* (New York: Charles Scribner's Sons, 1960), 58–59.

2. Jacques Maritain, *Creative Intuition in Art and Poetry*, Bollingen Series 35.1 (Princeton, New Jersey: Princeton University Press, 1977), 73.

I. Introduction

Some in the literary world might be surprised to learn just how much the American southern writer Flannery O'Connor was influenced by the philosophical framework of the French Thomist philosopher/metaphysician Jacques Maritain. This essay explores an illuminating correlation between Jacques Maritain's idea of the role of intuition in the development of the knowledge of being in the mind of a philosopher and Flannery O'Connor's idea of the role of the writer's art in the short story. By examining Maritain's essay "No Knowledge Without Intuitivity" in his late work, *Untrammeled Approaches*,[3] his treatment of intuition in *Creative Intuition in Art and Poetry*, and by looking at the collected essays of O'Connor in *Mystery and Manners*—most notably "Novelist and Believer" and "The Nature and Aim of Fiction"[4]—we can highlight the central role of intuition in both the philosopher's theoretical understanding of being and in the writer's art revealing it.

For Maritain, there are many senses in which the word "intuition" may be used.[5] If I may summarize here: often called a knowledge by connaturality, intuition means a knowledge or experience that involves both the human intellect and the senses in such a way that a person knows in a primarily non-discursive way. St. Thomas, in the *Summa theologiae*, famously contrasts the man who makes moral judgments through the concepts of moral science with the prudent man who needed only to consult his inclinations.[6] In attaining this knowledge, often called a "gut" knowledge by virtue of its employment of the senses, the knower does not abstract and disengage a universal concept or notion from the material object that is presented to it.[7] The knower is not aiming at scientific necessity but is

3. Jacques Maritain, *Untrammeled Approaches* (Notre Dame, Indiana: University of Notre Dame Press, 1996).

4. Flannery O'Connor, "The Nature and Aim of Fiction" in *Mystery and Manners: Occasional Prose*, edited by Sally and Robert Fitzgerald (New York: Farrar, Straus and Giroux, 1961).

5. To my knowledge, the best (and most thorough) treatment of Maritain's notion of intuition is in John G. Trapani Jr., *Poetry, Beauty and Contemplation: The Complete Aesthetics of Jacques Maritain* (Washington, D.C.: The Catholic University of America Press, 2011).

6. ST I, q. 1, a. 6, ad 3.

7. Jacques Maritain, *Art and Scholasticism and the Frontiers of Poetry*, translated by Joseph W. Evans (Notre Dame, Indiana: University of Notre Dame Press, 1974), 25; and *Distinguish to Unite or The Degrees of Knowledge*, translated by Gerald B. Phelan (New York: Charles Scribner's Sons, 1959), 2.

dealing with contingent or existential relationships in reality, which are often too complex to adequately treat scientifically. If the ordinary discursive process is the movement from sensory perception to abstraction and theory, perhaps one can see intuition as a temporary reversing or reverberation of it. As in judgment, one is returning to the phantasm or back to the sources of knowledge and thereby to the actual activity of individual persons and creatures. One needs only to think of parents "knowing" their child.[8] They know the child "inside out," as it were, by suffering the child's behavior. They know the child's tendencies—what the child will or will not do. A purely scientific knowledge would pale in comparison.

In ordinary scientific and discursive knowledge, the human mind draws from the phantasm and abstracts a form or a universal idea. When some entity is known through discursive knowledge, it is known through the concept that has been disengaged from its particular environment in space and time and has become, in a sense, both definite and timeless; intuition, on the contrary, is a process that uses something other than concepts in knowing reality. In the case of the poet, it is primarily through emotion that the poet or artist knows, and in the case of the Christian mystic it is through *agape* or God's love. Here, the senses that perceive and the imagination that grasps reality are vital, for the mind does not rely on disengaged universal concepts but rather on the sensual and the imaginative sources born in sustained direct contact with the sensible particulars of reality.

For both Maritain and O'Connor, intuition is a critical part of human rationality. It does what ordinary discursive and logical thinking cannot do: it develops the tools by which the philosopher or writer can expand their cognitive grasp of reality beyond their current paradigmatic, logical, or conceptual systems. It can do this because it does not, like ordinary discursive reasoning, only connect concepts at the same systematic and logical level, but rather can actually apprehend different levels of reality simultaneously.

II. Maritain

Displaying the influence of Aristotle and, more impressively, his mentor the philosopher Henri Bergson, Maritain claims that only intuition is fluid enough to develop the philosopher's mind in becoming adequate to

8. Maritain, *Creative Intuition*, 123n17.

understand reality fully. Maritain believes that Descartes and his progeny, because of the *Cogito* and the turn to the subject, are stuck within static mathematical and conceptually clear and distinct, atomistic and egalitarian frameworks of the mind alone. Cartesian and idealist concepts cannot of themselves develop or adapt to the realities to be known. And so, as Maritain says in *The Degrees of Knowledge*, the idealist framework is infinitely and univocally flat.[9] It ignores the reality of the whole process of coming to know being.

The key to understanding the critical role for intuition lies in the fact that the mind must be in constant contact and communication with being *before* it ever understands it. According to Maritain, this is how poetry is defined. It is "the intercommunication between the inner being of things and the inner being of the human self which is a kind of divination. [It] is the secret life of each and all of the arts."[10] Thus, there is always an intuitive underground and cognitive current or "trafficking" between the preconscious of the human being and the inner depths of things. Now, according to O'Connor, the writer must "stare" at it (reality), and "take a long look at it," in order to display reality and "plunge its depths."[11] Only intuition is fluid and powerful enough to accomplish this.

Maritain stresses the importance of intuition in his essay, "No Knowledge without Intuitivity." While the title says it all, he says some interesting things concerning it. Here, not unsurprisingly, he criticizes Descartes and modern philosophy. He notes that while Descartes correctly believed that one can intuit one's own mind, the same philosopher was in error when he held the idea that the mind need not continue its intuitive activity for discovering and seeing into reality. Descartes attempted to develop his philosophy through clear and distinct ideas and uniform systematic, deductive connections. And so the very concepts he used were homogeneous and ill-adapted, philosophically, to know fully the real. Maritain says, "With Descartes, reason is not controlled by the intuitivity of the mind turned toward the real, since the mind is turned solely toward itself. The philosopher remains shut up within his thought, clear ideas suffice for everything."[12] For Descartes, at precisely the point where "what is held to be true must be

9. Maritain, *Distinguish to Unite*, ix.

10. Maritain, *Creative Intuition*, 3.

11. Flannery O'Connor, "The Nature and Aim of Fiction", in *Mystery and Manners*, 77–78.

12. Jacques Maritain, *Untrammeled Approaches*, 320.

'adjusted,' reason is controlled only by itself: by its own power of constructivity, its own ease and satisfaction in putting together conceptual clarities."[13] For Maritain, this is a huge mistake, because the human intellect, as it becomes intentionally what it knows, needs to continue looking at the real and adjusting the nature and scope of its concepts and structure so that the intellect can adequately map out the real—one size will not fit all. The mind itself needs to grow!

We need to wake up to the fact that the order of the world may require more than our first logical attempts at coherent theories. Some modern philosophers seem to think that thinking should be automatic.[14] When I read the work of some naturalists, for example, I cannot help thinking that they think of the world as merely a vast Lego or Tinkertoy set. Their insistence upon mathematics as a heuristic for knowing the world is why the metaphor of the machine was so seminal to the early modern mind. It could only think of "reason" appropriating the world through clear and distinct ideas and mathematical measurement. It was fated to imagine the universe as a "machine," for it was the only way the universe could reveal itself through such a mindset. But, as Maritain claims, one need not accept this heuristic metaphor. He tries to wake us up in his *Approaches to God*:

> Let us rouse ourselves, let us stop living in dreams or in the magic of images and formulas, of words, of signs and practical symbols. Once a man has been awakened to the reality of existence and of his own existence, when he has really perceived that formidable, sometimes elating, sometimes sickening or maddening fact I exist, he is henceforth possessed by the intuition of being and the implication it bears with it.[15]

In *Untrammeled Approaches*, Maritain gives us an account of how reason should work. He reminds us that the idea that reality can be captured by concepts and logic alone is a crazy one (one may think of Star Trek's Dr. Spock, G. K. Chesterton's materialist madman in *Orthodoxy*, or even of Doc Martin from the eponymous BBC television show). Of course, concepts and logic are vital, but they need to be guided and "enveloped" by intuition. He summarizes his view by saying, "All by itself, and without the

13. Ibid., 320–21.

14. Maritain wrote: "Leibniz finally invents a logic and a language whose most wonderful characteristic is that it *dispenses from thinking*." See Maritain's discussion of this very point in *Art and Scholasticism*, 40.

15. Jacques Maritain, *Approaches to God*, World Perspectives Series, vol. 1, translated by Peter O'Reilly (London: George Allen and Unwin, 1955), 3.

control of the intuitivity of an intellect that is turned *toward* reality, the discourse of reason will inevitably go astray either by failing to branch off when it should or by heading down the wrong path."[16]

He illustrates why this must be so by the use of a metaphor. He asks us to imagine an explorer who has to travel through a strange country. The explorer prepares himself by reviewing an old map of where things are supposed to be (discursive rationality). Following upon the rational review of this map, he sends out a team of explorers to reconnoiter the terrain. They set out and discover that if they travel the direction he wants to go, they will run up against a swamp or a mountain lake. They must rethink their plan of attack. He thereupon sends out new mapmakers to draw up a new map (discursive rationality again), and then he proceeds with the journey.[17] The ability to change the map itself comes not from discursive thought, as that would maintain the conceptual status quo, but from intuition, for discursive thought connects the already conceived concepts and tries to connect them. Intuition rejects the current conceptual framework and reconceives the map.

Surprisingly, the advantage given by this experiential intuition lies in the ability to say "no." Intuition says "no" to the current conceptual plan,[18] and suggests new possibilities, which can then result in a change of plans.[19] It is this ability of experiential intuition to see into reality and to reject current conceptual systems of thought that lies at the heart of every great scientific discovery, says Maritain. It is at the origin of great mathematical and scientific reforms.[20] This concurs with what Thomas Kuhn wrote in *The Structure of Scientific Revolutions*. Just think of the moment when the scientist is at the end of his logical rope at the breakdown of an old paradigm and facing the beginning of a new one. Kuhn told us that when a scientist

16. Maritain, *Untrammeled Approaches*, 326.

17. Ibid., 314.

18. Ibid., 319.

19. This idea can be perhaps further illustrated by the use of E. F. Schumacher's notion of *adaequatio* or the ability of the mind to become adequate to the thing to be known (E. F. Schumacher, *Guide for the Perplexed* [New York: Harper and Row, 1977], 39–49). As an analogy, I will share a personal example of coming to know and appreciate Mozart's classic 41st symphony, the *Jupiter*. What at one time seemed like a collection of semi-random and boring sounds became exciting tonal vessels full of energy. My mind, through repeated listening and intuition, had adapted, had manufactured, the organizational intentional tools to grasp larger melodic and harmonic groupings and so could then interpret their powerful "movement" through the piece.

20. Maritain, *Untrammeled Approaches*, 312–13; *Creative Intuition*, 93n33.

is on the verge of an insight into a new paradigm he is not merely thinking logically, but in a fashion that would properly be characterized as aesthetic. According to Kuhn, "the importance of aesthetic considerations can sometimes be decisive" and "something must make at least a few scientists feel that the new proposal is on the right track, and sometimes it is only personal and inarticulate aesthetic considerations that can do that."[21]

Also worth noting in this regard is Karl Popper's idea that poetic intuition is actually critical to the scientist. He writes that "theories are seen to be the free creations of our own minds, the result of an almost poetic intuition, of an attempt to understand intuitively the laws of nature." He also says that "[a]mong the real dangers to the progress of science is not the likelihood of its being completed, but such things as lack of imagination."[22]

III. Flannery O' Connor

Flannery O'Connor claims that she cut her aesthetic teeth on Maritain's aesthetics.[23] Foremost and omnipresent in her essays is the emphasis on the writer writing for the good of the work alone and not for some ulterior purpose. She insists that "Art is a virtue of the practical intellect"[24] and that "St. Thomas said that the artist is concerned with the good of that which is made." The artist's concern should always be for the perfection of the work itself and not some ulterior motive. She illustrates this by saying, "The novel is an art form and when you use it for anything other than art, you pervert it. I didn't make this up. I got it from St. Thomas (via Maritain) who allows that art is wholly concerned with the good of that which is made; it has no utilitarian end. If you do manage to use it successfully for social, religious, or other purposes, it is because you make it art first."[25]

21. Thomas Kuhn, *The Structure of Scientific Revolutions* (Chicago: University of Chicago Press, 1970), 156–58.

22. Karl Popper, *Conjectures and Refutations: The Growth of Scientific Knowledge* (New York: Harper and Row, 1965), 192, 216.

23. "I have sent you *Art and Scholasticism*. It's the book I cut my aesthetic teeth on, though I think even some of the things he says get soft at times. He is a philosopher and not an artist but he does have great understanding of the nature of art, which he gets from St. Thomas." She was often recommending this book to others. Flannery O'Connor, *The Habit of Being: The Letters of Flannery O'Connor*, edited by Sally Fitzgerald (New York: Farrar, Straus and Giroux, 1979), 215–16.

24. Ibid., 216. This was a very liberating doctrine for her, according to biographer Brad Gooch in *Flannery: A Life of Flannery O'Connor* (New York: Little, Brown and Company, 2009), 162.

25. Flannery O'Connor, "Letter to Father J. H. McCown," in *The Habit of Being*, 157.

She upholds Maritain's—and St. Thomas's—criteria of beauty in her essay "Catholic Novelists and Their Readers" when she says to fearful writers (overly conscientious Catholics who suspect evil influences in their creativity) that their best defense against the devil taking over their work will lie in their strict attention to the order, proportion, and radiance of what they are making.

But I would prefer to focus on where she, in her practice, exemplifies some of the more interesting and perhaps lesser known aesthetic concepts of Maritain, more fully developed in his later works: the role of distortion or transfiguration of appearances in art; the penetration of the writer's vision into the depths of being; the ensuing vision of the existential texture of human existence. Art helps us to see into the mystery of the world.

1. *Distortion*

Flannery O'Connor was often accused of writing stories that were not "positive" enough. After all, some have claimed, if she were really a Catholic writer, should not she be inspirational and uplifting in her writing? On the contrary, she believed the novelist had the obligation to stare reality right in the face and show all of it, fully—the good and the evil. She criticizes novelists who, in trying to be edifying, "leave out half or three fourths of the facts of human existence."[26] Her thought on this was most succinctly illuminated in her discussion of Cardinal Spellman's novel, *The Foundling*. She writes, "The novelist who deliberately misuses his talent for some good purpose may be committing no sin, but he is certainly committing a grave inconsistency, for he is trying to reflect God with what amounts to a practical untruth. It's nobody's business to judge Cardinal Spellman except as a novelist, and as a novelist he's a bit short. You do have the satisfaction of knowing that if you buy a copy of his book, *The Foundling*, you are helping the orphans to whom the proceeds go; and afterwards you can always use the book as a doorstop."[27]

If we see the grotesque in her work, if we see the distortion, it is not by accident. On the contrary, it is critical to her writing. To get us to see why, she has first to remind us that understanding something is not the same thing as coming to understand it. To discover something is not the same as to have it handed to us. In her essay "Novelist and Believer" she talks about portraying

26. O'Connor, "Catholic Novelists and Their Readers," in *Mystery and Manners*, 175.
27. Ibid., 174–75.

the rite of Baptism and how hard that is. Given the secular nature of her readers, she knows that she has to jar them into some kind of emotional recognition of its significance. She says, "I have to make the reader feel, in his bones if nowhere else, that something is going on here that counts. Distortion in this case is an instrument, exaggeration has a purpose.... This is not the kind of distortion that destroys; it is the kind that reveals, or should reveal."[28] In her essay "Writing Short Stories," she writes, "The truth is not distorted here, but rather, a certain distortion is used to get at the truth. If we admit, as we must, that appearance is not the same thing as reality, then we must give the artist the liberty to make certain rearrangements of nature if these will lead to greater depths of vision."[29] You can compare this directly with what Maritain says about imitation and transfiguration in *Creative Intuition.*

In chapter six of of that book, Maritain raises the whole issue of imitation in art. After dismissing the idea of deceiving the eye as being opposed to the very nature of art, he enlists Aristotle in claiming that a genuine notion of intuition would involve the work's communicating a great amount of intuitive knowledge of some trans-apparent reality. Adding to this, he tells us that "St. Thomas insisted that art imitates nature *in her operation*—not in respect to natural appearances, but in respect to the ways in which nature herself operates."[30] He concludes that a truly genuine "concept of imitation affords a ground and a justification for the boldest kinds of transposition, transfiguration, deformation, or recasting of natural appearances."[31] The natural appearances are not what has been imitated but are instruments by which something trans-apparent or deeper is known.[32] For Maritain, the artist knows mystery. Instead of receiving the impressions of things in reality and then confining them by definition or reducing them to objects of utility,[33] he loves them enough to continue to suffer the actions of these natures.[34] If it is true, as W. Norris Clarke claims, that we know by the activity of things and people what kind of "actors" they are,[35] then it is also true that by letting go of the contours and conceptual outlines of

28. O'Connor, "Novelist and Believer," in *Mystery and Manners,* 162.

29. O'Connor, "Writing Short Stories," in *Mystery and Manners,* 97–98.

30. Maritain, *Creative Intuition,* 224.

31. Ibid., 225.

32. Ibid., 224–25.

33. Ibid., 335.

34. Ibid., 58.

35. W. Norris Clarke, S.J., "Action as the Self-Revelation of Being," in *History of Philosophy in the Making* (Washington, D.C.,: University Press of America, 1982), 63–80.

things and people by continuing to love and suffer them—and, perhaps stare[36]—the artist learns about their insides, their hidden meanings, energies, inclinations, and motives. In light of this, then, we must keep in mind that, for Maritain, what is most essential about humanity and things is neither immediately apparent nor obvious. Writing about the splendor of form, he reminds us not to forget that "being is intelligible *in itself*, but not necessarily *for us*, and remains most often obscure to us, either because its intelligibility in itself is obscured in matter or because it is too high and too pure for our intellect."[37] As Aristotle said, "For as the eyes of bats are to the blaze of day, so is the reason in our soul to the things which are by nature most evident of all."[38] It was "Descartes," Maritain judges, "with his clear ideas [that] divorced intelligence from mystery."[39]

2. *Descending the Depths*

Now O'Connor says that the writer is a kind of prophet and a prophet is—in a felicitous phrase she repeats often—a "realist of distances." Realism of this kind does not hesitate to distort appearances in order to show a hidden truth.[40] Now the problem for the novelist just may be "to know how far he can distort without destroying."[41] In order that his distortion may not destroy, O'Connor says that "he will have to descend through the darkness of the familiar, far enough into himself to reach those underground springs that give life to his work." Surely, these are the same underground springs referenced by Maritain in his definition of poetry? Continuing with O'Connor: "This descent into himself will, at the same time, be a descent into his region [in her case it was the South]. It will be a descent through the darkness of the familiar into a world where, like the blind man cured in the gospels, he sees men as if they were trees, but walking. This is the beginning of vision."[42] Maritain would describe that descent as the poet's intellectual descent within himself into the preconscious of his soul that is beyond concepts, where intelligence is raw and active, not set in place. Maritain had argued in *Creative Intuition* that in order for there

36. Maritain, *Creative Intuition*, 93–94.
37. Ibid., 161–62.
38. Aristotle, *Metaphysics*, 2.1, 993b9–11 (Ross).
39. Maritain, *Creative Intuition*, 162.
40. O'Connor, "Catholic Novelists," in *Mystery and Manners*, 179.
41. O'Connor, "The Grotesque in Southern Fiction," in *Mystery and Manners*, 50.
42. Ibid.

to be concepts and principles that could be known consciously, there had to be a preconscious life and power of the intelligence to fabricate them. I hold that it is to these underground springs of intelligence, burgeoning and flowing with non-conceptual awareness of the inner being of the self and the inner being of things that she is referring. Romano Guardini put it well when he said that "the roots of perception are in the heart."[43]

And from this posture, the writer stares at reality. A good writer must take a good long look at things. He must have an "angle of vision" that really sees what is physically there in front of him, but, in addition, can see past these appearances into their spiritual depths. "His problem is really how to make the concrete work double time for him."[44] He must depart or descend from the familiar. And, unlike the modern philosopher, he must have a distrust for the purely abstract. He must have a "respect for boundaries, a desire to penetrate the surface of reality and to find in each thing the spirit which makes it itself and holds the world together."[45] We must remember that "Art imitates nature in her operation!" The poet must have a keen sense of the inner unity and nature of the source of his agent's actions.

3. *Existential Vision*

What does the writer see when she gets there? What vision is embodied within the work that only the work can describe? "If the writer is any good what he makes will have its source in a realm much larger than that which his conscious mind can encompass and will be always a greater surprise to him than it can ever be to his reader."[46] O'Connor never tires of saying that what the writer arrives at is the "texture of existence." This is the realm of the knowledge of human identity and freedom where our human identity is not an abstraction, but an intuitive insight. Throughout his work, Maritain highlights this existential dimension as being primary in what he calls the "receptive intuition." The aesthetic experience is not about outward form, outward appearance, scientific facts, and so forth, but rather that realm that existentialists have always encouraged us to attend to: the realm of human individuals, freedom, choices, relationships, and all that can easily elude the philosopher's abstract methods.[47]

43. O'Connor, "The Church and the Fiction Writer," in *Mystery and Manners*, 144.
44. O'Connor, "Writing Short Stories," in *Mystery and Manners*, 98.
45. O'Connor, "Novelist and Believer," in *Mystery and Manners*, 168.
46. O'Connor, "The Nature and Aim of Fiction," in *Mystery and Manners*, 83.
47. For Maritain, the viewer receives a share or participation in the poet's original intuition.

O'Connor writes that what the short story writer discloses is "not to be found on the surface; it is not accessible to the poll-taker; it is not something that can become a cliché. It is not made from the mean average or the typical, but from the hidden and often the most extreme. It is not made from what passes, but from those qualities that endure, *regardless of what passes,* because they are related to truth. It lies very deep. In its entirety, it is known only to God, but of those who look for it, none gets so close as the artist."[48] We can find this in O'Connor's "A Good Man is Hard to Find," where the family characters face their moral identity through the haunting specter of death from the gun of a misfit as they get shot one by one. We can experience human vulnerability in her "Good Country People" when a Bible salesman steals the young woman's artificial leg. In movies, we can see the reverberating and infectious impact of an individual's character and actions upon the fabric of an entire society, as in *It's a Wonderful Life,* where George Bailey gets to see what the world would be like if he had never been born. What is revealed in all of this is not facts or theories, but neither is it an escape from reality. O'Connor writes: "I'm always highly irritated by people who imply that writing fiction is an escape from reality. It is a plunge into reality and it's very shocking to the system."[49] This reminds me

---

This includes a recognition of many things, discussed in several works: from *Art and Scholasticism,* the soul's own light, the splendor of the soul, the character of our souls, real spiritual radiances, and a world more real than offered to sense (25, 29, 59, 127); from *The Situation of Poetry,* the subjectivity of the artist and the communication between things in their act of existing (Jacques and Raïssa Maritain, *The Situation of Poetry: Four Essays on the Relations Between Poetry, Mysticism, Magic, and Knowledge,* translated by Marshall Suther, [New York: Philosophical Library, 1955; reprint, New York: Kraus Reprint, 1968]), 73, 79); from *Art and Faith,* allusions to the kingdom of God (Cocteau and Maritain, *Art and Faith: Letters Between Jacques Maritain and Jean Cocteau,* translated by John Coleman [New York: Philosophical Library, 1948], 90); from *Creative Intuition,* a reality more significant than in its logically interpreted appearances, existential relations between things, secrets perceived in things, correspondences, echoes, and intercommunications, the invisible, characters, attitudes, actions, passions, mores, radiance of the ontological mystery, basic presences or existential certainties, the irrefragable existence and exigency of intelligibility involved in things, certitude of the interiority of the human being and of its importance, a certitude that between man and the world there is a relationship deeper than any material connection, and a certitude that the impact of his freedom on his destiny shows man's life as a movement that is oriented and not just lost in the void and has to do with the whole fabric of being (30, 126–30, 224n10, 382); from *The Responsibility of the Artist,* a vision of a reality beyond reality (85); and from *Rouault,* the spiritual significance of what exists (and moves, and suffers and loves, and kills) (Maritain, *Rouault* [New York: Harry N. Abrams, 1952], 20ff). It can all be summed up by saying that what we receive through art is an existential knowledge of reality, reality as we often "experience" it.

48. O'Connor, "The Regional Writer," in *Mystery and Manners,* 58.

49. O'Connor, "Novelist and Believer," in *Mystery and Manners,* 168.

of what Henri Bergson said decades ago in *Laughter: An Essay on the Comic* when he wrote:

> The *individuality* of things or of beings escapes us, unless it is materially to our advantage to perceive it. Not only external objects, but even our own mental states, are screened from us in their inmost, their personal aspect. When we feel love or hatred, when we are gay or sad, is it really the feeling itself that reaches our consciousness with those innumerable fleeting shades of meaning and deep resounding echoes that make it something altogether our own? We should all, were it so, be novelists or poets or musicians.[50]

Now O'Connor says that "St. Thomas called art 'reason in making.'" The artist uses his reason to discover an answering reason in everything he sees. For him, to be reasonable is to find, in the object, in the situation, in the sequence, the spirit which makes it itself. This is not an easy thing to do. It is, according to O'Connor, to intrude upon the timeless."[51]

Samuel Butcher's analysis of Aristotle on imitation might be helpful in seeing the point here. According to Butcher, "Facial expressions, gestures, attitudes, are a dialect which nature herself has taught. They are living signs through which the outward frame follows and reflects the movements of the spirit. Painting and sculpture working through an inert material cannot indeed reproduce the life of the soul in all its variety and successive manifestations. In their frozen and arrested movement they fix eternally the feeling they portray.[52] O'Connor talks about children and the way they see things as analogous to the aim of the writer. She writes: "When a child draws, he doesn't intend to distort but to set down exactly what he sees, and as his gaze is direct, he sees the lines that create motion. Now the lines of motion that interest the writer are usually invisible. They are lines of spiritual motion."[53]

Why should we want all of this? O'Connor writes: "Our generation has been made to feel that the aim of learning is to eliminate mystery. For such people, fiction can be very disturbing, for the fiction writer is concerned with mystery that is lived. He's concerned with ultimate mystery as we find

50. Henri Bergson, *Laughter: An Essay on the Meaning of the Comic*, translated by Cloudesley Brereton and Fred Rothwell (New York: Macmillan Company, 1913), 152–54.

51. O'Connor, "The Nature and Aim of Fiction," in *Mystery and Manners*, 82–83.

52. Samuel Butcher, "Imitation as an Aesthetic Term," in *Aristotle's Theory of Poetry and Fine Art*, 4th ed. (New York: Dover Publications, 1951), 134–35.

53. O'Connor, "Remarks made at Hollins College, Virginia, 1963," in *Mystery and Manners*, 113.

it embodied in the concrete world of sense experience."[54] The writer's art and intuition is needed today more than ever. For as O'Connor writes, in almost a prophetic way, "For the last few centuries we have lived in a world which has been increasingly convinced that the reaches of reality end very close to the surface, that there is no ultimate divine source, that the things of the world do not pour forth from God in a double way or at all. For nearly two centuries the popular spirit of each succeeding generation has tended more and more to the view that the mysteries of life will eventually fall before the mind of man."[55]

This scientific materialist outlook on reality as well as the overreaching scientific habit of mind it engenders is as invisible as it is constricting. No facts will ever reveal to us our nearsightedness or our intellectual sclerosis. After all, facts will always be facts. We are in an age that increasingly denies the substance and soul of the human being, his freedom, and the significance of his being and action. We always insist on the scientific versus the manifest image of things, and so we are constantly seeing "less." And like the frog in the pot of water that is slowly brought to a boil, we will fail to know our peril before it is too late.

Now we can hope that through an appreciation of intuition and good writing such as O'Connor's, we can recover a vision of the universe that sufficiently rich in meaning to satisfy the human spirit. I would like to conclude with a quotation from Josef Pieper's *Leisure: The Basis of Culture* cited by John G. Trapani Jr. in his *Poetry, Beauty, and Contemplation*:

> Leisure is not necessarily present in … things like "breaks," "time off," "weekend," "vacation," and so on—[rather,] it is a condition of the soul.… [Leisure is] "non activity"—an inner absence of preoccupation, a calm, an ability to let things go, to be quiet. [It] is a form of that stillness that is the necessary preparation for accepting reality; only the person who is still can hear.… Leisure is the disposition of receptive understanding, of contemplative beholding, and immersion in the real. [It is the] surge of new life that flows out to us when we give ourselves to contemplation.[56]

54. O'Connor, "The Teaching of Literature," in *Mystery and Manners*, 125.

55. O'Connor, "Novelist and Believer," in *Mystery and Manners*, 157–58.

56. Josef Pieper, *Leisure, the Basis of* Culture, translated by Gerald Malsbury (South Bend, Indiana: St. Augustine's Press, 1998), 30–31, cited by John Trapani Jr. in *Poetry, Beauty, and Contemplation*, 146.

III

ANGELS AND EVOLUTION

MARIE GEORGE

What Are We to Make of Maritain's View that Angels are Intermediary Causes in Evolution?

I. Introduction

THERE IS NO DOUBT THAT intellectual custom exerts a force on all of us. Those of us who have grown up in a world where science has explained or at least offered plausible natural causes for so many phenomena cannot help but be taken a little aback by Maritain's suggestion that new animal species are the work of angels and are not solely the product of natural causes. Yet this is what he boldly proposes: "And the holy angels thank God for having permitted them, invisible as they are, to satisfy .... their devotedness as faithful servants, in the wise administration of these visible creatures, by controlling their structures with fanciful delight, by taking part in their evolution, always under God's governing and superelevating motions, by putting their art and their fantasy to work in furnishing all these specific forms, as varied as they are bizarre, with instincts which are themselves as varied as they are bizarre."[1]

In this essay I intend to examine whether this view could ever be verified, and then to consider arguments of fittingness both in favor and against it. I am going to assume that angels, purely spiritual beings endowed with

1. Jacques Maritain, "On the Philosophy of Nature (II): Concerning Animal Instinct," in *Untrammeled Approaches,* edited by Bernard E. Doering (Notre Dame, Indiana: University of Notre Dame Press, 1996), 144. Maritain was especially concerned with the origin of animal instincts which he argues is plausibly attributed to angels. However, I am going to focus on the more general thesis that angels play a role in evolution.

intelligence and will, exist.[2] I am also going to assume that the existence and action of creatures depends upon God, and thus I will not consider a materialistic explanation of evolution. I take it as a given that new species have originated from previously existing species. Evolution is the immediate result of change and only remotely of creation.[3]

Given the above assumptions, there are three possible explanations of the evolution of species: God could directly intervene and produce new species; God could produce them by the sole means of blind secondary causes; or God could produce them using angelic intermediaries (either alone or as complementing natural causes). The question, then, is whether there is any way to tell which method God uses to produce new species.

It is important to understand that "intervention" in the case of God does not refer to God's action insofar as it is always needed for natural things to exist and to act,[4] but rather refers to God's action producing an effect in the natural world that otherwise would not have occurred, at least not in that specific instance. Divine intervention occurs in the case of miracles and could in principle take the form of producing a substance by manipulating material things in the manner that a human chemist produces water, nylon, or Prozac; God could also intervene in evolution by directly flowing a substantial form into matter.

As for angelic intervention, it cannot take the form of a miracle (although in certain cases it might appear so to us). As Aquinas explains:

2. There are two sorts of philosophical arguments given for the existence of angels. One is based on the supposed eternal, non-natural motion of the heavenly bodies (see Aquinas, *De Potentia,* q. 6, a. 6). The other is based on the notion that the "chain of being" is gradually gradated, and there would be too big a gap between God and rational animals if there were no purely spiritual creatures (see *Summa contra Gentiles* II, chap. 91). All translations are my own.

3. See *Summa Theologiae* I, edited by Instituti Studiorum Medievalium Ottaviensis (Ottawa: Commissio Piana, 1953), q. 45, a. 8: "Others posited that forms are given or are caused by a separate agent through the mode of creation. This occurred to them out of their ignorance concerning form. For they were not considering that the form of a natural body is not a subsisting thing, but that by which something is, and therefore, since to become and to be created only properly belong to a subsisting thing . . . it does not belong to forms to become or to be created but to be concreated. However, what properly comes to be from a natural agent is a composite which comes to be out of the matter. Whence, creation is not mixed in the works of nature, but is presupposed to the operation of nature." Aquinas, in the *sed contra,* notes: "Augustine distinguishes the work of propagation, which is a work of nature, from the work of creation." Augustine regards the initial apparition of plants on the earth to pertain to the work of propagation and not to the work of creation (see ST I, q. 69, a. 2), and Aquinas regards this position as reasonable. Thus, Aquinas holds that new species may have appeared through generation rather than through creation.

4. See SCG III, chap. 55, "That God conserves things in being," and chap. 58, "That God is the cause of operating in every being that operates."

> Something is properly called a miracle when it occurs outside the order of nature. But it does not suffice for the notion of miracle if something occurs outside the order of a particular nature; because in this manner when someone threw a stone upwards, he would do a miracle, since this is outside the order of the nature of the stone. Therefore, something is said to be a miracle from this that it occurs outside the whole order of created nature. This, however, no one can do except God, for whatever an angel or any other creature does by its proper virtue, this occurs according to the order of created nature; and thus it is not a miracle.[5]

Angels, unlike God, are unable to directly cause substantial change by flowing substantial forms into matter.[6] According to Aquinas the *only* way they are able to directly act in the material world is by moving bodies from place to place; however, by doing so, they are also able to cause alteration and substantial change,[7] e.g., they could move a lit candle to a piece of grass, thereby burning it. (The reasoning behind Aquinas's somewhat puzzling position that the only change angels can directly cause is that of place is a subject for another essay. If the sun can directly alter something, one would think *a fortiori* an angel could do so.)

II. Can Biology Eliminate the Possibility of Angelic Intervention?

Is there some way of eliminating the possibility of angelic intervention? Just as the god-of-the-gaps is eliminated when a natural explanation is discovered, so too is the angel-of-the-gaps. For example, now that we have a scientific explanation of why certain flowers close at night, we no longer need to posit that fairies (or angels) shut them.[8] It seems then that if plau-

5. ST I, q. 110, a. 4.

6. In a number of places Aquinas reasons that angels cannot at will cause a substantial change on the grounds that like proceeds from like, and so a new composite of matter and form requires a composite being as its cause (see ST I, q. 65, a. 4 and q. 110, a. 2). Angels, however, can move material beings from place to place (see ST I, q. 110, a. 3). And in this manner they can bring about substantial changes: "What a lower power can do, the higher power can do, but in a more excellent mode and not in the same mode; just as the intellect knows sensible things in a more excellent mode than do the senses. And in this way the angel in a more excellent mode than bodily agents transmutes bodily matter, namely, by moving as a higher cause the bodily agents themselves" (ST I, q. 110, a. 2, ad 2).

7. See ST I, q. 110, a. 3.

8. See Elizabeth Palermo, "Why Do Flowers Close Up at Night?," http://www.livescience.com/34569-why-flowers-close-at-night-nyctinasty.html: "Plants that tuck themselves in for bedtime exhibit a natural behavior known as nyctinasty. Scientists know the mechanism behind the

sible scientific explanations of the evolution of new species are available, this weighs in favor of natural causes being responsible and the intervention of supernatural ones being unneeded.[9]

I think the convergent evidence commonly cited by biologists adequately establishes that new species have evolved. However, when it comes to showing in detail how any given species or feature of a species evolved, biologists have very little to offer. This is not surprising. First, it is a very small minority of biologists who devote themselves to the study of evolution; most biologists are cell biologists or geneticists. Secondly, this area poses many challenges, e.g., we often do not know what a given species' ancestor is and we can only extract so much information from fossils. Biologists do sometimes come up with plausible evolutionary pathways and propose reasonable intermediaries between species,[10] but overall our knowledge of how individual species evolved is very fragmentary, and what little we have applies to a tiny fraction of the species extant and extinct. Our inability to come up with specific accounts for the origin of all features and species means that we cannot in virtue of such accounts eliminate the possibility that angels are in some cases involved in the evolutionary process.

Does the general theory of evolution give reason to eliminate angelic intervention? Neo-Darwinian explanations all retain the core notion that evolution depends on variations which confer a selective advantage. Biologists commonly attribute variation to the following three causes: mutation, gene flow, and the genetic recombination that takes place in sexual reproduction, though some propose other causes as well.[11] I am going to focus on mutation, as all evolutionary biologists affirm that it has a role in evolution, and the point I intend to make concerning it—namely, that it involves chance causes—can be more simply made than it can in the case of the other two commonly named causes of variation (although it could be made in their case as well).

---

phenomenon: In cool air and darkness, the bottom-most petals of certain flowers grow at a faster rate than the upper-most petals, forcing the flowers shut."

9. I acknowledge that, to the extent that science proceeds through hypothesis, its conclusions lack absolute certitude, but at the same time they are supported, albeit in an imperfect manner, by evidence. Here is not the place to get into a discussion of the limits of science, but simply to assess in a rough way whether science offers plausible explanations for the evolution of species.

10. See Oliver Putz, "Hormone-Receptors and Complexity: Putting to Rest Another God of the Gaps?," *Theology and Science* 4, no. 3 (2006): 209–13, esp. 211.

11. See, for example, Kirschner and Gerhart's theory of facilitated variation: Marc W. Kirschner and John C. Gerhart, *The Plausibility of Life* (New Haven: Yale University Press, 2005).

So what are thought to be causes of mutation? The common answer is that it results from copying errors due to unspecified internal causes or to environmental agents, such as radiation, which cause DNA to break down. That a mutation proves to be beneficial is a matter of chance. In other words, usually DNA replication is successful, but it fails in the fewer number of cases; and in some cases the failed copies contribute to the production of a feature or behavior which proves beneficial to the organism's reproductive success. Whatever caused the failure was not tending to produce the beneficial feature or behavior, nor was the copying process tending to produce it, and so the apparition of the feature or behavior is a matter of luck.

The reason I focus on the element of chance in mutation is because chance events in some cases can be traced back to an intelligent cause. Aquinas gives numerous examples of this:

> For nothing prohibits that which is *per accidens* to be taken as one by some intellect; otherwise the intellect could not form this proposition: "The one digging a grave finds a treasure." And just as the intellect can apprehend this, so too it is able to bring it about: as would be the case if someone, knowing that a treasure was hidden in a certain place, would incite some peasant ignorant of this to dig a grave there. And thus nothing prevents those things which here are done *per accidens*, as luck and chance events, to be reduced to some ordering cause which acts through intellect.[12]

Also:

> Although all things, even the least things, are divinely dispensed ... nothing nevertheless prohibits something to happen by chance and fortune. For something is fortuitous or casual with respect to a lower cause when something is done outside its intention or tending (*intentionem*), which nevertheless is not fortuitous or casual in regard to a higher cause, as it is not done outside its intention; as it manifests in the case of a master who sends two servants to the same place, so that one is unaware of the other; the encounter of the two is casual as to both of them, but not as to the master. In this manner, therefore, when some things happens outside the intention or tending (*intentionem*) of secondary causes, they are fortuitous or casual in respect to those causes; and they can simply speaking be called casual, because an effect is denominated simply speaking according to the condition of proximate causes.[13]

12. ST I, q. 116, a. 1.

13. *Compendium Theologiae,* in *Opuscula Theologica,* vol. 1, edited by Raymundi A Verardo, O.P. (Rome: Marietti, 1954), q. 137. See also *Commentary on the Metaphysics,* bk. 7, lec. 6, no. 1403.

The element of chance in the scientific explanation of evolution is compatible, then, with a further explanation that involves intelligent beings who have orchestrated the chance event. Angels can intervene in the process of DNA replication, e.g., they can change the position of certain base pairs so that it results in a useful mutation.[14] Since the DNA replication process tends to produce an exact copy, its failure to do so in such cases is a matter of chance (just as would be true if a physical cause, instead of an angel, interfered in it, resulting in a mutation). However, from the point of view of the angel who intervenes, it is not chance.

One might wonder, then, whether we would be able to detect the artistic intervention of angels. Those who argue in favor of Intelligent Design (ID) maintain that in principle we are able to recognize new species as being the products of an intelligent being as proximate cause, similar to how a plant scientist can recognize that a given strain of plant has been genetically modified (though perhaps not with absolute certitude). According to Intelligent Design theory, there exist features of organisms that are not functional unless all the parts are present; such features cannot arise in a gradual fashion and therefore must be assembled by intelligent agents outside of nature, such as angels.[15] Aristotle, observing that among the things that come to be as a result of art some can come to be either from art or

14. To get a more concrete idea of where angels could intervene, see William K. Purves, Gordon H. Orians, and H. Craig Heller, *Life: The Science of Biology* (Sunderland, Massachuesetts: Sinauer Associates, 1998), 382: "DNA sequencing has revealed that mutations occur most often at certain base pairs in human DNA. These 'hot spots' are often located where cytosine residues have been methylated to 5-methylcytosine.... The explanation of this mutation phenomenon has to do with the natural instability of the bases in DNA. Either spontaneously, or with chemical prodding, the cytosine residues can lose their amino group and form uracil. But the cell nucleus has a repair system that recognizes uracil as being inappropriate for DNA.... The fate of 5-methylcytosine that loses its amino group is rather different, since the result of that loss is thymine, a natural base of DNA. The uracil repair system ignores this thymine. However, since the GC pair is now a mismatched GT pair, a different type of repair system comes in and tries to fix the mismatch. Half the time, the repair system matches a new C to the G, but the other half of the time, it matches a new A to the T, resulting in a mutation."

15. I am giving Michael Behe's version of ID. William Dembski speaks in terms of "specified complexity," which he claims is present in organisms (e.g., their DNA) and cannot come about by natural causality; whence the need of an intelligent being to install it in living things. See Michael Behe, "The Modern Intelligent Design Hypothesis: Breaking Rules," in *God and Design: The Teleological Argument and Modern Science*, edited by Neil A. Manson (London: Routledge, 2003), 277: "Thus, while I argue for design, the question of the identity of the designer is left open. Possible candidates for the role of designer include: the God of Christianity; an angel—fallen or not; Plato's demiurge." See also Dembski's "The Chance of the Gaps" in the same volume.

nature, whereas others can come to be only from art, tries to determine why this is the case.[16] While we can readily agree that a house is not going to be assembled as a result of natural causes, it is not entirely clear that it is impossible for the medicines and fabrics that humans synthesize to form naturally, albeit it is doubtlessly very improbable that this would ever occur. This is the often-cited problem with ID: we do not know for sure what is beyond the range of chance when it comes to the formation of organic features. So I do not think that if angels intervene in evolution we would be able to recognize with certainty that they have done so.

Regardless of whether ID is true or whether a scientific explanation in terms of physical causes and chance is true, in neither case can angelic intervention be ruled out on scientific grounds. Science cannot eliminate the possibility that a given individual chance result which could occur naturally has been orchestrated by an intelligent being. Scientists in some cases propose plausible natural pathways to explain the origin of certain complex biological features but generally are unable to ascertain the specific cause of a given mutation and all the more so when the events in question occurred in the past.[17] For example, it is reasonable to think that the glucocorticoid receptor arose from an ancestral corticoid receptor as the result of gene duplication followed by two point mutations;[18] however, specifically what caused the three errors in DNA replication lie hidden in the past.

As for ID, which argues for the intervention of intelligent causes other than humans in evolution, science cannot eliminate it either. For although scientists have shown in a few cases that certain complex biological features could develop from simpler ones in a stepwise fashion, contrary to ID claims,[19] realistically it cannot do so in every case due to the limitations of investigating extinct species' metabolic functions, genomes, and even details concerning gross body parts (not to mention that intermediary species are often lacking). To claim that natural causality suffices to explain

16. See *Commentary on the Metaphysics*, bk. 7, lec. 8.

17. Scientists may be able to reasonably ascertain the cause of mutations that they provoked by the use of certain chemical agents, and perhaps might be able to determined such agents (or radiation) were present at the time of key evolutionary changes.

18. See Putz, "Hormone-Receptors and Complexity," 211.

19. Michael Behe claimed that Factor XII was part of the irreducibly complex clotting system. However, as biologist Kenneth Miller point outs: "Once again, however, a nasty little fact gets in the way of intelligent design theory. Dolphins lack Factor XII (Robinson, Kasting, and Aggeler 1969), and yet their blood clots perfectly well." Kenneth Miller, "The Flagellum Unspun," http://www.millerandlevine.com/km/evol/design2/article.html.

the origin of specific features in the absence of specific explanations is an appeal to ignorance. Just because certain features turn out not to be irreducibly complex does not mean that all will turn out to be such. Science, then, cannot eliminate the possibility of angelic intervention either in the more extreme form favored by ID or in the more subtle form where angels orchestrate chance events.

Maritain himself thinks that angelic action should be undetectable—that angels should only enter the picture at the point where science no longer has anything to say. After asking the question, "But how can the angels cooperate in the government of the material universe?" Maritain offers the following answer: "Is it by transporting continents and mountains, or by causing molecules to change places? No, let us rather entertain the idea that they act on matter . . . in the realm of microphysics—where that kind of invisibility which matter enjoys by reason of its indetermination with regard to our measures is in a relationship of propriety or affinity with the invisibility of the angelic motions."[20] Maritain offers a weak argument based on "propriety" for his conclusion that angels' actions occur at that level—namely, the similarity between our inability to know determinately what goes on at the quantum level and our inability to see angelic actions. (This argument also applies to the angels-orchestrating-chance-events view that I propose.[21])

III. Objections to Angelic Intervention in Evolution Drawn from the Philosophy of Science

A science-related concern, similar to one raised by some of those who investigate divine action in nature, is that angelic action would violate the laws of nature. Although angelically-caused motions might appear to us to

20. Maritain, "Animal Instinct," in *Untrammeled Approaches*, 149.

21. Those who are familiar with discussions about the nature of divine causality will recognize the explanation I offer regarding how angels can interact in a seamless way with natural causes as similar to ones that are offered to explain divine action in the natural world. For example, Ian Barbour maintains: "Quantum events have necessary but not sufficient physical causes. If they are not completely determined by the relationships described by the laws of physics, their final determination might be made directly by God. What appears to be chance . . . may be the very point at which God acts." Quoted in Michael J. Dodds, *Unlocking Divine Action* (Washington, D.C.: The Catholic University of America Press, 2012), 127. Michael Dodds documents views of this sort, and goes on to argue against them as offering suitable explanations for divine action (see *Unlocking Divine Action*, chap. 4, 119–59). However, I think this type of argument offers a suitable way for angelic creatures to act in the natural world, though I am unable to ascertain whether quantum events are adequate instruments to use for directing evolution.

violate certain laws of nature, they in fact do not do so, since scientific laws describe interactions of purely natural entities. To every action *of a physical agent* there is an equal and opposite reaction. One might object that certain biological features or species produced by angels would never naturally occur. However, the same could be said of at least certain GMOs produced by humans (and similarly for synthetics, such as nylon), and yet we do not violate natural laws in producing such things. Again, angels' direct agency is limited to moving a thing from one place to another, and their doing so is no more contrary to nature than our moving a heavy body upwards. One might still object that angels cannot cause things to move since they would have to so without applying any force. This would result in an increase in the amount of energy in the universe, a clear violation of the law of the conservation of energy. However, the law that energy can neither be created nor destroyed applies only to a closed system, which the universe is not known to be.[22]

One might object that if angels were to intervene in evolution, our understanding of nature in terms of laws would break down. However, all, or virtually all, the angelic intervention we have been talking about would have occurred before humans appeared on the planet, and as such was not something that could be directly observed; at most such interventions could be inferred in a limited number of cases, if it could be inferred at all.[23] If one were to currently witness an evolutionary event brought about by angelic action, ignorant of its cause, one would not feel compelled to revise the laws of nature, because what occurred would be the exception and not the rule. Errors in observation and measurement happen all the time in science without scientists rushing to jettison the laws of nature. The same is true even if the unusual occurrence were to be attributed to a miracle (though, again, angels by their own power cannot perform miracles): the cancer researcher

22. One might object that since energy and matter are convertible, putting more energy into the world is tantamount to creation. This apparent problem overlooks the operational nature of definitions in physics. Matter and energy as construed by physics are not the same as substance and accident. When I move a hamster from the floor back into its cage, neither I nor the hamster undergo substantial change. While the hamster is moving, its motion is an accident, i.e., it is a modification of the substance that is the hamster. If there is any substantial change, it would be in the breakdown of ATP to ADP in my muscles; this would not be a creation, however. That an angel moves something does not even require a substantial change of this sort; much less does it require creation.

23. Those of the ID school claim that one can infer from irreducibly complex biological features that there are intelligent causes, such as angels.

who believes that some cancer patients have been miraculously cured does not despair of finding a cure for cancer. Angelic intervention would have to be more than occasional and its effects would have to be observable for it to interfere with our ability to recognize the regularities in nature that we express in the form of laws.

A third science-related reason to question whether angels are involved in evolution is that scientists for the most part do not willingly embrace any vision of the universe that would render scientific research futile. As Einstein puts it: "Subtle is the Lord, but malicious he is not. Nature hides her secret because of her essential loftiness, but not by mean of ruse."[24] If there are gaps in the natural world when it comes to immediate causes that can only be filled by supernatural beings, then scientists are going to be searching in vain for natural causes. This problem is acute if the ID thinkers are correct. Scientists will be seeking evolutionary explanations of how parts and pathways originated when in fact they are the work of angels. However, if angels only enter in at the point where science invokes chance and offers no further explanation, scientific inquiry into the evolution of species is not rendered vain. ID thinkers, of course, will counter that if only these scientists embraced ID, they would know the search for natural causes in certain specific cases is in vain. This brings us back to the question of whether any synthetic is beyond the reach of chance.

Setting aside ID, however, one can still raise questions about the reasonableness of the assumption that all natural phenomena can be explained without invoking supernatural intervention. That scientists seek explanations in terms of natural causes does not commit them to holding that everything is explicable in this manner. At the same time, though, the extent of science's ability to explain things is delimited by the abilities of natural causes. Those who are conversant with science and who acknowledge divine action generally find Howard J. Van Till's notion of nature's "functional integrity" attractive:

> The creation was gifted from the outset with *functional integrity*—a wholeness of being that eliminated the need for gap-bridging interventions to compensate for formational capabilities that the Creator may have initially withheld from it so it is accurately described by the *Robust Formational Economy Principle*—an affirmation that the creation was fully equipped by God with all of the resources, potentiali-

24. Albert Einstein quoted by Abraham Pais in *"Subtle is the Lord": The Science and Life of Albert Einstein* (Oxford: Oxford University Press, 1982), 253.

ties, and formational capabilities that would be needed for the creaturely system to actualize every type of physical structure and every form of living organism that has appeared in the course of time.

I believe that the universe exists now only because its Creator has *given it being* and continues to *sustain it in being* from moment to moment.... Each of its resources, potentialities, and capabilities can be celebrated as a *gift of being* that is indicative of the character and intentions of the Creator, ... indicative of both the Creator's *creativity* (in the action of conceptualizing something that would accomplish the Creator's intentions) and the Creator's *generosity* (in the act of giving such integrity and fullness of being as this robustly gifted universe appears to possess).... The *more* robust the universe's formational economy is, the *more* the universe owes to its Creator for the richness of its being. In the context of this consideration I find it especially ironic when Christian opponents to evolution appear to argue the contrary position: the *less* robust the universe's formational economy, the *more* it needs a Creator or Designer.[25]

To the extent that angels contribute more to evolution, natural things contribute less. But that natural things contribute less seems to entail either that God withheld from natural things capabilities that he otherwise would have endowed them with (which does not seem in keeping with his generosity), or that he did not withhold them and angels are doing things that natural things could do (which seems unlikely, as such angelic activity would be superfluous). I will return to this objection later on.

At this point we have seen that objections based on the claims that scientific law would need to be revised if angels were to intervene in evolution and that their intervention would contravene scientific law are not valid. Earlier we saw that scientific discoveries could not rule out the possibility that intelligent beings are intermediary causes in evolution. Pace ID, neither can we rule out the possibility that natural causes alone are. And so to decide between the two, we are left with arguments from fittingness.

IV. Arguments from Fittingness in Favor of Angelic Intervention

Arguments from fittingness are weak arguments even when one has no doubt about the occurrence of an event to be explained. If one is certain that

25. "Evolutionary Creation (Theistic Evolution) and Functional Integrity (Fully Gifted Creation, Robust Formational Economy Principle), excerpts from the writings of Howard Van Till," http://www.asa3.org/ASA/education/origins/methods-hvt.htm.

the event has occurred, then one can come up with suitable reasons for its occurrence; yet, short of interrogating the agent in question, one could never be sure of having hit upon the real reasons for its occurence. But where one is not even sure that the event has occurred, arguments from fittingness are even less certain. In the case of angelic intervention in evolution, we are left with extremely tenuous arguments of the latter sort, as we do not know for a fact that the angels have so intervened.

In order to judge which sort of secondary cause God more fittingly uses, it is helpful to understand why God uses secondary causes in the first place:

> Divine goodness has a twofold perfection: one in itself, according as, namely, all perfection is super-eminently contained in it; a second according as it flows into things, namely, according as it is cause of things; whence it is congruent with divine goodness that both [perfections] be communicated to the creature, so that, namely, the created thing would not only have from divine goodness that it would be and would be good, but also that it would bestow being and goodness on another.[26]

The above supplies grounds for an argument of fittingness applicable to evolution that eliminates the possibility that God causes new species to arise by direct intervention.[27] In keeping with his goodness, it is reasonable to think that he is going to cause it through intermediaries to which he communicates the good of causality. But which is it? Natural causes alone or natural causes and angels?

The continuation of Aquinas's discussion of the causality God imparts to rational creatures as opposed to non-rational ones is relevant here:

> Among higher creatures, however, those in the highest degree near to God are rational creatures which to the likeness of God exist, live, and understand; whence not only from divine goodness is it conferred upon them that they flow into other things, but also that they retain the same mode of inflowing by which God flows; namely, through will and not through the necessity of nature. Whence he governs all lower creatures both through spiritual creatures and through more worthy corporeal creatures; but he provides through corporeal creatures in this manner that

26. *De Veritate*, q. 5, a. 8.

27. See ST I, q. 103, a. 6, ad 2: "If God alone would govern, causal perfection would be subtracted from things." See also ad 3: "Not only does it pertain to the perfection of a terrestrial king that he have an executor of his governance, but it also pertains to the king's dignity; for the power of the king is rendered more illustrious by the order of the ministers."

he does not make them provident, but agents only; whereas he provides through spiritual creatures in this manner that he makes them provident.[28]

Aquinas goes on to say that even among rational creatures there is an order, human providence being limited to "few things, namely, as to human things and those things which are able to come into use for human life," whereas "the providence of the angels is universal and is extended over all corporeal creatures; and therefore it is said by both the saints and by the philosophers that all bodily beings are ruled or governed by divine providence through angelic intermediaries."[29]

Two main reasons can be offered for why it is more fitting that God uses angelic intermediaries than natural intermediaries alone in the production of new species. The first has already been mentioned above: namely, God in imparting the goodness of causality to things imparts it to certain things in the same mode in which he himself possesses it, namely, as intelligent, and thus as capable of exercising providence. We can add to this first reason that since what is best in created things is the order of the universe which consists in part of a hierarchy of different beings,[30] it seems that the production of various species is the sort of thing where the execution of the divine plan most appropriately involves intelligent intermediaries who understand this order—and not simply blind natural causes that God could have programmed, so to speak—to produce the same result.

Maritain gives a variation of the above argument that looks to individual species and not to the biosphere taken as a whole—namely, that the artistry involved in the various species is fittingly brought about in part by intelligent beings:

If you consider in particular the evolution of organisms, are you not struck by a characteristic trait, the element of play, of humor, of wit, in the sense of that imaginative invention that makes one laugh,[31] in short the element of the amusement of the artist, which appears, along with a host of other elements, luxuriousness, sumptuousness, beauty in the world of the evolution of species.... In my opinion

28. *De Veritate,* q. 5, a. 8.

29. Ibid.

30. ST I, q. 103, a. 4, ad 1.

31. We can be sure that Maritain does not mean to attribute the material faculty of imagination to the angels. Rather where a human artist, e.g., an architect, uses imagination to produce the plan for a specific house from his general knowledge of how to design houses, the angel uses its innate concepts, for these concepts are not simply generic plans but contain in act knowledge of its particular realizations. See ST I, q. 55, a. 2, "Whether angels know particulars."

all of this means that God, who created things from nothing, without making use of any intermediary, but who governs through created intermediaries, has directed evolution through the intermediary of angelic intelligences.[32]

Angelic intelligences, from the first moment of their existence, are endowed by God with the plans or notions of creatures: "In the mind of the angel are likenesses of creatures that are not received from the creatures themselves, but from God.... Whence Augustine says ... that 'just as the notion (ratio) by which a creature is composed exists in the Word of God prior to the creature itself which is composed, thus also the knowledge of the same notion comes to be first in the intellectual creature, and thereafter is the very composition of the creature.'"[33]

Accordingly, angels are fitting agents for actualizing in the real world the notions that exist in their minds (that is, subsequent to the initial creation of material beings, which is God's work alone.)[34] Thus, Aquinas proposes that: "Participated forms in matter are not reduced to some per se subsisting forms as the Platonists held, but rather to intelligible forms or to angelic understanding from which they proceed through motion."[35]

Of course, Aquinas did not think in terms of evolution where one species arises from a previously existing one, but only to species arising after creation; however, what he says applies to evolution as well. Again, although angels cannot immediately produce a new substantial form in matter, they can move material agents both to prepare the matter and then to act on matter which is in immediate potency to a new substantial form; the material agents in question could have moved to those places, but otherwise would not have—at least not in that case. Thus, angels can move matter to cause DNA copy errors, and they can do so as well to influence the other sources of variation, i.e., gene flow and recombination in sexual reproduction. In this manner, they can cause variations that are needed for new species, as well as ensuring the presence of whatever other causes are

32. Maritain, "Animal Instinct," in *Untrammeled Approaches*, 149. Maritain also mentions in passing another reason for angelic mediation, namely, that in evolution there is "a passage from the inferior to the superior." Aquinas agrees that a higher being must account for this, but leaves it open as to whether this is God himself or an angel (see *De Potentia*, q. 3, a. 11, ob. 13 and ad 13). Maritain thought that it was especially appropriate that angels, as intellectual beings, were intermediary causes of animal instincts, insofar as instinctive knowledge requires an intelligent cause other than the animal that possesses it. See "Animal Instinct," 145.

33. ST I, q. 55, a. 2, ad 1.

34. See ST I, q. 45, a. 5.

35. ST I, q. 65, a. 4, ad 2.

necessary for speciation. This could be a way, then, that "participated forms in matter are reduced ... to intelligible forms or to angelic understanding from which they proceed through motion."[36]

The second reason that it is fitting that God employ angels as intermediary causes in evolution is that doing so increases interactivity among parts of the universe, and hence increases the perfection of the universe. Aquinas maintains that: "What is best, however, in created things is the perfection of the universe which consists in the order of distinct things. For in all things, the perfection of the whole surpasses the perfection of the individual parts."[37] He further holds that "[t]he order of the universe includes in itself both the conservation of the diverse things instituted by God, and the motion of them; because according to these a twofold order is found in things, namely, according as one thing is better than another, and according as one thing is moved by another."[38] Certainly the interactions of angels with the material realm could be restricted to the care of humans, but if angels were also involved with non-rational creation by playing a role in evolution there would be more interactivity among the parts of the universe, and thus it would be a better universe.[39]

V. Objections, Based on Fittingness, to Angelic Intervention in the Natural World

There are several objections to the notion that angels govern material creation, in general, and the course of evolution, in particular. One is that angels' work in material creation seems to involve the subordination of what is higher to what is lower. Aquinas responds:

> To the extent that something is of more perfect virtue and more eminent in a grade of goodness, to that extent it has a more common appetite and seeks and works the good in things more distant from itself.... Therefore it is not unfitting if the motion of the heavenly bodies and the actions of their movers are said to be in

36. Ibid.

37. SCG II, chap. 45.

38. ST I, q. 103, a. 4, ad 1.

39. See ST I, q. 61, a. 3: "It seems more probable that the angel was created simultaneous with the bodily creature. For angels are a certain part of the universe. For they do not constitute a universe that is per se one, but both they and the corporeal creature come together in the constitution of one universe, something that appears in the order of one creature to another; for the order of things to each other is the good of the universe."

some manner for the sake of the bodies which are generated and corrupted, which are less worthy than they are; but intending the generation of these, they intend their own good and divine likeness as ultimate end.[40]

The more extensive a being's causality is, the more like to God the being is. Just as God's causality extends to every creature, even the least, without implying any subservience on his part to them, so too the angels' causality exercised over material creatures does not imply subservience on their part to material creation.

A second objection stems from the principle of subsidiarity, i.e., that "execution of least things befits a lower power proportioned to the effect:"[41]

Two things are required for divine providence: the ordering and the execution of the order. The first of the two come about through a cognitive power; whence those who are of more perfect cognition are said to be orderers of other things. The second comes about through an operative power. Things stand in an opposite manner in regard to these two. For to the extent that ordering is more perfect, to that extent it descends further to the least thing. The execution of least things, however, befits a lower power proportioned to the effect. In God, however, the highest perfection as to both is found. For in him are the most perfect wisdom for ordering and the most perfect virtue for operating. It is necessary, therefore, that he disposes the orders of all things through his wisdom, even of the least, and that the least or lowest things are executed through other lower powers, through which he operates, as a universal and higher power [*virtus*] through a particular and lower power. It is suitable, therefore, that there are lower agent powers that are executrices of divine providence.[42]

It follows from this that there is a hierarchy in secondary causality; higher beings do not do things that lower beings can do. On this principle, "the superior angels are never sent on exterior missions"[43] to the corporeal realm, and members of the lowest order of angels are the guardians of human beings.[44] Accordingly, it would seem then that angels should rule over humans, but not over things so lowly as non-rational bodies. Humans, being

40. SCG III, chap. 24.

41. SCG III, chap. 77.

42. SCG III, chap. 77. The chapter is entitled: "That the execution of divine providence comes about by means of secondary causes."

43. See ST I, chap. 112, a. 4: "To be sent on an exterior mission properly belongs to an angel according as it acts in regard to some corporeal creature from divine command.... Whence it pertains to these [lower] orders to be sent in exterior ministry, but not, however, to the four superior ones."

44. See ST I, q. 113, a. 3.

lower than the angels, stand between the angels and material creation, and consequently they are the ones that ought to preside over material creation. Aquinas himself raises a similar objection:

> What is allotted to one by reason of his dignity does not belong to what does not have like dignity. But according to Jerome [commenting on Mt. 18:10: "their angels always see," etc.], "so great is the dignity of souls that each and every one of them has an angel deputed to their care." This dignity, however, is not found in bodily creatures. Therefore they are not committed to the providence and ordination of angels."[45]

One response to this objection was already mentioned above (DV 5.8), namely, that human beings do not have the intelligence to preside over the whole of material creation (at most we know to avoid species extinction and destruction of unique ecosystems),[46] and yet it is fitting that some intelligent being act as a secondary cause executing God's providence over material creation. The angels' execution of this charge does not conflict with the special care they exercise over humans:

> Just as all corporeal things are subject to divine providence, and nevertheless it is said to concern human beings alone on account of a special mode of providence, so too although all corporeal things are subject to the governance of angels, nevertheless that they are more specially deputed to the care of humans is attributed to the dignity of souls.[47]

We are of special concern to the angels because we are closest to them, for we and they are created in the image of God and are capable of sharing in the beatific vision. It remains appropriate, however, that the material realm

45. *De Veritate*, q. 5, a. 8, ob. 6.

46. Theologian Daniel P. Scheid wants to affirms that we humans need to be helping nature as a whole to flourish, but ends up tacitly admitting that we lack the knowledge to do so: "As the only self-provident creatures, humans are called to contribute to the ordered interconnections among creatures (nature's 'beauty, diversity, and integrity') and to move other creatures to goodness ('fostering its productivity').... Humans must foster nature's ability to create new life and harmonious interconnections.... They ought to approach this task cautiously.... Humans should not presume to know for certain what will bring about greater flourishing. At times, people have attempt to 'improve' nature only to find that they could not have anticipated the repercussions, (e.g., bringing nonnative plants such as kudzu to America, only to have the kudzu dominate much of the countryside in the southern United States). The order among creatures in nature is fantastically complex, and though humans are called to promote the flourishing of nature and enhance its fecundity, they must undertake this task with humility." Daniel Sheid, "Saint Thomas Aquinas, the Thomistic Tradition, and the Cosmic Common Good," in *Green Discipleship* (Winona, Minnesota: Anselm Academic, 2011), 143–44.

47. *De Veritate*, q. 5, a. 8, ad 6.

be governed by intelligent intermediary beings and angels have the knowledge relevant to this task—knowledge that we lack.

Another response that can be offered to the objection that angels should only take care of humans and not of the rest of material creation is that angels care for humans in part by ruling over material creation:

> Care [*custodia*] is shown to a human being in two ways. In one way, particular care, according as an individual angel is deputed to the care of individual human beings.... In another way is universal care. And this is multiplied according to diverse orders; for to the extent that an agent is more universal to that extent it is higher. Therefore, in this manner, the care of the human multitude pertains to the order of Principalities or perhaps to the Archangels.... Further the Virtues have care over all bodily natures.[48]

A third objection to angelic oversight of non-rational creatures argues that it is superfluous: God in the initial creation produced all the diverse life forms that would occupy the earth, some of them in act and others in "seminal principles" (*rationes seminales*), i.e., in the active and passive powers of created things.[49] Therefore, the activity of angels is not needed when it comes to the apparition of new species of living things. This objection resembles one that Aquinas raises: "Bodily creatures are ruled by divine providence in this manner that they are ordered to an end through their natural operations which follow upon their determinate natures. Since the determinate natures of natural bodies are directly from God and are not from spiritual creatures, it seems that natural bodies are not ruled by means of spiritual substances."[50] Aquinas responds:

> Although the institution of nature through which corporeal things are inclined to an end is immediately from God, nevertheless the motion and action of them is able to be through angelic intermediaries; just as, although the seminal principles (*rationes seminales*) are in lower nature from God alone, nevertheless they are helped through the providence of farmers that they may go forth into act; whence,

48. ST I, q. 113, a. 3.

49. II *Sentences*, d. 13, q. 1, a. 1: "In the works of the six days, nature was so instituted that the principles of nature then established subsisted in them, from which they were able to propagate other things through mutual action and undergoing; and therefore it is necessary that at that time being was conferred on them and both active and passive powers, which Augustine calls seminal reasons, from which subsequent effects were produced. Therefore, when it comes to the being of these principles, this assumes the work of creation through which the substance of the elements of the world was produced in being."

50. *De Veritate*, q. 5, a. 8, ob. 4.

just as the farmer governs the growth of a field, so too every act of help or direction (*administratio*) given to a bodily creature is administered by angels.[51]

Farmers help plants grow by watering, providing fertilizer, removing weeds, and killing pests. The natural ability of plants to sprout from seed and grow can only be actualized when other natural things are available, such as water and nutriments, and when impediments are removed. Farmers insure these things. More plants grow to maturity due to the farmers' efforts than without them. Similarly, the forms of certain species lie in the potency of matter, but can only be actualized by certain other natural agents; however, angels can insure the presence of these agents.

This seems to be one of the forms of help that Aquinas has in mind when he says angels provide help to material creation:

> And therefore since like becomes from like, the cause of corporeal forms is not to be sought on the part of some immaterial form; but something composite, according as this fire is generated from this fire. In this manner, therefore, corporeal forms are caused, not as influxes from some immaterial form, but as matter reduced from potency to act by some composite agent. But because a composite agent, which is a body, is moved by a created spiritual substance, as Augustine says in III *De Trinitate*, it follows further that bodily forms are also derived from spiritual substances, not as it were by streaming in forms, but as by moving to forms. The species of the angelic intellect, which are certain seminal principles (*seminales rationes*) of bodily forms, are, however, further reduced to God as the first cause.[52]

The species in the angelic intellect are rightly called by analogy certain seminal principles, insofar as they constitute practical knowledge as to the production of natural things, and not simply knowledge as to their nature.[53]

Two questions remain, the first of which is: Is it more fitting that angels are involved in some or all cases of the evolution of species? Aquinas compares the angels to farmers who are responsible for more seeds growing to maturity than would without their intervention. Would a certain number

51. *De Veritate,* q. 5, a. 8, ad 4. See also, *Quodlibet* 9, q. 4, a. 5, ob. 3 which argues that angels do not act on lower bodies "by leading from potency to act, because nature suffices for this." Aquinas responds, "Although natural agents are able to lead from potency to act, nevertheless not so perfectly as can an Angel." Aquinas draws the notion that angels act like farmers in producing new species from Augustine; see *De Trinitate,* bk. 3, chap. 8. Note that Augustine hold that demons, as well, can act in this manner.

52. ST I, q. 65, a. 4.

53. See SCG II, chap. 100: "For it [the angel] has intelligible species from its likeness to the first intelligible species of the divine intellect which certainly is not abstracted from things, but is productive of things." See also ST I, q. 55, a. 2.

of species arise naturally without angelic intervention, angels being involved only in events like the Cambrian explosion? Or are angels involved in the origin of every new species? I am going to punt on this question, as I fail to see any convincing way of answering it. The second question is one that has been discussed above in a slightly different form: What constitutes the most fitting way angels might intervene in the evolution of species?

It seems that it should come about in a manner that allows for the maximal amount of causality on the part of material natural agents. On ID-type scenarios, some of what God gives to angels by way of intermediary causality he could have given to material natural causes (although some IDers might disagree). Though in the angels-orchestrating-chance-events scenario God also turns over to angels causality he could have given to material beings,[54] in contrast to ID accounts, he does so minimally and in such a way that it does not render certain forms of scientific research inherently futile.[55] It seems appropriate that angels do the least possible amount of physical work compatible with their creative oversight; even though this work is not laborious for them, it is more appropriately carried out by lowly blind material agents. After all, it is not the job of human architects to lay the bricks of the buildings they design. Thus, I think that the notions that "the execution of least things ... befit[s] a lower power proportioned to the effect"[56] and of provident beings giving direction can be put together in a manner similar to that which occurs when a labor-saving device is guided by a human being, e.g., a rototiller directed by a farmer. The rototiller is a work of human art that is meant to do brute work, but it requires the guidance of the farmer. Nature is a work of divine art, but one that requires further direction by angels to produce new species, or at least some of them. This vision maximizes the sort of causality appropriate to both kinds of beings.[57] Angels are not needed to cause DNA replication (except perhaps at

54. Angels perhaps were involved in the chance event that is thought to have caused the extinction of the dinosaurs by directing the giant asteroid that purportedly struck the Earth.

55. There is a recent theory that posits that quantum effects influence mutations so that they do occur more frequently in a manner that is adaptive rather than purely random. Even if theory is correct, the quantum causality is not claimed to be uniformly effective, and so an element of chance still remains. See Johnjoe McFadden and Jim Al-Khalili, "A quantum mechanical model of adaptive mutation," *BioSystems* 50 (1999): 203–11.

56. SCG III, chap. 77.

57. The long periods of time over which evolution occurs and the irregular manner in which it proceeds support the notion that natural causes acting on their own play a large role in evolution.

its very origin), but they may be needed to give it a direction it would not take on its own so that mutations leading to new species arise. This kind of division of labor is also suggested by Aquinas's position that angels cannot directly cause any form of change other than local motion. Thus, while angels can guide material things into the right position, the material things do the rest.[58]

It is not clear, however, that Aquinas favors this proposed division of labor which seeks to maximize natural causality, for he holds that many more things go on in the natural world due to the action of immaterial beings than the natural philosopher would hold:

> This argument proceeds according to the opinion of Aristotle who posited that the heavenly bodies are moved by spiritual substances.... But he did not posit that there would be some spiritual substances that had immediate governance over lower bodies, with perhaps the exception of human souls. And he held this because he did not consider operations other than natural to be exercised in lower bodies, for which the motion of the heavenly bodies sufficed. But because we posit many things to come about in lower bodies in addition to the natural actions of bodies, things for which the virtues of the heavenly bodies do not suffice, therefore, according to us, it is necessary to posit that angels have immediate governance not only over the heavenly bodies, but also over the lower bodies.[59]

Aristotle posited the existence of angels because he thought that the movements of the heavenly bodies were eternal and needed unmoved eternal agents to cause them.[60] Nowadays we realize that the heavenly bodies are made of the same materials and obey the same laws as earthly bodies, and so angelic causality is not needed.

What does Aquinas have in mind when he says "many things come about in lower bodies in addition to the natural actions of bodies, things for which the virtues of the heavenly bodies do not suffice?" In response to an objection in the same question, Aquinas says:

> However, the holy Doctors held, as did the Platonists, that spiritual substances were set over corporeal things as overseers. For Augustine says: "Each and every visible thing in this world has an angelic power set over it." And Damascene says: "The devil was from those angelic powers that preside over the terrestrial order." And Origen says commenting on "When the ass saw the angel" (Num. 22:23) that

58. See ST I, q. 110, a. 2, ad 2: "The angel in a more excellent mode than bodily agents transmutes bodily matter, namely, by moving as a higher cause the bodily agents themselves."

59. ST I, q. 110, a. 1, ad 2.

60. See Aristotle, *Metaphysics*, bk. 12, chaps. 7 and 8.

"there is work in the world for angels, who preside over the beasts and over the birth of animals and over the growth of trees, plants, and the rest of things."[61]

Angels presiding over the birth of animals seems about as necessary as their opening flowers in the morning. It smacks of the sort of magical world depicted in medieval bestiaries which is antipathetic to scientific inquiry. Aquinas himself gives as a reason for why substantial forms cannot be directly caused by angels that like generates like. The cow is a sufficient immediate cause of a calf; no angelic intervention is necessary.[62] While I've argued that it is appropriate for angels to be involved in the production of new species,[63] and while I acknowledge their role in protecting humans, I am at a loss to see why else they would be intervening in the material world. It seems right that they should have some sort of oversight over the whole of nature, but what exactly this consists in other than assisting the production of new species escapes me. In any case, we can be sure that Aquinas does not want to render what goes on in nature the patchwork of natural and supernatural causes following no rhyme or reason.

VI. Conclusion

At this point, however, I am going to leave off my speculations as to the extent of angelic causality in evolution,[64] and reiterate my main conclusions.

61. ST I, q. 110, a. 1, ad 3.

62. See ST I, q. 65, a. 4: "And therefore, since like becomes from its like, some immaterial form is not to be sought as cause of corporeal forms." See also *Commentary on the Metaphysics*, Bk. 7, lec. 7, no. 1431–35.

63. God's providence extends to species in a way that it does not extend to individual plants and animals, and thus it is fitting that intelligent beings have governance over the apparition of species, while not having oversight of individual non-rational beings as such. See *De Veritate*, q. 5, a. 3: "But corruptible things cannot have perpetuity except in the species; whence the species themselves are provided for for their own sakes, but the individuals belonging to them are not provided for except for the sake of conserving the perpetual being of the species."

64. An interesting question is whether the fallen angels had any role in evolution. It has been addressed by a number of thinkers; see Benedict Ashley, *Theologies of the Body: Humanist and Christian* (Braintree, Massachusetts: Pope John Center, 1995), 654–57, and Travis Dumsday, "Natural Evil, Evolution, and Scholastic Accounts of the Limits on Demonic Power," *Pro Ecclesia* 24, no. 1 (2015): 7–84. (Dumsday cites a number of other authors who consider this view.) Some examine whether the particular case of the sort of pain experienced by certain animals, the sort that Darwin found troubling, is reasonably attributed to demonic influences in evolution: "There seems to me too much misery in the world. I cannot persuade myself that a beneficent and omnipotent God would have designedly created the Ichneumonidae [wasp larvae] with the express intention of their feeding within the living bodies of caterpillars, or that a cat should play with

First, science cannot rule out angelic intervention in evolution as it is unable to identify the specific chance causes involved in key evolutionary changes that have occurred in the past, even if it may, in certain cases, be capable of plausibly reconstructing the sequence of changes.

Secondly, objections drawn from the philosophy of science to the effect that angelic intervention would introduce irregularities preventing us from knowing the laws of nature or would involve violation of the laws of nature were shown to overlook that science routinely ignores outliers and that the laws of nature, formulated as they are to describe the interactions of natural causes, do not exclude the possibility of non-natural causes acting in an artistic manner in the world. It is conceded, however, that extensive angelic intervention in the natural world would frustrate those seeking scientific explanations of things occurring in nature.

Thirdly, it is fitting that angels have a role in the production of new species for two reasons. First, it is fitting that God in his goodness impart causality to some beings in the manner in which he exercises causality, namely, intelligently. The sorts of effects most appropriate to these provident beings are those in which the order that is the product of intelligence shows forth most plainly; these effects are the various species and their order relative to one another. Although God could bring about such order using blind natural causes alone, the latter alone are not the most appropriate agents for these artistic tasks. Secondly, angelic intervention in evolution makes for a more interactive universe, and therefore for a more perfect universe. Those versions of angelic intervention that allot the greatest possible causal integrity to non-rational creatures are best in keeping with God's overflowing goodness, according to which he "not only makes things to be, but also to be causes."[65]

mice." Charles Darwin, Letter of May 22, 1860, addressed to Asa Gray http://www.thenewatlantis.com/publications/darwins-world-of-pain-and-wonder. My essay shows that demons are capable of directing the production of new species, but does not consider whether God would allow such intervention or whether the aforesaid natural evils are in need of being attributed to a malevolent cause, rather than simply being evils that naturally arise due to the contingency of nature (falling under Aquinas's notion of the "necessity of matter"; see *De Malo*, q. 5, a. 5).

65. SCG III, chap. 70.

MARK MOES

Maritain, Mascall, Pendergast, and Ashley

Untrammeled Approaches to the Doctrine of Original Sin from an Evolutionary Perspective

JACQUES MARITAIN SPECULATES in chapters 6 and 7 of *Untrammeled Approaches* about the transmission of original sin and about the role of the angels in the evolution of animals. Speculations on the same topics by other Catholic thinkers appeared in the decades either shortly before or shortly after the publication of *Untrammeled Approaches*—speculations which appear to complement and dovetail with Maritain's views. After looking at Maritain's speculations about the role of the angels in evolution in chapter 7, we shall attend to speculations published by the Anglican Thomist Eric L. Mascall, the Jesuit Richard Pendergast, and the Dominican Benedict Ashley, that treat not only of the role of the angels in evolution but also of the implications of that role for our understanding of the doctrine of original sin. Then we shall take note of Maritain's discussion of the doctrine of original sin in chapter 6 and, with the aid of Father Anthony Zimmerman's interpretation of that doctrine in his *Evolution and the Sin in Eden*,[1] articulate a brief interpretation of the doctrines of original sin and concupiscence that integrates the suggestions of all four thinkers.

1. Anthony Zimmerman, *Evolution and the Sin in Eden* (Lanham, Maryland: University Press of America, 1998).

I. Maritain on the Pure Spirits and the Evolutionary Process

In chapter 7 of *Untrammeled Approaches* Maritain reflects upon animal instinct, which he defines as the complex ensemble of innate, coordinated mental operations for determinate ways of acting common to all animals of a species and adapted to an end of which the animal is generally not conscious. He is especially interested here in the problem of the provenance of the innate "knowledge" involved in animal instinct (e.g., concerning particular suitable foods and ways of protecting offspring, defending against enemies, and healing wounds), which the animal brings into play without conscious learning or development. Maritain writes, "The cosmos and its intelligibility demands that there be such knowledge; but it is not the animal that has it."[2]

Maritain prefaces his hypothesis concerning the explanation of such complex animal instinct with a discussion of some general principles of his theistic cosmology. First, he recalls that pre-human animals receive their being from God in a way different from the way in which human animals and created pure spirits receive theirs. Whereas human souls and created pure spirits receive their being from God in a direct act of creation, all merely material creatures, including pre-human animals, receive their being through the mediation of pre-existing material powers of nature. The animal soul receives its being as mediated by a long material process extending back through evolutionary time, by the created cosmos and the sub-creative powers at work in it. Secondly, he notes that material things embody two contrary aspirations—the aspiration to maintain themselves in being, on the one hand, and the aspiration to "rejoin the Creator as much as possible and to attain to the divine similitude ... [by] tending to pass beyond the degree of perfection in which matter is found in this or that case."[3] This latter aspiration in the evolutionary process embodies itself in a succession of mutations such that, at crucial junctures, under the direction of the first Cause, new species emerge. This aspiration or evolutionary *elan* is a tendency of active powers given by God to this or that

2. Jacques Maritain, *Untrammeled Approaches*, translated by Bernard Doering (Notre Dame, Indiana: University of Notre Dame Press, 1997), 137n9.

3. Ibid., 141–42.

creature whereby the creature in quasi-Lamarckian fashion[4] itself works at raising to a new degree of perfection its living lineage, helping somehow to prepare and to fashion new and higher structures for other living beings which will cross over the threshold of a new species when their material substrate is properly prepared.[5]

Yet the mode in which *pre-human* animal species receive their being, according to Maritain, is not conditioned and mediatized *solely* by the evolutionary *elan* mentioned before but also by the activity of the pure spirits. The angels, it is true, are not "instruments of the creative Act" of God, since no creature can participate in Creation itself, but they are rather sub-creative beings who receive from God the mission to administer the visible world.[6] The divine Wisdom allows the angels to influence the formation of the "mass of psychic and physical structures" emerging in the evolution of the pre-human animal world, which the evolutionary *elan* of matter calls for and prepares in animals. And God delights in the work of the angels as "artists" influencing evolution in ways expressing their "sense of the richest and most joyous fantasy." Since it is fitting, according to Maritain, for God to entrust the angels with the preparations for the formation of human beings,[7] it is reasonable to speculate that the knowledge presupposed by this or that animal instinct—for example the knowledge presupposed by the swallow's instinct to rub celadine on the eyes of young swallows whose eyes don't open properly—ultimately derives from the knowledge of the angels.[8]

4. On various relationships between nature and nurture, on different levels and units of natural selection, and on some recent views on quasi-Lamarckianism in genetics, see Robert Wesson, *Beyond Natural Selection* (Cambridge, Massachusetts: MIT Press, 1991). See also Matt Ridley, *The Agile Gene: How Nature Turns on Nurture* (New York: HarperCollins, 2003). See also Eva Jablonka and Marion J. Lamb, *Evolution in Four Dimensions: Genetic, Epigenetic, Behavioral, and Symbolic Variation in the History of Life* (Cambridge, Massachusetts: MIT Press, 2005).

5. See Philip Fothergill, *Evolution and Christians* (London: Longmans, Green, and Co., 1961), 188–93.

6. Maritain cites St. Thomas's ST I, q. 100, *De Veritate,* q. 5, a. 8, and SCG III, chaps. 78, 83; he also cites St. Augustine's *De Trin.,* III and St. Gregory's line: "In hoc mundo visibili nihil nisi per creaturam invisibilem disponi potest."

7. For arguments in favor of this view of the rational "fittingness" of the angelic influence upon the evolutionary process, see Marie George's essay in this volume.

8. Maritain further speculates that it is the non-deterministic realm of subatomic matter which provides the "window" through which the influence of the angelic intelligences passes into the evolutionary process. He suggests that the angels act on matter in the realm of microphysics, where the kind of invisibility which matter enjoys by reason of its indetermination with

II. Eric Mascall on Evil, Evolution, and the Fall

In 1956, Eric L. Mascall—Cambridge-trained mathematician, Professor of Historical Theology in the University of London, and Episcopal Priest of the Oratory of the Good Shepherd—published his Bampton Lectures under the title of *Christian Theology and Natural Science*.[9] Two sections of this excellent and still highly relevant set of lectures are worthy of our attention in the context of our discussion of Maritain's speculations on the role of the angels in evolution: section 6 of chapter 1, entitled "Evolution and Pre-Human Evil," and section 3 of chapter 8, entitled "Evolution, Evil and the Fall." In these sections Mascall maintains, with a focus somewhat different from Maritain's, that the development of the general theory of organic evolution has prompted contemporary theologians to revisit the "Hebrew tradition which identified the serpent of the Genesis-story with the devil (in *Wisdom* 2.24)"[10]; this revisiting suggests limitations of a traditionally popular Christian view, articulated in connection with oversimplified views of Scriptural inspiration and inerrancy: namely, that all evils, both moral and physical, derive somehow from the first sins of embodied *human* beings. Knowing what we now do about the past history of the Earth and of man, maintains Mascall, contemporary theology no longer needs to suppose that, before man appeared, everything was going precisely as God ideally intended it to go. And theology has ready at hand the views held from the beginning that, before the creation of man, sin had already occurred[11] in the angelic realm, and that the angels occupied themselves, among other things, with administering and tending to the evolving material world. If these views are true—views which clash considerably with the modern mechanistic-idealistic-deistic views of God's relation to the created world, on the basis of which modern formulations of the atheological argument from evil are articulated—and if God's intention was that the realms of matter and spirit were to be linked together in intimate union so that the lower levels of this cosmos were to be under the surveillance

regard to our measures is in a relationship of propriety or affinity with the invisibility of the angelic motions.

9. Eric L. Mascall, *Christian Theology and Natural Science* (London: Longmans, Green and Co., 1956).

10. Mascall, *Christian Theology*, 32.

11. The temporality of this verb has to be interpreted analogically if the angels live and operate not in physical time but in "aeviternity."

and care of the higher, then it seems reasonable to suppose, says Mascall, that defection and rebellion in the angelic realm should drastically disorder, hamper, and distort the carrying out of God's ultimate intentions in the material world.

An acknowledgment of the existence of pre-human evil, moral in respect of the sin of the fallen angels and physical in respect to the results of the disordered exercise of their administrative occupations, should caution theologians against making much use of the sort of "arguments from design" for theism that were articulated in the modern post-Cartesian era by theologians who, in debate with Naturalists and Deists, argued as if the angelic realm did not exist and the angelic Fall never happened. It is true that the physical evil of the "cruelty of nature red in tooth and claw" can be exaggerated and misconceived.[12] But nevertheless, suggests Mascall, a theologian who neglects the angelic Fall might well be troubled by certain forms of parasitism in nature, for example in the life cycle of the malarial parasite *Plasmodium*.[13] The whole process can be seen as the story of

12. Although Mascall does not mention this, Alfred Russell Wallace, the co-discoverer of the theory of evolution by natural selection, points it out in his profoundly interesting essay "Is Nature Cruel? The Uses of Pain," chapter 19 of his *The World of Life: A Manifestation of Creative Power, Directive Mind and Ultimate Purpose* (New York: Moffat, Yard and Company, 1911). In chapter 20 of that work, Wallace maintains that a full understanding of the evolutionary process requires an understanding of the role of the angels in the evolutionary process. However, Wallace, a non-Christian freethinker, says nothing about any *sin* of the angels. He only claims that to afford any rational explanation of the world of life we must postulate the continuous action and guidance of higher intelligences. "If, as I contend," writes Wallace, "we are forced to the assumption of an infinite God by the fact that our earth *has* developed life, mind, and ourselves, it seems only logical to assume that the vast, the infinite chasm between ourselves and the Deity is to some extent occupied by an almost infinite series of grades of beings, each successive grade having higher and higher powers in regard to the origination, the development, and the control of the universe" (p. 423).

13. Mascall describes it as follows: *Plasmodium* is injected into the human bloodstream with the dose of poison injected during a mosquito bite. The parasite is carried to the liver, where it enters a parenchyma cell. It multiplies by the thousands by asexual division until the cell bursts, when some of the parasites enter fresh liver cells and repeat the process and others attack the red cells of the blood, which in turn burst so that the young can escape into the bloodstream to attack red cells as the parent did. In an infected human host, millions of infected cells break down simultaneously about twice a week, disgorging the parasites and with them poisons highly injurious to the human host and which cause a paroxysm of fever. The parasites then prepare for a sexual stage of existence, each one turning into an immature male or female form which, instead of bursting its cell, settles down and waits until another mosquito bites the human sufferer. The blood drawn into the mosquito's stomach contains red cells inhabited by these immature sexual forms which rapidly develop into mature sperm-cells and ova. Fertilized *Plasmodium* ova subdivide into hundreds of cells which break off as separate individual parasites and swarm in

securing the existence of a single-cell parasite at the cost of lives superior to it in the scale of life, scourging with misery and death entire regions of the Earth which might without it be happy places. "Evolution" has adapted *Plasmodium* to a life cycle that slaughters man. (It is a life cycle exhibiting the kind of "ingenuity" or "knowledge," possessed without conscious learning or development, concerning particular suitable foods and ways of producing and protecting offspring, which Maritain attributes, in its happier instances, to the activity of the good angels.)

Mascall suggests that the theologian must ask, when he hears about such biological phenomena, how this kind of thing has come about in a world which is the creation of a good and almighty God. He thinks it a happy chance that Christian theology did not have to wait for the researches of micro-biologists to learn that something had gone very badly wrong with God's world. But he worries about the way in which it has often been taught that man's original fall away from God, presumed to be the first case of the personal rebellion against God's ordering of the world originating from within the material order, was alone responsible for introducing disorganization into man's nature and relationships, impairing his spiritual faculties and throwing his bodily life out of joint. From the point of view of this teaching, man's mortality and liability to physical disease are consequences of the original human rejection of grace and of nothing else. But it does not make much sense to him to think that the unbalanced condition in which some parasites and viruses can survive only at the expense of the human host's life or happiness (of course many parasites are harmless to their hosts) has its origin in the sin of Adam and Eve. It may be fine and good to say that much human suffering can be attributed to the human rebellion against God working its way out in the mistreatment of nature and of man. It may be true that man experiences his suffering as an evil and not a means of sanctification because of his condition of alienation from God. It may also be true that the pain of sub-rational animals, unaccompanied as it is by the self-conscious distress that rationality and the power of imaginative memory and anticipation add to physical pain, does not constitute suffering in any way comparable with human suffering. Nevertheless, the existence of realities such as the life cycle of *Plasmodium* makes it almost

the mosquito's blood, especially in the poison gland in the mosquito's head [how does the parasite know how to migrate especially to the poison gland?], where they are ready, the next time it bites, to infect a fresh human being. See *Christian Theology and Natural Science*, 297–99.

impossible to interpret the course of pre-human evolution as free from distortion and deviation.

Hence Mascall thinks it important to bring back into play in the modern context the doctrine held from the beginning of Christianity that angels—pure spirits, exercising a sort of administrative authority over the material world—had sinned before man, and the doctrine that man's own sin of unbelief may have been provoked by influences proceeding from the fallen spiritual realm. Attention to these old doctrines may put a new light upon the way in which much modern apostasy from God is often based upon the atheological argument from natural evil propounded from a standpoint that denies the existence of the pure spirits altogether. For the result of angelic sin may well have been, according to Mascall, to introduce into the material realm a disorder manifesting itself in a distortion of the evolutionary plan.[14] This he thinks a reasonable theory because it seems to be a general law that the lower orders in creation should be governed by, and have a certain dependence upon, the higher ones. He finds the suggestion more compelling because the doctrine of the angelic Fall was not originally postulated in order to account for the existence of natural evil in the material world before man, but rather was stored away in the faith tradition in readiness for answering a problem that would not arise until the emergence of evolutionary biology in the nineteenth century.

III. Richard Pendergast's *Cosmos*

In 1973, the year of the publication of *Untrammeled Approaches,* the Jesuit Richard J. Pendergast published *Cosmos,* whose penultimate chapter considers evolution and original sin from an evolutionary perspective and speculates about the role of angels in evolution. Pendergast emphasizes that the material cosmos is a hylomorphic system with a definite unity, and that in the life realm, ecosystems and populations of organisms evolve in interaction with each other and with the constraints set both by physics and chemistry and by the geological evolution of the Earth and of the solar system. But at the root of the cosmic process, he says, is "an intelligent be-

14. Mascall cites Illtyd Trethown, *An Essay in Christian Philosophy* (London: Longman's, Green, and Co., 1954) as having propounded a similar view, a view that one of the results of the fall of the angels was the disorganization of the material universe over which the fallen angels had charge. See Mascall, *Christian Theology,* 301–302.

ing or beings whose symbolizing activity produces the material structures of the universe."[15] According to the Catholic views of the divine perfection and of evil as privation, evil can only have entered the cosmos by way of defective creaturely symbolizing activity. (Though he uses different terminology, Pendergast's speculations here dovetail with Maritain's thoughts on the source of human and angelic sin in the "non-consideration of the rule."[16]) And though it is clear that man is a source of evil in the world, he cannot be the only source. The pervasiveness of moral and natural evil in the cosmos, proffers Pendergast, is best explained by the hypothesis that the unity of the present cosmos is grounded in a society of symbolizers to some extent in conflict with one another, rather than in a single personality. The unity of the present cosmos is less like the unity of a human body or of a single mind than it is like the unity of a fragmented culture vivified by conflicting intentions. For Pendergast, "the inner dynamism of things has been corrupted and so the evolutionary process which flows from it is also corrupt,"[17] and "our present world is the result of an evolutionary process which is probably ten billion years long and which went awry from the very beginning."[18] The existence of the angels as "sub-creators" of the visible material structures of the universe is rejected by modern post-Cartesian thinkers only because of their "Deist" prejudice that the universe is an impersonal world machine.

Pendergast attempts to integrate the foregoing views on cosmic evil with the traditional doctrine of original sin in the following way. Original sin *originatum* is the present sinful state of man in which he is inclined to moral evil and is subject to suffering and death experienced as traumatic. Original sin *originans* is the historical act or acts by which intelligent creatures introduced evil into nature and into human history, resulting in orig-

15. Richard J. Pendergast, *Cosmos* (New York: Fordham University Press, 1973), 149. Pendergast uses this term following Karl Rahner, "Theology of the Symbol," *Theological Investigations* (Baltimore, Maryland: Helicon, 1966); and Rahner, *On the Theology of Death* (New York: Herder, 1961).

16. See James G. Hanink, *Aquinas and Maritain on Evil* (Washington D.C.: The American Maritain Association, distributed by The Catholic University of America Press, 2013), especially the papers of Mary Catherine Sommers, Siobhan Nash-Marshall, Jonathan Sanford, Laura L. Garcia, and Michael D. Torre. Maritain's term "rule" needs a lot of unpacking. Suffice it here to say that he closely associates "non-consideration of the rule" with the saying of Christ in the Johannine Gospel: "Apart from me you can do nothing" (15:5).

17. Pendergast, *Cosmos*, 166.

18. Ibid., 171.

inal sin *originatum*. Though traditionally original sin *originans* was attributed solely to Adam and Eve, theology might now better attribute it in part, especially in respect to the natural evils consequent upon it, and in light of modern knowledge about the unity of the evolutionary cosmos, to the activity of some of the fallen angelic powers.[19] Traditional theology taught that original sin *originatum* consisted in the *absence* of sanctifying grace and the gifts of the Spirit (and of certain preternatural gifts), an absence resulting from the *loss* of these gifts on account of human sin. But the pervasiveness of moral and natural evil in the cosmos suggests that the state of original sin *originatum* into which humans fell after the loss of the gifts is a quite helpless subjection to evils "deeply rooted in the present world order ... that affect even structures below the human level which antedate man's appearance on the planet."[20] Man's failings are "bound up with his evolutionary background and with general characteristics of the whole structure of the universe."[21] Many of man's vestigial sexual and aggressive "open" instincts,[22] psychological results of man's evolutionary bodily heritage,[23] are no longer very appropriate for a rational being, especially in modern

19. Pendergast attempts to relate this view to the Scriptural account of the Fall in *Genesis* 2 and 3 on pages 163–72 of his chapter. He also makes use of Heinrich Schlier, *Principalities and Powers in the New Testament* (New York: Herder, 1961). On pages 169–70 he writes: "Even if one feels it is necessary to retain the idea of the Fall of man is a historical event ... one would still have to admit that this event is a secondary one and that there must have been a Fall in which the Principalities and Powers rebelled against God.... Today we need to retain Saint Paul's profound insight into the physical solidarity in sin and death of the present world order."

20. Pendergast, *Cosmos*, 155.

21. Ibid., 156. Later on page 162, Pendergast writes: "Even if a new Adam and Eve were to start afresh on some distant earth-like planet, it seems virtually certain that their descendants would face essentially the same problems as we do. In other words, the present order of the cosmos is such that, without a special gift of God, disorder (concupiscence) will inevitably afflict man in both his concupiscible and irascible sense-appetites.... The higher order entity is never able to dominate and order totally the subordinate entities of which it is composed. The finality by which the subordinate structures are ordered to the good of the superordinate ones is weak compared to the finality by which they are ordered to their own good. Man's problems are not unique to him. They are the problems of the whole cosmos.... This universe is substantially good, but it is infected with evil."

22. Obviously, instinct does not operate the same way in humans and in sub-human animals. Pendergast suggests that man's "open instincts" correspond roughly to the scholastic "sensory appetite" and "irascible appetite."

23. Maritain writes at the end of section III of chapter 6 of *Untrammeled Approaches*: "The soul such as God creates it is pure and immaculate; it is by reason of its union with the body that, at the instant of its creation and infusion, it is made to participate in the original transgression and receives the weaknesses and disorders that come from it."

circumstances.[24] The parable of the wheat and the tares, however, may be taken to indicate that the good which God wants to create requires that evil be allowed to take its course this side of the New Creation promised in Scripture.

IV. Benedict Ashley on the Pure Spirits and the Evolutionary Process

In his *Theologies of the Body: Humanist and Christian*, the Dominican Thomist Benedict Ashley notes that references to intelligent superhuman created pure spirits, some good and some evil, are deeply embedded not only in Scripture, in general, and in the recorded sayings of Jesus, in particular, but also in the Church's liturgy, in the writings of the Fathers, and in many non-definitive but important documents of the councils and popes.[25] Not only pre-rational mythological religions, but all traditional religions, refer to such spirits and even claim acquaintance with them. Among the world religions, only Secular Humanism tends to exclude such beings from its ontology, and Secular Humanist objections to their existence seem to derive from nothing more profound than a residual Deism that characterizes the world as an impersonal machine. Ashley offers a number of reasons for believing that the biblical references to angels and devils are to be understood as inspired and true assertions.[26]

24. Pendergast provides an interesting discussion of "open human instincts" of sexuality and aggression on pages 156–63. He relies heavily upon the (now somewhat dated) discussions of human evolutionary psychology in Konrad Lorenz, *On Aggression* (New York: Bantam Books, 1967); *Man and Aggression*, edited by Ashley Montague (Oxford: Oxford University Press, 1968); and Anthony Storr, *Human Aggression* (New York: Atheneum, 1968).

25. Benedict Ashley, *Theologies of the Body: Humanist and Christian* (Braintree, Massachusetts: Pope John Center, 1995), 646. Ashley's discussion of the angels and evolution is on pages 646–59.

26. Benedict Ashley's speculations about the fallen angels having distorted the evolutionary process resonate with the work of a variety of contemporary philosophers of religion. Like Ashley, these thinkers are in part concerned to respond to non-theistic humanists who argue that the deliverances of the sciences of nature provide evidence against the existence of the transcendent and perfectly good God of Christianity. These humanists, among whom some of the more brash and vocal are Philip Kitcher, Richard Dawkins, and William Rowe, typically appeal to some version of "the Darwinian problem of evil," which consists in the claim that the vast and unquantifiable array of non-human animal suffering connected to the predation, pain, and death that is endemic to the evolutionary process counts as evidence against the existence of God. See Michael Murray, *Nature Red in Tooth and Claw: Theism and the Problem of Animal Suffering* (Oxford University Press, 2008). Non-theists standardly maintain that a good God would never have allowed demonic sin to have such widespread negative consequences, and would never have cre-

First of all, the existence of angels and devils has an intimate connection with the central doctrine of the victory of Christ over sin. In the biblical understanding God rules history through the powers and principalities who are both good and evil and who are, to a greater or lesser degree, limited in wisdom. Such powers rule the nations, and God directly rules only his chosen people. God entrusted the governance of history, cosmological and human, to the powers, but while some have remained faithful to him, others have set themselves up as autonomous and so have become, so to speak, sub-creative sub-contractors who do bad work.[27] The Messianic age begins with the life and death and resurrection of Jesus, which begins the process of undoing the results of the distorted ministrations of those fallen powers and principalities whose authority is to be revoked in the age to come. The Gospel makes no sense apart from this scheme, Ashley insists, and to deny the existence of these superhuman powers is to trivialize the New Testament teaching both on the human need of salvation and on the magnitude of Christ's work.

A second reason for believing in the reality of the angels and devils, according to Ashley, is that the modern scientific world picture has not eliminated a cosmological argument for the existence of superhuman intelligences as necessary factors in a consistent modern cosmology. Modern cosmology attributes the existence of the Sun to galactic processes that go back to the original Big Bang, and it asserts that in our region of space, at least, a biological evolution to more complex forms and to man has gone on in spite of the fact that the universe as a whole is ever tending toward entropic decay. Ashley maintains that the counter-current to entropy which has led to man can only be accounted for scientifically by appealing not to natural laws but to a *history* of a long sequence of events produced by unique concurrences of the four natural forces, a sequence that could have turned aside at any point and is guided by no known natural law or cosmic code. The source of new information constituting more complex life systems is simply the contingent *history* of situations in which recognized particles

---

ated a world in which so much natural evil was possible in the first place. Murray discusses ways in which theists might combine the demonic sin hypothesis with other approaches to the problem of natural evil in order to constitute a more persuasive theodicy capable of gaining a hearing among defenders of the "Darwinian problem of evil" argument against the existence of God.

27. See Benedict Ashley, *Choosing a World View and Value System* (New York: Alba House, 2000), 306.

and forces act.[28] Though it is sometimes maintained that human life is just an accident bound to happen sooner or later in infinite time, modern science suggests that cosmic processes do not go on infinitely. We still need to posit the existence of superhuman intelligences guiding natural events. It is increasingly recognized that the Darwinian theory of natural selection is not a complete explanation for the long historical scenario required to produce the complexity of the human brain. It is not implausible to suppose that the universe as a whole includes pure spirits whose presence does not override or replace physical laws and processes but uses them to guide evolution, as human chemists produce complex chemicals by ordinary natural processes, chemicals that would not occur in nature without human activity. Moreover, since the history of evolutionary process exhibits imperfect unity, lack of smoothness, and a great deal of conflict, it would seem that we need to posit a number of imperfect intelligences working sometimes at cross purposes in guiding evolution.

Ashley points out that one of the modes of creative thinking that has paid off richly in contemporary science is *extrapolation* or pattern thinking, exemplified in Mendeleev's extrapolation of the periodical table of the elements from the physico-chemical patterns known to him. The evolutionary view of the world presents us with a pattern of a great variety of natural kinds, from atoms to the most complex of living forms, and we are always looking for "missing links" to complete this pattern. When we discover in our physical universe a human species which introduces a wholly new principle of living behavior that involves semiosis and creative thought, we naturally conjecture that the single human species is not the only exemplification of this kind of life. If we accept that the world has been created by an infinite intelligence, we are struck by the incongruity of the size of the gap between human embodied intelligence, on the one hand, and divine omniscience, on the other. It is not unreasonable, therefore, to follow Aquinas in accounting for this gap by positing the existence of a large range of created intelligences so powerful as not to require a body in their mental activity.[29]

28. See Benedict Ashley, "Causality and Evolution," *Thomist* 36 (1972): 199–230, esp. 212.

29. Compare the arguments articulated by Marie George in her essay in this volume. Ashley reminds us that, according to Aquinas, these beings are not essentially bound, as things in the material world are, to prime matter, which is the ontological basis of the peculiar spatiotemporal quantity and individuality of material beings; but they are *virtually* related to the material world of energy, space, and time to the extent that they can influence its development and express their creativity within it to some degree. Aquinas thought of them as knowing by means of innate

An objection to the existence of the created pure spirits, often made from the point of view of Secular Humanism, is that there is no good physical evidence for their existence and activity. But perhaps, suggests Ashley, because their influence is usually subtle enough not to disturb or override physical law,[30] their action becomes evident, not primarily in disturbance of the natural order, but rather in that *course of human and cosmic history* that is determined not as much by natural law as by chance and by human and angelic free will. This supposition leads Ashley to articulate another set of reasons, over and above Scriptural references and the evolutionary and cosmological extrapolation arguments, for believing in the existence of angels. He singles out three aspects of human and cosmic history that might be especially illuminated by the doctrine of the angels.

The first aspect has to do with the possible role of the evil spirits in encouraging the "mysteries of iniquity" of internal dissensions and moral corruptions in the history of the Christian Church—antisemitism, Gnosticism, Constantinian secularization, schisms, wrangles over Christology dividing East from West, Renaissance corruption, the dividing of Christendom in the Reformation, defections following Vatican II, and the like. He suggests that what is most diabolic is not open and militant atheism, but the efforts of the evil ones to gain control over whatever is *good* in the world by turning *good against good*, influencing human beings to use this or that religious truth as a weapon against this or that other religious truth. Ashley also mentions extraordinarily inhuman events such as the Holocaust, which could not have occurred without the concurrence of many forces

ideas in a purely intuitive and non-discursive manner, the more powerful of them knowing by means of fewer and fewer innate ideas in proportion to the degree of integration of their knowledge, the knowledge of the highest angel approaching the perfection of God's knowledge. All the angels know innately, with different degrees of clarity, the whole material and spiritual universe in its fundamental order, enjoying in the mirror of this universe a *natural* knowledge of God, as opposed to an infused knowledge by grace. But the angels cannot know the exact course of future history by means of their innate ideas. They are not only contemplative but also active as God's messengers and ministers, in the latter capacity guiding the course of nature and of history. As our human intelligence has control over our material bodies, so angels can affect natural processes.

30. Ashley suggests that angels may communicate with humans by a subtle action on the brain by which we are assisted in our thinking to synthesize the information we have gained by ordinary learning processes in such a way as to arrive at more secure and penetrating insights, perhaps even by "visions" or "apparitions." God, he says, probably maintains the ordinary course of natural events in such a way as, in respect to the subsidiarity of secondary causes, to restrict the number of paranormal events that we might otherwise expect on the hypothesis of the existence of the angels.

not under human control, and mentions the possible role of evil spirits in the occurrence of corrupt polytheistic cultures worshipping false gods.

The second aspect has to do with the apparent role of good spirits in the appearance of righteous and holy men and women outside of Israel and the Church, including inspired leaders such as the Buddha, Confucius, and Socrates. Ashley's idea is that what comes from the good angels is whatever has been especially remarkable in history in extraordinary human creativity (such as the "Greek miracle" or extraordinary artistic masterpieces in general) and in the good stewardship of God's gifts, that the action of the good angels is seen in the carrying out of divine Providence in the face of obstacles set by bad angels, and that the action of evil spirits is seen in the way God's antecedent will has been in part frustrated by angelic sin. Ashley does not discuss testimonies to the existence of the angels by persons who claimed to have experienced encounters with them, but it is interesting that one of the greatest mathematicians who ever lived, Srinivasi Ramanujan, describes his mathematical findings as revelations to him of a "goddess" Namagiri.

The third aspect of history that might be illuminated by the doctrine of the angels has to do with that with which Mascall and Pendergast were concerned: the possible role that the evil angels might play in the explanation of the problem of physical and pre-moral evil and animal suffering in the evolutionary process itself. Ashley admits that the Darwinian universe seems in important respects to be "red in tooth and claw" in the carnal warfare of "survival of the fittest," though it has also been found that symbiosis and cooperation between life forms contribute importantly to evolution. It may seem that the organic food chain, with its apparent overproduction of offspring and high mortality rates of young animals, is essential to evolution. Large numbers in gamete production and in reproduction are necessary in order that there be lots of genetic variability as raw material for adaptive change and plenty of food for higher life forms. But the grosser aspects of selection like struggle, predation, parasitism, or physical catastrophe can seem repulsive. It can seem unnecessary that natural selection would lead to the extinction of a species because it has developed oversized horns or spines. It can even seem strange that organisms are genetically programmed to live only for a certain limited time, though it is apparent that this is essential to the rise of higher life forms in the present world order.

Moreover, the powerful and unruly aggressive instincts of the "irascible appetite" that is genetically programmed in the human race because of the survival needs of proto-humans can seem troubling to the theist who believes in the perfection of goodness in the Creator. Human aggressiveness, often leading to irrational violence, can seem to be an obsolete vestige of a need to fight off enemies that no longer exist. Sometimes, apparently, human aggressiveness becomes libidinized in the pursuit of sadistic or masochistic sexual pleasure, or turned back on persons in depression, suicide, or intra-family violence. Some speculate that the human unconscious contains a sort of phylogenetic memory of the whole previous course of evolution, and that the tensions in that course are mirrored in the temporal tensions in the unconscious. Humans seem to have inborn fears of falling, snakes, and the dark, corresponding to the chief dangers posed to tree-dwelling ancestors inhabiting a world of nocturnal predators, and in states of lowered cortical activity the brain seem to replay the age-old warfare among reptiles and mammals. Non-analytic parts of the brain, unaware of time relations, may not discriminate between ancestral "memories" and memories of events that have occurred in a person's lifetime.[31]

Given these troubling features of apparent natural and pre-moral evils, it is not unreasonable to suppose, since the intrinsic governance of the universe is the responsibility of the angels, some of whom have set themselves against God's plan and thereby disturbed the universe to its entropic foundations, that the course of evolution could have followed a smoother path toward the production of an Earth suitable for human intelligence and of the evolution toward humankind than it actually has.[32] It is reasonable to sup-

31. Of course, it is also true that in our present condition aggressiveness must be and often is aimed not at destroying order but at overcoming disorder and creating order through self-defense in just conflict, art, technology, and moral discipline.

32. See Benedict Ashley, *Choosing a World View and Value System: An Ecumenical Apologetics* (New York: Alba House, 2000), 303–307. Ashley writes: "We may suppose that if the good angels had governed the process of cosmological evolution it would have been smooth and gentle with much less waste and emptiness, and biological evolution would have come about by symbiosis, or cooperation, among living things rather than by their competition to survive. The history of evolution, therefore, might have been very different, but God would have insured that it would ultimately have climaxed in the creation of intelligent bodily humanity as supreme in the material world. Thus there seems no scientific reason, either physical or biological, that humanity might not have evolved very directly through an evolutionary line where animal pain could have been avoided, although this possibility staggers the imagination." Ashley notes also the remarkable fact, mentioned earlier, that Alfred Russell Wallace, the co-discoverer with Darwin of the theory of evolution through natural selection, wrote a book called *The World of Life: A*

pose that the history of evolution, including aspects of the food chain and of natural selection and of the current unruly state of inborn human aggressiveness and irascibility, reflects a civil war among the cosmic intelligences.[33]

V. Jacques Maritain and Anthony Zimmerman on Original Sin

Considerations such as the foregoing lead to complementary considerations concerning the Christian doctrine of original sin. Let us begin these by considering Maritain's remarks on original sin in chapter 6 of *Untrammeled Approaches.* In this chapter Maritain lays out a neo-Thomistic account of the evolutionary origins of man, together with his "*petit vehicule*" or little wisdom on the state of man before and after the Fall. In a postscript at the end of the chapter, Maritain remarks that the unity of the human species is guaranteed by each human's possession of a spiritual and immortal soul separating him from the overdeveloped animals preceding him, even while maintaining that each new human being receives his *full human nature* by virtue of biological lineage and hereditary transmission. The Judeo-Christian tradition that man was created in the state of grace must somehow be reconciled with the tradition that every new human being since "Adam" is born with a nature deprived of grace and wounded in its being by reason of this hereditary transmission.[34]

Manifestation of Creative Power, Directive Mind and Ultimate Purpose, in which Wallace concluded that evolution involved more than natural selection and was guided by the creative intelligence of the angels whom God put in charge to give historical direction to evolutionary processes.

33. See Travis Dumsday, "Natural Evil, Evolution, and Scholastic Accounts of the Limits on Demonic Power," *Pro Ecclesia* 24, no. 1 (2015): 71–84. Dumsday points out that in recent literature the connection of natural evil to the sin of the angels has been developed in most detail by the Protestant theologian Gregory Boyd in his *Satan and the Problem of Evil: Constructing a Trinitarian Warfare Theology* (Downer's Grove, Illinois: InterVarsity Press, 2001), although it was articulated earlier by a variety of philosophical theologians such as C. S. Lewis, Eric Mascall, Terence Penelhum, and Alvin Plantinga. The connection was also articulated mythically in J. R. R. Tolkien's creation story in his *Silmarillion,* the *Ainulindale.* Dumsday is concerned in his paper with the worry that attributing natural evil to the evil spirits might be heretical insofar as it implies an excessively large degree of demonic control over nature and the evolutionary process, even reminding some theologians of Gnostic attributions of physical nature to an evil demiurge over whom God has no control. Dumsday argues that various Scholastic claims actually allow for demonic intervention and interference in animal evolution. Dumsday suggests that an angel or a demon, like a human artist, might introduce new "sub-created" or "artificial" forms by employing *already existent potential dispositions* of things.

34. Maritain thinks that this reconciliation requires that we adopt monogenism, the view

At the end of section III, Maritain makes another important remark about original sin. He lays out Thomas's teaching that original sin is contracted by the human soul at the very instant of its infusion: "The soul such as God creates it is pure and immaculate; it is by reason of its union with the body that, at the instant of its creation and infusion, it is made to participate in the original transgression and receives the weaknesses and disorders that come from it." Because mortal bodily nature is distorted, so is the human soul. He says that by inheritance the child pays the price of the disturbances which have arisen in his long hereditary line, inheriting disorders of temperament that expose the child to difficulties in its intellectual or moral activity. He goes even further by saying that even disturbances which have arisen more recently, during the lifespans of his parents—disturbances due to pathogenic agents, to conditions of physical or social milieu, or to psycho-somatic disturbances resulting from moral transgressions—can incline the child toward evil. Certain profound moral disorders in the parents' lives can have destructive psychosomatic repercussions, perhaps capable in some sort of quasi-Lamarckian way of attaining the gonads themselves, which thus become bearers of alterations which are then transmitted. In such cases, added on to the disorder which affects all human nature due to its entire evolutionary history, the child receives hidden in its body the germ of neurotic disturbances and perverse moral inclinations.[35]

Now let us compare Maritain's remarks with some views about original sin from Anthony Zimmerman's 1998 book *Evolution and the Sin in Eden.*[36] Zimmerman supposes that the creation of our first ancestors in the state of grace need not mean that there was nothing out of order in their bodily inheritance.[37] It might mean rather that God gave them, in the period in

---

that the first humans came into existence at the same time by a temporally indexed divine act of *love of election* or *love of choice* (compare C. S. Lewis's teachings about the selectiveness God exercises in His providential acts), so that we can preserve the tradition of the hereditary transmission of original sin.

35. In another work, Maritain writes: "All of the dead hidden in my heredity weigh in me upon my destiny. Their dreams and their poisons which are fermenting within me are the hidden evil through which I am lost. For in every hereditary line there are particular disequilibria and disorders which, to the extent to which the determinism of matter is at play, inexorably push the unfortunate survivor toward the abyss." See *Moral Philosophy: An Historical and Critical Survey of the Great Systems* (New York: Charles Scribner's Sons, 1964), 356.

36. Anthony Zimmerman, *Evolution and the Sin in Eden: A New Christian Synthesis* (Lanham, Maryland: University Press of America, 1998).

37. C. S. Lewis in *The Problem of Pain* suggested that the Satanic corruption of the beasts contributed to the Satanic corruption of man because one result of man's Fall was that his ani-

which they separated from their parent population because of linguistic and social barriers, certain extra-natural capacities, perhaps including infused theological, intellectual, and moral virtues, together with a primordial revelation about his reality and plans for mankind. Presumably these gifts would have been given in order to supplement their natural intelligence in such a way as to correct and to compensate for the distorted aspects of their animal inheritance, to enable them to deal calmly with and to "politically govern"[38] drives and passions and emotions imperfectly integrated because of the contingencies of their evolutionary past. It was their rejection or neglect of this gift and calling that constituted human original sin *originans* in the sense of an action in history, symbolized by the deed of "eating from the tree of the knowledge of good and evil."

But original sin is not only an original act but also an inherited state of being (an originated state of sin), an inherited *disposition* to do unholy and inhumane things. It is concupiscence, a *consequence* of the original rejection or neglect, whereby the first parents lost the communion with God that enabled them to domesticate internally the unruly and disturbed psychological dispositions they had inherited from their (angelically disturbed) animal ancestors.[39] These dispositions are bound up with phylo-

mality fell back from the humanity into which it had been taken up. Without the aid of infused grace, man could no longer rule his animality. Gregory Boyd has suggested more recently that the pre-Adamic Eden did not encompass the whole earth, but was only a providentially protected enclave from which humanity's mission to re-take and remake God's fallen world would have begun had it not been for the human Fall.

38. See Zimmerman, *Evolution*, chapter 10. See Aristotle, *Politics* 1.2, and Aquinas's comment at ST I-II, q. 17, a. 7. Aristotle's view is a development of the analogy of the *psyche* to the *polis* in Plato's *Republic*. Aquinas says "reason 'governs' the irascible and concupiscible appetites not by a despotic supremacy which is that of a master over a slave, but by a politic and royal supremacy, whereby are governed the free, who are not wholly subject to command." This saying implies that the drives and the emotions, however distorted they may be, are not *morally* bad unless badly governed and wrongly expressed. Sexuality, bodily appetite in general, and aggression, when properly and rationally *governed*, disciplined, and *educated*, can serve the person and the group. As sources of energy that are not under automatic rational control, the drives and emotions function, in accordance with Socrates' image in the *Phaedrus*, as more or less unruly horses needed to drive the chariot man. Though the horses, especially the sexual horse, sometimes need stern discipline, they can serve no purpose at all if they are harmed or killed. (The imperfect integration of reason with the drives and emotions has been illustrated by a much-cited work of brain science. See Paul MacLean's *A Triune Concept of the Brain* [Toronto: University of Toronto Press, 1973].)

39. To achieve a fuller understanding of the meaning of concupiscence from an evolutionary standpoint would require engaging in a project that goes beyond the purview of this essay—the project of opening up explorations of the potential significance for moral theology of the new

genetically older structures inherited from the brutes, capacities for kinds of sexual, aggressive, and dominant behavior that become in man, insofar as he rejects grace, even worse for being allied to rational and increased imaginative powers.[40] Understood in this way, it is obvious why original sin is something that spread through the species not only by imitation but by propagation. Of course, it is not moral guilt that human children inherit genetically from their parents, but rather slavery to these disabling dispositions and deficiencies that follows upon the loss of virtuous communion with God.[41]

Moreover, if in the unfallen state man had the power to domesticate the unruly aspects of his psyche, it need not follow that Augustine's speculation is right that unfallen man was nearly an angel, having no potentially unruly dispositions at all. Nor need the doctrine of concupiscence mean that the natural endowments of intellect and will were utterly corrupted in fallen man; it need only imply that after the Fall humans henceforth needed divine aid in order to successfully carry out the project of correcting and

---

(putative) science of evolutionary psychology, with its interesting theories concerning innate human predispositions. For an interesting textbook introduction to this new field, see David M. Buss, *Evolutionary Psychology: The New Science of Mind* (Boston: Allyn and Bacon, 1999).

40. Saint Paul's notion of *sarx* is that of "an obscure but invincible complicity that the power of darkness finds in us, inherited in fact with our earthly nature and bound to the present state of it ... dominated by an external power ... introducing its enmity against God at the very sources of our action." See Louis Bouyer, "The Two Economies of Divine Government: Satan and Christ," in *God and His Creation*, edited by A. M. Henry (Notre Dame: Fides Press, 1955), 469–78. Bouyer argues that in Rabbinic Judaism the Torah or Law included the pattern of creation in the mind of God, including all the laws of human society *and* of nature. Both kinds of law, according to this tradition, were distorted under the influence of the fallen angels. The role of sinful angels in the economy of creation as "mediators" of the Torah turned out to involve the deception of man and the distortion of the cosmos. Thus Saint Paul represents God in Christ, paradoxically, as delivering man from God's own Law and God's own "wrath" (I Thes. 1:10; Gal. 3:13). See C. S. Lewis, *Miracles: A Preliminary Study* (London: MacMillan, 1947); and Brian Wicker, *The Story-Shaped World: Fiction and Metaphysics: Some Variations on a Theme* (Notre Dame, Indiana: University of Notre Dame Press, 1975), chapters 3–4.

41. On the meaning of the Immaculate Conception of Mary, her preservation from the first moment of her conception in immunity "from all taint of original sin ... by a singular privilege and grace of almighty God" (DS 2804), see Benedict Ashley, "Moral Theology and Mariology," in *The Ashley Reader* (Washington D.C.: Sapientia Press, 2006), 162. He discusses how the virginal conception not only marks and communicates to mankind a new beginning that will overcome any inherited elements from the biological and phylogenetic past that might otherwise disturb her perfect communion with God the Father, but also how and why her virginity was bound up with her vocation to be utterly dedicated to God alone in perfect faith, faith of the kind which, before it was lost, preserved the first parents from being overcome by concupiscence in their unfallen state.

compensating for the distorted aspects of the animal inheritance. Nor need we think that physical death, a destiny already necessitated by the entropic nature of the evolutionary cosmos in which the first humans were embodied, was primarily a retributive punishment for original sin in the sense of an original sinful act.[42] The punishment was (in part) that humans after the Fall *suffered*[43] their physical death with a fear conditioned by their having fallen out of faithful communion with God.[44]

If the foregoing considerations are helpful in making sense of the tradition that original sin spreads through the species not only by imitation but by propagation and genetic inheritance, it remains nevertheless true that concupiscence as a disposition to live in a non-virtuous and ungodly way is a deficiency that can be passed on to human offspring, and even enhanced and exacerbated in them, not only by one or another genetic route but by a distortion in the pattern of the *education* received from their parents, guardians, and teachers. Hence imitation, in some broad sense, is another channel through which original sin can be transmitted. The ripple effects of sinful acts and behaviors on the community as a whole, and especially on the basic community of the family, come to constitute the "sin of the

42. There are a number of senses in which it is true that "death is a punishment for sin." Yet all three terms in that formula—"death" and "punishment" and "sin"—need disambiguation. Does the formula refer to physical death or to spiritual death? Does it speak of punishment as deterrent or retributive or reformative or as some combination of these? Does it speak of sin as an act or as a disposition? For an illuminating discussion of the meaning of the formula, see Josef Pieper, *Death and Immortality* (South Bend, Indiana: Saint Augustine's Press, 2000), chapters 4–6. There are also a variety of senses in which Jesus' atoning death might be characterized as a taking upon himself of a punishment due to our sins. On various aspects of punishment and sanction, see Jacques Maritain, "The Notion of Sanction," chapter 9 of *An Introduction to the Basic Problems of Moral Philosophy* (New York: Magi Books, 1990). Two brilliant formulations and discussions of Aquinas' interpretation of the Atonement can be found in Eleonore Stump, *Aquinas* (London: Routledge, 2003), chapter 15; and in Richard Purtill, "Justice, Mercy, and Atonement," in *Reason to Believe: Why Faith Makes Sense* (San Francisco: Ignatius Press, 2009), 187–203. Purtill points out that Jesus, strictly speaking, was not *punished* for our sins, but only suffered for our sins.

43. See *The Catechism of the Catholic Church* (New York: Catholic Book Publishing Company, 1994), no. 1018.

44. Of course, God can use the fear of death for transformative purposes, as in Tolstoy's story "The Death of Ivan Ilyich." The prospect of death can function as a deterrent or reformative punishment, as much as death itself can function as a retributive one. No doubt God allowed the angelic Fall in the eternal knowledge that the death trends introduced into nature by angelic sin would put a brake on fallen man's tendencies toward self-deification. The old belief that the physical evils that afflict the Earth were connected *in some way* with the sin of the first parents had some truth in it.

world" into which each human child is born.[45] In order to shelter children from the "sin of the world," good parents ought routinely to "rebuild the wall around the Garden of Eden for their children" by forming them in virtue in a loving family life.

This type of family life, supported by the Church and the sacraments, is an important means—a more than merely biological means—whereby virtue and grace are transmitted to human persons, in cooperating with God in countering and, to some extent, overcoming the effects of the transmission of original sin. If the loving communion of family life is analogous to the loving communion with God that is the effect of the presence of sanctifying grace to a willing soul, we might suppose that just as true parental love is not to be a saccharine and false love that spoils the children, so too God's love is not a love that communes with members of the human family indiscriminately. As Zimmerman says, God does not give the pearl of grace to members of the human family who will not treasure and appreciate it, but restores his original gift only to persons who properly belong to the community of the faithful, inside or outside the institutional church, who ask for it, either personally or through their parents or guardians. Baptism in the broadest sense—by water in the Church's sacrament or by desire or martyrdom—is the humble request to God for the restoration of His loving communion. In the original Eden this communion would flow to each new person through the loving education he received from graced parents or guardians. So long as all humans were communally committed to holiness and justice, God could lovingly provide the gift of his loving grace to each new member of the species at the moment of conception. But in our world, instead of casting pearls before swine, God waits for parents to come forward voluntarily to request with faith the gift of grace for themselves and their children. He has provided the Church and sacraments to aid them in making and sustaining this request.

45. See Ashley, *Theologies of the Body: Humanist and Christian*, 351, where Ashley says modern theology conceives original sin "not merely as a single act at the beginning of human history but also as the accumulation of evils produced by sins committed throughout the ages in complicity with the first sin of the human community, which has distorted our cultural world, our earthly environment, and even our individual persons from the moment of our conception as bodies living spiritually in a state of alienation." On pages 372–85, 415–23, and 613 Ashley offers biological speculations on the origin of man combined with profound interpretations of the *Genesis* accounts of the origin of man and of original sin both as a transgression and as a state of being.

IV

LOVE, MARRIAGE, AND SEXUALITY

MICHAEL PAKALUK

The Meaning of Sex Differences and Marriage in Maritain

I. Introduction

In discussing sex differences and the meaning of marriage here, I take myself to be addressing a restricted community: namely, those who hold that masculinity and femininity exist and are really different; that they have the character of a gift or talent, and that therefore, like other talents, we should respond by developing and accentuating them, not suppressing or attempting to eradicate them; that these traits belong to a kind of natural endowment which represents the intention of a Creator God and therefore have a teleological purpose, and indeed an ultimate purpose; also, that we are not reasonably free to reject these traits—or, rather, that to do so is like rejecting a fundamental principle of natural law, carrying with it all the same illogic and disastrous unintended consequences. St. Thomas says that the Ten Commandments represent God's fundamental intention for the human family, and therefore that no commandment admits of being dispensed with, in special circumstances or in cases of necessity, through considerations of *epieikeia*,[1] and the same holds, I think, of male and female. Or at least I shall so suppose, and I take myself to be addressing those who think similarly or are at least prepared to entertain these things. It is obvious that this community is not that of the broader society in which we live, or of the elite cultures. Each day gives new proof, such as a recent

1. "If therefore there be any precepts which contain the very preservation of the common good, or the very order of justice and virtue, such precepts contain the intention of the lawgiver, and therefore are indispensable," etc. ST I, q. 100, a. 8, resp.; and see ad 1, 2.

headline that officials in a public schools district do not quite know how to deal with high school guys who are wearing dresses to school and arguing that there is no reason why they should not be allowed to dress up like girls, if they want, since girls can wear outfits traditionally worn by guys.[2]

Once we make this point about the two communities, the familiar question arises: What should be the task of a Catholic philosopher—to speak to the narrower community on its presuppositions and attempt to develop a view on rich metaphysical principles which will not be widely believable, or to attempt to say something to win the conviction of the broader community on attenuated principles which might be widely endorsed? Catholic intellectuals have generally taken the second approach. Not wanting to appear to be "sexist"—that is, to be the sort of person who posits false distinctions between the sexes in order, it would be suspected, to advance his own interests or the interests of his group—and not wanting to say anything that might seem to imply or endorse any kind of inequality between male and female, in the external forum we make schematic assertions such as "male and female are equal but complementary," and in the internal forum we are content to see a view of sex differences arising implicitly, although without definite commitment and precise articulation, in spiritual writings, such as John Paul II's reflections on the different roles of Mary and Joseph.[3]

II. Procreation and Sex Differences in Classical Philosophy

As for philosophy, the classical inheritance on these matters constituted a coherent and deeply interesting view. It has generally been rejected, and Maritain rejects it too, for both ethical and scientific reasons; yet we have nothing suitable to replace it with, and certainly Maritain's alternative is not preferable. So let me state that view, consider Maritain's objections to it, and then say something about why Maritain's view should be rejected.

In considering the classical view—deriving from Aristotle, and adapted and changed in an important respect by St. Thomas—it is useful as a preliminary to distinguish three questions. The first is the question of *sex de-*

2. See for example, "Teen boys don dresses to protest school dress code," *Miami Herald*, February 2, 2016.

3. See John Paul II, *Mulieris dignitatem* (1988); and *Redemptoris custos* (1989).

termination: What makes it so, that a developing human being becomes a male rather than a female—what is the causal mechanism? The second is the question of *sex difference*, that is, in what does the distinction between male and female consist, and what is its meaning? And the third is the question of *procreation*, that is, what is the connection between sex difference and procreation? The failure to distinguish these questions can easily lead to misunderstanding. For example, the notorious claim on the classical view, that a female is, as it were, a *mas occasionatus*, a misfired male, is in the first instance a claim about sex determination—how an embryo turns out to be female; whether it implies also a view of sex difference is a different matter, as we shall see.

To understand the classical view, one must begin with procreation, because male and female are understood as being causes of procreation—to be a male, on this view, is to be a certain kind of cause, and to be a female is to be a complementary cause, of procreation. The procreation of a new human being is a type of causation—it is genuine causation and, indeed, a paradigm of causation—which is distinct from making: The parents cause the existence of the child but not through any kind of process or action that can be described as a making. It is because they cause the child that they are responsible for the child. On this view, to look about the human race and to notice two types, male and female, is to see separate, isolated, and clearly identifiable types of causes of new human beings. The cause must be the father and the mother, not something mother and father supply, otherwise procreation risks turning into making. Suppose the father supplied the oxygen and the mother hydrogen, they would be making water, not procreating water. There are obviously many difficulties to raise about this approach, but that is the basic outlook and rationale.

As for the meaning of procreation—or, why living things procreate in a continuous process—St. Thomas follows Aristotle in holding that it is something noble and divine. One might recall the famous passage in *De Anima*, 2.4 (415a26–b7), where Aristotle says that every existing thing aims to imitate God, the ultimate good, in the way in which it is able. Mortal beings, he says, as they are mortal, cannot, of course, imitate God's eternity individually. However, suppose mortal beings could cause something like to themselves to come into existence; in that case they could achieve in a certain manner, generically, what none could achieve on its own individually. So that is precisely the reason, he thinks, why some things reproduce:

in order to imitate God's eternity better than things that cannot reproduce. On this view, procreation becomes a divine common good: divine, because it takes place in order to imitate God and achieve eternity, in a way; and a common good, because it shows the characteristics of a common good—that is, individuals can claim what the community achieves and yet the price they typically have to pay is some sacrifice of their own advantage.

Obviously on a Christian conception involving the coming into existence of eternal souls with the vocation to life with God in heaven, procreation becomes even more divine. But if procreation is understood in no more than in this Aristotelian way, as an individual's participation in a divine common good, it already has significant, admirable ethical implications, which are clearly on display, for example, in book III of the *Oeconomica* attributed to Aristotle. Consider a couple of the norms found there. A good wife, he writes, should be as devoted to her husband when he fails at his efforts as when he is a success, because "he has indeed bought her with a great price—with partnership in his life and in the procreation of children; than which things naught could be greater or more divine."[4] Note that the passage draws explicit attention to the sacrifices it is expected the husband has already made to his personal advantage in order to have children with the wife. "To find partners in prosperity is easy enough," the Aristotelian author adds, "but only the best women are ready to share in adversity." The husband receives similar advice on a similar basis: "The rules which a good husband will follow in treatment of his wife will be similar, seeing that she has entered his home like a suppliant from without, and is pledged to be the partner of his life and parenthood; and that the offspring she leaves behind her will bear the names of their parents, her name as well as his. And what could be more divine than this, or more desired by a man of sound mind, than to beget by a noble and honored wife children who shall be the most loyal supporters and discreet guardians of their parents in old age, and the preservers of the whole house?"[5]

Now I think the morals of our society hardly ever rise to the level of

4. "Magno enim precio [45] empta fuit, societate namque vite et protectione liberorum, quibus nil maius nec sanctius fieret." (The text survives only in a Latin translation).

5. Vir autem leges a similibus adinveniat uxoris in usu, quoniam tamquam socia filiorum et vite ad domum viri devenit, relinquens filios genitorum viri et sui nomina habituros.quibus quid sanctius fieret aut circa que magis vir [70] sane mentis studebit, quam ex optima et preciosissima muliere liberos procreare, senectutis pastores quasi optimos et pudicos patris ac matris custodes ac tocius domus conservatores.

the gentle nobility and sweet affection of the sentiments conveyed in these and like passages of this pagan author. But what I next want to draw to your attention, in connection with the meaning of procreation, is how in this passage it is taken for granted that "the procreation of children" covers the entire process, from the generation of the mere life of the offspring, all the way through to the education to maturity of an adult man or woman. Procreation in a human being is regarded not as a five minute thing, or a nine month process, but rather as an action extending twenty or more years. St. Thomas says this explicitly in multiple passages—in a human being, he says, because of the need for the body to develop, and the soul to be educated in the virtues and with knowledge, procreation, properly speaking (not metaphorically, but strictly) involves first begetting, then nurturing and sustaining the child begotten, and finally educating the child who is nourished. Of these three—existence, nurture, and education—the last is the most important, because it is the ultimate goal.[6]

So these things must be understood in connection with anything said in the classical tradition about procreation. Therefore, if we read somewhere that woman was created as a helper of man for the purposes of procreation, such a claim must be understood, not, basely, as referring to the sex act, but rather as meaning that, for that action extended over twenty plus years, which includes nurture and education, the wife is an indispensable helper—or, better, that the task cannot suitably be done alone but is managed well only by the two together.

In a similar vein, the notion of the division of household tasks cannot be understood independently of the tasks of nurture and of education. The assertion in the classical tradition that a wife is a helpmate for daily household tasks includes, to be sure, the idea that even without children household life goes easier and well if, besides a servant (whom one orders around and

6. See for example as a reliable expression of St. Thomas's thought ST Suppl. q. 49, a. 2, "Objection 1: It would seem that the goods of marriage are insufficiently enumerated by the Master (Sent. iv, D, 31), namely 'faith, offspring, and sacrament.' For the object of marriage among men is not only the begetting and feeding of children, but also the partnership of a common life, whereby each one contributes his share of work to the common stock, as stated in Ethic. viii, 12. Therefore as the offspring is reckoned a good of matrimony, so also should the communication of works. ... Reply to Objection 1: Offspring signifies not only the begetting of children, but also their education, to which as its end is directed the entire communion of works that exists between man and wife as united in marriage, since parents naturally 'lay up' for their 'children' (2 Cor. 12:14); so that the offspring like a principal end includes another, as it were, secondary end."

treats as an instrument), a husband has a companion and partner to share tasks in a suitable and complementary way; however, in a typical household, where the couple has children, it is understood that most of these tasks will be carried out in such a way, too, as to educate the children in skills and virtues—that such tasks provide sustenance is obvious.

This mention of the servant or slave makes it appropriate to point out that Aristotle in several places—and he is followed by St. Thomas—rather sharply upbraids a man for misguidedly treating a wife (and sons too) as a servant (see *Pol.* 1.1, 1252a34–b9, 1.12, 1259a37–b10). That is how the illiberal peoples such as the Persians act, Aristotle says (*Nic. Eth.* 8.10, 1160b27). Now note that the idea that husband stands to wife as active to passive principles in causation, or as form to matter,[7] is of a piece with this outlook. Matter and form never operate together in such a way that the form appears as violent, or even in such a way that it is noticed as something distinct.[8] Similarly, that the soul is the form of the body implies precisely that it does *not* manipulate the body from without, as on a crude dualist picture, in the manner of an instrument or tool. That is why Aristotle is prone to compare the relationship of husband and wife to different, collaborating, authorities in an aristocratic form of government (*Nic. Eth.* 8.11, 1161a22–25)—and indeed he regards the marital relationship as the "source and spring" of collaborative political action in society in general, where one finds and wants to realize authorities with distinct competencies, each not fully contained in the authority of the other (*Eud. Eth.* 1242b1; *Pol.* 2.2–6).

So all of the following, on the classical view, are bound up with the idea that the woman is a helpmate to the man for purposes of procreation: being a noble and esteemed partner in a divine activity, making like sacrifices for a common good, collaborating in providing sustenance for the couple and for offspring, supplying a necessary element for education in virtue and knowledge, and practicing and setting an example of a difficult virtue which is crucial to republican forms of government: namely, compromise and cooperation with other authorities who have distinct competencies.

7. For example, "In omnibus enim viventibus perfectis in quibus est sexus distinctio, femina se habet ut patiens et materiam ministrans, et mas se habet ut agens et formam inducens, ut in 15 de animalibus dicitur," *Super Sent.*, lib. 2 d. 20 q. 1 a. 2 co. (*De Animalibus* was a compilation of Aristotelian biological treatises).

8. "It is not necessary to ask whether soul and body are one, just as it is not necessary to ask whether the wax and its shape are one, nor generally whether the matter of each thing and that of which it is the matter are one," *De Anima* 2.1, 412b6–8.

III. Maritain versus St. Thomas on Procreation

Given Aristotle's noble view of marriage, it is highly inaccurate to summarize the classical view, as Maritain does in *Untrammeled Approaches*, as "woman is ordained to breed," as if procreation were breeding.[9] Yet that remark, flawed as it is, is based additionally on an outright misreading of St. Thomas, when Maritain draws an invidious comparison which is not found in the text. The text in question is St. Thomas's discussion of why, in the creation account, the creation of woman is specially mentioned, and not just the creation of human beings, humanity, or "man" in the inclusive or unmarked sense, which would refer of course to every variety of human being, such as the old, the infirm, or children. St. Thomas says something highly interesting here, which represents, I believe, his significant improvement on the Aristotelian view:

> Some living things do not possess in themselves the power of generation, but are generated by some other specific agent, such as some plants and animals by the influence of the heavenly bodies, from some fitting matter and not from seed: others possess the active and passive generative power together; as we see in plants which are generated from seed; for the noblest vital function in plants is generation. Wherefore we observe that in these the active power of generation invariably accompanies the passive power. Among perfect animals the active power of generation belongs to the male sex, and the passive power to the female. And as among animals there is a vital operation nobler than generation, to which their life is principally directed; therefore the male sex is not found in continual union with the female in perfect animals, but only at the time of coition; so that we may consider that by this means the male and female are one, as in plants they are always united; although in some cases one of them preponderates, and in some the other. But man is yet further ordered to a still nobler vital action, and that is intellectual operation.[10]

9. Jacques Maritain, *Untrammeled Approaches*, edited by Bernard Doering (Notre Dame, Indiana: University of Notre Dame Press, 1997), 154.

10. ST I q. 92, a. 1, resp.: Sunt enim quaedam viventia, quae in seipsis non habent virtutem activam generationis, sed ab agente alterius speciei generantur; sicut plantae et animalia quae generantur sine semine ex materia convenienti per virtutem activam caelestium corporum. Quaedam vero habent virtutem generationis activam et passivam coniunctam; sicut accidit in plantis quae generantur ex semine. Non enim est in plantis aliquod nobilius opus vitae quam generatio, unde convenienter omni tempore in eis virtuti passivae coniungitur virtus activa generationis. Animalibus vero perfectis competit virtus activa generationis secundum sexum masculinum, virtus vero passiva secundum sexum femininum. Et quia est aliquod opus vitae nobilius in animalibus quam generatio, ad quod eorum vita principaliter ordinatur; ideo non omni tempore sexus masculinus feminino coniungitur in animalibus perfectis, sed solum tem-

Now notice that he is presenting a scale of greater perfection among creatures: those that do not reproduce, those whose highest activity is to reproduce (plants), those which have a higher activity than reproduction (animals, who have the power of sensation), and those which have an even higher activity than sensation and reproduction (human beings). This is of course the hierarchy of types of soul that Aristotle gives in *De Anima* II.2–3. The remark that "man is yet further ordered to a still nobler vital action" must therefore refer to human beings, rational animals—and, not surprisingly, we find in the Latin that St. Thomas uses *homo* at this point: *Homo autem adhuc ordinatur ad nobilius opus vitae, quod est intelligere.* He dispenses with referring to *mas* and *femina* and uses *homo*. But Maritain misses that and takes him to be referring to males, in contrast with females: "It follows from this," Maritain says, "that in truth man alone corresponds perfectly to the definition of human nature … for he is ordained *ad nobilius opus vitae, quod est intelligere,* whereas woman is ordained to breed."[11] Thus, as I said, Maritain not only presupposes a debased understanding of procreation in man, but also introduces an invidious comparison which is not in the text.

His false step here causes him to overlook St. Thomas's innovation. It is St. Thomas's idea, and not Aristotle's, that as one moves up the hierarchy of perfection in souls, the reproductive powers become separated as a result of the introduction of a task which is higher, *nobilius*. Now St. Thomas simply states that it is so in order to establish that the separate creation of male and female in man is meant to be a sign of the higher calling of man to contemplate. Yet this idea is extremely suggestive and is open to greater development. I shall mention three implications.

The first is the obvious point that for St. Thomas the meaning of male and female is found also in the separation of the two sexes and not simply in the possibility of their combination. On the Aristotelian picture, it looks

---

pore coitus; ut imaginemur per coitum sic fieri unum ex mare et femina, sicut in planta omni tempore coniunguntur vis masculina et feminina, etsi in quibusdam plus abundet una harum, in quibusdam plus altera. Homo autem adhuc ordinatur ad nobilius opus vitae, quod est intelligere. Et ideo adhuc in homine debuit esse maiori ratione distinctio utriusque virtutis, ut seorsum produceretur femina a mare, et tamen carnaliter coniungerentur in unum ad generationis opus. Et ideo statim post formationem mulieris, dicitur Gen. II, erunt duo in carne una.

11. In the original, "Il suit de là qu'à vrai dire seul l'homme répond parfaitment à la definition de la nature humaine (dont la difference spécifique est d'être doué d'intelligence et de raison), car il est ordonné « ad nobilius opus vitae, quod est intelligere » (même article), tandis que la femme est ordonnée à engendrer," *Approches sans Entraves*, (Paris: Fayard, 1973), 189.

as though what male and female principally testify to is what male and female accomplish when combined—not unlike, say, if one saw a puddle of gasoline in one corner of the room, and a match in the other, one might be drawn to consider what would happen if the match were lit. That is, male and female serve, as it were, as natural signs of the divine common good of procreation. But for St. Thomas the *separation* of these powers, and not solely the possible combination of the sexual powers, has signification as well—as though someone might place a gun in one cabinet under lock and key, and the ammunition in another, to signify and express that he regards himself as living primarily in a peaceable society.

A second thought is that, surely, in human beings the sexual powers need to be separated additionally, beyond their being located in different types of human beings, as *that* sort of separation is already found in non-rational animals, and so it would do no more than signify the greater nobility of sensation over reproduction. But we possess an even more noble activity, which needs to be appropriately marked, by its own kind of separation. This additional separation, we might speculate, as it marks something distinctively human, would appropriately be accomplished through the use of the distinctively human powers of reason and will, operating too in a social manner throughout a society and manifested in cultural norms rather than through the brute distribution of the different powers in different biological organisms. But what would be that rational and freely willed ordering, found in a society, which would keep the sexual powers properly separate but also indicate their reasonable combination when appropriate? Well, this is just a description of marriage and practices of marriage. On this view, marriage regarded as a "natural institution" becomes the societal means whereby the separation and combination of the sexual powers in man are rationally governed in such a way as to testify to the higher vocation of man to the use of his reason. That marriage, as we have seen, is also that institution through which offspring are educated up to the point of attaining the virtues, even the intellectual virtues, confirms this point. Of course, on a Christian conception the existence of persons committed or consecrated to the single life provides an additional signification complementary to that of marriage.[12]

12. Note that Pope St. John Paul II never ceased to emphasize that the celibate and married vocations each testified to and supported the other, for example, "In the light of Christ's words, and also in the light of the whole authentic Christian Tradition, it is possible to deduce that this

A third reflection is this. It is a commonplace in St. Thomas that there are two uses of reason, namely, that consisting in the application of reason to action, which he calls the "active life," and that consisting in its application to the consideration of truth, which he calls of course the "contemplative life."[13] I take it that when St. Thomas says, in that article we just considered from the *Summa*, that man is ordained to understand, *intelligere*, he means, more precisely, that there is an ordering here: man is ordained, primarily and preferably, simply to understand—that is, to contemplate—but he is also ordained, in a secondary and less preferable sense, to use his understanding in action. As I said, this is common Thomistic doctrine, and it makes sense to understand it as implicit in the passage, because man is set apart from the non-rational animals through both uses of his reason. It follows that the sexes, in their rational separation and possibility of combination, would testify, too, to this twofold difference in man's vocation to reason. But if so, then to which would male testify, as it were by attribution, and which female?

It is clear that on this view the female sexual power in separation from the male corresponds most fittingly to the use of reason in its primary form, contemplation. The female, the woman, does so because the efforts of the male, the man, are, on this view, directed outside the home primarily, to support the home and to realize suitable conditions within it, so that his work looks like it is for the sake of the woman's work within. (As if to testify to this, consider that in English the term "matrimony" comes from the Latin word for "mother" and means "motherhood," *mater-munus*: thus, to get married is to agree to free up, from the world of work and business, a space in which motherhood can be practiced.) Again, as on the classical view, the female sexual power is the receptive power, then, as contemplation is receptivity to form, the contemplative life corresponds best to the female. Thus, for instance, in the homilies on Ezekiel by St. Gregory the Great, which St. Thomas likes to cite as a guide to the contemplative life and its distinc-

---

renunciation is at the same time a particular form of affirming that value from which the unmarried person consistently abstains, following the evangelical counsel. This can seem paradoxical. Nevertheless, it is known that many statements in the Gospel are paradoxical, and those are often the most eloquent and profound. Accepting such a meaning of the call to continence for the sake of the kingdom of heaven, we draw a correct conclusion, holding that the realization of this call serves also—and in a particular way—to confirm the nuptial meaning of the human body in its masculinity and femininity," John Paul II, "Celibacy for the Kingdom Affirms Marriage," General Audience of May 5, 1982.

13. See ST II-II, q. 179.

tion from the active, St. Gregory refers to a human being as at work ordering the world as "he," but he refers to a human being, as turning to God to contemplate, as a "she," since the soul is a "she": When the soul turns to God, to allow itself to be ordered by God, in the way in which the soul had formerly been ordering the world, then, in its receptivity, it is referred to as "she."[14]

But as I said, Maritain misses this important innovation of St. Thomas and its implications, because of his low view of human procreation as mere breeding and his misreading of the passage.

IV. Maritain versus Aristotle and St. Thomas on Sex Determination

Maritain is also to be faulted for his handling of the rather infamous claim in Aristotle, accepted by St. Thomas, that a female embryo originates through a kind of misfiring of a process which would produce a male—that is, that a female is *quasi mas occasionatus*.[15] Observe first of all that the phrase is offered as a metaphor, "as if" or "as it were" (Greek *hōsper*), not a scientific statement. Secondly, as mentioned above, it concerns the mechanism by which the sex of an embryo is determined to be female. It would be irresponsible, then, to pull the phrase out of this context and apply it straightforwardly to a mature woman, but Maritain does this and in various passages says that, according to Aristotle and St. Thomas, "woman is a man that nature accidentally botched up."[16]

14. "Then the first step is to compose oneself, the second to see the like of this composure, the third to rise above oneself and by intention to submit to the contemplation of the invisible Creator. But one by no means composes himself unless he has first learned to curb the apparition of earthly and heavenly images from his mind's eye and cast out and tread down whatever of sight, hearing, smell, touch and taste occurs to his bodily thought, in order that he may inwardly seek such as is free thereof. For when he ponders these things he turns, as it were, some bodily shadows inwards. Then all things are to be driven away by the hand of discernment from the mind's eye so that the soul may regard herself as she was created, above the body but below God, so that being quickened by her superior she may quicken the inferior which she administers. . . . When therefore the soul thinks of herself without bodily images she has already entered the first door. But this door leads on to the other in order that something from the nature of Almighty God may be contemplated. So the soul in the body is the life of the flesh, but God Who quickens all is the life of souls," and so on. St. Gregory the Great, *Homilies on the Book of the Prophet Ezekiel*, book two, fifth homily, section 9, translated by Theodosia Tomkinson (Etna, California: Center for Traditionalist Orthodox Studies, 2008).

15. The phrase is from Michael Scot's Latin-Arabic translation of Aristotle, *De Animalibus* (made in Toledo, Spain, c. 1220), corresponding to τὸ γὰρ θῆλυ ὥσπερ ἄρρεν ἐστὶ πεπηρωμένον, *De Generatione Animalium*, 2.3, 737a27–28.

16. *Untrammeled Approaches*, 154.

Consider the phenomenon which Aristotle wanted to explain. There are two discrete types, male and female, and any offspring's being one or the other seems a random and independent event. At the same time, there seem to be causal factors which can tilt the odds in one direction or the other (Aristotle and St. Thomas both cite a popular view that the direction of the wind could do this); moreover, it seemed to Aristotle that female children typically resembled the mother more than the father. We saw that he wants to say that there are two sexual powers, which correlate to each other as active to passive. His theory of sex determination is an elegant attempt to account for all these things. The male seed carries the active power of the man, and its corporeal vehicle and manifestation is a high degree of heat in the male seed; the female seed carries the passive power, and its vehicle and manifestation is a low degree of heat. (Understand the active power as just the power of initiating a new human organism and the passive power as just the power of receiving the initiation of a new human organism. In saying that the one is active, the other passive, one is by no means assuming that either is something simple; rather, each would have the complexity of a human organism, but the male somehow has this complexity in an active way while the female in a receptive way). The male seed acts in the female seed, with the goal or "intention" of initiating, not simply a new human organism, but rather a new male organism, that is, one which would in turn have the power of initiating a new human organism. The male seed must properly be described as aiming to do this, because of the general principles of Aristotelian physics: first, that every active agent acts to assimilate the recipient to itself, and second, that the proper specification of a power must refer to the maximal effect that the power is able to accomplish (if a strong man can lift 500 pounds, it is inaccurate to describe his strength as "the power to lift 300 pounds"). So simply in the description of the action of the male seed, to say that it is doing anything less than aiming to produce a human organism with active power would be mistaken. Anything else which results from its action as its effect would be, so to speak, incidental to *its* goal as properly described.

Now, on this theory, if the male seed is not hot enough, or the female seed is too cold or in some way less accepting of heat, then the male seed does not succeed in its purpose, and a living human organism results, but not one with active generative power. Aristotle describes the conversion of the effect from passive to active as all or nothing: The male seed has to act upon the female seed with a certain degree of vigor and heat, otherwise the conversion is not effected, and there is a kind of lapsing of the effect into the alternative state, of possessing passive power only.

Now that there are only two possible states of the effect—male or active, and female or passive—shows that the difference between male and female is not itself a matter of chance, and is not one of degree. A female is not a deficient male, because deficiencies show great variety in kind and degree (consider all the ways an arrow could miss its mark). Again, that the female results almost exactly half the time, even though the mechanism has a random element, shows that the mechanism itself is not random, and that, if one considers "nature" overall, then females are intended just as much as males, and they are good in their kind, not "botched." Aquinas says as much in the article Maritain refers to. Here is the Latin first:

> Ad primum ergo dicendum quod per respectum ad naturam particularem, femina est aliquid deficiens et occasionatum. Quia virtus activa quae est in semine maris, intendit producere sibi simile perfectum, secundum masculinum sexum, sed quod femina generetur, hoc est propter virtutis activae debilitatem, vel propter aliquam materiae indispositionem, vel etiam propter aliquam transmutationem ab extrinseco, puta a ventis Australibus, qui sunt humidi, ut dicitur in libro de Generat. Animal. Sed per comparationem ad naturam universalem, femina non est aliquid occasionatum, sed est de intentione naturae ad opus generationis ordinata.[17]

This gets wrongly rendered in the standard translation:

> As regards the individual nature, woman is defective and misbegotten, for the active force in the male seed tends to the production of a perfect likeness in the masculine sex; while the production of woman comes from defect in the active force or from some material indisposition, or even from some external influence; such as that of a south wind, which is moist, as the Philosopher observes (*De Gener. Animal.* iv, 2). On the other hand, as regards human nature in general, woman is not misbegotten, but is included in nature's intention as directed to the work of generation.

The mistake is in the representation of the contrast between *natura particularis* and *natura generalis*. Aquinas intends the former phrase to refer to the nature of the male seed, not the nature of the woman, as the translation has it. He intends the second phrase to refer to all of nature regarded as a teleological system, not human nature. His point is that, as I said, an

17. ST I, q. 92, a. 1, ad 1.

embryo which turns out female represents a falling short in what the male seed should properly be said to be aiming to accomplish, but the system, containing a random element by which half of human offspring turn out to be female, is definitely not random and in no way fails in what it aims to accomplish. Curiously, in *Untrammeled Approaches,* Maritain glosses this distinction correctly, but then he persists in referring derisively to Aquinas's view that "a woman is a botched up man."

I am struck by Maritain's anomalous treatment of the Thomistic view of sex differences. Typically he gives St. Thomas the benefit of the doubt and finds the Thomistic text a fruitful source of philosophical intuitions. In *Untrammeled Approaches* he goes so far as to defend, for example, the Aristotelian theory of stages of embryonic development,[18] and he minutely investigates the presumed properties of the resurrected body, even speculating about the nature and quality of the fluid which fills its non-functional intestines.[19] However, when it comes to the philosophical treatment of sex differences, he sharply dismisses the Thomistic view, and proposes his own theory, independent of Thomistic texts.

V. Problems with Maritain's View of Sex Differences

It is not that Maritain has a superior view of sex difference. He agrees that male and female are complementary, but he does not say what they are complementary for. "What has to be said," he writes, "is that man and woman are equal in human value and dignity, but that they share differently in the qualities of that nature, in such a way that what one has in greater measure compensates for what the other has in lesser measure, and that the *human being* finds its complete expression only in *man and woman taken together.*"[20] But this is confused. Does a male lack features which a woman has, and vice versa? Then no one person has human nature; it is something shared between beings. But then Christ would not be *perfectus homo,* because his nature would need to be joined with that of a woman to be completed. Yet if male and female differed only in the degree of qualities, why should it be that males are always lesser than females in the same qualities,

18. Maritain, *Untrammeled Approaches,* 91–118.

19. Ibid., 404: "The intestines will be there too, as will all the other organs. Since they will have nothing more to do in the way of digestion, they will be filled, certainly not with foul superfluities, but with the most noble of fluids," he says, citing St. Thomas, ST q. 80, a. 1, ad 2.

20. Maritain, *Untrammeled Approaches,* 155; emphasis in original.

and vice versa? This is unexplained. Or how could we know that no male with particularly strong qualities all round did not have even to a greater degree than any female those qualities which most males had to a lesser degree than females, and vice versa? Maritain's assertion looks totally unsupported. And needless to say, the presence of different degrees of qualities hardly establishes complementarity. Again, on Maritain's view, it would be theoretically possible to combine male and female qualities into a single super-human being, with all the qualities to a high degree, but that is obviously absurd.

Maritain gives two different analogies for the difference between male and female. Sometimes he says it is like the differences among the races.[21] But this view is useless, it seems to me, as it arises, I believe, from a discredited type of ethnography that was popular in the 1920s and 1930s. In other places he says that male and female differ as do right and left hands.[22] This is a relationship known in science as "chirality," after the Greek work for "hand." The right and the left hand are symmetric and mirror images, yet they are not the same, since no transposition of the right hand in space can make it overlap with the left hand.[23] But there are all kinds of problems in this comparison. Note first of all that pairs of chirals, as chirals, are not complementary: The thumb on one hand indeed complements the other fingers on that hand, and it is the presence of the opposing thumb which makes the hand chiral, but the left and right hands taken as a pair do not complement each other through being chiral, as hands without thumbs can equally be folded or matched to each other. In nature, right- and left-handed molecules, in fact, usually interfere with each other, and scientists will have procedures to remove one type, to leave a pure substance. Again, if the right and left hands really were apt analogues of male and female, then, because of the presence of hands and sexes in daily life, one would

21. Ibid, 158. See also 100: "We must affirm, on the one hand, not only the essential equality of all human beings as such ... but also the human complementarity of the great racial families in the variety of qualities which distinguish them, each one having more than the others in certain respects, and less than the others in other respects. I might add that once this racial psycho-somatic differentiation of the human being has been established, it is in the intellectual and cultural order that its development has continued and will continue."

22. Ibid, 159: "Let us say, if you like, borrowing a metaphor from the chemists who tell us of dextrogyre or levogyre tartaric acid, that from its creation the soul of a man is dextroversly individualized and that the soul of a woman is levoversly individualized."

23. One might quip that Maritain with this theory gives a new twist to the idea of sexual orientation.

find the corresponding comparisons throughout our language, and yet we find nothing of the sort. The left hand stands in for things which are wrong or disturbing ("sinister"), not feminine (or masculine). A left-handed complement is not a feminine (or masculine) complement; a right-hand man is not a masculine (or feminine) man.

As for procreation, Maritain anticipates Richard Dawkins and holds that procreation is the species' way of instrumentalizing the individual for the continuation of the species.[24] He takes a reductive view of romanticism and says that its "essential aim" is "sexual attraction and satisfaction." Our imaginations dress up this sexual impulse and give it an intoxicatingly false appearance. Thus the task of marital love for Maritain is "to transmute romantic love, or what existed of it at the beginning, into real and indestructible human love, and really disinterested love, which does not exclude sex, of course, but which grows more and more independent of sex, and even can be, in its highest forms, completely free from sexual desire and intercourse, because it is essentially spiritual in nature—a complete and irrevocable gift of the one to the other, for the sake of the other."[25]

These views seem to me disastrously wrong on every front. Marriage in its ordinary human manifestation—I exclude very special cases such as the betrothal of the Mother of God to St. Joseph—does not find its highest expression (he does not say a *possible* expression, or a *sometimes praiseworthy* expression) in a condition "completely free from sexual desire and sexual intercourse." Romantic love is not, for persons raised in innocence, correctly described as a desire for sexual satisfaction; rather, it is modest and actually shrinks from physical contact—it strikes us rather as a delight

24. Dawkins has said notoriously that "a chicken is DNA's way of making more DNA." Maritain in this connection refers to the influence of his teacher in biology, Alfred Giard (after whom Giardia is named): "If Giard's ideas retain a certain importance for me, it is above all because they call attention to the fact that the gonads in each living being are ordained not to serve and perfect the individual life of that particular living being, but to work out in it those elements which will bring another living being into existence." Maritain rather creepily adds (and the contrast with the Thomistic theory is striking): "I mentioned above apropos of the spermatozoon and the ovule, which by their union bring into existence another living being. It could be said that in such species, particularly in the human species, the male organism—the soma of the man—and the female organism—the soma of the woman—are, each in its particular case parasitically preyed upon by its eventual future child as by a stranger, but from its own flesh, which is being prepared in the new being. It seems to me that these are psychological elements which have far-reaching importance." Maritain, *Untrammeled Approaches*, 100n13.

25. Ibid., 184. See also *Reflections on America* (Garden City, New York: Doubleday, Image Books, 1958), 80ff.

in the existence and possible gift of the other. That lovers, for example, see the beauty of the world with particular intensity, and think this beauty belongs especially to them, is not a trick played by the imagination but a true insight that we would do well to preserve. And romantic love in a healthy marriage does not "transmute" in the sense of being replaced but continues through, since so much of daily life in a happily married couple will continue to have the character of courtship and mutual gift.

What was it that caused Maritain to go so wrong on these topics? Was it a kind of Manicheism which I have argued is discernible in his distinction between persons and individuals?[26] Or was it a deficiency in philosophical method, which emphasizes the intuition of abstract objects, and which therefore can be led away from an attention to what Aristotle called *phainomena* and *endoxa*, as generating the pertinent *aporiai*? Did he fall prey to the common error of wanting to affirm the equality of the sexes so strongly that he said very weak things about their differences? Was he simply befuddled about sex, as can happen so easily to us, on account of original sin, as his views on contraception in his correspondence with Bishop Journet might seem to indicate? One draws back from the hypothesis that he was inappropriately generalizing from his own unusual relationship with Raïssa—*We Have Been* Friends *Together* is the title, not "lovers" or "one flesh." Whatever the explanation, we can regret that Maritain did not carry out in this case what he does so adeptly in so many other cases and give us a rich harvest of insights into the Thomistic view of sex differences.

26. See my "The Light of the Truth of the Gospels for the Common Good," in *Proceedings of the XIII Plenary Session*, Pontifical Academy of St. Thomas (Vatican City: Libreria Editrice Vaticana, 2013).

MATTHEW MINERD

Maritain and the Metaphysics of Sexual Differentiation

I. Introduction

With the numerous controversies today regarding gender identity, women's rights, and the repudiation of societal structures merely by the mention of "patriarchy," the Church has an interest in being engaged in vexed questions pertaining to the nature of man and woman. Encouraged by the testimony of the first two chapters of Genesis, she unflinchingly can proclaim that the human person, in his or her very structure as male and female, is created in the image and likeness of God. Of course, the articulation of this point has had its vicissitudes in the history of Christianity.[1] The papacy of John Paul II has encouraged a thorough evaluation of the language concerning the relation of the sexes, stressing their complementary nature.[2] Likewise, in his writings on marriage, Dietrich von Hildebrand poetically expresses what he takes to be the complementarity of human personhood expressed in male and female sexual differentiation. Indeed, on such matters, von Hildebrand has expressed himself quite eloquently and directly:

1. Consider merely the treatment chronicled in the thorough and fair study, Prudence Allen, *The Concept of Woman, Vol. 2: The Early Humanist Reformation, 1250–1500* (Grand Rapids, Michigan: William B. Eerdmans, 2002). Also, Prudence Allen, *The Concept of Woman, Volume 3: The Search for Communion of Persons, 1500–2015* (Grand Rapids, MI: Eerdmans, 2016). Also, see Prudence Allen, "Man-Woman Complementarity: The Catholic Inspiration," *Logos: A Journal of Catholic Thought and Culture* 9, no. 3 (2006): 87–108.

2. See the recent compilation *Pope John Paul II Speaks on Women*, edited by Brooke Williams Deely (Washington, D.C.: The Catholic University of America Press, 2014).

> For the person who has freed himself from this basically mistaken tendency today, which still haunts modern psychology, it is not difficult to see that the difference between man and woman is not only a biological one, but that it concerns two different original types of the spiritual person that is man. Although we must also guard against the not uncommon exaggeration of this difference, it still remains correct that in man and woman we are confronted with two fundamental types of mankind, with their specific values, with their specific missions, and with their specific supplementary gifts.[3]

However, for a Thomist, one wishes to ground such assertions within a slightly more robust metaphysical account. Sadly, it seems that most discussions about Aquinas and the relation of the sexes tend to get lost in polemics regarding his use of Aristotle's biology of the female.[4] Often, an *apologia* is made for Aquinas when, in fact, there is so little said by Thomas that it would be better for Thomists to claim that this was not his primary focus than strenuously to defend his writings against detractors. Because of the relative barrenness of such an apologetic and defensive approach, this essay will not enter into the details of these debates. Instead, in the hopes of advancing a broadly Thomistic position, I wish to discuss some suggestive remarks made by Maritain concerning the metaphysics of sexual differentiation.

In the essay "Let Us Make for Him a Helpmate Like to Himself," Maritain addresses the question of the relation of the sexes in a manner that

3. Dietrich von Hildebrand, *Man, Woman, and the Meaning of Love* (Manchester, New Hampshire: Sophia Institute Press, 2002), 103–104. Also, see the striking statements in Dietrich von Hildebrand, *Marriage: The Mystery of Faithful Love* (Manchester, New Hampshire: Sophia Institute Press, 1997), 13: "It would be incredibly superficial to consider as a mere biological difference the distinction between man and woman, which really shows us two complementary types of the spiritual person of the human species."

4. On what might be called the "positive register" defending Aquinas, see Joseph Hartel, "The Integral Feminism of St. Thomas Aquinas," *Gregorianum* 77 (1996): 527–47; Michael Nolan, "The Aristotelian Background to Aquinas's Denial that 'Woman is a Defective Male,'" *The Thomist* 64 (2000): 21–69; Rosalind Smith Edman, "Feminism, Postmodernism and Thomism Confront Questions of Gender," in *Postmodernism and Christian Philosophy*, edited by Roman T. Ciapalo (Washington, D.C.: American Maritain Association, 1997), 97–106; and Joseph Francis Hartle, "*Femina Ut Imago Dei in the Integral Feminism of St. Thomas Aquinas* (Rome: Editrice Pontificia Università Gregoriana, 1993).

On the "negative register" among thinkers who kindly dissent from Aquinas, we can include the text of Maritain under consideration here: Jacques Maritain, "Let Us Make for Him a Helpmate Like to Himself," in *Untrammeled Approaches*, translated by Bernard Doering (Notre Dame, Indiana: University of Notre Dame Press, 1997), 151–64; and Prudence Allen, *The Concept of Woman, Vol. 2*, 127–52. Also, see the introductory remarks of Brooke Williams Deely in *Pope John Paul II Speaks on Women*, 1–12.

helps to build positively on Aquinas's metaphysics *without* denying the problematic texts in the corpus. Maritain uses the manner of individuation proper to the spiritual soul as the principle for explaining the unique complementarity found in the case of male and female human persons. Sadly, Maritain's metaphysical remarks in the aforementioned paper have generally been overlooked.[5] This state of affairs is unfortunate, for his reflections provide a salient link from a rich Thomistic metaphysic to the positive insights expressed in the writings of Catholic phenomenologists like von Hildebrand and Pope St. John Paul II.

This essay is meant only to be an initial attempt to clear the ground, not a full-blown attempt at discussing the metaphysics of sexual differentiation. Thus, it is not my goal to undertake the extensive textual work needed for a full study that would guarantee Maritain's "Thomistic credentials." Likewise, I am not looking to respond to the intramural debates on these matters among contemporary Thomists. Finally, I am not aiming to integrate these insights into the Magisterium of John Paul II concerning the complementarity of the sexes. To undertake any of these tasks would be to present a pastiche of texts at best. Instead, I wish to draw attention to an issue indicated in a short text by Maritain and to pay attention to the *problem itself*. My goals are thus partly interpretive (inasmuch as Maritain's text represents the "guiding star" of this essay) and partly didactic (inasmuch as I intend to elaborate Maritain's position with slightly more clarity than is found in his own exposition). The upshot is to bring the principles of Thomistic metaphysics to bear on a problem that has perhaps heretofore been more ably handled by figures like von Hildebrand and John Paul II than by Thomists who often find themselves involved in presenting some form of defense of Aquinas's texts concerning females.

II. A Unique Form: Maritain on Modal-Essential Differentiation in the Human Form

In the essay in question, Maritain exemplifies *in actu exercito* precisely how the supernatural order can elevate cognition of the purely natural or-

5. I recall a conversation with Sr. Prudence Allen several years ago during which I recommended the essay to her. She kindly accepted such remarks from a junior philosopher. The text is discussed in her recent volume from Eerdmans, though it seems that Brooke Williams Deely also had extended conversations with her on these matters as well.

der. In the text, he is not exactly proceeding as a "research worker" on behalf of theology.[6] The reflections at the beginning of the essay are not, strictly speaking, of a theological nature. Instead of proceeding from the *habitus* of theological science, his reflections proceed as "a *reading of the* [scriptural] *text* as would be done by *any Christian in search of intelligibility*."[7] Therefore, it is a reading that proceeds under the light of faith, though not in the scientific manner proper to theological science. In this faith-directed reading, Maritain attempts to understand the implications of the Genesis narrative vis-à-vis the nature and dignity of the human person. While reading a supernatural narrative, guided by the supernatural light of faith, Maritain will draw attention to a truth that, of itself, is natural—though our poor, weak intellects are more quickly guided to it by revelation than by the unaided light of reason.

In the midst of a critique of Aristotle's and Aquinas's dicta concerning the nature of women, Maritain proposes what will be his primary philosophical thesis later in the essay. He states that the Genesis passage declares that the human male and female each "share differently in the qualities of that [i.e. human] nature."[8] He is quite clear that he does not hold that the differences of sex as shared with the animal kingdom are the "most basic foundation" for this difference. Instead, it is in the individual nature that the human person is differentiated in one way as *being-man* and another as *being-woman*.[9] Such a statement is strikingly similar to the aforementioned passage from von Hildebrand![10]

After some further discussions focusing on the text in Genesis and its general repercussions, Maritain "hands off" the problem to the domain of philosophical wisdom and its natural intellectual lights. His thesis is that within the single species of humanity, there are two sub-specific types. He uses the example of racial differentiation but immediately notes that the cases are not the same. Indeed, the parallel is really metaphorical or analogical at best. In the case of racial differentiation, accidental traits play the

6. See Jacques Maritain, *On the Grace and Humanity of Jesus*, translated by Joseph W. Evans (New York: Herder, 1969), 11–12.

7. Maritain, "Let Us Make," in *Untrammeled Approaches*, 151; emphasis in original.

8. Ibid., 155.

9. See ibid.

10. Let us note, however, that he goes on to say that inasmuch as sexual differentiation (especially as regards reproduction) is for the sake of the species, it is "parasitic" on the personhood of the person! We will return to the troublesome nature of this language on several occasions below.

primary role, whereas what he is stating about the male and female sexes pertains to the very nature of the human person. He contrasts the case of the human person to the sexual differentiation of animals, which he takes to be of the purely functional order.[11]

In the case of the human person, it is a matter of the essence itself being "turned" in a given direction (so to speak) precisely because of its ordering to the given male or female body of which the soul will be the form. In a footnote, he remarks that he is speaking of what might be called a sub-specificity of the modal-essential order, by which he means "a mode of the human essence itself."[12] To explicate this insight further, he remarks that this situation is due to the peculiar mode of individuation proper to the human soul. Whereas the animal soul is individuated by the matter that it informs, the human soul is individuated *as ordered to* the matter it informs. Though he does not directly state it here, the distinction has to deal with the way that the spiritual soul is a self-subsistent form destined to be the form of the body. He struggles with the language to use, proposing an analogy to the case of left-handed and right-handed chirality—as though one would say that a male soul would be "dextroversly" individualized and a female soul "levroversly" individualized because of their respective ordering to the matters of which they are respectively the forms.[13] In using this expression, he is merely searching for a way to express the idea that one and the same thing takes on two different structural forms. Thus, a metaphorical analogy is established: "As the left hand is to the right, so is the human male complementary to the human female." It is nothing more than a metaphor, as he openly admits.[14]

11. See ibid., 158–59.

12. Ibid., 158n5.

13. See ibid., 159.

14. I stress this point against those who would critique his overall discussion on account of such a brief (and self-admittedly groping) example. Granted, neither chemical isomers nor even mere human hands are complementary (as Maritain *does* hold the sexes to be) merely because of their chirality. However, he merely is searching for the metaphor of how two forms can take on such different "turns" to their essential structure. These are *untrammeled* approaches, after all.

A philosopher must not *argue* from metaphors. However, whenever one is breaking new ground, it is sometimes necessary to use them to orient one's thought. Indeed, the critic should note that even Maritain's *very* sober student, Yves Simon, has said the same. See Yves R. Simon, *Work, Society, and Culture*, edited by Vukan Kuic (New York: Fordham University Press, 1971), 168: "The use of metaphors in philosophy proper must either be rejected or at least strictly controlled; but in the phase of discovery, in the introduction to a subject, nothing is more natural than to use metaphors. In fact, a rich metaphorical imagination is an indispensable privilege of

In the next section, I am going to unpack the meaning of Maritain's remarks, which I think merit careful consideration. Alas, however, Maritain's wording is infected with the same class of problems that one finds throughout his treatment of the bipolarity of "person" and "individual."[15] In this chapter, he speaks of a spiritual and a carnal pole in the human person, insisting repeatedly that he is concerned with the spiritual pole (and its concomitant repercussions on the whole person). By using such language, he attempts to avoid drawing an equivalence between mere physical differentiation and the modal-essential complementarity that he wishes to explain.

The language of "two poles" pushes him so far as to assert that there is a "harmonic correspondence" between the so-called carnal and spiritual poles.[16] This distinction risks a kind of dualism that locates the *whole* of human personhood in its spiritual roots. While it is true that personhood extends only to those beings that are intellectual, it is also the case that the human person, unlike the Divine Persons of the Trinity and the personhood proper to the angels, is unique in not being wholly immaterial. Because the notion of person denotes a whole (namely, a subsistent individual of a rational nature), it is not possible for the human *person* to be a person except in a state of union with the body. The immaterial soul is only a part of the substantial whole and therefore cannot be considered a person when it is separate from the body.[17]

A recent essay by Federico Tedesco has ably probed aspects of this issue. It is Tedesco's contention that the root of Maritain's theme concerning "person and individual" is found in his theory of subsistence. In particular,

all creative philosophers. Philosophy will begin when metaphor is transcended, but in the introduction to philosophy we have to use metaphorical analogies."

15. See Maritain, *Education at the Crossroads* (New Haven, Connecticut: Yale University, 1971), 9–10. See also Jacques Maritain, *The Person and the Common Good*, translated by John J. Fitzgerald (Notre Dame, Indiana: University of Notre Dame Press, 2009), 31–46; Maritain, *Scholasticism and Politics*, edited and translated by Mortimer J. Adler (Indianapolis, Indiana: Liberty Fund, 2011), 56–67; Maritain, *Three Reformers: Luther, Descartes, Rousseau* (New York: Scribner, 1942), 14–28. Note that Maritain cites Garrigou-Lagrange's *Le sens commun*. See Reginald Garrigou-Lagrange, *Le sens commun: La philosophie de l'être et les formules Dogmatiques* (Paris: Nouvelle Librairie Nationale, 1922), 333. See also Garrigou-Lagrange, *Beatitude: A Commentary on St. Thomas' Theological Summa, Ia IIae, qq. 1–54*, translated by Patick Cummings (St. Louis: B. Herder, 1956), 75.

16. See Maritain, "Let Us Make," in *Untrammeled Approaches*, 160.

17. See Aquinas, *In III Sent.* d. 5, q. 3, a. 2 ad 2. Also, Aquinas, *De pot.* q. 9, a. 3 ad 14. Maritain states same at *The Degrees of Knowledge*, translated by Gerald B. Phelan et al. (Notre Dame, Indiana: University of Notre Dame Press, 1995), 246. Likewise, see the same point in Maritain, *On the Church of Christ*, translated by Joseph Evans (Notre Dame, Indiana: University of Notre Dame Press, 1971), 247n5.

this issue comes to the foreground in Tedesco's opinion when one considers Maritain's position that, "The body subsists with the subsistence of the soul."[18] Tedesco argues, at some length, that Maritain does not handle the notion of subsistence operative in this manner of stating the problem. The problem comes down to whether or not the subsistence of the spiritual soul is *complete*, rendering the soul (as thus subsisting) wholly incommunicable. This would make the soul to be a *quid* that in fact cannot be communicated to the human composite. We would be faced with a subsistent soul that at best could be extrinsically added to the body.

Tedesco draws at length from Aquinas, Cajetan, and Poinsot to argue on behalf of a doctrine of degrees of perseity. In particular, it is necessary to explain how the spiritual soul can subsist in an incomplete manner *as a part* without shattering the unity of the human person.[19] In this essay, it is impossible to enter into a full evaluation of Tedesco's assessment of Maritain. Clearly, in the *Degrees of Knowledge* (quite proximate to passages cited by Tedesco), Maritain affirms the incomplete nature of the separate soul.[20] However, he does not discuss at length how this relates to the nature of subsistence, thus failing to discuss the degrees of perseity that Tedesco rightly indicates are important for parsing these matters carefully.

Briefly stated, an internal dissonance remains within Maritain's position. He does claim that the completion of human nature requires the subsistence of the soul precisely as the form of the body. However, he can also seem to speak of the antagonism of matter against personality.[21] I think the best way to recover a partial resolution of this antithesis is to note the way the historical destiny of mankind plays into Maritain's remarks in the essay we are considering from *Untrammeled Approaches*. To acknowledge the historical destiny of the human person would be tantamount to acknowledging the exigencies of embodied existence—history being intrinsically linked to matter-bound temporality. To understand this reading of Maritain, I will turn now to a fuller treatment of the metaphysics undergirding his assertions.

18. This position remained to the end of his career. See Jacques Maritain, *On the Church of Christ*, 247n5.

19. See Federico Tedesco, "From Maritain to Aquinas: Beyond the Polarity between Individual and Person," in *Human Nature, Contemplation, and the Political Order: Essays Inspired by Maritain's* Scholasticism and Politics, edited by Peter Karl Koritansky (Washington, D.C.: The Catholic University of America Press, 2014), 76–82.

20. See n. 17 above.

21. See Maritain, *The Degrees of Knowledge*, 247.

III. Drawing Out Maritain's Point

Let us begin with sub-human animals. In this case, the act/potency relationship is dominated by the form/matter relationship. Consider a group of dogs. Within the group, there are a number of social roles that are played based upon age and sex. In order to understand the whole range of "dog life"—i.e., the full amplitude of the formal cause of these animals—we must consider all of the animals. There is a kind of perfection in working of the power of estimation in the young dogs learning to accommodate themselves to the environment. There are properties of maternal care to be found in the females that will not be expressed in the males. The adult males will express potencies that will be actualized neither in the young nor in the females. Likewise, dogs of different breeds will exemplify various aspects of "dog life" in numerous ways.

The important—quite critical—question is: What is the root of this differentiation? That is, are they differences on the side of form or on the side of matter? If matter is the source of individuation, we must recognize that the individuality of each dog expresses itself in more than mere numerical multiplication. Matter and quantity are not the same. The accident of quantity allows for the differentiation of homogeneous parts outside of each other. Matter, on the other hand, is potency for form.[22] Are the dogs individuated by their matter?[23] What we see in all of these dogs is a single form of life, detectable and similar in all of the instances.[24] To understand

22. A clear exposition of these points can be found in Joseph Owens, *An Elementary Christian Metaphysics* (Houston, Texas: Center for Thomistic Studies, 2011), 166–70.

23. It would be a travesty of historical sensibility to ignore the numerous controversies that such claims involve. However, we can only point to the learned studies such as those of Jorge Gracia as evidence of the fact that many great minds have puzzled over how one should exactly formulate these points. This paper is not the place to make grand claims regarding Thomas's own position. See Jorge J. E. Gracia, *Introduction to the Problem of Individuation in the Early Middle Ages* (Washington, D.C.: The Catholic University of America Press, 1984); and *Individuation in Scholasticism: The Later Middle Ages and the Counter-Reformation, 1150–1650*, edited by Jorge J. E. Gracia (Albany, New York: SUNY Press, 1994). For a quite insightful remark on the principle of individuation, see Étienne Gilson, *The Spirit of Medieval Philosophy*, translated by A. H. C. Downes (New York: Charles Scribner's Sons, 1940), 193–200, 464n5–466n7.

24. Here, I am choosing my words quite carefully, for the formal unity of the species is nothing positive but instead is only a negative unity of non-division. This doctrine, that of Poinsot, does run dangerously close to the Ockhamist position regarding maximum similarity between unique individuals as being the grounding for specific unity. However, this is an issue to be adjudicated elsewhere. See John of St. Thomas, *Material Logic,Cursus philosophicus, Ars Logica* par. 2, edited and translated by Yves R. Simon, John J. Glanville, and G. Donald Hollenhorst (Chicago:

the nature of each dog's activity, we look to their shared life as well as to the life that they share with the rest of the world. The question we must ask is, Is the form different among these dogs? Do their different manners of life express a difference in formality?

We must come to know substantial essences by means of the accidents that express that essence, looking for true properties that signify directly and uniquely the activity of the given substantial essence.[25] Do the activities of these dogs recommend to us any kind of activity that is wholly separate from matter? So far as we can tell, the animals are engaged in a form of life that wholly has its terminus in temporal existence. Even the kind of quasi-societal life of the pack is still oriented to the practical judgments that will be made by the animal's particular power of estimation. The activity of the animals is mundane, even if it is not relegated to the mere brute *hic et nunc*.

The activity of the dog, so far as we can tell, bespeaks of a mode of existence that is material. The form can only be expressed in its totality by means of the various potentialities of matter into which it is received. The differences among the dogs, though significant and various, arise from the different matters in which they subsist. One form of life, expressible in the world of motion and change, finds various expressions in various material substrates. The form of life is individuated *by* the matter.

We turn next to the case of the angel. Unique in its own species, the angel has no principle of individuation in the same way spoken of before. With utter formal difference separating each immaterial substance from the next, no question arises regarding how one form of life is experienced in many different individuals—at least on the standard Thomistic account.[26] Instead, each angel is essentially unique, and so the term "individual" takes on a new register. It does not indicate the presence of an act/potency relationship between the form of the angel and some sort of matter. Instead, the individuality of the subsistent angel is nothing more than the fact that this given essence subsists in itself, receiving its act of existence immediately, not through the further principle of prime matter. Of itself, the angelic essence remains in potency to existence. However, lacking the potency that comes

---

Chicago University Press, 1955), q. 3, a. 3 and a. 6 (pp. 102–14 and 130–40). Also, see John C. Cahalan, "On the Training of Thomists," *The Future of Thomism*, edited by Deal W. Hudson and Dennis W. Moran (Notre Dame, Indiana: American Maritain Association, 1992), 138n12.

25. See Maritain, *The Degrees of Knowledge*, 215–24, especially 221n8.

26. Various texts could be cited. See the early opusculum, Aquinas, *De Ente*, c. 4 and 5. Also, ST I, q. 50, a. 4.

from matter, it does not need to express its essence by means of the imperfect actuality that is motion.

Now, these considerations soar quite quickly into analogates that are far above the beginning steps that must be taken by mere philosophical wisdom. Here, I am buttressed by the angelic musings of the Thomist tradition, but we would do well to remember the humility of Thomists like Poinsot, whose detailed discussions of angelic matters are found in the *Cursus Theologicus*, not his philosophical writings.[27] Yes, it is true, "He who has not meditated on the angels will never be a perfect metaphysician."[28] However, let us also remember that to speak of purely spiritual natures is a quite lofty affair in metaphysics, calling for intellectual humility on behalf of human knowers who must begin the quest of knowledge with the material quiddities that are the proportionate object of our intellection in our current state.

Returning to the case of the dogs, the act/potency couplet is twofold. The essence of the dog is in potency to the actuality of its own substantial existence. This existence adds *no quidditative note*, but it makes all the difference as to whether the dog is dead or alive. However, the essence itself can only receive and exercise this existence by being incarnate in its particular matter. Thus, the form of dog life exists only by holding in existence the flux of various material changes that arise from its material constitution. It is matter that makes possible the expression of this life form—*as a principle of potency*, not as a separate *quid* that must be joined to the form extrinsically. The imperfect actuality (i.e., movement[29]) of its activity is the expression of this matter-bound potency.

We are about to make the critical transition, so several summary points should help to clarify my trajectory. There are certain forms of life that terminate solely in spiritual and immaterial activities—completely and utterly. In this august order are found the angelic hosts. Here there is no question of a relationship between matter and form, though the act/potency relationship remains with regard to existence and essence. (It is not our task in this paper to show how angelic agency relates to act and potency in

27. See the remarkable study John Deely, "The Semiosis of Angels," *The Thomist* 68 (2004): 205–58.

28. See Maritain, *The Degrees of Knowledge*, 235.

29. See Aristotle, *Metaphysics*, 1049b18–34. Also, Yves Simon, "The Philosophy of Change," in *The Great Dialogue of Nature and Space*, edited by Gerard J. Dalcourt (Albany, NY: Magi Books, 1970), 59–86.

a manner that is different from the act/potency relationship found in the motion of hylomorphic beings.[30])

Then, there is the case of hylomorphic beings in which the act/potency relationship of existence/essence can only be actualized if the essence is understood in terms of form/matter. The form can only express all of its virtualities by the progressive actualization of its matter—and in light of this fact, it can only express itself in a most fleeting manner through the history of the individual material substance. Note again, however, that we are not here confronted with three *quids*: (1) a form, (2) a matter, and (3) an individual made up of a stitched-together combination of the first two. The form has *no* subsistence except insofar as it is informing the matter. Such a form is not a pure act of existence; thus, it must have the potency proper to its particular grade of actuality.

We thus come to the case of the human soul, which is much more problematic. The human soul is the form of the body. As such it is the actuality principle of the human composite. However, we know also that the human person is an agent capable of acts of intellection and appetition that proceed from principles that are not bound wholly to matter. This is no simple feat for the philosopher to prove. Given the requirement of all intellection to turn to the phantasm, it is easy to think that all of our potencies are tied to materiality. Still, the universal objects of intellection reveal (in various degrees) the immateriality of the soul—even though this immateriality is intimately linked to our physical constitution.[31] Thus, the subsistence of the human composite is a unique case—a spiritual subsistence for an embodied creature.

The dog subsists in its matter. The angel subsists in its very form. The human person subsists in its soul as the form of the body. I can think of no better way to summarize the state of affairs than in the words of Anton Pegis: "In short, the human soul is literally substance *as* the form of the body."[32] The separate soul is not a person; it lacks the completion of its na-

30. But it should be noted that the points of transition between the embodied and the angelic will be most ably found in the explanation of the immanent activities of sensation, perception, and intellection, which most closely approximate the kind of perfect actuality pertaining to immaterial agency.

31. This profound problem is noted by Yves Simon regarding the instrumental causality proper to the phantasm in intellection. See Yves R. Simon, *Introduction to Metaphysics of Knowledge*, translated by Vukan Kuic and Richard J. Thompson (New York: Fordham University Press, 1990), 113–27.

32. See Anton Pegis, *At the Origins of the Thomistic Notion of Man* (New York: MacMillan, 1963), 39.

ture, which precisely *as form* is ordered to be *the form of the body*. The very nature of the soul, as a self-subsistent reality, finds its perfection only in communicating that existence to the body. Lacking that communication, its state is imperfect, even if it is possible for it to have a preternatural manner of knowing.[33]

A great mystery is contained in these words, and it is not surprising that God has chosen to reveal in Genesis the complementarity of male and female. In the case of the dogs, form is expressed *only* in materiality. In order that this particular form of life may express itself in all its amplitude, it must exist in many individuals. Such is the destiny of the matter-bound animal. Yes, it speaks to the majesty even of such matter-bound forms—they are not exhausted by their individuals. What we call "dog life" must be expressed in the various individual substances that express through imperfect actuality this form of life—i.e., through the medium of motion and change.[34] Still, there is one formal actuality involved here, differentiated by its various material supposits.

What we call "human life" is quite different—and, here we see that we are in the midst a set of analogical terms.[35] The form of the dog is not exhausted in each individual dog. The form of the angel is wholly exhausted by the given angel. The human form, insofar as it is a form and can subsist in itself (akin to the angel, different from the dog), can only perfectly subsist insofar as it is actually informing the particular matter of a given person (akin to the dog, different from the angel). Like the dog, humanity is not exhausted in any particular individual. But here is where the rub comes

33. For a careful textual study concerning the separate soul's knowledge, see John Wippel, "Thomas Aquinas on the Separated Soul's Natural Knowledge," in *Thomas Aquinas: Approaches to Truth*, edited by James McEvoy and Michael Dunne (Dublin: Four Courts, 2002), 114–40. See also Mark Spencer, "The Personhood of the Separated Soul," *Nova et Vetera* 12, no. 3 (Summer 2014): 863–912. Spencer, however, concludes that the separate soul is a person. The essay remains a veritable goldmine for texts. However, it is arguable that we await a full study of the problem of the separate soul in a purely philosophical manner (i.e., not in one that merely dialectically plays various texts off of each other). This holds even in light of the work of Fr. Woodbury on the topic. See Austin Woodbury, *Natural Philosophy, Treatise Three: Psychology*, (Latrobe, Pennsylvania: The John N. Deely and Anthony Russell Collection, St. Vincent College), 794–814, nn. 942–59 .

34. Recall the importance of this fact, eloquently expressed in Jacques Maritain, "Sign and Symbol," in *Redeeming the Time*, translated by Harry Lorin Binsse (London: Geoffrey Bles, 1943), 191: "The sign involves the whole extent of moral and human life; it is in the human world a universal instrument, *just as is movement in the physical world*" (emphasis added).

35. For further explication of this manner of speaking of analogy, see Yves R. Simon, "On Order in Analogical Sets," in *Philosopher at Work*, edited by Anthony O. Simon (Lanham, Maryland: Rowman and Littlefield, 1999), 135–71.

in—*qua form,* it has a particular kind of destiny in being related to a given sort of matter.

This is no insignificant affair. It means that the soul itself—i.e., *qua form*—is intrinsically modified because of its orientation to the substantial whole of which it is a part. Even in its imperfect state of separation, the soul remains individuated by this orientation.[36] Granting the complexities of genetics,[37] this nonetheless means that the form of life exhibited by the male *soul* will differ from that of the female *soul* in a way that is more intimate than the mere case of the dog. Lacking a better manner of expression, we could say that the possibilities contained in the form of life proper to human existence are superabundant in a way that qualitatively surpasses the case of the dog. To explain the nature of femaleness in dogs is to explain the *essence of dog life,* though only noting particular activities that can be exercised thanks to the individuation in a particular matter. However, to explain the nature of femaleness in humans is to explain the *essence of female human life*—it is a unique mode of human life, more unique than is the case of "dog femininity." This all is a long way of stating what Maritain states succinctly in writing, "[The human soul] is masculine or feminine *by virtue of the typical form of its very being.*"[38]

36. See Aquinas, *De Ente,* cap. 5; *ST* I, q. 76, a. 1, ad 6.

37. As regards the baseline needed for determining sexual differentiation, taken from a scientifically informed, Thomistic perspective, see Nicanor Pier Giorgio Austriaco, "The Specification of Sex/Gender in the Human Species: A Thomistic Analysis," *New Blackfriars* 94 (2013): 701–15.

38. See Maritain, "Let us Make," in *Untrammeled Approaches,* 159. On this topic, the reader would profit from reading the remarks of Fr. Garrigou-Lagrange, who considers briefly how the human soul is substantially differentiated by its ordination to the body (though not essentially so). He explains it as being a *predicable* accident of the substantial nature (i.e., *not* an accident in a predicamental sense). This topic opens up many interesting related issues, for it draws to light the *unique vocation of every individual to make known some particular refulgence of human nature's amplitude.* A careful philosophical reflection on this matter would consider how the unique human case differs from that of animal ensoulment and that of angelic specific differentiation. These are lofty matters of metaphysics, requiring supple analogical reflection and carefully selected data from which to structure such analogical reflection. See Reginald Garrigou-Lagrange, *Le réalisme du principe de finalité* (Paris: Desclée de Brouwer, 1932), 344–46.

This point is well summarized in remarks by Fr. Austin Woodbury, a student of Fr. Garrigou-Lagrange and often a disciple of Maritain. See Austin Woodbury, *Natural Philosophy, Treatise Three: Psychology,* n. 934Ab: "[There is a certain correspondence between the human intellect and the senses] in the order of entity (and of intellectivity), for, since the intellective soul, as will be shown hereunder, is created *not only IN* the body *but also ACCORDING TO the body,* there results to the intellective soul and to its intellect a more perfect entity and a more perfect intellective vigour from a more perfectly disposed organism, especially according as the organs of the internal senses, seated in the cortex, are the more perfectly disposed for the func-

The individual dogs express a kind of "trans-temporality" insofar as the individual exists for the sake of the species. There is also a kind of trans-temporality in the acquired characteristics of the animal, which is able thus to embody something of a history of acquired characteristics. However, it is uniquely characteristic of the human person to be able to draw to himself or herself *more* than mere physical "history." Human persons, together in moral agency, fashion a true history in the project of cultural life. The human person has a uniquely historical character—the temporal and spiritual progress lived in the *combined* orders of intentional and natural existence.[39]

Thus, for all of the infelicitous manners of expressing himself in the given essay, I believe that Maritain is on the correct pathway when he writes, "Masculine or feminine typicity is not a mere functional or genital typicity. It is a typicity *of nature* (of individual nature) ordered to the temporal and spiritual progress of the human species toward its end, and implying a differentiation in the qualities of the soul, and which includes as one of its properties, however necessary it may be, the genital function related to human animality."[40] Merely speaking within the natural order (as distinguished from—though superelevated by[41]—the supernatural order of the life of grace), this temporal and spiritual progress is the kind of historical expansion that Maritain hints at in many places when he treats the problem of the historical expansion of our knowledge of the natural law and the historical conquest of freedom in the moral life.[42]

---

tions of sensitive lie. Wherefore, not only is the intellect the better furnished with the objects of its knowledge, but also *the intellect is of greater intellective vigour and penetrativeness IN ITSELF*" (emphasis added, uppercase in original). Fr. Woodbury cites Aquinas, *In* II *De Anima*, lect. 19; ST I, q. 79, a. 5; q. 85, a. 7.

39. See Pegis, *At the Origins of the Thomistic Notion of Man*, 45–59. An excellent continuation in this vein can be found in Armand Maurer, *St. Thomas and Historicity* (Milwaukee, Wisconsin: Marquette University Press, 1979).

40. Maritain, "Let us Make," 159. To understand this point adequately, see also160–61: "That idea in vogue today which, by reducing the whole problem to a single carnal pole, considers sex and the genital function as the basic foundation from which derive and according to which are explained all the other differentials which distinguish the being-man and the being-woman is, as I hope I have shown, a basic error which vitiates our entire perspective on the human being. It's like trying to explain the genius of Mozart by the biochemical activities of his spleen or his liver."

41. This issue was dear to Maritain throughout his works. For the purposes of our discussions here, see Jacques Maritain, *On the Philosophy of History*, edited by Joseph W. Evans (New York: Scribner, 1957), 119–32.

42. See Jacques Maritain, *Christianity and Democracy* in *Christianity and Democracy and the Rights of Man and the Natural Law*, translated by Doris C. Anson (San Francisco: Ignatius, 2011), 33. Maritain, *On the Philosophy of History*, 99–126; 138. Jacques Maritain, *La loi naturelle ou loi non écrite*, edited by Georges Brazzola (Fribourg: Éditions Universitaires, 1986), 33 and 183–200.

Male and female human persons are given to each other as partners in this task not merely from a functional and physical order, but even as complementary at the very root of our individual immaterial natures. Yes, as incarnate beings, the male and female sexes are coordinated toward each other for the propagation of the species as well as the domestic life. However, it is necessary to go further, for otherwise it is quite difficult to see how human sexual differentiation is much different from the kind of accidental differentiation found in the animal order. In order to be truly human, sexual differentiation must bear the mark of the intentional/moral existence that we exhibit in our activity as historical and cultural beings. Masculinity and femininity provide two complementary manners of establishing and living this embodied form of spiritual existence.

At this point, we should register again concerns with Maritain's remarks about sexual reproduction being parasitic upon the personhood of the human person.[43] "Person" is analogical in scope, a point that Maritain himself notes elsewhere: "Man and angel are both *persons,* and in that light not parts but real *wholes;* for the person signifies in itself wholeness. Neither man nor even the angel are persons in the perfect and absolute state, but they are in a real sense persons,—however wretchedly that condition of person is realized in man."[44]

It is unfortunate that he makes the rhetorical flourish that he does in the essay we have been considering, for it does stress infelicitous aspects of his often-revisited distinction of "the individual" and "the person." Still, given his other remarks about human personhood, it is most charitable to point out the constructive and positive élan of his reflections (without naively exonerating the conceptual issues that *undeniably do* arise because of the strained separation of individuality and personhood). In the Godhead, personhood is purely a subsistent relation.[45] In the angels, personhood is the concrete supposit of the angelic essence existing in itself. Each angelic person exhausts the totality of its particular grade of actuality. In humans, however, personhood is only exercised by the concrete supposit that re-

Jacques Maritain, *Neuf Leçons sur les Notions Premières de la Philosophie Morale* (Paris: Téqui, 1951), 54–59. Jacques Maritain, *Man and the State* (Washington, D.C.: The Catholic University of America, 1998), 76–107, especially 89–94.

43. I believe that these remarks should be balanced against the brief, though important, reflections that Maritain undertakes in Maritain, *La loi naturelle ou loi non écrite,* 170–75.

44. Jacques Maritain, *St. Thomas and the Problem of Evil* (Milwaukee, Wisconsin: Marquette University Press, 1942), 11.

45. See ST I, q. 29, a. 4.

quires matter as a secondary principle of potency in order that there be any existent whatsoever. It is not enough that the soul subsist in itself. It must subsist in itself as informing the body. Unlike the case of the angels—for whom each angel lives a unique specific form of life—humanity is revealed only in many individuals.

This is the very notion of human personhood—to be poor, but also to have a destiny in history. Humanity is understood only if we see it as a unique form of life that expresses its full amplitude in the historical and cultural conquest of freedom—bringing all things into subjection to the truth that specifies the intellect and the good that specifies the will. Let us recall Maritain's own sage words from *Freedom in the Modern World*:

> It is proper here to add that reason has to do more than to recognize the order that issues from the Creative Mind. There is an order that it is the office of reason, as practical reason, to make: it is, to be exact, the order of human acts and operations which (in the teaching of St. Thomas) defines the field of ethics. Continuing and collaborating with the Divine action, reason has at every moment to fashion in conformity with the Eternal order the contingent and perpetually renewed order of works of time: *facere veritatem* [to make the truth], in the Gospel phrase. ... The whole order of human life is not ready-made in nature and in things; it is an Order of Freedom; it has not just to be discovered and accepted: it has also to be made.[46]

Similarly, related to the question of the unique kind of personhood lived by Man, recall Maritain's remarks in *Scholasticism and Politics*, stressing the historical mission embedded in the nature of human personhood:

> As to the human person, he is but a person in embryo. He is, as with all created persons, not only subject to realities other than himself as to the specifying objects of his knowledge and of his will, but he is also subjected to laws he has not made, as measures regulating his actions. And this is the first defeat, inflicted upon the aspirations of the person as such, a defeat far deeper in men than in angels.
>
> Moreover, the human person is involved in all the miseries and fatalities of material nature,—the servitudes and the needs of the body, heredity, ignorance, selfishness, and the savagery of instincts. This is the second defeat, inflicted upon the person as such, and this defeat originates not in the transcendence of God, but in the burden of nature.
>
> The human person! This unfortunate being, threatened by the entire universe, which seems ready to crush him, pretends to be a whole, to be a person! He is, indeed, a whole and a person! He is a person in the metaphysical root of personality.

46. Jacques Maritain, *Freedom in the Modern World*, translated by Richard O'Sullivan (New York: Gordian Press, 1971), 79–80.

But for subjects both spiritual and bodily, which participate in the same specific nature, which are opaque to themselves, and whose normal state is movement, this metaphysical root, hidden in the depths of being, manifests itself only through a progressive conquest of itself by itself, accomplished in time.

Man must win his personality, as well as his freedom, and he pays dearly for it, and runs many risks. He is a person in the order of doing only if his rational energies and virtues, and love, give such a face to the torrential multiplicity which inhabits him, and freely imprint on him the seal of his radical, ontological unity. In this sense, the one knows real personality and real liberty, while the other does not.[47]

There may be something of a "history" of the angels, but in that case, the term is used analogously to human history—just as angelic duration is only analogously akin to our temporal existence, which is lived in the midst of motion that is numbered according to "before" and "after."[48] Humans, not angels, establish history by linking the past to the present, all with a hope for greater fulfillment in the future. The human spirit is poor—lacking that brilliant actuality that we find in the angelic hosts. However, in its particular poverty, it also shines forth with its own peculiar, *human* superabundance. Strictly speaking, non-spiritual beings have no moral and cultural history. However, for humans, there is indeed such a history. Among the ways that *human persons—qua embodied human persons*—fulfill their destination *as persons* is by cultivating the orders of moral and cultural life.

In human nature itself is inscribed one very important means of living this life—procreation. What else does the duty of educating children mean than to become the stewards and cultivators of society itself?[49] The family is a primordial source from which springs forth the very preservation, stewardship, and continued expansion of humanity's moral and cultural life. It is *in* the family—as the activity constituting a natural society enduring through all of life's many vicissitudes—that culture first blossoms forth from human nature. The primary duty of education, falling to the parents, is really a summons to partake in an important aspect of *human* personhood—to live as moral and intellectual beings in an historical manner. Pro-

47. Jacques Maritain, *Scholasticism and Politics*, edited and translated by Mortimer J. Adler (Indianapolis, Indiana: Liberty Fund, 2011), 134–35.

48. See Yves R. Simon, "Time," in *The Great Dialogue of Nature and Space*, edited by Gerard J. Dalcourt (Albany, New York: Magi Books, 1970), 129–37.

49. Maritain was aware of this exigency as well, as is testified by the remarks cited above from *Loi naturelle*, 171–75.

creation is a mark *par excellence* of the historical and moral destinies of the human race.

Thus, one should take care to avoid the pitfalls of Maritain's occasional expressions regarding the individual and the person. As humans, we are persons only insofar as we are individuals. There is no other way to consider the matter. Nonetheless, it would be churlish to rebuke Maritain entirely, given that in other places, he shows an awareness of the precise points that should qualify his occasional rhetorical excesses. Therefore, as regards our particular concern in this essay, it is appropriate to end with Maritain's own words, which easily surmount the inadequacies of some otherwise-infelicitous manners of stating the matter:

> But there is another and far higher end which the Ancients did not mention here because the dimension of time and of historical progress was not sufficiently clear and operative in their thinking. What humanity was created for was to advance here on earth, to lead here an ever higher temporal and cultural life and at the same time an ever higher life of the spirit, and finally to enter into the Kingdom of God and of the beatific vision. ... It is to better assure the progress of the human species toward this end that from the very beginning human nature was divided between two distinct subspecific types complementing each other. And this is precisely why from the creation of Eve it was necessary that the qualities which distinguish femininity from masculinity be different and complementary.[50]

50. Maritain, "Let Us Make," in *Untrammeled Approaches*, 157.

NIKOLAJ ZUNIC

Maritain's Concept of Virtue as a Form of Movement and its Application to Human Generation

I. Introduction

IN AN ESSAY entitled "Towards a Thomist Idea of Evolution," from his book *Untrammeled Approaches*, Jacques Maritain introduces his readers to a novel understanding of the concept of virtue, which he takes to be the form of a movement. Maritain's objective in this essay is to present a Thomistic interpretation of the scientific theory of evolution. By relying on a hylomorphic theory, Maritain is able to explain certain aspects of human generation and development in a richer and more nuanced way than one normally encounters from the typical evolutionary perspectives, which tend to be barren of philosophical insight. I use Maritain's concept of virtue to analyze and challenge not human evolution as such, as Maritain did, but a certain form of assisted reproduction known as *in vitro* fertilization. I discern in Maritain's Thomistically inspired doctrines the principles of an extremely valuable philosophical hermeneutic of human generation that can help us to see the problems of a technological approach to the production of human life.

I open the essay with a discussion of the ethics of *in vitro* fertilization, especially the views propounded by the inventor of IVF, Dr. Robert Edwards. I follow this with an in-depth treatment of a Thomistic hylomorphic analysis of human nature in terms of the subtle relationship between body and soul. Having laid this conceptual ground, I then venture to offer a substantive critique of *in vitro* fertilization by arguing for its immorality. The final part of the essay broaches the topic of the teleological structure of human life which the practice of *in vitro* fertilization, on my argument, derails. My basic conclusion is that *in vitro* fertilization is wrong because it impedes the natural development of a genuinely human life by disembedding the person from its lived human context right at the origin of its temporal existence.

II. The Ethics of *In vitro* Fertilization

How human beings are conceived, generated, and born has become an ethically controversial subject since the first successful human *in vitro* fertilization procedure in 1978. Dr. Robert Edwards (1925–2013), a British physiologist, and his colleague, Dr. Patrick Steptoe (1913–1988), a British obstetrician and gynaecologist, are credited with the development of this new method of artificially fertilizing an ovum with a sperm outside of the human body, usually done in a test tube or Petri dish, resulting in a human being or what is colloquially referred to as a "test tube baby."[1] The first IVF procedure in 1978 produced a baby girl named Louise Brown who is alive and well to this very day in England, having gone on to marry and bearing two children of her own. Since that first procedure, millions of babies around the world have been produced by means of IVF. IVF has been widely regarded as a wonderful remedy for infertility.[2] Our civilization generally lauds and approves of IVF, so much so that Dr. Edwards was awarded the Nobel Prize in Physiology or Medicine in 2010 for his work. Today, *in vitro* fertilization is a commonplace procedure of which many infertile couples, unmarried women, and homosexual and lesbian partnerships avail themselves to fulfill their desire to have children.

Despite this virtually universal approbation, IVF is not without its critics. When the procedure was first developed, many people, as with any novel practice, were suspicious about the moral acceptability of an unnat-

1. Patrick Steptoe commented on the nomenclature adopted for the product of IVF in the following way: "The press coined the phrase 'test-tube babies,' which has been associated with the procedure ever since, although it mistakenly gave the impression that babies would be grown entirely outside the human body." In "Historical Aspects of the Ethics of *in Vitro* Fertilization," *Annals of the New York Academy of Sciences* 442 (1985): 573–76, esp. 573.

2. Many ethicists point out that IVF does not actually cure infertility but only circumvents infertility to produce a baby. The causes of an individual's or couple's infertility are not directly addressed by the procedure of IVF.

ural or artificial method of creating human beings.[3] The spontaneous reaction of many was that IVF seemed to be contravening the laws of nature or at least not being in accord with the way nature intended human beings to be generated. This objection from the unnaturalness of the procedure carries with it some intuitive conviction but usually, though not necessarily, lacks the requisite philosophical rigor and insight. The biggest problem here is how to define the concept of *nature* and how to make a persuasive case for the immorality of an act based on its being contrary to nature. For it is not clear at all that an act that is "contrary to nature" is in fact morally wrong.[4] For example, the act of fasting—intentionally refusing to eat food for some period of time—is contrary to the natural orientation of an organism to nourish itself and thus to sustain its life, but one would not judge fasting to be immoral; in fact, fasting can be highly moral, as an act of self-abnegation or simply as a healthy lifestyle choice.[5] Other examples that go against our natural inclination for self-preservation include abstaining from sexual activity despite our natural human inclination to reproduce (e.g., the vow of priestly celibacy); or willingly enduring pain and even risking one's own life, such as in situations of employment (e.g., a fire fighter or soldier) or parents sacrificing their well-being for the sake of their children (e.g, raising a family in arduous circumstances) despite our natural inclination for self-preservation. In sum, this line of argumentation is not always compelling.

The main sorts of arguments that one usually comes across with respect to IVF are utilitarian in kind. These include arguments that invoke the onerous costs involved, the invasive nature of the procedure, the (long-term) health risks posed to the baby, the emotional toll on the parents, or the

3. See Robert G. Edwards, "The Bumpy Road to Human *In Vitro* Fertilization," *Nature Medicine* 7, no. 10 (October 2001): 1092: "Ethicists decried us, forecasting abnormal babies, misleading the infertile and misrepresenting our work as really acquiring human embryos for research. They announced that IVF did not cure infertility, as women remained infertile after having an IVF baby. My response was to put forward spectacles, false teeth and heart transplants. Popes were critical and rigid Protestants were sometimes vicious."

4. Such a line of argumentation admittedly conflicts with a more traditional or classical approach to ethical reasoning. Ancient Greek philosophy regularly adopted the terminology of an act being "contrary to nature" (*para phusin*) to argue for its unacceptability. For example, Plato famously denounced homosexual acts as *para phusin* (unnatural or contrary to nature). See John Finnis, "Law, Morality, and 'Sexual Orientation,'" in *Human Rights and Common Good, Collected Essays: Volume III* (Oxford: Oxford University Press, 2011), 334–52, esp. 336–39.

5. This example is borrowed from Patrick Lee and Robert P. George, *Conjugal Union: What Marriage Is and Why It Matters* (Cambridge: Cambridge University Press, 2014), 12–14.

discernment regarding the allocation of government funds when so many other areas of health care are in need of increased financial support. But as with all forms of utilitarian argumentation, IVF is not judged to be intrinsically bad on this account; the problem lies only with some of the consequences, not with the act itself. Thus, all one needs to do is to minimize or eliminate the perceived harm done and the procedure will be free of any and all utilitarian objections.[6]

Robert Edwards, the IVF pioneer, was a vociferous advocate for the moral permissibility of IVF. In a paper entitled "The Scientific Basis of Ethics," Edwards outlines the foundation of his ethical thinking on this topic, which can be summarized in four points.[7] First, Edwards is clear that at least with respect to IVF, and ostensibly even beyond the medical domain, ethics, in his view, is grounded in science. That is, ethical principles are taken from scientific knowledge. He writes, "The basis for my ethical stance is grounded firmly in biological knowledge, for I believe that no other fundamental basis is available."[8] This is a problematic understanding of ethics for not only does it reduce ethics to a crude scientific materialism, but Edwards does not appear to be aware of the fact-value distinction, first raised by David Hume and echoed by countless other philosophers in his wake, which suggests

6. Some ethicists judge IVF to be completely safe for both child and mother. See Thomas A. Shannon, "Ethical Issues Involved with In Vitro Fertilization," *AORN Journal* 53, no. 3 (September 1990): 627: "What is important about in vitro fertilization is that the procedure does not present a risk of harm to the fertilized ovum or substantially increase any risks to the mother." Most ethicists claim that IVF is ethically acceptable, such as in Claire L. Pouncey and Ray V. Haning Jr., "The Status of the Ethics of *In vitro* Fertilization in 1985," *Forensic Science International* 30 (1986): 129: "The practice of *in vitro* fertilization has been accepted by most to be ethical." These views appear to be egregiously ignorant of the empirical facts and philosophical arguments which demonstrate the problems with IVF. Not only are there serious moral objections to IVF, such as the argument based on the dignity of the human person, but there are a number of health and medical risks involved in IVF. For a treatment of the moral arguments against IVF see Teresa Iglesias, "*In Vitro* Fertilisation: The Major Issues," *Journal of Medical Ethics* 1 (1984): 32–37, and Paul Ramsey, "Shall We 'Reproduce'? I. The Medical Ethics of In Vitro Fertilization," *Journal of the American Medical Association* 220, no. 10 (June 5, 1972): 1346–50. For a list of all associated health risks with IVF see the information fact sheet, "In Vitro Fertilization (IVF): What are the Risks?," published by the American Society for Reproductive Medicine, accessible on-line at: http://www.reproductivefacts.org/globalassets/rf/news-and-publications/bookletsfact-sheets/english-fact-sheets-and-info-booklets/in_vitro_ fertilization_ivf_what_are_the_risks_factsheet.pdf

7. R. G. Edwards, "Introduction: The Scientific Basis of Ethics," *Annals of the New York Academy of Sciences* 442 (May 1985): 564–70. The appendix to this article lists all of Edwards's articles and essays between 1966 and 1984 which discuss the ethics of reproduction and *in vitro* fertilization.

8. Ibid., 565.

that one cannot derive moral judgements ("ought" statements) from judgements of fact ("is" statements).[9] As any well-educated philosopher recognizes, science simply does not provide the principles of ethics.

Second, although he has established his ethical views as originating from his understanding of science, he unwittingly contradicts this position by stating that certain ethical positions are correct or acceptable because they are consistent with popular social opinions. He seems to want to defend the rectitude of certain ethical assertions by referring to society's approval of them.[10] However, this praise for democratic ideals, as expressed in this *argumentum ad populum*, is betrayed by Edwards's elitist and tendentious view of society, as he decries opinion polls and petitions organized by pro-life groups which oppose IVF, while endorsing only those citizens who are properly educated in science as Edwards himself is and who have arrived at the same conclusions as Edwards regarding IVF.[11] As regards his deference to social opinion, Edwards clearly wants to have it both ways.

Third, fertilization does not constitute the beginning of life. According to Edwards, life is continuous; it does not begin discretely with fertil-

9. This is by no means intended to suggest approbation of the philosophical rationale for the fact-value distinction, as developed by Hume and his adherents. No doubt, there are cogent counter-arguments to the fact-value distinction which demonstrate the untenability of this proposition. My point here is simply to indicate that Edwards does not even seem to be aware of this elementary doctrine which is common knowledge in the world of philosophy.

10. "How, then, can we judge the value of early embryonic life in relation to the principles of ethical behavior that are ingrained in law and obeyed by society? ... A fetus at 3 months of gestation is different from a newborn child, a difference reflected in the laws of society, which often accepts abortion but not infanticide." See also p. 566: "Research may therefore be carried on human embryos, but only for urgent clinical reasons, such as the treatment of infertility, the alleviation of genetic disorders, detection of the causes of human anomalies, analysis of the relationships between embryonic and cancer cells, and the development of fetal tissue for use in transplantation. These studies cannot wait, for they are too urgent. They demand that a very early embryo be judged as less than an adult or a child suffering from severe disorders. Such standards are already held by society." Edwards, "The Scientific Basis of Ethics," 565.

11. "I would like to illustrate briefly these remarks in relation to the situation in my own country. We face societal and political debates this year on the recommendations of the Warnock Committee, a governmentally appointed committee that has made recommendations concerning the ethics and practice of artificial insemination and *in vitro* fertilization. There are already hints of a hostile response to the recommendations in this report, with large-scale petitions against any research on embryos or surrogate mothers being submitted to Parliament, organized by strong pro-life lobbies. Emotions have been aroused, and many signatures have been obtained outside of supermarkets, or in response to newspaper advertising. *Those who are unknowing or unthinking can easily make snap decisions on fundamental topics under these circumstances. But what is the value of these signatures? How much thoughtful understanding and enquiry do they represent?*". Ibid., 567; emphasis added.

ization. To quote Edwards on this matter, "Fertilization is obviously very important, but is not the only decisive moment in establishing human life.... Fertilization is an essential step, but merely one of a long succession of essential stages in the establishment of the individual."[12] He is very dismissive of those he calls "absolutists," such as Roman Catholics, who claim that "fertilization begins human life."[13] The problem with this second point is that Edwards commits the fallacy of equivocation with respect to the concept of life: he uses it with a broad signification to mean "any living thing," which naturally can include oocytes and sperm, but also applies the same use of the term to designate an individual human being.

Finally, Edwards holds that human dignity and human rights are accorded to human beings on a gradated scale. The value of an embryo is less than that of a full-grown adult; rights are not absolute or inalienable but are given to persons at different stages of life. As Edwards writes: "Rightly or wrongly, a severe mental defective with kidney failure will not be given equal rights with a normal family man in the queue for limited numbers of dialysis machines. The rights of a 'brain-dead' adult on a life-support machine are severely diminished, even his right to life. Rights vary throughout life—to drive a car, to sign checks, or to vote."[14] Edwards asserts that his own view lies midway between the absolutists, who maintain that the embryo is equal in worth and dignity to mature human beings, and the standpoint that the embryo is utterly worthless. Despite his attempt to show that he values the embryo to a limited extent, this idea of a fluid and changing human dignity can be challenged philosophically on many fronts. Not only does Edwards ignore the true basis of dignity in our very human nature, which is present at conception and remains until death, but he confuses different kinds of rights: namely, basic human rights and conventional civil rights. The right to life cannot be treated on the same level with the right to drive a vehicle.

My purpose in highlighting Edwards's ethical views on IVF is to demonstrate how philosophically weak and shallow they are. Yet even if his ethical beliefs are shot through with logical errors and fallacies, it must be admitted that these beliefs are shared by multitudes of individuals in our world who are just as convinced about the moral goodness of IVF as Edwards is. Given

12. Ibid., 565.
13. Ibid., 567.
14. Ibid., 566.

the kinds of moral reasoning that are often involved in assessing the ethical nature of *in vitro* fertilization, it is not surprising that the vast majority of people do not judge this procedure to be morally objectionable. No doubt, the critics of IVF have their work cut out for them. However, arguably the most significant and seemingly insurmountable datum which stands in the way of any and all moral objections to IVF is that the procedure results in a real, living human being. Nobody can deny that a human being is the product of IVF—Louise Brown and millions of others are proof of this fact. The human beings produced by means of IVF are just like any human being: they have the same human nature and the same human dignity. Even the Catholic Church, which condemns the practice of IVF and judges it to be gravely immoral, affirms the inherent dignity and worth of the human beings who are created from this process.[15] Such persons should be treated with the same moral concern as anybody else. This incontrovertible fact—that a living human being is produced from IVF—is what strikes most people as the strongest and most persuasive reason for the moral acceptability of IVF. The bioethicist Arthur Caplan summarizes this point in this way:

> Test tube baby technology is seen by almost every American as pro-life technology. Normally those who worry about this technology say: Is this the right way to make a baby? Is this an acceptable way to make a baby? I think most Americans say: Who cares? If you get babies, and infertile couples want them, and they're the biological offspring of those couples, and those couples don't have many other options (adoption being something that's relatively difficult to do), then this is a great technology.[16]

Does this mean, therefore, that *in vitro* fertilization is truly morally acceptable? Is it true that there are no cogent arguments one could offer to demonstrate that IVF is morally wrong? The broader issue here deals with how human beings are conceived, generated, and born and the relationship of human sexuality to the procreation of new human life. Does it matter that human beings can be produced by means of technology outside of the human body while being at the disposal of other human beings' intentions

15. *Catechism of the Catholic Church* (Doubleday: New York, 1994), paragraph 2376: "Techniques that entail the dissociation of husband and wife, by the intrusion of a person other than the couple (donation of sperm or ovum, surrogate uterus), are gravely immoral. These techniques (heterologous artificial insemination and fertilization) infringe the child's right to be born of a father and mother known to him and bound to each other by marriage. They betray the spouses' 'right to become a father and a mother only through each other.'"

16. http://www.pbs.org/wgbh/americanexperience/features/interview/ethical-questions/

and projects? The purpose of my paper is to attempt to formulate an argument that artificial forms of reproduction, of which the exemplary case is IVF, are morally unacceptable. But to do this I need to first present the philosophical ideas which lie at the basis of this ethical judgement.

III. The Philosophical Principles of the Origins of Human Life

Modern science has clarified the material basis of human life in the male and female sex cells or gametes, namely, the sperm and ova (oocytes). Since the invention of the microscope in the 17th-century and especially since the invention of ultrasound technology in the 1950s, along with advances in genetics and human physiology, we now know exactly what happens during the reproduction process that results in an individual human being: the sperm fertilizes an ovum, leading to the combination of the chromosomes of both sex cells (a process known as syngamy), which results in a genetically unique individual living organism (a new genotype) with its own developmental trajectory. This knowledge of the reproductive process is so universal and obvious today, taught in schools and part of the common sense worldview of educated persons, that it comes across as trite and mundane when presented like this. However, its very *obviousness* and *matter-of-factness* is precisely what may obstruct a deeper and more encompassing understanding of the dynamics and nature of human generation. When we assume that we know exactly what something is, we are less open to seeing it from a different perspective or even to learning more about it. In short, the epistemic posture of certitude can, strangely, occlude our vision of reality.

The main problem with this knowledge of reproduction is that it is *merely* scientific or biological. It is culled from empirical observation and thus is strictly conditioned by sensory perception. Jacques Maritain has written much about this kind of mental attitude or standpoint towards reality which characterizes modern science, something he calls "empiriological knowledge," which means that the mind resolves its concepts in the sensible—in other words, the mind focuses exclusively on what the senses convey to it about reality.[17] Modern empiriological science, despite is many achievements, artificially reduces reality to the sensible domain and does not ac-

17. See Jacques Maritain, *Distinguish to Unite or The Degrees of Knowledge*, translated by Gerald B. Phelan (Notre Dame, Indiana: University of Notre Dame Press, 1995), 156–59.

cord any credibility to the intellect to penetrate to the very being of things, which would give us "ontological knowledge." The upshot here is that modern science does not give us the whole truth, but only a one-sided tale, and a very deficient account at that. The human mind must be permitted to grasp and understand the reality which we are dealing with in all its richness and depth. When such freedom is given to the intellect, we have entered the philosophical realm, for philosophy is nothing other than the free exercise of the intellect in its pursuit of the truth. When we are considering the phenomenon of human generation, the origin of human life itself, what can philosophy contribute that science has overlooked or ignored?

There are two important areas that philosophy can elucidate and correct with respect to certain scientific misunderstandings or misrepresentations concerning human life. The first deals with the principle of life. What makes something to be alive? Aristotle argued millennia ago that matter by itself does not make something to be alive. It is form, more precisely a special kind of form, which makes certain kinds of matter to be alive. I do want to rehearse the entire argument of *De anima*, but it might be worth repeating Aristotle's fundamental insight here: if matter were the principle of life, then all material things would be alive, which is clearly false.[18] Therefore, there must be something different from the matter which, furthermore, informs the matter of living things that makes them to be alive. Philosophers call this substantial form of a living body a soul. The soul is distinct and different from the body, yet it is the form of the body and thus unified with the body, both together constituting "one thing." There are three fundamental properties of the soul: (a) it is the substantial form of a body; (b) it is the actuality of a body; and (c) it is the principle of unity of a body.

The second thing that philosophy can add to this discussion is a notion of human nature. What is a human being? The traditional Aristotelian conception of the human being is that it is a particular kind of body animated by a rational soul. It is the presence of mind or intellect which is unique to human beings, not found in any other thing, whether animate or inanimate. It is the distinctive kind of soul, one which is rational or intellective, that constitutes the very nature or essence of a human being.

18. Aristotle, *On the Soul*, translated by J. A. Smith, in *The Complete Works of Aristotle*, volume 1, edited by Jonathan Barnes (Princeton, New Jersey: Princeton University Press, 1984), 2.1, 412a17–22: "Now given that there are bodies of such and such a kind, viz. having life, the soul cannot be a body; for the body is the subject or matter, not what is attributed to it. Hence the soul must be a substance in the sense of the form of a natural body having life potentially within it. But substance is actuality, and thus soul is the actuality of a body as above characterized."

The relationship between the rational soul and the human body is a complicated one. On the one hand, the rational soul is unified with the body as its substantial form. Thus, the body and soul constitute one thing (*unum simpliciter*). On the other hand, what makes the rational soul different from other kinds of soul is the presence of spirit, that is, the power to execute acts which transcend matter. The human being is capable of two such acts: knowing and willing. The operations of knowing and willing transcend the body and are not reducible to bodily functions. In this way, the rational soul, in its capacities of knowing and willing, is spiritual and thus is independent of the body. It is precisely in understanding this delicate relationship between the human body and rational soul, as unified and yet also distinct, that makes all the difference to a genuinely philosophical conception of human nature. The human being is indeed a unity of a material body and a spiritual soul. Furthermore, the spiritual soul is not reducible to or explained away by the material body. This relationship is further complicated by the indispensable Aristotelian principle that the body and form must fit or harmonize together appropriately. We can call this *the principle of fittingness*. The body must "fit" the soul and the soul must "fit" the body, just as a lock and key fit together, or to use an Aristotelian example, how the concave and convex sides of a nose fit together.[19] The basic insight guiding the principle of fittingness is that the soul must be suitable for the kind of body that it informs and animates. This rules out the possibility that one could have a body which is animated by a radically inappropriate or incompatible form, such as having a rational soul be the substantial form of a stone, or conversely, the form of a stone be the substantial form of a living human being.

In his essay, "Toward a Thomist Idea of Evolution," Jacques Maritain

19. See Fred D. Miller Jr., "Aristotle on the Separability of Mind," in *The Oxford Handbook of Aristotle*, edited by Christopher Shields (Oxford: Oxford University Press, 2012), 309: "Items are separate in account (*logos*) when they have different definitions, neither of which makes reference to the other. Things may be separable in definition even though they are not spatially separable. For example, an arc of a circle is both concave (from the inside) and convex (from the outside). Although concave and convex have different definitions which do not refer to each other (respectively, 'bending up' and 'bending down'), they are spatially inseparable because any arc which is concave is also convex and vice versa." For instance, see Aristotle, *On the Soul*, 3.10, 433b20–25: "To state the matter summarily at present, that which is the instrument in the production of movement is to be found where a beginning and an end coincide as e.g. in a ball and socket joint; for there the convex and concave sides are respectively an end and a beginning (that is why while the one remains at rest, the other is moved): they are separate in definition but not separable spatially."

presents some very useful philosophical concepts and distinctions to help us understand what is going on in the generation of a human being.[20] Both Aristotle and St. Thomas Aquinas taught that the human being passes through several stages of development from conception to maturity. These stages are based on a certain movement of substantial transformation: a substance undergoes corruption, after which a different substance is generated. Thus, at conception and for the first number of weeks the life of the fertilized ovum, blastocyst, or zygote is animated by a vegetative soul because its only functions at this stage are nourishment and growth. Then once a certain further development is attained the embryo lives by a sensitive soul because it is now able to experience sensations, such as pain. Finally, once the brain and nervous system are sufficiently developed the fetus is animated by a rational soul because now the material conditions of the body are in place to sustain the kinds of activities that are proper to a rational soul. Therefore, to reiterate, the human embryo passes through three distinct stages of life during its development, "where the fetus lives first by plant life, then by animal life, and finally by human life."[21]

If the rational soul is what makes a human being to be distinctively human, then this implies that the zygote/embryo/fetus only becomes human with the introduction of the rational soul and not before. This Aristotelian-Thomistic doctrine has come to be known as the delayed hominization or ensoulment thesis because it proposes that the embryo is not originally a human being and only becomes so once it acquires a rational soul, for, once again, it is the rational soul which is the substantial form of the human being, something that emerges roughly in the third trimester of pregnancy.[22] Many people reject this doctrine of delayed hominization because they believe that it opens the door to the moral permissibility of abortion, an act which is intrinsically evil. The purported danger can be summarized in the following way: if the zygote is not formally human, due to its not possessing a rational soul, then it would not be a moral outrage to abort it, for the abortion would not be of a human being. This Aristotelian-Thomistic doctrine of delayed hominization *seems* to support such a line of argumentation. So, to counter this potential threat, it is maintained that the fertilized ovum *is* a human being or even a person at

20. Jacques Maritain, "Toward a Thomist Idea of Evolution," in *Untrammeled Approaches*, translated by Bernard Doering (Notre Dame, Indiana: University of Notre Dame Press, 1997), 85–131.

21. Ibid., 92.

22. See David Albert Jones, *The Soul of the Embryo* (New York: Continuum, 2004), 109–24.

conception. As attractive as this assertion may be, a rigorous philosophical outlook on the issue cannot submit to it. It is understandable why someone would be motivated to affirm the humanity and personhood of the zygote—namely, to bestow upon it a much needed dignity and respect—but a deeper philosophical analysis of the situation does not support such a contention. This position of "immediate animation," that is, the view that the rational soul is somehow present immediately at conception instead of later on during the gestational development, violates the Aristotelian principle of fittingness, which holds that the matter must fit its form. The problem with the doctrine of immediate animation is that a blastocyst does not have the requisite material constitution in place to sustain a rational soul. In other words, the body of a blastocyst does not "fit" a rational soul. For if one accepted the premise that the rational soul is the substantial form of a blastocyst, then anything could have a rational soul—a stone, a lake, a house. The moment one accepts a logical impossibility as valid, then anything is possible, even self-contradictory propositions such as "a stone is a man."

Jacques Maritain is unequivocal in his endorsement of this Thomistic position on human generation. His words could not be clearer: "But I have no intention of abandoning St. Thomas' views on human generation; I consider them true and singularly enlightening."[23] He also writes: "To admit that the human fetus, from the instant of its conception, receives the intellective soul, while the matter is still in no way disposed with respect to it, is in my view a philosophical absurdity. It is just as absurd to call a fertilized ovum a *baby*."[24] And later on in the same chapter he also asserts, "Thus the two reasons proposed by modern theologians [that of abortion and the dogma of the Immaculate Conception] to insist that the rational soul is infused from the very first instant of conception are invalid. And, by virtue of the considerations which I have just indicated, the theory that the rational soul is infused from the very first moment of conception is philosophically untenable."[25] Maritain is not alone among philosophers in sup-

23. Maritain, "Toward a Thomist Idea of Evolution," in *Untrammeled Approaches*, 92.

24. Ibid., 93.

25. Ibid., 94. Contrast this last claim of Maritain's with the statements of William E. May, a Catholic bioethicist, who vehemently opposes the doctrine of delayed hominization: "The attempted rehabilitation of the 'delayed hominization' theory is philosophically untenable, and untenable on *Thomistic* grounds in light of what we *know* about the process of human generation." See *Catholic Bioethics and the Gift of Human Life* (Huntington, Indiana: Our Sunday Visitor, 2000), 163.

porting the Thomistic position: Elizabeth Anscombe also accepts it.[26] The physician and bioethicist Leon Kass expresses a similar conviction when he writes: "Granting that a human life begins at fertilization and develops via a continuous process thereafter, surely—one might say—the blastocyst itself can hardly be considered a human being. I myself would agree that a blastocyst is not, in a *full* sense, a human being—or what the current fashion calls, rather arbitrarily and without clear definition, a person."[27] Even the Magisterium of the Catholic Church does not teach that the rational soul is infused at the moment of conception.[28] This is why official Catholic teaching uses very specific language when it refers to the treatment of the human embryo. The Church always teaches that the embryo should be treated "as" a person, not that it "is" a person.[29] It emphasizes the moral disposition that one should adopt with respect to the embryo, rather than the embryo's actual ontological status.

The fear that many have of the doctrine of delayed hominization is that it seems to deny any value and humanity to the embryo in its earliest stages of life. It is certainly true that many theologians and philosophers

26. See G. E. M. Anscombe, "Embryos and Final Causes," in *Human Life, Action and Ethics*, edited by Mary Geach and Luke Gormally (Exeter, United Kingdom: Imprint Academic, 2005), 46: "I have for long myself had doubts about what is called 'immediate animation' and might more aptly be called 'immediate hominisation.'" For a comprehensive discussion of this issue of delayed hominization and for the traditional philosophical support for it, see Joseph F. Donceel, S.J., "Immediate Animation and Delayed Hominization," *Theological Studies* 31, no. 1 (1970): 76–105.

27. Leon R. Kass, M.D., *Life, Liberty and the Defense of Dignity* (San Francisco: Encounter Books, 2002), 88, emphasis in original.

28. See Congregation for the Doctrine of the Faith, "Declaration on Procured Abortion" (Nov. 18, 1974), in *Medical Ethics: Sources of Catholic Teachings*, 3rd ed., edited by Kevin D. O'Rourke and Philip Boyle (Washington, D.C.: Georgetown University Press, 1999), 37n19: "This declaration expressly leaves aside the question of the moment when the spiritual soul is infused. There is not a unanimous tradition on this point and authors are as yet in disagreement. For some it dates from the first instant, for others it could not at least precede nidation. It is not within the competence of science to decide between these views, because the existence of an immortal soul is not a question in its field. It is a philosophical problem from which our moral affirmation remains independent for two reasons: (1) supposing a later animation, there is still nothing less than a *human* life, preparing for and calling for a soul in which the nature received from parents is completed; (2) on the other hand it suffices for this presence of the soul be probable (and one can never prove the contrary) in order that the taking of life involve accepting the risk of killing a man, not only waiting for, but already in possession of his soul."

29. See Congregation for the Doctrine of the Faith, *Instruction on Respect for Human Life in its Origin and on the Dignity of Procreation: Replies to Certain Questions of the Day* (Sherbrooke, Quebec: Éditions Paulines, 1987), 17: "The human being must be respected—as a person—from the very first instant of his existence."

use this doctrine as a subterfuge for their pro-choice or pro-abortion commitments, arguing that Catholic teaching somehow supports the moral permissibility of abortion. However, such a use of the doctrine of delayed hominization is unwarranted and downright fraudulent. Direct abortion has always been and remains an intrinsic evil. This is the constant teaching of the Catholic Church. Furthermore, Thomas Aquinas and Jacques Maritain explicitly condemn abortion, despite their adherence to the doctrine of delayed animation/hominization. The way to argue for the moral impermissibility of abortion is not to circumvent or discard the theory of delayed hominization, which is philosophically justified, but to attempt to discover another cogent argument which vindicates both the humanity and dignity of the human embryo.

Maritain does this with the Thomistic distinction between virtual and formal human nature. The fetus which has the rational soul has human nature *formally*, but prior to this stage of development the embryo has human nature only *virtually*. The term "virtually" should not be interpreted along the lines of our contemporary, colloquial usage of this term as meaning "almost" or "nearly," terms which suggest that human nature is not present yet, but rather in the etymological sense of the Latin *virtus*, meaning "power," "strength," or "forcefulness." Maritain emphasizes that in this context "virtually" signifies "really." When we say that human nature is virtually present in the human embryo, we are affirming that human nature is *really* present, but just not formally. The concept of virtual human nature does not imply that the embryo is not human or does not possess human nature. *Au contraire*! The point of this concept is to introduce a subtle distinction between two kinds of reality: formal and virtual reality. In this way, Maritain affirms that the human embryo is indeed human, but only virtually, that is, *really*—a truth which makes abortion morally impermissible while it becomes formally human only later in its growth process. But this understanding and use of the term "virtual" may appear unusual to some. Is Maritain justified in interpreting the term "virtual" in this way by positing a different kind of reality, distinct from "formal reality"? I believe that he is. First, reality is not a univocal term. As Aristotle wrote long ago, reality (being) is spoken of in many different ways. No doubt, reality is an analogical concept; the reality of physical things is analogically proportional to the reality of divine being. Second, the word "virtue," although traditionally understood ethically as an exemplary character trait, certainly connotes different meanings more in line with its root etymology based on the Latin noun *vir* meaning "man," suggesting "strength," "valour," or "manliness." Third, in our contemporary world the adjective "virtual" is widely used in the phrase "virtual reality," which denotes the world of cyberspace and electronic communication via the internet. Virtual reality, in this sense, is one that is different from physical or material reality but which is nonetheless real, not imaginary or fictitious. Therefore, although Maritain is certainly not using the term "virtual" to refer to cyberspace, a contemporary audience would have no problem in grasping the meaning of the phrase "virtual reality." Ironically, it is arguable that the traditional ethical concept of "virtue"—and not that of "virtual reality"—might prove to be more mysterious to today's Western societies.

IV. The Moral Wrongness of *In vitro* Fertilization

It is a popular strategy at present for those who seek to defend the humanity of the embryo to point to its genetic code. Since the conceptus has human DNA, therefore it is clearly human and not a member of another animal species.[30] This line of argumentation is considered by many to be definitive in proving that the fertilized ovum is indeed human, even a human being. However, the error of this argument is that it reduces human nature to the biological or physical level; it purports that our humanness is strictly an aspect of our physical body (our DNA). We have already discussed that for the Aristotelian-Thomistic standpoint our human nature derives from our substantial form—our rational soul—and not from our matter or body. To assume that our genetic code constitutes fully and completely our human nature is to misrepresent our proper essence by reducing it unjustifiably to our bodily constitution. The chief defect of this argument is the denial of a spiritual element to our human nature. Our rational

30. See Congregation for the Doctrine of the Faith, *Instruction on Respect for Human Life*, 18: "This Congregation is aware of the current debates concerning the beginning of human life, concerning the individuality of the human being and concerning the identity of the human person. The Congregation recalls the teachings found in the *Declaration on Procured Abortion*: 'From the time that the ovum is fertilized, a new life is begun which is neither that of the father nor of the mother; it is rather the life of a new human being with its own growth. It would never be made human if it were not human already. To this perpetual evidence ... modern genetic science brings valuable confirmation. It has demonstrated that, from the first instant, the programme is fixed as to what this living being will be: a man, this individual-man with his characteristic aspects already well determined.'"

soul is not produced by our body or by our chromosomes. Since our rational soul is a spiritual soul and since spirit transcends matter, matter itself cannot produce something immaterial or spiritual—or to use Thomistic language, the rational soul is not *educed* from the animal body nor from the sensitive soul. This is why the rational, spiritual soul must be held to be infused into the body by God. The rational, spiritual soul is created directly by God and introduced into the human body from without. This doctrine of the infusion of the rational soul directly challenges the proposition that our humanness is found only and wholly in our DNA. If what makes us human is to have a rational, spiritual soul and if God is the author of this rational, spiritual soul, then our DNA does not define our humanness, if for no other reason than that it does not possess spirit.

What makes the procedure of *in vitro* fertilization morally reprehensible is that it reduces the human being to its biological reality. In other words, it denies the spiritual essence of the human being. By treating the human being as nothing more than the gametes fused together into a new individual organism, the persons involved in this process fail to recognize the true humanness of the fertilized ovum. This is a defect of human understanding, a failure to acknowledge what makes us truly human. We are more than our bodies—we have a spiritual essence which transcends our bodies. This is why one of the main criticisms of IVF is the argument that the actors in this procedure are treating the human embryo as an *object* and not as a *person*.[31] This reduction of the embryo to the status of an object or product in turn changes the nature of the relationship between the parent and the child, from one of equality to one of inequality. John Finnis puts this point eloquently:

> Products as such are assigned their meaning and value by the human makers who produce them, and the consumers who use them, and so the status of any product precisely as such is *sub*personal. That initial relationship, of those who choose to *produce* babies with the babies they produce, is inconsistent with, and so inherently impedes, the communion which is appropriate in any relationship among persons concerning the basic aspects of their personal well-being, their fundamental good. In short, the relations of producers to product is a relationship of domina-

31. See John Finnis, "C. S. Lewis and Test-Tube Babies," in *Human Rights and Common Good: Collected Essays Volume III* (Oxford: Oxford University Press, 2011), 273–81, at 278: "The essential conditions of the IVF child's origin, on the other hand, tend to assign this child, in its inception, the same status as other objects of acquisition. The technical skill and decisions of the child's makers will have produced, they hope, a good product, a desirable acquisition."

tion, which in itself is contrary to the dignity and equality which is appropriate to the parent-child relationship.[32]

The clinician who is combining the sex cells and the "parents" who have given consent to this procedure are treating the embryo as a product, as something sub-personal, as a merely material object. As morally repugnant as this may be, on one level it is not totally surprising since it is true, as we have been arguing, that the conceptus is not *formally* human until much later on in its development. To a certain extent, people can be forgiven for believing that the zygote is not a full human being because it does lack the form of the rational soul which is the *sine qua non* of our formal humanness. The line of defense which holds that the zygote is a human being because it possesses human DNA is, as I argued above, a spurious argument because it relies on a false and misleading conception of human nature: namely, one that judges our humanness to be identified solely with our material body.

Yet the zygote is undeniably human. No reasonable person would suggest that it is not. After all, the individuals who are engaged in the process of IVF are certainly cognizant that they are dealing with a human embryo and not the embryo of some other animal species. A human child, to be blunt, is exactly what individuals who pursue the course of IVF are aiming to procure. It goes without saying that the whole process of IVF would be a complete and utter failure if we did not know that the embryo was human. In that case the end which is intended, which is the birth of a human baby, would not be achieved. However, we need to clarify how exactly and in what way the zygote or conceptus, prior to the infusion of the rational soul, is human. We have already broached Maritain's notion of a virtual human nature. Let's examine this idea more closely, for it contains the key to identifying what precisely is morally objectionable with IVF.

Maritain explains that the concept of "virtue" in this context denotes the form of a movement. This form is not entitative, as with a thing or object, but is transitive, in the sense that it exerts a power or force onto something. This is not an outlandish interpretation of the concept of form, for both Aristotle and Aquinas recognized it. For instance, there are forms of material things in the world, such as stones, tables, and houses, but there are also forms as powers or capacities such as sight (the power to see as

32. John Finnis, "On Producing Human Embryos," in *Intention and Identity: Collected Essays Volume II* (Oxford: Oxford University Press, 2011), 299; emphasis in original.

the form of the eye) or hearing (the power to hear as the form of the ear). Aristotle tells us that if the eye loses the power to see in a case of blindness then the eye ceases to be an eye.[33] The power to see is the form of the eye and if the form is the actuality of the thing that it informs, then if the form is no longer present, the thing itself also goes out of existence. In the case of blindness, we still say that the blind man has "eyes," but we speak equivocally here—those are not *really* eyes. For the very being or substance of an eye is "to see" and once this power is removed, then the eye ceases to be what it is. Virtue, on Maritain's interpretation, is the form of a movement, a process, a development, a spiritual force or forcefulness that is present and communicated in a movement. Moreover, virtue belongs to the instrumental order, in the sense that virtue makes use of things for it to be communicated. It requires physical things which it utilizes as tools or instruments to convey transitively its form to something else. Remember: it is a transitive form, not an entitative form.

Maritain gives three examples to illustrate this specific meaning of "virtue."[34] First, when I speak and use language I am conveying my thoughts through my voice to someone else. The virtue of my intelligence is communicated in and controls the movement of the exhalation of air when I speak intelligibly to people. Contrast this situation with someone who reads a book out loud, such as at a lecture or church liturgy, and is merely mechanically mouthing the words without understanding them. Here the spoken words would not be directed by and communicating the intelligible understanding of the words. In this second situation, virtue would not be present in the spoken words. The words would come across as empty, without force, spiritless. Second, consider the artistic talent of Michelangelo.

33. Aristotle, *On the Soul*, 2.1, 412b18–22: "Suppose that the eye were an animal—sight would have been its soul, for sight is the substance of the eye which corresponds to the account, the eye being merely the matter of seeing; when seeing is removed the eye is no longer an eye, except in name—no more than the eye of a statue or of a painted figure." See also St. Thomas Aquinas, *Commentary on Aristotle's* De Anima, translated by Kenelm Foster, O.P., and Silvester Humphries, O.P. (Notre Dame, Indiana: Dumb Ox Books, 1994), 78–79: "If, he says, the eye were a whole animal, its soul would be sight; for sight is the essential form of the eye; which in itself is the material condition of sight; in the same way as an organic body is the material condition of a soul. Once sight is lost, the eye is no longer an eye, except in the sense that a stone or painted eye may be called an eye equivocally (this term is used when the same name is given to essentially different things). Remove, then, what makes an eye really an eye, and there is left only the name. And the same argument applies to the animate body as a whole: what makes it an animate body is its form, the soul. This removed, you have a living body only equivocally."

34. Maritain, "Towards a Thomist Idea of Evolution," in *Untrammeled Approaches*, 97–99.

His artistic genius as a sculptor is communicated by virtue of his chisel and into the marble he is sculpting. His arms, hands, and chisel are expressing his genius. It is clear that his spiritual talent as an artist is communicated instrumentally and moves or passes through his bodily limbs and tools and it makes its physical mark on the marble slab in the real world which is transformed into a magnificent work of art. Third, the composer of a symphony writes down his music into notes in a score which the musicians of an orchestra play. The composer's musical creativity is played by virtue of the score and the musicians and the musical instruments. There is a movement from the composer's mind through the sheet music and into the musicians and their instruments which is ultimately received by the audience. In each of these examples the movement of speech, sculpting, or music has a specific form which we call "virtue." It involves a process, in the instrumental order, by which something spiritual (a thought, an intuition, a talent, an inspiration) is manifested physically (a spoken word, a marble sculpture, a musical symphony) through a meaningful process.

Maritain gives us the following definition of virtue: "virtue is *the form of a caused movement by which the action of the efficient cause, when it is not instantaneous, controls the whole instrumentality which leads to the final effect, as long as the process of causation lasts*."[35] Maritain also emphasizes that virtue depends on *formal* causality, not on *efficient* causality.[36] This is an important point. The form of the movement (the virtue) is not due to the agent (the speaker, the sculptor, the composer)—that is, the efficient cause—but inheres in the meaningfulness and directionality of the movement itself. One could say that the particular movement or operation or activity has a momentum all its own, just as when a bowler launches a bowling ball down a lane—the rolling ball has an intelligible trajectory in its movement after the bowler has separated himself from the ball. After all, the composer of the musical score is not the one who is actually performing the music, though the form of the score is the movement of the music. Similarly, the lector at a church Mass is reading the Bible, but it is the understood meaning of the words which is the form of the movement of the reading itself. And it is the form of the sculpture which Michelangelo is set on creating which passes through his arms, hands, and chisel—not Michelangelo himself, who is the efficient cause.

35. Ibid., 99.
36. Ibid., 98.

Having discussed all this, what does this particular concept of "virtue" have to do with human procreation and the procedure of *in vitro* fertilization in creating human embryos? Maritain tells us that the human embryo has human nature *virtually*. What does this mean? The humanness of the embryo is derived, not from its possessing a rational soul (an entitative form), but from its participation in a movement which was begun by its parents. The embryo is human because it resides in a meaningful movement of procreation initiated by its parents and terminating in its becoming a full and independent human being. When a man and a woman engage in the generative or conjugal act, they initiate the movement of procreation. Yes, the conjugal act is procreative, in the sense that a new human being can be conceived and born from this act. But what is happening here is that the man and the woman are participating in an act—called the generative or conjugal act—which has a certain form or intelligibility embedded in it, irrespective of the motivations or intentions of the man and woman (their efficient causality). The procreative process bestows human nature upon the newly conceived conceptus because it is part of a unique process or movement which generates a new human being. The form of the movement of procreation—its virtue—is the communication of and the passing of human nature from the parents to the embryo, instrumentally, by virtue of the gametes (sperm and ovum). Human nature is transmitted to the embryo from its parents in the procreative act. Of course, we are speaking about human nature in its fullness, both physical and spiritual, that is transferred to the embryo from the parents. The physical part of that nature is in the gametes that constitute the biological reality of the embryo. However, the spiritual part of that human nature is the *form of the movement* of human generation and development. The embryo is a participant in a movement, a process whose inherent form or meaning is to generate and give birth to new human life.

What *in vitro* fertilization does is to remove the embryo from this human-generating movement of procreation. The embryo produced in a Petri dish does not participate in the life-generating movement of the parents initiated by the conjugal act and sustained by the body of the mother. Not only does IVF reduce the embryo to a mere physical object and thus depersonalizes it, but it robs it of its life-sustaining and life-nurturing environment in the body. The human being is not only a specific individual organism but is determined in its fundamental essence by intersubjectivity, that is, the union of persons, which is nothing other than the love expressed by the man and woman in the conjugal act. It is true that the *matter* of the embryo undergoes its own internal development in accordance with its genetic code. This is why the embryo does indeed begin to undergo mitosis and growth in the Petri dish even though it is not being sustained in this *movement* by the human form of its parents. However, simple cell division is not to be equated with a truly human development. For as we have been arguing, the zygote is not formally human but derives its humanness from participating in a uniquely human-generating act, that being the conjugal act of the parents. So, the basic problem of IVF is that it deprives the embryo of its humanness right at the beginning of its life, a humanness that is not ontic or entitative but is a distinctive process of becoming: the movement of becoming fully and formally human.

The upshot of this reflection on the beginnings of human life is that human nature and human dignity are essentially linked to human procreation, that is, the way in which human beings are conceived, generated, and born. Our culture tends to downplay the manner by which human life is originated, considering it to be all the same. But what so many do not recognize is that our earthly origins need to be preserved in a continuum with the spiritual union of love of our parents which enshrines an interpersonal dimension into the very core of our being. In her acerbic commentary on the dehumanizing consequences of *in vitro* fertilization, Elizabeth Anscombe does not mince her words:

> Procreation by the male in the female is intrinsic to the mode of a new human life's coming about by human operation. Why? It is because what the operation is bringing about *is* human life. Fatherhood—which means procreation—and motherhood—which means conception—are a very important part of the human relationships constituting the life of man. Making human zygotes in a dish or test-tube is an enormity because the operator is a manufacturer—even if he uses his own semen—not a father. ... The child who is conceived by a mother, and who has a father, is not unequal to them. I think people have hardly considered what will be the status of babies who have not even grown inside a woman and been born.[37]

The problem with so much of contemporary reproductive technology is that the human being is regarded in solely entitative terms, reduced to the

37. G. E. M. Anscombe, "The Dignity of the Human Being," in *Human Life, Action and Ethics*, edited by Mary Geach and Luke Gormally (Exeter, United Kingdom: Imprint Academic, 2005), 70–71; emphasis in original.

status of a thing or object, and as such is capable of being manipulated. What is ignored is the crucial truth that to be human means to be involved in a movement sustained by one's parents. This movement is what we call a human life and this aspect of one's humanity has to be present right at the beginning of one's existence. Expressed differently, human beings are not static things, like rocks, but are the movement of life itself. To be human is to move, to change, to grow, in specifically human ways.

V. The Teleological Structure of Human Life

If human beings are constituted by a movement, which is the cause of their generation and which carries them forward throughout life, as a ship out at sea, this movement must have a goal or end. Every movement is teleological in its nature. It goes somewhere, aims at a target, is geared towards an end. This final cause of the movement bestows upon the movement its purpose and impetus. As Aquinas argues, the final cause of a process is the true explanation for the process without which the process would cease to be. The final cause is "the reason for which the efficient cause acts; in short, as the cause of causes ... the final cause tells us the reason for which things exist."[38] For it is incoherent for there to be a movement without there being an end towards which it is directed.

The final cause must be present at the origin of the movement. The movement does not gain its final cause at some later moment but is determined by the final cause right at the outset. In this way the parents who engage in the conjugal act are already participating in the final cause of the movement of their sexual congress that will result in the conception of a human life. It is helpful to understand the sexual act itself as containing a teleological structure: people engage in sex for a certain end. The Catholic tradition has emphasized that the conjugal act has two inseparable ends: a unitive and procreative end. The sexual act expresses the love between the spouses and also moves in the direction of the generation of new life. However, even before the couple enter into the act of sexual congress, there is the fact of sexual attraction which motivates the individuals to embrace each other in this way.

38. Étienne Gilson, *Thomism: The Philosophy of Thomas Aquinas*, 6th ed., translated by Laurence K. Shook and Armand Maurer (Toronto: Pontifical Institute of Medieval Studies, 2002), 74.

Saint John Paul II, known also by his given name of Karol Wojtyla, has given this appetitive feature of human sexuality the name *the sexual urge.*[39] The sexual urge is distinguished from the sexual instinct. Instinct has a merely biological, reflexive, and automatic meaning, something that an organism executes without much thought or volition. In this way the sexual instinct is a product of biological evolution in which human beings spontaneously find themselves sexually attracted to persons of the opposite sex. By contrast, the sexual urge is full of meaning and significance because it is anchored in the recognition of values. A certain consciousness of values is inherent in the sexual urge. The values that are pertinent in this regard are moral and spiritual ones, such as the distinction between good and evil, and between the person and an object—the former which has an absolute value and the latter possessing a conditional one. What this suggests is that the sexual urge involves thought, moral awareness, judgement, and choice. It is not an impersonal force thrusting individuals impetuously into each other's arms, but signifies the truly human manner by which human beings engage each other in forms of life that favor the expression of our sexuality. These include the many different customs and rituals that have been developed in our civilization over time, such as courtship, betrothal, and marriage.

Yet the most important aspect of the sexual urge is its teleological structure. It has a purpose and end. Its meaningfulness and coherence are ultimately due to its being focused on a particular target of its movement of attraction. Wojtyla calls the sexual urge "a vector of aspiration":

> When we speak of the sexual urge in man we have in mind not an interior source of specific actions somehow 'imposed in advance,' but a certain orientation, a certain direction in man's life implicit in his very nature. The sexual *urge* in this conception is a *natural drive born in all human beings, a vector of aspiration* along which their whole existence develops and perfects itself from within.[40]

Wojtyla is adamant that this sexual urge is in all human beings, in the sense that it is a distinctively human property. He describes it as a drive, a force, some power that channels human beings to move in a certain direction. But what is this end towards which the sexual urge is geared? The end of the sexual urge, Wojtyla tells us, is the existence of the human species. It

39. Karol Wojtyla, *Love and Responsibility*, translated by H. T. Willetts (San Francisco: Ignatius Press, 1981), 45–54.

40. Ibid., 46; emphasis in original.

is responsible for the very existence of the human species. In this way the sexual urge is constitutive of humanity, not simply in terms of its essence, but also its existence. This is why Wojtyla writes that the sexual urge has an existential and not a biological significance:

> The existence of the whole species *Homo* depends directly on [the sexual urge]. The species could not exist if it were not for the sexual urge and its natural results. ... Human kind can be maintained in being only so long as individual people, individual men and women, human couples, obey the sexual urge. It furnishes ... what we may call material for love between persons, between man and woman. ... The proper end of the urge, the end *per se*, is something supra-personal, the existence of the species *Homo*, the constant prolongation of its existence.[41]

When a human couple engages in the conjugal act, they are participating in a procreative act, one that can generate new human life. This new human life is not only an individual, which it certainly is, but also represents the human species. We can make sense of this proposition if we keep in mind that the sexual urge, the appetite that motivates us to engage in sexual acts, does not belong to us *qua* our individuality, but *qua* our humanity, as members of the human species. In other words, the sexual urge is not unique to us as individuals, but ushers from our human nature itself which is universally present in all human beings. Therefore, when a man and woman engage in the conjugal act they are participating in an act that has a significance for the human species as a whole. The baby who is generated from this act is not only an individual human being but is also a being who has a universal human nature and thus possesses a value that transcends his individuality.

It is arguable that today we have lost sight of this dimension of human procreation which embeds its meaning on the level of the species as a whole. Too many people view the sexual act as having only an individual meaning, restricted to their own individual bodies and agency and desires. In truth, the force which propels human beings into sexual acts and which is responsible for human reproduction attains to a truly transcendent end. Aristotle described the act of reproduction in *On the Soul* as a participation in eternity and divinity, in a passage that deserves to be quoted at length:

> For any living thing that has reached its normal development and which is unmutilated, and whose mode of generation is not spontaneous, the most natural act

41. Ibid., 51.

> is the production of another like itself, an animal producing an animal, a plant a plant, in order that, as far as its nature allows, it may partake in the eternal and divine. That is the goal towards which all things strive, that for the sake of which they do whatsoever their nature renders possible. The phrase "for the sake of which" is ambiguous; it may mean either the end to achieve which, or the being in whose interest, the act is done. Since then no living thing is able to partake in what is eternal and divine by uninterrupted continuance (for nothing perishable can for ever remain one and the same), it tries to achieve that end in the only way possible to it, and success is possible in varying degrees; so it remains not indeed as the self-same individual but continues its existence in something like itself—not numerically but specifically one.[42]

The desire for sexual intimacy between persons of the opposite sex can be legitimately understood as a desire for eternity. It is anchored in the human self-awareness of mortality. Because human beings die, they naturally desire in this life to aspire to eternal life, to a status of immortality, which clearly cannot be attained in this individual physical body. Therefore, the way this eternity is pursued and brought about in this life is through the act of reproduction which creates new human life. Through this procreative act the human species continues to exist beyond the finite time span of an individual human life. In short, the individual person will die one day, but the human species will endure, seemingly forever, and this is all owing to the sexual urge whose proper end is the existence of the human species.

This temporal dimension of the sexual urge and the sexual act is an important one to consider. The human being who has the sexual urge within him is the same being who is cognizant of his own mortality, that his days on this earth are numbered. Human sexuality is very much tied to the mortality of human life. The way human beings live is to pass through different stages of development: the gestational development in a mother's womb, followed by birth, then infancy, adolescence, adulthood, old age, and death. This passage from one moment to another, from earlier phases of life to later ones, is the very substance of the human experience of time. Time forces upon human beings the consciousness of our own mortality. But simultaneous to this self-awareness is the attention paid to the other. What I mean by this is the orientation towards other human beings ensconced in our nature. We move toward forming relationships with others precisely because we perceive our own life as finite and destined for an eventual

42. Aristotle, *On the Soul,* 2.4, 415a27–415b8.

death. The formation of relationships, such as in the marriage between a man and woman, serves the end of attaining some hold on eternity, albeit imperfectly in this temporal life. The love which binds a married couple together partakes in a transcendent, imperishable domain which is the heart of divinity. This is why the procreative act between a man and woman is not only a movement towards eternity but also divinity, as Aristotle suggests. The sexual act has a direct connection with God, in the sense that the trajectory of the movement embedded in the sexual urge leads to the end of eternal life which is the very essence of God.

Those individual human beings who are produced by *in vitro* fertilization have their life's trajectory frustrated because they were not generated through a truly human conjugal act. What is missing for such individuals is this underlying impulse of love that should have been the motivating force in their parents' relationship with each other and which should have been concretely present at the very origin of their child's life. The sin of artificial forms of reproduction is to ignore the profound meaning of human life as a participation in eternity and to replace it with a counterfeit philosophy of life which treats human beings as manipulable things. For what is at stake in this discussion is the meaning of human life itself which philosophy constantly seeks to address: Why was I born? What is the purpose of my life? By nature, my existence is supposed to be due to the sexual urge. Yet modern reproductive science and the political societies which support it through legislation understand human beings as constructible, like products in a factory. As I have argued in this essay, human beings are not reducible to mere matter—that is, to their bodies—but need to be sustained by a human environment which is saturated with love and spirit. This does not mean that all hope is lost for such individuals; they may still acquire the momentum of the movement of life which *God,* and not their parents, established at the foundation of the world. Nonetheless, it is inexcusable for human beings intentionally to injure another human being's natural movement of life by resorting to the immoral practice of *in vitro* fertilization.

V

FAITH, CHURCH, AND PRIESTHOOD

ROMANUS CESSARIO, O.P.

Sacrifice and Priesthood

Maritain's Still *Untrammeled Approaches*

I. Maritain as Harbinger

THE ESSAYS THAT I WILL discuss from Maritain's *Untrammeled Approaches* exhibit how much philosophical flair helps to illuminate the most profound theological realities of the Catholic religion. To be sure, Maritain's two essays on sacrifice and priesthood, respectively, exhibit his acumen as a philosophical theologian. However, I selected them for another reason. Each reveals Jacques Maritain as an early critic—one both prescient and astute—of directions in Catholic theology that would gain prominence after the Second Vatican Council. These directions, moreover, still require critical appraisal. More poignantly then, one might describe Maritain as a Cassandra figure, a harbinger of things to come. Why? These two essays contain subtle warnings about misguided theological moves that can catch Catholic theologians off guard, as it were. So, as Father Lonergan says, this essay aims to shift the probabilities.

Maritain raises, albeit obliquely, a first caution concerning the sacrifice that stands at the heart of the Eucharistic liturgy. As I have pointed out elsewhere, the notion of the Eucharist as a sacrifice received scant attention during the composition of the Second Vatican Council's 1963 constitution of the liturgy, *Sacrosanctum concilium*.[1] This trimmed treatment resulted in an eclipse of sacrifice both in theological prose about the Eucharist and

1. See Romanus Cessario, O.P., "The Sacraments of the Church" in *Vatican II: Renewal Within Tradition*, edited by Matthew L. Lamb and Matthew Levering (Oxford: Oxford University Press, 2008), 129–46.

in the popular Catholic imagination. One concrete sign of this mentality appears in the reduced number of Mass intentions for both the living and the dead that pastors report receiving from their parishioners. Likewise, the enormously rich suite of commentaries that since the sixteenth century sought to explain how in the Catholic Mass Christ's sacrifice on Calvary achieves re-enactment without repetition—including those writings that developed within the Thomist commentatorial tradition—have fallen out of even most seminary instruction. This turn of events ought to give one moment for pause. Priests who do not know that they sacrifice each time that they celebrate Mass suffer a handicap when it comes to the practice of pastoral charity. Their nescience shrinks their communication with the source of divine love as clogged arteries impede the flow of blood to the heart.[2] All the difference in the world exists between a priest who knows that, at the altar, he stands with Christ on Calvary, Victim and Priest, and the priest who thinks that he presides over a communitarian symbolic activity—for example, a shared meal. This difference does not necessarily affect the validity of the Eucharistic conversion that occurs at each Mass. However, the difference shows up in the psychological dispositions of the priest celebrant and, sadly, oftentimes in what is communicated to the congregation in the symbolist priest's words and gestures.

The intrinsic relationship that exists between the priest and the sacrifice of the Mass introduces the second of Maritain's themes—namely, the place of the priest, his identity, within the hierarchical structure of the Church. At the same time that *Sacrosanctum concilium* left underdeveloped the notion of sacrifice, *Lumen gentium*, the dogmatic constitution on the Church promulgated in 1964, brought new attention to the relationship of the common priesthood of the faithful to, as we say today, the ministerial priesthood. The conciliar text runs, "The common priesthood of the faithful and the ministerial or hierarchical priesthood, though they differ in essence and not simply in degree, are nevertheless interrelated: each in its own particular way shares (*participant*) in the one priesthood of Christ."[3] Although this text was not designed to surrender easily to a Lutheran interpretation, many Catholics, in fact, began to discourse as if they were Lutherans. That

2. For further discussion, see Romanus Cessario, O.P., "'Circa res . . . aliquid fit': Aquinas on New Law Sacrifice," in *Theology and Sanctity*, edited by Cajetan Cuddy, O.P. (Ave Maria, Florida: Sapientia Press, 2014), 99–119.

3. Vatican Council II, *"Lumen gentium,"* in *Decrees of the Ecumenical Councils*, vol. 2, translated by Norman Tanner (London: Sheed and Ward, 1990), 857.

is, they spoke as though it were orthodox to confess that—in the words of one Baptist theologian—"every Christian is someone else's priest, and we are all priests to one another."[4] Not a few Catholics in Europe and the United States also attempted to act as if this undifferentiated egalitarianism were Catholic doctrine. However, such a distortion of Catholic teaching —that is, one that denies the essential difference between priest and layman—wreaks havoc on the Church. Priests who do not recognize who they are precisely as priests suffer from a handicap more parlous than what arises from their remaining nescient about their identity as sacrificers. Such priests fail to consider their "spiritual existence," to borrow an expression from *Pastores dabo vobis*.[5] For his part, Maritain prefers to focus on the functions of the priest, though without his reducing completely the sacred priesthood to a functional specialty within the Christian community.

Today many of the missteps in Catholic theology that multiplied after 1965 have been to some extent corrected by subsequent magisterial determinations. Still, as declining Mass attendance and other noxious symptoms reveal, these salutary indications have not always been followed. However, it exceeds the objectives of this communication to put Humpty Dumpty back together again. Instead, let Maritain's thought-provoking essays remind us how to think rightly about two irreplaceable elements of the Catholic religion: sacrifice and priesthood. Maritain knew that both Eucharistic sacrifice and priests remain indispensable constituents of Catholic life and practice. What is more important, the Church follows his untrammeled path, as again *Pastores dabo vobis* reminds us: "Priests, as ministers of sacred things, are first and foremost ministers of the sacrifice of the Mass (see *Presbyterorum Ordinis*, 13): The role is utterly irreplaceable, because without the priest there can be no eucharistic offering."[6]

II. The Catholic Thinker

What are the specific questions about the Eucharist and priesthood that Maritain helps us to explore? Mention, first of all, goes to the sacrifice of

4. Timothy George, *Theology of the Reformers* (Nashville, Tennessee: Broadman and Holman Publishing Group, 2015), 96.

5. Pope John Paul II, *Pastores dabo vobis* (1992): no. 21.

6. *Pastores dabo vobis*, no. 48. For further discussion, see Romanus Cessario, O.P., "Aquinas on the Priest: Sacramental Realism and the Indispensable and Irreplaceable Vocation of the Priest," in *Theology and Sanctity*, 133–50.

the Mass which, in words Maritain cites approvingly, "is *identically the very sacrificial act of Calvary*."[7] Then comes the "indelible character" of Holy Orders which priests receive at their ordination. This tenet of the faith invites theologians to explain properly the sacramental character's nature and supernatural effects in both the person and the actions of priests.[8] Both essays appear in the collection *Approches sans Entraves*, first published at Paris in 1973, the year that Maritain died. The first essay, "The Sacrifice of the Mass," falls under the sub-heading, "A Look at Theology (I)." The second essay, "*Apropos* of the French School," falls under the sub-heading of "A Supplement to the Book *On the Church of Christ*."[9] Maritain's essays on the sacrifice of the Mass and the Catholic priesthood originally were published in 1968 and 1971 respectively. Their compositions date, then, from the period shortly after the Second Vatican Council (1962–1965). Maritain, nonetheless, knew that the theological issues to which he turned his attention owed their origins to discussions that transpired during a period that followed an earlier ecumenical council, the Council of Trent, celebrated during a time in the history of the Church that produced its own contradictions and resolutions.

The Catholic Reform that follows the sixteenth-century Council of Trent (1545–1563) opens up a vast field of historical and theological investigation. Maritain, as his essay on the *Three Reformers* indicates, understood deeply the ruptures—religious (Luther), philosophical (Descartes), and moral (Rousseau)—that affected European life from the start of the sixteenth century.[10] He also realized that the Catholic Reform arrived later in France than in other places of Catholic Europe. The flourishing of the post-Tridentine reforms, the Catholic Reform, followed a tumultuous period of civil discord in *la belle France* known as the French Wars of Religion (1562–1598). In his informative study of seventeenth-century France, *Church, Society and Reli-*

7. The words are from Cardinal Journet; see Maritain, "The Sacrifice of the Mass," in *Untrammeled Approaches*, translated by Bernard Doering (Notre Dame, Indiana: University of Notre Dame Press, 1997), 351.

8. See *Catechism of the Catholic Church*, no. 1582: "The sacrament of Holy Orders, like the other two, confers an indelible spiritual character and cannot be repeated or conferred temporarily."

9. Maritain, *Untrammeled Approaches*, 424–41; see Maritain, *On the Church of Christ: The Person of the Church and Her Personnel*, translated by Joseph W. Evans (Notre Dame, Indiana: University of Notre Dame Press, 1973).

10. See Jacques Maritain, *Three Reformers. Luther, Descartes, Rousseau* (New York: Apollo Editions, 1970), 4.

gious Change in France 1580–1730, Joseph Bergin has shown that despite the fire and ashes that characterized the late sixteenth-century civil conflict in France, "so much of the energy and initiatives for religious change at work during the early part of the seventeenth century were rooted in the experiences of those earlier decades."[11] Maritain further understood that the Catholic Reform made of seventeenth-century France, especially in light of the seventy-two year reign of the French King, Louis XIV (1643–1715), a rich seedbed both for renewal of the Church and for worldwide missionary activity. Think of the North American martyrs. For all of his Frenchness, however, Maritain's investigations, especially on the Eucharist, take account of Catholic authors from other parts of Europe. By contrast, when he treats the priesthood, Maritain opposes one of the luminous figures of early seventeenth-century French spiritual renewal.

These essays, which clearly exhibit the work of one justly called a philosophical theologian, evoke various historical issues and contexts.[12] In other words, to grasp fully Maritain's analytical genius, we need to recall the post-Tridentine history of Catholic theological investigation. The first essay about the identicalness of the sacrifice of the Mass with the sacrifice of Calvary returns us to the sixteenth-century debates that emerged around the Council of Trent's teaching and canons on the most holy sacrifice of the Mass.[13] The second discussion brings us back to the start of the seventeenth century when the luminous Pierre de Bérulle (1575–1629), priest, cardinal, and statesman, launched a reform of the diocesan clergy through the establishment in 1611 of the French Oratory, the *Société de l'Oratoire de Jésus et de Marie Immaculée.*

III. A Saraband of Competing Explanations

We consider first the essay on the sacrifice of the Mass which grows out of a 1965 seminar that Maritain gave at Toulouse to the Little Brothers of Jesus. However, before we turn to the essay, we should recall the enormous energy that, from the start of the early modern period until the early twentieth century, Catholic theologians devoted to accounting for the

11. Joseph Bergin, *Church, Society and Religious Change in France 1580–1730* (New Haven, Connecticut: Yale University Press, 2009), 3.

12. For example, see the description used by the German-American philosopher, Nicholas Rescher, in his *Autobiography: Revised edition* (Frankfurt: Ontos Verlag, 2010), 60.

13. Session 22 held on 17 September 1562. See *DS* nos. 1738–60.

fact that the Mass remains a real and true sacrifice. One indication may be gleaned from the general or analytical tables of the *Dictionnaire de Théologie Catholique*, which appeared in 1951. Volume sixteen, part one, devotes seven columns, cols. 1350–1356, to the indexing alone of what theologians after Trent—not a few of them French authors—wrote about the essence and the efficacity of the Mass. These opinions represent the various efforts of Catholic theologians to tweak the definition of sacrifice that Aquinas gives in the *Summa theologiae* so that it will apply to the Tridentine canons that teach authoritatively about the "divine sacrifice which is performed (*peragitur*) in the Mass."[14]

These tables classify the significant authors under three general headings. The first general conception explains the Mass as a sacrifice because the priest does something that serves as a representative act of the sacrifice of the cross. Subdivisions of this general category include: (1) broad formulations and (2) specific theories. Each of the theories listed under this heading seeks to identify what precisely the priest does in order to represent Calvary. Under the first subdivision, broad formulations, one finds three different estimates about which priestly action during the Mass in fact represents sacrifice: (1.1) the fraction rite, (1.2) the communion rite, or (1.3) the double consecration. Some thirteen different theologians espoused one or another of these three approaches; the majority of them, however, followed the sixteenth-century Thomist author Thomas de Vio Cardinal Cajetan (1469–1534). He identifies the double consecration—separate words pronounced over the dual species of bread and wine—as a figurative immolation that resides at the heart of the Eucharistic celebration.[15]

Under the second subdivision, particular theories, one finds, first, the developed opinion of the Jesuit Gabriel Vasquez (d. 1604): namely, that the consecration itself represents the real sacrifice of Calvary, whereas the Mass itself can only be described as a relative sacrifice since the victim remains without change. And in second place, the theory of another Jesuit, Leonard Lessius (d. 1623), which holds for the Mass as a "virtual" immolation and so, argues this theologian, recalls without re-enacting the sac-

14. For Aquinas's definition of sacrifice, see ST II-II, q. 85, a. 3 and ad 3. For Trent, see *DS* no. 1746.

15. See his *De missae sacrificio et ritu adversus Lutheranos*, chap VI: "immolatitio modo repraesentans."

rifice of Calvary. And lastly, there develops a slight variation on the above theories, one elaborated especially by the French Bishop Jacques-Bénigne Bossuet (d. 1704). He sees in the sacramental separation of the Body and Blood of Christ, that is, of the two species "mystiquement séparés," an appearance of death in the Jesus-host. This sacramental separation effects a mystical immolation (which is distinguished from a virtual one), such that the words of consecration function as a sword that slays Christ under the appearances of bread and wine.[16]

The second general category of explanations includes authors who argue that sacrifice is assured by a change in the matter or in the victim. Although there are earlier authors who point directly to the "destruction" of the bread and wine, this thesis is identified with the Jesuit Francis Suarez (d. 1617), who made transubstantiation itself the change that assured sacrifice because of the destruction of the bread and wine. Critics, however, note that this Renaissance scholar remained satisfied with leaving the Mass specifically and essentially distinct from the sacrifice of the Cross. The Jesuit saint, Robert Bellarmine (d. 1621), taught that the immolation affected Christ himself, that is, the consecration prepares the victim and the communion destroys it. Another Jesuit cardinal, John de Lugo (d. 1660), speaks about an annihilation, in which the glorious Christ is destroyed in his human mode of existence.

The third general category includes those authors who present the Mass as an oblation of the sacrifice of the Cross, whether by Christ himself or by the Church. This thesis is associated with the aforementioned Cardinal de Bérulle and his Oratory and spread even as far as the United States in the person of the scholarly Francis Patrick Kenrick, Archbishop of Baltimore (d. 1863).

This catalogue does not result in an airtight categorization of theories. Instead, a close inspection of the authors cataloged displays cross-fertilization among them. Since more than a hundred published authors appear in the *Dictionnaire,* what else may one reasonably expect to discover? Further, this entry does not include the countless pious authors who, in order to present the Mass as a sacrifice, summarized and popularized these theories in

16. For further information, see Romanus Cessario, O.P., "Sacrifice, Social and Sacramental: The Witness of Louis Billot, S.J.," *Nova et Vetera,* English Edition, 14 (2016): 127–49. In this essay, however, I do not address the underlying difference in explanatory concepts that distinguish thinkers such as Billot from mainline Thomist authors such as Cajetan.

their manuals of devotion and prayer books. Each one played a part in the valiant effort of the Catholic Counter-Reform to preserve authentic Catholic teaching about the Blessed Sacrament of the Altar. Contrary to pluralist optimism, diverse theological opinions do not always edify. In fact, Maritain employs a colorful metaphor to describe the band of theologians who used their ingenuity to defend the Tridentine canons. He compares them to the saraband: that is, a dance in triple time that resembles the farandole, a lively Provençal terpsichore in which the dancers join hands and, forming a chain, wind in and out.[17] This chain of theologians, however, filled quarto page after quarto page of printed tomes that populated the library shelves of Catholic intellectuals.

IV. Double Consecration and Eternity

Maritain begins his discussion of the Mass with reference to the defective theories: those that seek either to separate the sacrifice at the Mass from the one on Calvary or to introduce sacrifice into the glorious Christ. He then acknowledges his indebtedness to Swiss Cardinal Charles Journet (1891–1975) for his teaching that the Mass remains identical with the very sacrificial act of Calvary—that is, of the passible Christ. Maritain, however, respectfully demurs from following Journet's complete explanation. For his own reasons, Journet bracketed the Thomist view that "all moments of time are *physically* present to the divine eternity" in favor of an explanation that invoked the operative application of a spiritual power to each Mass celebrated.[18] Maritain thinks that more should and can be said. He wants to argue that "by means of the sacrificial sign the divine omnipotence makes us present at the sacrifice of the cross as it is eternally preserved in heaven."[19] It reveals something of Maritain's spiritual depth that the austere Saint Peter Damian (d. 1072) supplies the intuition for Maritain's explanation of the "eternal sacrifice."[20] Christ's death took place at an instant of time in the world; it now stands "eternally present to the eternal instant of God."[21]

17. Maritain, "A Look at Theology (I): The Sacrifice of the Mass," in *Untrammeled Approaches*, 351.

18. Ibid., 352.

19. Ibid., 356.

20. For instance, Maritain suggested that Thomas Merton send the Prior of the Carthusians in Rome a copy of his book, *The Seven Storey Mountain*. See Thomas Merton, *The Sign of Jonas*, (New York: Houghton Mifflin Harcourt, 2002), 174.

21. Maritain, "A Look at Theology (I)" in *Untrammeled Approaches*, 357.

The principal agent of this sacrifice can only be the glorified Christ, whereas the instrumental cause of the sign that we behold, the double consecration, as Catholic teaching makes clear, remains the Catholic priest and him alone. Only the Catholic priest enacts the two distinct moments of consecration that represent the separation of Christ's Body and Blood. Let Maritain's own words summarize his teaching:

> The sacrificial sign of the double consecration is a sign with existential implications which the glorious Christ uses in order to reactualize for us, by a miracle of His omnipotence, that sacrifice which, when he was passible here below, he accomplished under Pontius Pilate, and which at each Mass, is once again *there*, as present at a certain moment of our time.[22]

Maritain's account of the sacrifice of the Mass entails "a miraculous presence at an event with regard to the time (not the space) at which it took place."[23] The double consecration signifies an event which took place in the past and which is present to the divine eternity. Calvary remains unique, *semel*, once and for all, as the *Catechism of the Catholic Church* states.[24] Still, at a given moment of time, our time, when the priest celebrates Mass, we stand face-to-face with that sacrifice "by a miracle of the divine omnipotence."[25] Carthusian spiritual teaching comes to mind, "Stat Crux dum volvitur orbis."

Maritain then turns to consider the common phrase that the Mass proceeds in a bloodless manner. He argues that were this true, then there would be no sacrifice. Sacrifice requires doing something destructive to the victim. The appeal to mode or "unbloody manner," in Maritain's view, does not run deep enough into the metaphysics of the sacrificial representation. Maritain rather points to the "mode of presence to our time," not the mode of the putative bloodless sacrifice. "Brains were racked," he says, to make the sacrifice itself a bloodless one.[26] Instead, Maritain affirms: "This is a mode of presence proper to the sign by the means and the power of which, at a given moment of our time, we find ourselves contemporary to the sacrifice of Christ on Calvary."[27] Maritain, of course, did not know

22. Ibid., 364.
23. Ibid.
24. *Catechism of the Catholic Church*, no. 1367.
25. Maritain, "A Look at Theology (I)" in *Untrammeled Approaches*, 369.
26. Ibid., 370.
27. Ibid., 371.

that the *Catechism of the Catholic Church* would maintain the reference to "unbloody manner" as found in the documents of both Trent and Vatican Council II.[28]

Maritain completes this essay by examining magisterial texts on the sacrifice of the Mass. He also points out why appeals to heavenly immolations, as if the glorious Christ were dying again, cannot do justice to Catholic doctrine or, one may add, to common sense.

V. At Odds with Bérulle?

As I have indicated at the beginning of this essay, Maritain also turns his attention and analysis to the spiritual identity of the Catholic priest. In order to understand the momentousness of his argument, it is necessary to recall that one of the major supports for priestly formation after the Council of Trent sprung from the powerful seventeenth-century spiritual movement known as *L'École Française*, the French School. To cite only the success of the Sulpicians, one may fairly assess that the French School provided the blueprint for priestly formation that, arguably, has lasted since 1641 until the present day. At the source of this French School stands the figure of Cardinal Pierre de Bérulle (1575–1629), whom Maritain describes as "a confused, mystical Platonist."[29] The saintly cardinal, in Maritain's view, makes an elision between the sacerdotal office seen as a function and—for the diocesan priesthood—as a state of perfection. Maritain of course observes the obvious: consecrated persons, those who pronounce vows, commit themselves to a state of life by one act, whereas priests are obliged to perform many acts, principally sacramental, in order to fulfill their mission in the Church. The point at stake follows what Aquinas says about the states of perfection.[30] "The religious state," affirms Aquinas, "is constituted by the three vows."[31] Maritain considers Bérulle's making of an "imperceptible step" from function to a state of life wrongheaded.[32] However, while one may grant that consecrated life and the clerical state remain distinct vocations within the Church, to argue today that the cleri-

28. See *Catechism*, nos. 1367 and 1369.

29. Maritain, "*Apropos* of the French School," in *Untrammeled Approaches*, 425.

30. Aquinas's treatment of this question appears conveniently in *Summa theologiae* II-II q. 184, especially a. 8: "Whether parish priests and archdeacons are more perfect than religious."

31. ST II-II q. 186, a. 7.

32. Maritain, "*Apropos* of the French School," in *Untrammeled Approaches*, 427.

cal state does not entail its own perfections runs counter to certain emphases in recent magisterial teachings on the priesthood.

Bérulle's waxing lyrical on priests' belonging to the order of Christ's humanity and his explaining that priests receive their identity in some way because of the hypostatic union, on Maritain's account, do not square with sound theology. He may have been right. However, Maritain goes on to question the classical formulation that the priest comes forth as another Christ. *Sacerdos est alter Christus* of course shaped pre-conciliar Catholic clerical piety, and the concept is not altogether absent from post-conciliar magisterial teaching.[33] For his part, Maritain argues that the French School misunderstood the grandness of the priest's place in the Church. Instead, he asserts that "what makes for the grandeur of the priesthood is not a more perfect state of life than that of the ordinary people of God, it is the holy function exercised in the Church for the salvation of souls."[34] In a word, Maritain wants to identify the priest by appeal to the immense and capital importance of priests' functions in the Church, especially their Eucharistic grandeur. To return to the theme of the first essay on the Eucharistic sacrifice, Maritain exclaims in italics, "at each Mass Christ dies for us."[35] The priest enacts this sacrifice. Therein lies his grandeur.

Such grandeur still does not prohibit Maritain from wondering whether priestly celibacy will always be rigorously enforced in the Church of the Latin rite. He also considers it normal to expect that the diocesan priest will someday earn his own living by manual or other labor; "on condition of course," Maritain stipulates, "that the time required for the exercise of his priestly functions is not drastically reduced."[36] All in all, Maritain conceives a fairly particular view of what diocesan priesthood entails. His ecclesiological vision resembles that of the Eastern Churches where bishops and monks serve the religious and spiritual needs of the lay faithful, while the ordinary priests are restricted to serving as liturgical functionaries.

Let me conclude where I began, with Maritain the prophet. Maritain's effort to render a philosophically satisfying account of what the Church

33. In *Pastores dabo vobis*, no. 11, Pope John Paul II calls for "an awareness of the specific ontological bond which unites the priesthood to Christ the high priest and good shepherd." Again, "By the sacramental anointing of holy orders, the Holy Spirit configures them in a new and special way to Jesus Christ the head and shepherd" (no. 15).

34. Maritain, "*Apropos* of the French School," in *Untrammeled Approaches*, 440.

35. Ibid., 441.

36. Ibid., 439.

holds about the sacrifice of the Mass and the sacrifice of Calvary merits widespread recognition among Catholic theologians. Most catechetical efforts to explain the reality of the Catholic Mass do not advert sufficiently to what stands at the heart of the Eucharist. As a result, most people (outside of traditionalist groups) have forgotten that the Mass enacts the sacrifice of the cross. To my mind, this eclipse of Catholic teaching accounts for the sharp decline in Mass attendance that sociologists observe throughout Western Europe and the United States. Additionally, Maritain raises consciousness about the required devotion that offering and attending Mass requires, a devoutness that also includes one's making the right preparation for participating in the Mass.

Maritain's views on the priesthood raise questions of a different kind. Bérulle, whom Maritain criticizes, sought to restore dignity to the diocesan or secular clergy, not to religious clerics, such as monks and friars and clerks regular. Today, however, the Church stresses less the difference between priestly functions and states of life; for example, religious no longer can claim exemption from the local bishop, and all priests working in a given diocese belong to the local presbyterate. Then there is the admonition that comes from Pope Saint John Paul II: "The priest should continually renew and deepen his awareness of being a minister of Jesus Christ by virtue of sacramental consecration and configuration to Christ the head and shepherd of the Church."[37] The language that the Church uses in *Pastores dabo vobis* points beyond what a priest does. However, contemporary Catholics can learn from Maritain's clarifications on the French School. Maritain clearly affirms the high respect that Catholics should show to their priests on account of their indispensable role as ministers of the Eucharist. They alone can bring us for one or two minutes into contact with eternity.

37. *Pastores dabo vobis*, no. 25.

HEATHER M. ERB

Towards an Aristotelian Prologue to the Spiritual Life

Ecclesial Themes in Maritain and Aquinas

I. Introduction

REGINALD GARRIGOU-LAGRANGE and Cardinal Journet gathered much fruit from the recognition that the place from which one begins theology influences the place where one ends it. With this fact in mind, Garrigou-Lagrange combined the inductive and deductive approaches in his studies on mystical theology,[1] so that neither the data of great mystics or scriptural exegesis nor the perennial themes in theology would be ignored. Journet discerned the links between ecclesiology and spirituality, outlining the Church's features of apostolicity and unity within an Aristotelian causal framework,[2] showing that only the eyes of supernatural faith, not a sociological model, could access knowledge of the Bride of Christ in Herself, or grasp Her mission in the world. Their insights were prescient, in that the post-conciliar era has ushered in experiential, psychologized spiritualities,[3] and, more recently, an "outward bound" eccle-

1. Found in Garrigou-Lagrange, *The Three Ages of the Interior Life*, vol. 1 (Rockford, Illinois: Tan Books, 1987), 10–13. Cf. Garrigou-Lagrange, *Christian Perfection and Contemplation According to St. Thomas Aquinas and St. John of the Cross*, translated by Sister M. Timothea Doyle (St. Louis, Missouri: Herder Book Company, 1937), 16–23.

2. Charles Journet, *The Theology of the Church* (San Francisco: Ignatius Press, 2004).

3. The interest in Catholic spirituality circles (and in priestly formation) in "self-help" spirituality, Jung, New Age, and psychological topics signals the overhauling of pre-conciliar Catholic spirituality. John A. Sanford, Ronald Rolheiser, Thomas Moore, Anthony de Mello, S.J., and Robert Kennedy, S.J., among others, led the way to a psychological understanding of Catholic

siology[4] which substitutes an ecumenical focus for theological principles grounded in realist metaphysics.[5]

Influenced by the prudence of both Garrigou and Journet, Maritain developed a trio of themes in his final work, *Untrammeled Approaches*, which are forgotten signposts in the contemporary landscape of spirituality: (1) the Church as a transcendent, eternal Person,[6] (2) the Church triumphant as the life of the blessed, and (3) the Church as the spotless Bride of Christ.[7] A retrieval of these motifs is not only an intellectual but also a pastoral challenge to the modernist view developed by Tyrell a century ago,[8] which interprets revelatory experience as strictly historical and personal, segregating it from propositional dogmatic truth. Maritain's Thomistic roots bar him from a strictly authoritarian, juridical ecclesiology—wrongly feared by interpreters of Journet—and tie him to several Aristotelian premises of the spiritual life that grow into a distinctive ecclesiology.

By his use of Aristotelian-style prologues, Aquinas sometimes organized his treatises' subject matter around the four causes of being. A similar approach can be used profitably to combine the inductive and deductive methods of his mystical theology, which bear fruit in Maritain's three ecclesial themes. Although today we see a return to the source of Aristotle in

spirituality. Garrigou warned of the substitution of doctrine and theological principles for an exclusively descriptive analysis of so-called mystical states. Cf. Heather M. Erb, "Natural Mysticism: Gateway or Detour? Aquinas, Maritain, and the Core/Contextualist Debate," in *Redeeming Philosophy: From Metaphysics to Aesthetics*, edited by John Conley (Washington, D.C.: The Catholic University of America Press, 2014), 23–53.

4. On Francis's "outward bound" Church, which prioritizes moving out to the "peripheries" in ecumenical and missionary endeavors, over an "inward looking" Church focused on doctrine and ritual, see, e.g., Andrea Gagliarducci, "Pope Francis: The Criteria of the Church 'Outward Bound'," *Monday Vatican* (1 February 2016).

5. On the impact of the modernist notion of truth on the Church today and its relation to Thomism, see Heather M. Erb, "Modernism and the Growing Catholic Identity Crisis: Thomistic Reflections and Solutions," *Studia Gilsoniana* 4, no. 3 (July–September 2015): 251–83.

6. Jacques Maritain, *Untrammeled Approaches*, translated by Bernard Doering (Notre Dame, Indiana: University of Notre Dame Press, 1997), 443–94; cf. Maritain, *The Church of Christ: The Person of the Church and Her Personnel*, translated by Joseph W. Evans (Notre Dame, Indiana: University of Notre Dame Press, 1973).

7. See Maritain, *Untrammeled Approaches*, 381–402; 443–94.

8. George Tyrell was expelled from the Jesuit order for his sundering of dogma and propositional truth from subjective, experiential piety. See Tyrell, *Through Scylla and Charybdis, or The Old Theology and the New* (New York: Longmans, Green, and Company, 1907). Tyrell's view is discussed in Hans Boersma, *Nouvelle Théologie and Sacramental Theology: A Return to Mystery* (New York: Oxford University Press, 2009), 18–22.

Aquinas's theology,[9] several factors influenced the delay of this appreciation. First, rejection of neo-scholastic metaphysics by early twentieth century figures (such as Blondel, Marechal, and Rousselot) resulted in their replacement of deductive systems with emphasis on the will. Second, De Lubac and Bouillard represented the movement away from an Aristotelian metaphysical view that emphasized an autonomous nature within an ordered system of ends. Third, there was the liturgical, historical model of theology favored by Chenu and von Balthasar, to the exclusion of the insights of neo-scholastic system-building. According to Hans Boersma,[10] these various thinkers' rejection of a "neutral" concept of being and prioritizing of faith over rational deduction favored the move away from Aristotle.

In studying the Aristotelian roots of Aquinas's mystical theology,[11] we find his spirituality and ecclesiology intersecting, overhearing, and, at points, mutually grounding each other. Ecclesial themes such as the ones we will consider make sense only in light of the soul's progress towards God, but spiritual progress in Thomistic terms is through the priestly action of Christ, in the Holy Spirit as the life-giving Soul of the Church.

The mutual influence of spirituality and ecclesiology is notable in Maritain, whose rich metaphysical approach provided both the foundation and link between these two domains. In this chapter, I argue that Maritain's three ecclesial themes signify important but neglected final causes in spiritual growth. One can study them as descriptive of the four marks of the Church (one,

9. For example, Gilles Emery and Matthew Levering, editors, *Aristotle in Aquinas's Theology* (Oxford: Oxford University Press, 2015).

10. See Boersma, *Nouvelle Théologie and Sacramental Theology*, as summarized by Matthew Levering in "A Return to Mystery" (*First Things*, March 31, 2010): "De Lubac claims that the Aristotelian emphasis on the natural order of ends, when taken up within Christian scholasticism, promotes secularization by positing a 'pure nature' separate from the order of grace." Cf. Maurice Blondel, *L'action: essai d'une critique de la vie et d'une science de la pratique* (Paris: Alcan and Presses Universitaires de France, 1893); Marie-Dominique Chenu, "Nature, Man, and Society in the Twelfth Century: Essays on New Theological Perspectives in the Latin West," in *Medieval Academy Reprints for Teaching*, no. 37, translated and edited by Jerome Taylor and Lester Little (1968; reprint, Toronto: University of Toronto Press, 1997).

11. Although Aquinas did not develop a mystical theology in the later sense of a spiritual manual for direction, or mystical treatise as such, he did provide the metaphysical, theological, and affective principles for such (which were drawn on by St. John of the Cross, for example), and in this sense, one can discern the lineaments of mystical theology within his writings. Various terms have been used to describe his mystical theology, such as "spiritual theology," "spirituality," "mystical theology," etc. Cf. Garrigou-Lagrange, *The Three Ages of the Interior Life*, 2:640.

holy, catholic, and apostolic[12]), or in their power to draw to fulfilment our "universal call to holiness"[13] and to sustain hope amid adversity. Joining the two approaches is an example of the combined deductive/inductive methods of mystical theology recommended by Garrigou. Of interest here is the role of beatitude and the Beatitudes in setting the stage for the contemplative character of the final cause of the spiritual life.[14] For Aquinas, perfect happiness consists in knowing the intellect's object as it is in itself: namely, truth in its fullness. But since beatitude is not an isolated intellectual act, it involves an ecclesial dimension of the grafting of the communion of saints, as a perfected Bride, onto Christ.

Second, I examine the Aristotelian moorings of Aquinas's mystical theology, as they help frame the deductive side of an Aristotelian prologue to the spiritual life, focusing on the remaining three causes (formal, material, and efficient), with emphasis on some examples of the efficient cause. This approach contrasts with the modernist project of replacing neo-Scholastic frameworks with a focus on culture, history, and, vaguely, "life" as starting points for exploring spiritual themes.[15] Aquinas's Aristotelian commitments are also at work in his distinction between sanctifying grace and charity, in a discussion featuring the role of secondary causes.

II. The Mystical Body of Christ as the Basis for Maritain's Three Ecclesial Motifs

Maritain's three motifs are joined to the Pauline theme of the Church as the Mystical Body, which is often interpreted as a reorientation of ecclesiology to the communal view of the Church as the "people of God" hailed in Vatican II.[16] Maritain's motifs are linked to the theme of the Mystical Body

12. See *Catechism of the Catholic Church*, nos. 811–70.

13. Vatican II's Dogmatic Constitution on the Church, *Lumen Gentium*, no. 40 invokes the universal call to holiness based on Matthew 5:48, "So be perfect, just as your heavenly Father is perfect." Pope John Paul II also appeals to the teaching in his 2000 Apostolic Letter, *Novo Millenio Ineunte*, nos. 30–32.

14. See e.g., Servais-Theodore Pinckaers, O.P., "The Sources of the Ethics of St. Thomas Aquinas," in *The Ethics of Aquinas*, edited by Stephen Pope (Washington, D.C.: Georgetown University Press, 2002), 17–29, and Georg Wieland, "Happiness (Ia-IIae, qq. 1–5)" in the same work, pp. 57–68.

15. Aquinas balances the primacy of the intellect in the process of justification, with the notion that all of sanctity originates in the will (*In 1 Sent.*, d. 10), a rational appetite.

16. The influence of Yves Congar is seen in Vatican II's *Lumen Gentium* no. 9, which provides what would become the popular description of the Church as the people of God. Congar

because they all concern a unity which stands both at the base and the summit of the spiritual life. The term "Body of Christ" refers analogously to the Eucharist[17] and to the members, both visible and invisible, of the Church,[18] established by the life of sacraments and Word, through which we progress in union with Christ. Yet participation in the sacraments only commences the spiritual life of grace, whose eschatological fullness is signified in the motifs of the spotless Bride of Christ, the eternal Person of the Church, and the blessed in heaven. Taken together, Maritain's motifs function as a final cause of the interior life, since the end which draws the rational creature is the fulfilment of the life of grace in our total happiness and goodness.

Applying an Aristotelian perspective to Maritain's motifs illumines Aquinas's dovetailing of the natural and supernatural orders in his discussion of human perfection. A final cause acts in the manner of perfecting a subject: in this case, the human soul. "A being capable of perfecting another after the manner of an end," says Aquinas, is called "good."[19] The Church is at once the Mystical Body of Christ, the Bride, and the blessed in heaven. Together, these are supremely lovable in the order of perfection and actuality.[20] These realities act on the soul as eschatological influences,[21] giving our hope and charity the anchor of faith by which we cling to the promises of Christ.

---

spearheaded the study of the role of the laity in the Church in his various works, especially *Jalons pour un théologie du laïcat. Unam Sanctam* 23, translated by Donald Attwater as *Laypeople in the Church: A Study for a Theology of Laity* (Westminster, Maryland: Newman Press, 1965). Cf. Rose M. Beal, *Mystery of the Church, People of God: Yves Congar's Total Ecclesiology as a Path to Vatican II* (Washington, D.C.: The Catholic University of America Press, 2014).

17. See the *Catechism of the Catholic Church*, nos. 1346 and 1331, citing various Pauline and magisterial documents.

18. Ibid., nos. 752 and 779. Pius XII's encyclical *Mystici Corporis* emphasizes the theme of the Mystical Body to a greater degree than do later magisterial documents on ecclesiology.

19. *De veritate*, q. 21, a. 1. At ST I, q. 5, a. 1, Aquinas says that the notion of goodness is rooted in that of desirability, which itself is rooted in perfection and actuality.

20. However, the Church on earth is full of sinners, so theologians have held the truths of a "holy yet sinful" Church in tension, while explaining the distinction in different ways, and from different motives. Maritain deals with this side of ecclesiology in both *Untrammeled Approaches* and *On the Church of Christ*. My analysis of the ways in which Maritain's three ecclesial motifs can be said to act as final causes in the spiritual life does not supplant the neo-scholastic approach which assigns a causal structure to spiritual progress (e.g., the Holy Ghost as an efficient cause of spiritual growth through the habit of sanctifying grace; beatitude as the final cause of spiritual growth). On the contrary, these two approaches mutually complement one another, since ecclesiology, metaphysics, and mystical theology are inseparable in a Thomistic framework of the spiritual life.

21. The trio of ecclesial realities will not be fully realized and recognized by all until the end of time, but in their eternal verity they can ground the ascent of soul by purifying and strengthening our spiritual intentions. The first in intention is the last in execution, says Aquinas (ST I-II,

III. Maritain's Three Ecclesial Motifs and the Spiritual Life

In *Untrammeled Approaches,* in the chapter entitled "*A propos* of the Church of Heaven," Maritain grounds the Church triumphant in the unity of the Mystical Body of Christ, by which the Church militant, penitent, and triumphant are "one person," living what he calls a "great human life"[22] in relation to God and each other. The "humanism of the saints," including the uncanonized "immense mass of the poor and little people of God"[23] even in heaven, corrects both sentimentalist devotion and our indifference to the invisible. For, even if we cannot imagine them, we can love them, especially in the universal prayer of the Church, the liturgy, more than through popular piety. Aquinas bases his Augustinian view of the relatively small number of the elect on the notion of a good which surpasses the common state of nature.[24] The beatific vision, Aquinas reasons, exceeds the common state of nature, and the majority of men are deprived of grace through the corruption of original sin, resulting in the minority being saved. If one includes among the elect both angels and men, however, the number of the elect probably exceeds that of the damned. Maritain, unlike Aquinas, reasons that salvation is not like a high point of natural perfection which surpasses the common state of nature, but is entirely supernatural, resting on the boundless mercy of God shown in the wounds of Christ, which reverse those of original sin and raise us by grace to friendship with God. While Aquinas appealed to divine mercy in his notion that few would be saved, Maritain refers to divine mercy as justification for the majority whom he believed are saved. It is likely that Maritain's argument is an extension of the optimism of Garrigou on the "normalcy" of holiness as a fulfilment of the life of grace,[25] and of Pius IX's view that invincible

q. 1, a. 1, ad 1). Of course the primary final cause in the spiritual life is the beatific vision itself, but the communal character of salvation means that more proximate final causes (such as the ecclesial realities examined by Maritain) are fitting objects of hope *in via*.

22. Maritain, *Untrammeled Approaches*, 382.

23. Ibid., 387.

24. ST I, q. 23, a. 7, ad 3: "The good that is proportionate to the common state of nature is to be found in the majority; and is wanting in the minority. The good that exceeds the common state of nature is to be found in the minority, and is wanting in the majority.... He has chosen some for that salvation, from which very many in accordance with the common course and tendency of nature fall short." It is also important to avoid reading Aquinas's texts on this question through a Reformation lens; he lacked a theory of double predestination.

25. For Maritain's view, see *Untrammeled Approaches*, 391. For Garrigou-Lagrange's position,

ignorance and obedience to the natural law "engraved in the heart of all by God", are measures by which many attain eternal life.[26]

Furthermore, what is "normal" and what is "more frequent in point of fact" often differ, and the common state of humanity destines us directly for paradise, not for hell or even purgatory. The soul's revolt against God and its refusal of redemptive work here below may be frequent, but it is abnormal in terms of the soul's nature.[27] Maritain's view has the advantage of providing psychological continuity between the Church militant and triumphant, removing the latter from the fringes of spiritual life, while reversing the "progressive collapse of the practical exercise of the virtue of hope." This occurred due to the consciousness of human unworthiness and misery, which he blamed partly on Baroque manuals of piety that denied the universal call to holiness which was reinstated in Vatican II.[28] Whether the constantly renewed conversation between heaven and earth leads us to fraternal charity, to interior peace and joy, or even to the dunghill of Job through which we enter into eternal life, he says, its law is as necessary to spiritual progress as is sowing to reaping. In addition to its role as a final cause of the spiritual life, the Church triumphant brings about our spiritual growth through a Thomistic law of the supernatural order—namely, that "the intentions of heaven are carried out on earth by means of certain conditions." Unlike the ordinary regime of non-rational creatures and the ordinary regime of men receiving goods from divine liberality through their prayers,[29] there is the extraordinary regime wherein men receive without asking, often through the prayers of members of the Mystical Body.

The interrelation of Maritain's ecclesial motifs underscores their role as final causes in the spiritual life, in drawing believers from an embryonic state of charity in sanctifying grace and the sacrament of baptism to the fullness of participation in the life of Christ through His Church. The

---

see *Christian Perfection and Contemplation*, 127; *Predestination*, translated by Dom Bede Rose, O.S.B. (B. Herder Book Company: St. Louis, Missouri, 1939), 217–19.

26. See: Pius IX, *Quanto Conficiamur Moerore* (1863): no. 7: "Because God knows, searches and clearly understands the minds, hearts, thoughts, and nature of all, his supreme kindness and clemency do not permit anyone at all who is not guilty of deliberate sin to suffer eternal punishment."

27. Maritain, *Untrammeled Approaches*, 392–93.

28. Ibid., 393–95. In particular, Maritain is referring to the clericalist error of the French school.

29. On Maritain's division of the "three regimes" of Providence, see Maritain, *Untrammeled Approaches*, 398–99.

Church's effect of holiness in relation to Her sinful members in the temporal order marks Her as the Bride of Christ, in addition to being the triumphant communion of saints and the Personality and Soul of the Church as the Spirit, distinct from Her sinful personnel.

Maritain's discussion of the spotless Bride of the *Song of Songs* is an exegetical complement to his more systematic treatment of the topic in his late work, *On the Church of Christ*, as well as to more recent systematic theologies. Present in both works is the distinction between the Church's supernatural Person (sometimes called Her "personality"), which advances in charity through time, and the Church's often sinful personnel. The latter's activity as a proper rather than a merely instrumental cause exposes the Church's members to sin and error.[30] The Church is an "ontological person embracing all the members of God's people within one supernatural personality which transcends the natural personality" of each member and is given to the Church by reason of the image of Christ that she carries within her.[31]

Along with the Person/personnel distinction, there are two other points which, for Maritain, add to an explanation of the paradoxically "holy yet sinful" Church. The existential state or "state of life" of a priest is distinct from his sacerdotal function of administering grace through the sacraments in the mission of redemption.[32] The religious or consecrated state in life is a "state of perfection" still to be acquired, and the sacramental character does not make priests into "super-Christians."[33] They are not conjoined instruments in their priestly acts in a way analogous to the humanity of Christ in the hypostatic union. Bérulle, Maritain argued, confused sacerdotal character with the grace which stems from it. These distinctions, then (the Church's person vs. Her personnel; the priest's function vs. his state of life) combine with Maritain's exegetical work on the Church as Bride in the *Song of Songs* to illumine aspects of the paradox of a holy yet sinful Church.

Whereas Pius XII's 1943 encyclical *Mystici Corporis* focused on the visi-

30. See e.g., ibid., 452 and 456; cf. Maritain, *On the Church of Christ*, 241, where he concludes his findings succinctly.

31. Maritain, *Untrammeled Approaches*, 452. Maritain uses the terms "person" and "Person," and "bride" and "Bride" variably, depending on whether he is discussing the meaning of the terms generically, or applying them to the Church.

32. Maritain develops this distinction as a critique of the French School, in particular, of Bérulle's spirituality, which leaned towards clericalism, in "A Supplement to the book *On the Church of Christ—A Propos* of the French School," in *Untrammeled Approaches*, 425ff.

33. Maritain, *Untrammeled Approaches*, 427; cf. 429.

ble character of the Church as necessary for salvation,[34] Maritain, inspired by Journet's view of the Holy Spirit as the formal cause of the Church,[35] parallels the Second Vatican Council's ecclesiology by including in the Church its invisible members, such as the just of Israel and all members of God's people who belong to the Church in a "tendential" and "virtual" way.[36] The just of Israel are by extension, but in a proper way,[37] the Bride of Yahweh; Israel herself as the chosen people are the Bride, in an imperfect manner, due to a defect of grace, as are those not participating the fullness of the faith. The invisible quality of the Church's Person in certain situations is demanded, then, by two facts: the first concerns the scope of the Church, as the ensemble of those souls living in the state of grace and charity,[38] which, as pre-Christian, could not operate as a visible social body. Second, the "Person/personnel" distinction explains the Church's indefectible holiness in Her magisterial teaching and sacramental functions, despite sin among her visible members.

In the chapter on the *Song of Songs*, Maritain gives both a temporal and eternal dimension to the Church as Bride of Christ and identifies her as both the Church militant and triumphant, the most intimate reality of the Church as Person through the ages. The Church as Bride is Maritain's preferred reading of the text, in contrast to two other meanings—namely, the Jews as God's chosen ones, and John of the Cross's nuptial reading of God and the soul in mystical union.

34. On the visible nature of the Church's body, see: *Mystici Corporis* no. 14. Cf. nos. 16 and 41. At no. 62, Pius XII distinguishes a "moral body" from a "mystical body." The former's members are united in a common end, external to each of them. The latter's members are also united by an intrinsic vivifying principle: in this case, the soul of the Church, which is the Holy Spirit, who leaves an uncreated gift of sanctifying grace in each member as a principle of new life.

35. See, e.g., Charles Journet, *The Theology of the Church*, translated by Victor Szczurek (San Francisco: Ignatius Press, 2004). While the created soul of the Church is sanctifying grace and the infused virtue of charity, the Church's uncreated soul is the Holy Spirit, as the form of the body, which is Her members.

36. See e.g., *Untrammeled Approaches*, 450ff. The notion of "tendential" sanctity was introduced by Journet to defend the sanctity that is fitting to the ordained as something not due to their own merit, but by reference to the Church's sanctity. See Journet, *The Theology of the Church*, 223.

37. That is, the just of Israel participate to a degree in the actual spousal reality of the Church, and are not the Bride in a mere metaphorical sense.

38. Maritain, *Untrammeled Approaches*, 450n11. In this footnote, he explains the way in which the just of Israel and the entire chosen people of God are members of the invisible Church. He also notes that Aquinas (*In 4 Sent.*, d. 27, q. 3, a. 1) designates the "Synagogue" as the "bride" of Christ in an improper sense. The term "synagogue" is used equivocally, in that it can mean either the religious regime under which Israel lived or those men who exercised authority over Israel and sent Christ to his death.

In the temporal order, the Bride advances in charity through history towards perfect union with the Bridegroom in the beatific vision. Maritain challenges a Patristic and modern reading of *Song of Songs* 1:5–6, where the beloved exhorts the lover not to gaze at her because she is burnt dark black, even though she is also beautiful.[39] He rejects the reading which interprets her blackness as her sinful personnel, and as the straying Israel.[40] Instead, the Bride is black because she has been burnt by the sun of history, while toiling in the vineyard of prayer, contemplation, suffering, and active works, as a wandering exile on earth.[41] He states, let us not imagine "that she is black because of the faults of her members and of her personnel. She suffers from these faults, she does penance for them, but they are completely foreign to her personality. If she is black, if she has a dark complexion; it is the sun of history that has burnt her ... she is obliged by the heirs of the first sin to watch over the vines, and this is a difficult task. She is the guardian of the vineyard of her Spouse, she has to strengthen and constantly preserve in this vineyard the faith in the truth of divine revelation." The Bride, he says, is "love itself" and since the Bridegroom knows this love must grow to reach perfection, he does not waken her—her heart is already awake: "I beseech you, says the Spouse in the Canticle, *be careful not to waken, not to stir up love again*" (*Song of Songs* 2:7).[42]

Far from being limited by the sins of her members, the patience of the Person of the Church is a sorrowful enduring of the infirmities of the flock committed to her care by her Spouse, and her mysterious sleep refers to Her continued presence to Her members through the dark and sinful periods in Church history, in a silent ardor of contemplation—the parallel of "sleep" and "night" inspired by John of the Cross is not accidental.[43] This sleep is the "highest and most hidden activity, the one that is the most important in the life of the Church."[44] Echoing John of the Cross's various as-

39. "My mother's sons were angry with me, they made me keeper of the vineyards but my own vineyard I have not kept." *Song of Songs* 1:6 (NRSV).

40. For example, Gregory of Nyssa. See *Untrammeled Approaches*, 470.

41. See ibid., 472–73.

42. Ibid., 455.

43. Ibid., 464–65. Although Maritain's reference to the Canticle concerns the contemplation of the sinful members of the Church, there is a discernible link to St. John of the Cross's description of the night of the spirit as a purgative, divine contemplation which displaces our natural powers (*Dark Night of the Soul*, Pt. 2, chap. 4.2). Cf. *Dark Night* Pt 2, chap. 5.2, on the reasons this divine wisdom is darkness, affliction, and torment for the soul (namely, its excessive power, and the soul's baseness and impurity).

44. Maritain, *Untrammeled Approaches*, 465. In no. 34, Maritain attributes the sleep of the

cending nights, he describes the third sleep of the Bride (*Song of Songs* 5:2) as a dark night empty of the sweetness of contemplation, an agony of being engulfed in a sense of abandonment by God—a state reflected in both the rise of Protestantism and the post-conciliar confusion.[45]

In sum, inspired by John of the Cross's reading of the Canticle, and deploying his own notion of the Person of the Church who progresses in time towards perfection while undergoing sufferings and purifications to attain higher levels of charity, Maritain holds his three ecclesial themes in a fruitful tension. The indefectible Person of the Church is closely linked to the Bride of Christ in history, who is open to the world's misery in a heroic devotion to contemplation and works of mercy. It is She who wages battle, protecting Christian morality from the foxes threatening on all sides, until at last, she is woken by her Beloved for eternity as the Church triumphant, for, as the text says, "love is stronger than death … its flames are a blazing fire, deep waters cannot quench it" (*Song of Songs* 8:6–7).[46]

III. Views Complementary to Maritain's

The Church's eternal and temporal dimensions are studied by theologians—such as Journet, Nicolas,[47] Bouyer,[48] Nichols,[49] and, as we have seen, Maritain—and are used to unravel the paradox of a holy yet sinful Church.

Bride as the "sleep of contemplation" to Aquinas (in Aquinas's second commentary on the Canticle, which Maritain notes had been attributed to Aquinas).

45. Maritain, *Untrammeled Approaches*, 468. In both this work and in *The Peasant of the Garonne*, translated by Michael Cuddihy and Elizabeth Hughes (New York: Holt, Rinehart and Winston, Inc., 1968), Maritain expresses the role that temporal events in the drama of salvation history have in advancing the spiritual purgation of the soul, in part due to their effect on the Church. In *The Peasant of the Garonne* (47–48), he presents salvation history in terms of spiritual warfare, tasking the Christian with the role of wresting control of souls from the devil in his own domain—the world.

46. Maritain, *Untrammeled Approaches*, 475. For Maritain's reference to the Bride of Christ as guardian and defender of the Faith, see *Untrammeled Approaches* 473: "She is the guardian of the vineyard of her Spouse; she has to strengthen and constantly preserve in this vineyard the faith in the truth of divine revelation … to advance theological wisdom, even canon law, to watch over Christian morality, to defend this precious vine from the young foxes which ceaselessly threaten it on all sides."

47. Jean-Hervé Nicolas, *Synthèse dogmatique: De la Trinité à la Trinité* (Fribourg: Editions universitaires de Fribourg, 1985).

48. Louis Bouyer, *L'Eglise de Dieu: Corps du Christ et Temple de l'Esprit* (Paris: Cerf, 1970).

49. Aidan Nichols, *Figuring out the Church: Her Marks and Her Masters* (San Francisco: Ignatius Press, 2013).

Without unpacking this paradox, the ecclesial aspect of the soul's final cause is obscured and muted. While Maritain's exegesis provides a more experiential, inductive contribution to mystical theology and ecclesiology, Nichols's recent work complements Maritain's by adding an eschatological dimension in a systematic discussion of the Church's holiness.

Paradoxes are home to distinctions, and Nichols's discussion of the "holy but sinful Church" is no exception. First, the Church's holiness, making her the spotless Bride of Christ, requires both sanctifying principles[50] (that is, the complete, coexisting ensemble of sanctifying measures, such as sacraments, Scripture, theology and Magisterium) and sanctified members (that is, the *vera Ecclesia* has enough holy members "for a humanly inexplicable holiness to appear there as the proper effect of the sanctifying principles bestowed by Christ on his people"[51]). Second, the holiness of the Church's perfection is analogous across its members, ascending from the common sanctity of the ordinary laity, to the more perfect holiness facilitated by the evangelical counsels, and culminating in the rare heroic sanctity of saints. Third, while the Augustinian and Thomistic idea of the mystical Body of Christ is useful in this discussion, the modern focus on its invisibility is complemented by the distinction between ontological and eschatological holiness.[52]

St. Augustine clarified his theology of the Mystical Body in response to the Donatists and the Pelagians.[53] The Church's holiness comes from its Head and through union with the Head, into the members, including the visible hierarchy. It is incomplete on earth but will become absolute at the end of time. Against the Pelagians, the offer of divine grace can coexist both with human original sin and concupiscence and with reliance on God for growth in holiness. The vital, organic, and ordered unity of the Mystical Body secures the Church's holiness in this view.[54]

50. Ibid., 36–38.

51. Ibid., 38. The context of Nichols's discussion is the argument that the Roman Catholic Church is the *vera Ecclesia,* drawing on material from the Patristics, especially St. Augustine, and the Scholastics, especially Aquinas.

52. The distinction between the Church's ontological and eschatological holiness is discussed by Nichols (*Figuring out the Church,* 51–53) and echoed by Bouyer (*L'Eglise de Dieu,* 607).

53. Augustine addressed the Pelagian and Donatist heresies at several points in his career. See e.g., *Psalmus contra partem Donati* (394 AD); *Contra Donatistas* (400 AD); *Contra epistulam Donati heretici liber unus* (405 AD); *De natura et gratia liber unus* (413 AD); *Contra duas epistulas Pelagianorum libri quattour* (421 AD).

54. St. Augustine's Christological focus permeates his ecclesiology. See e.g., *In Psalmos* 91, no. 13: "The Holy City is not the Church of this country only, but of the whole world as well: not that of this age only, but from Abel himself down to those who shall to the end be born and

De Lubac's view of the Church as a *complexio oppositorum*—both Bride of Christ and harlot, a woman saved from prostitution and the Bride of the Lamb[55]—is also complementary to Maritain's. The Protestant temptation to detach the Mystical Body from the visible Church appeared in Luther's severance of the sinful visible, temporal, hierarchical Church from the eternal, invisible, and holy Church, making the former a merely human creation composed of sinners. But in fact, as de Lubac stressed, the Church Herself is both human and divine, for there is only one Church, bathed in glory even as it is living and progressing in time.[56] De Lubac cites history and temporality as the locus of the sinful aspects of the Church, but the Church's splendor is that She walks in both time and eternity, towards the divine life of the Trinity.[57]

Nichols's two-pronged approach to dissolving the paradox of a holy yet sinful Church, or a "chaste harlot," invokes participation and eschatology. Church members sin *qua* individuals, but they repent and conform themselves to Christ through the sacraments, *qua* members of the Body of Christ, such that the Church possesses a "repentant holiness" on earth and an eschatological flowering in heaven. Both Bouyer and Aquinas echo this eschatological interpretation—Bouyer by replacing the Bride motif with the "Betrothed" motif,[58] and Aquinas by giving a mystical interpretation to

believe in Christ, the whole assembly of the Saints, belonging to one city; which city is Christ's body, of which Christ is the Head. There, too, dwell the Angels, who are our fellow citizens: we toil, because we are as yet pilgrims: while they within that city are awaiting our arrival. Letters have reached us too from that city, apart from which we are wandering: those letters are the Scriptures . . . the Head is not separate from the Body, and both are spoken of as one." *Nicene and Post-Nicene Fathers*, first series, vol. 8: *St. Augustine: Exposition on the Psalms*, translated and edited by Philip Schaff (repr., Peabody, Massachusetts: Hendrickson Publishers, 1989).

55. See Dennis Doyle, *Communion Ecclesiology* (New York: Orbis Press, 2000), 58–59, citing de Lubac, *Catholicism*.

56. De Lubac develops this theme in *The Splendor of the Church*, translated by Michael Mason (San Francisco: Ignatius Press, 1986), 82–85. The paradoxical glorious and pilgrim status of the militant Church are expressed in *Mystici Corporis* nos. 46–47, as well as in the *Catechism of the Catholic Church*, no. 827.

57. De Lubac, *The Church: Paradox and Mystery*, translated by James R. Dunne (New York: Alba House, 1969), 14. Cf. Henri de Lubac, *The Splendor of the Church*, translated by Michael Mason (San Francisco: Ignatius Press, 1986). Pius XII details the activity of the Church in each soul beautifully in *Mystici Corporis*, no. 39, as Christ continually gives interior guidance as the "Shepherd and Bishop of our souls," interiorly sanctifying the Mystical Body's members through the Word and sacraments, calming the "turbulent passions" (no. 51). The encyclical expresses the communication of abundant grace from Head to members in various concrete ways.

58. Louis Bouyer, *L'Eglise de Dieu: Corps du Christ et Temple de l'Esprit* (Paris: Cerf, 1970), 607, as cited in Nichols, *Figuring out the Church*, 53.

the wedding at Cana in his *Commentary on the Gospel of John*: the marriage between Christ and the human souls of His Church will be consummated only in the nuptial chamber of heavenly glory.[59] Here, the Church's visible holiness is one of recovered innocence, but one "on the way" to fulfilment, a partial participation in the fullness of grace belonging to the Bridegroom. For Aquinas, the person of the Church is present in the liturgy and common prayer—the Lord's Prayer, he says, is pronounced in the "common person of the whole Church."[60] The participation and eschatology motifs inform the Church-as-Bride motif, while the notion of Church as supernatural Person, more developed by Maritain, deciphers her holiness on earth.

IV. Formal and Efficient Causes of the Spiritual Life: Aristotelian Influences on Aquinas's Mystical Theology

We have now seen how Maritain's three ecclesial motifs play the role of final causes in the spiritual life, drawing the soul towards glory and full participation in God's life through membership in the life of the Church. This is complemented by Aquinas's use of formal, efficient, and material causes in his understanding of the spiritual life. Although he wrote no treatise analyzing the spiritual life and its causes, his theology of grace is directed by metaphysical principles that provide such an analysis, specifically in terms of his Aristotelian commitments. In contrast to the modernist lopsided emphasis on affectivity and its muting of speculative reason, Aquinas rests numerous facets of his theology firmly on Aristotle.[61]

59. Aquinas, In 2 Joannem l.1, no. 338: "In the mystical sense, marriage signifies the union of Christ with his Church.... It will be consummated when the bride, i.e., the Church, is led into the resting place of the groom, i.e., into the glory of heaven." *Thomas Aquinas: Commentary on the Gospel of St. John*, translated by Fabian Larcher, O.P. and James A. Weisheipl, O.P. (Albany, New York: Magi Books, 1980).

60. ST II-II, q. 83, a. 16, ad 3. The person of the Church is understood as indefectibly holy here, since the sinner does not lie in pronouncing and intending the words of the prayer as consonant with the mind of the Church, "although his words do not apply to him personally" so he is deprived of the fruit of his prayer.

61. Aristotle's influence even appears in his mystical theology, in his statement in the SCG IV, chap. 42 that "the ultimate salvation of man is that he may be perfected in his intellectual aspect by the contemplation of the First Truth." However, However, Aquinas develops his own distinctive theory of virtue, locating infused virtue at its heart (ST I-II, q. 55, a. 4; q. 56, a. 6). For Aquinas, no strictly true virtue is possible without the theological virtue of love. On modernism and its impact on Catholic spirituality, see e.g., Heather M. Erb, "Modernism and the Growing Catholic Identity Crisis," 265–69.

Aquinas's Aristotelian approach grounds his frequent comparisons of the natural and supernatural orders through causal analogies. Just as the themes of organic unity and growth mark a natural being's tendency towards a state of integration and finality, so they also figure in the spiritual life, appearing as the soul's ordered progress in the virtues and Gifts, in contemplation, and the sacraments. This pastorally effective approach to the spiritual life involves discerning a path of perfection in which predictable patterns of fulfilment are at work, where the final cause is primary in power, gently drawing the power of the efficient and formal causes towards it.[62]

Materially, human nature and its spiritual powers provide the stuff out of which the spiritual ascent is launched and sustained. In a way analogous to the role of the Holy Ghost as the "form" of the Church, as its life-giving soul,[63] the form of the spiritual life, what gives the soul its Christian character, is the presence of the virtues and Gifts, by which God's gift of created grace propels us, by divine direction and an increase of charity, to our supernatural destiny. Aquinas clarifies that although God is the life of the soul after the manner of an efficient cause, His grace is present in the soul after the manner of a formal cause, sustaining the acts of the infused virtues in the manner of a permanent supernatural habit which is a created accidental form.[64] By this form, the soul is disposed to the infused virtues which relate it to its higher end, union with God, in the same way that natural

62. For the order among causes as applied to the spiritual life, see below. Positing an order of spiritual development through the causes does not minimize God's power to control natural causes as He sees fit. God is in no way subject to the order of secondary causes; rather, that order stems from His own mind and will (ST I, q. 105, a. 6).

63. Aquinas bases this notion on 1 Cor. 12:12–14. See Aquinas, *Commentary on the Apostle's Creed*, article 10: "We see that in a man there are one soul and one body; and of his body there are many members. So also the Catholic Church is one body and has different members. The soul which animates this body is the Holy Spirit." *The Sermon Conferences of Thomas Aquinas on the Apostle's Creed*, translated by Nicholas Ayo, C.S.C. (Notre Dame, Indiana: University of Notre Dame Press, 1988). Aquinas's view grounds Journet's revision of the manualist approach. The formal cause of the Church, according to several manualists (detailed by Daniel A. Triulxi, "The Tract, *De Ecclesia Christi*, in "The Seminary Manuals Predating the Second Vatican Council," unpublished [1986]) is the Church hierarchy, whereas the material cause is the laity. Journet broke with this juridical view, drawing on Patristics by making the Holy Spirit the formal cause of the Church, as its life-giving principle.

64. ST I-II, q. 110, a. 1, ad 2. We will not treat every aspect of efficient causality in the spiritual life, such as Christ's headship in the Church, which causes the sacraments to transmit grace to His members (e.g., ST III, q. 8). See also ST I-II, q. 110, a. 2 on how grace is a "quality" in the soul, as an accidental form coming to it from without, as an imperfect participation in the divine goodness.

reason's light makes us capable of the acquired virtues.[65] And as making the infused virtues possible, this grace does double duty, as formal cause and as an intrinsic efficient cause of our spiritual life. Created sanctifying grace[66] is present in the soul's essence as a form caused by God, constituting the basis of the spiritual life, whose essence is the lived reality of the infused virtues, their acts and fruits.

But what does Aquinas say about the efficient causes of the spiritual life? God is the principal efficient cause, bestowing on the rational creature a share in the divine nature, made possible through a similitude or likeness in him.[67] Other than this principal efficient cause, there are the subordinate efficient causes of Christ and the sacraments, which communicate grace. As the Head of the Mystical Body, Christ transmits grace to the members by instituting the sacraments, the bath of regeneration.[68] This occurs by the external promptings of the Holy Spirit,[69] and by the internal created habit of sanctifying grace which activates the Gifts and virtues in us. Aquinas's explanation of God's decision to invest rational creatures with a created form of grace, instead of moving them directly and ineluctably towards goodness in every act, reveals his commitment to an Aristotelian system of causes, and to the importance of secondary causes.

65. Cf. ST I-II, q. 110, a. 3: "For as the acquired virtues enable a man to walk in accordance with the natural light of reason, so do the infused virtues enable a man to walk as befits the light of grace."

66. The *Catechism of the Catholic Church*, no. 2000: "Sanctifying grace is a habitual gift, a stable and supernatural disposition that perfects the soul itself to enable it to live with God, to act by his love. *Habitual grace*, the permanent disposition to live and act in keeping with God's call, is distinguished from actual graces which refer to God's interventions, whether at the beginning of conversion or in the course of the work of sanctification." This is based on Aquinas's distinction, found at ST I-II, q. 110, a. 2.

67. ST I-II, q. 112, a. 1. Cf. ST I, q. 42, a. 1, ad 1: "Everything, insofar as it actually is, acts and tends towards what suits it in terms of its form."

68. ST III, q. 8 on the headship of Christ causing grace in the members of the Mystical Body. See ST III, q. 62, a. 1 on the role of the sacraments as efficient causes of grace. Both Christ's humanity and the sacraments are instrumental causes of grace, fully dependent on the power of the principal cause for their power and efficacy (ST I-II, q. 112, a. 2, ad 1).

69. See e.g., ST I-II, q. 68, a. 1 on the higher mode by which we operate when prompted by the *instinctus* (promptings) of the Holy Spirit, in the Gifts. The Gifts, he says, are the higher perfections by which we are disposed to be moved by God. By them, we "become amenable to divine inspiration." We need these higher dispositions in order to become "proportionate" to the mover, viz. God: "The more exalted the mover, the more perfect must be the disposition whereby the mobile is made proportionate to its mover."

1. *Sanctifying Grace and our Supernatural End*

Aquinas invests the creature with its own mode of traversing the infinite, in a way that avoids Pelagianism, on the one hand,[70] and pantheism, on the other, which joins us to God by a union of nature, not of grace, shrinking our will's role in the spiritual life.[71] Aquinas frames his arguments on grace in Aristotelian terms, particularly in his insistence that grace is needed for salvation, since actions must be proportionate to their end, and that grace is a spiritual form or quality implanted in us to facilitate this conformity.

Sanctifying grace is the axis of the spiritual life by elevating the soul's essence, giving it a new mode of existence by which its powers are capable of the theological virtues. In Aristotelian terms, he argues that the soul's essence is not the same as its powers, but a source of them, as act is prior to potency and as subject is to accidents.[72] If they were identical, the soul's operations would be ceaseless. He based his view on Aristotle's distinction between first and second actuality,[73] a philosophical distinction enabling him to explain the penetrating nature of a grace which established a new platform for spiritual existence called "recreation."[74]Just as the soul's powers flow from its own hidden essence, so grace is the font from which the infused virtues and sevenfold Gifts flow into the soul's powers.[75]

At ST I-II, q. 109, a. 5, Aquinas identifies sanctifying grace as a condition of eternal life. Eternal life requires grace, he argues, since actions are proportionate to their end:

> Acts conducing to an end must be proportioned to the end. But no act exceeds the proportion of its active principle; and hence we see in natural things, that nothing can by its operation bring about an effect which exceeds its active force, but only such as is proportionate to its power. Now everlasting life is an end exceeding the proportion of human nature, as is clear from what we have said above (ST I-II, q. 5, a. 5). Hence man, by his natural powers, cannot produce meritorious works proportionate to everlasting life; and for this a higher force is needed, viz. the force

70. *Contra* the Pelagians, grace is needed to attain our final end: ST I-II, q. 109.

71. In the analogous notion of "life" we see the priority of the natural order in the order of discovery, contrasted to the natural priority, or priority in perfection, of the supernatural order.

72. See e.g., ST I, q. 77, a. 6.

73. Aristotle, *On the Soul* 2.1, 412a22–28.

74. ST I-II, q. 110, a. 4: "Through the 'nature of the soul' he participates in the divine nature according to a certain similitude, through a certain regeneration or recreation."

75. See e.g., ST III, q. 62, a. 2. The distinction between the soul's essence and its powers, then, is basic to Aquinas's theology of grace and the spiritual life.

of grace [*virtus gratiae*]. And thus without grace man cannot merit everlasting life; yet he can perform works conducing to a good which is natural to man, as 'to toil in the fields, to drink, to eat, or to have friends,' and the like.

Eternal life is a final cause, drawing the soul through the efficient cause of elevating grace. The order of causes is from final, to efficient, to formal[76]: just as a craftsman, with a view to his product, applies action to his axe, which cuts by being sharp, so we attain our end by applying the infused virtues, which operate through the form of grace in the soul. God gives the creature a form by which to attain its end, working intimately through its being.

Aristotle also is of use in the argument that grace is a form implanted in us to achieve conformity with our supernatural end. We have seen that Aquinas distinguishes the soul's essence, nature, or substance, and its powers, through which we make the journey to God. Just as the soul's powers flow from its essence, so does our entering into God's knowledge and love through faith and charity flow, as it were, from sanctifying grace. His argument for the essence/powers distinction follows from the priority of act: "The soul, in terms of its essence, is an actuality. Therefore, if the very essence of the soul were the immediate basis of its operations, then anything that has a soul would always actually have the operations associated with life ... one finds, however, that what has a soul is not always in actuality as regards the operations associated with life."[77] Grace penetrates to the soul's mysterious essence, then, and influences the powers with an elevated mode of acting in a habitual manner. Aquinas concludes: "For as man in his intellective power participates in the divine knowledge through the virtue of faith, and in his power of will participates in the divine love through the virtue of charity, so also in the nature of the soul does he participate in the Divine Nature, after the manner of a likeness, through a certain regeneration or re-creation."[78] Cruciform conformity affects the way in which we know, love, act, and suffer—a theme contemplated by John of the Cross, a student of Aquinas' thought, in his meditation on God touching the "substance" of the soul in contemplation.[79] Further, the love by which we are

76. Cf. ST I, q. 105, a. 5 on the order of causes.

77. ST I, q. 77, a. 1. On this topic, see Robert Pasnau, *Thomas Aquinas on Human Nature* (Cambridge: Cambridge University Press, 2002), 151–57. Aquinas argues that created grace is prior to the theological virtues as a subject is prior to its powers, at ST I-II, q. 110. a. 3.

78. ST I-II, q. 110 a. 3.

79. Language facilitated perhaps by Aquinas's reflections, but terminology which caused Maritain alarm in *The Degrees of Knowledge*.

disposed and drawn to God is unlike human love in that God's love is not a response to an already existing good, but a love which makes its object worthy of love.[80]

2. *Efficient Causes of Spiritual Growth: Aquinas versus the Lombard*

Aquinas relates Peter Lombard's view that neither grace nor charity set up something in the soul since there is no intermediary between God and the soul any more than there is a mediator between the body and its life-giving principle, the soul.[81] While faith and hope are from the Holy Ghost by the intermediaries of the intellect and will, the Lombard saw charity as the Holy Ghost Himself present immediately to the soul's essence.[82] But Aquinas replies that an efficient cause (here, the Holy Ghost) works through a created form, and that endowing things with principles of their own self-motion signals a powerful, not a weak, agent. In the case of grace, God provides the soul with an elevating form which enables a connatural similarity (or proportion) between the soul and God.[83] The will is not moved coercively, or as an instrument, but retains its causality to act/not to act as a voluntary principle. As he says elsewhere,[84] "every agent which does not act according to its proper form but only because it is moved by another, is an agent only instrumentally, as an axe is an agent only inasmuch as it is moved by a woodsman."

Drawing on Aristotle's metaphysics of substance, he continues, just as accidents inhere in subjects, powers and their virtues flow from a ground—the soul's essence. Charity is to the will as grace is to the soul's essence—one is an operative, the other, an entitative habit from which the virtue

80. This, according to Rudi te Velde, in his *Aquinas on God: The "Divine Science" of the Summa Theologiae* (Farnham, United Kingdom: Ashgate, 2006), 168n44.

81. Aquinas discusses Augustine's and the Lombard's identity of charity and the Holy Spirit in the soul in the treatise on grace as well as on the virtue of charity, once again using Greek metaphysics in his solutions (of sanctifying grace [ST I-II, q. 110, a. 1] and charity [ST II-II, q. 23, a. 2]). ST II-II, q. 23, a. 2 presents the Lombard's view. Cf. *De caritate* 1.

82. Peter Lombard, *Sententiae in IV libris distinctae*, I, d. 17, c. 6.1. The context of the question concerns whether the Holy Spirit is the same as the love by which we love our neighbor and God.

83. ST II-II, q. 23, a. 2. God gives the soul a created form (grace) by which the virtues and Gifts are exercised. However, "God is the life of the soul in the manner of a mover, and not in the manner of a formal principle" (*De caritate* 1, ad 1).

84. *De caritate* 1.

grows, making our soul to an extent proportioned, or connatural, to heaven. Charity fits us for participation in God, and grace is a habitual gift and principle needed for this end, enabling us to be led by God's hand, sweetly and promptly, towards beatitude.[85]

But even if grace is a habit intervening between the essence of the soul and its powers, on the one hand, and the infused virtues, on the other, we may still wonder why the principle of our spiritual life is not the Holy Ghost Himself (i.e., uncreated charity). The Holy Ghost, after all, moves or prompts (*instinctus)* the soul interiorly in the Gifts, and His name is "Love," the first gift through which all other goods proceed.[86] At several points in his career, Aquinas treats the question of whether charity is something created in the soul or the Holy Ghost Himself.[87] There are several reasons why he answers the question in the negative.

First, if sanctifying grace were not a created habit, but the Holy Ghost Himself, pantheism would ensue. For the Lombard, our wills are united to the Holy Spirit in a way similar to the two natures in Christ. He used an analogy to explain this: Just as color is the product of light and a transparent medium, so charity is the product of the Holy Ghost and the will. Against the Lombard, Aquinas points out that the union of natures in the hypostatic union differs from the union of the Holy Ghost and the human will. In the hypostatic union, "numerically the same act belongs at once to a divine Person and to the human nature assumed." Here, Christ's two natures perform an identical act. But the union between the will and the Holy Spirit is a lesser union. In this latter case, "the will of one or another saint is not assumed into unity of the Holy Spirit's supposit." [88]

Further, if the Holy Spirit is itself the virtue of charity, occasionalism results, with God as the only cause and creatures merely providing the "occasion" for divine action.[89] We would lack both a free response to the

85. ST I-II, q. 110, a. 3 on charity in the will, and grace in the soul's essence. Grace works formally, he states (ST II-II, q. 23, a. 2 ad and 3).

86. The Holy Spirit's names are "Love" and "Gift": ST I, q. 37, a. 1; q. 38, a. 2.

87. E.g., *De caritate* 1; *In 1 Sent.*, d. 17, q. 1, a. 1; ST II-II, q. 23, a. 2.

88. Aquinas explains the Lombard's analogy in his study of the issue at *In 1 Sent.*, d. 17, q. 1, a. 1, sol.

89. On occasionalism and Aquinas's solution to it, see *Stanford Encyclopedia of Philosophy*, "Nicolas Malebranche" entry: https://plato.stanford.edu/entries/malebranche/#Occ. Aquinas's objection to Islamic occasionalism (posited to magnify divine omnipotence) lay in the fact that creatures are true secondary causes—a fact evident to the senses and necessary for scientific explanation (creatures' natures are needed to explain effects).

offer of grace and a stable foundation for virtue, being as mere axes in the woodsman's hands.[90] Our wills are not moved to charity by coercion, or even as instruments—the very meaning of love presupposes that we have rational appetites and have the freedom to act or not to act.[91] Neither pleasure in acting nor merit in achieving would exist, if there were no intrinsic formal principle grounding the theological virtues.[92]

Aquinas also draws on Aristotle's metaphysics in another argument against making the Holy Ghost identical to charity in the soul. It is the mark of a more perfect agent to induce a form by which a thing reaches its end—forms are a sign of God "keeping an order" in things.[93] Habits of the soul require an active interior principle. Aristotle's focus on the natural order also provides the backdrop once again. Aquinas gives an *a fortiori* proof from the natural order: God provides for nature by giving creatures principles to attain their natural ends; so much more so does he provide for souls.[94] Aristotle's notion of habit appears again in another argument against the Lombard's identification, in a reason taken from "actual love." Without a habit of grace, grace is reduced to mere actual grace or a transitory event. This entails denying that we are in a state of grace when we are not actually loving and denies the Spirit's disposing or preparing the soul to love, before we actually love, in order that we might love well and easily.[95] Again, God does not coerce our soul, or use it as a tool, but abides in it—hence the Scriptural language of grace as a pledge, seal, fountain, and seed of glory.[96]

Finally, the argument for a distinction between the Holy Ghost and created charity in the soul is not a denial of God's presence in our spiritual life. The Holy Ghost, Aquinas says, exists in those with created charity, moves them to acts of love, "as he moves all things to their own actions by which they are inclined by their own proper forms." The order between primary

90. *De caritate* 1c: "Every agent which does not act according to its proper form but only because it is moved by another, is an agent only instrumentally, as an axe is an agent only inasmuch as it is moved by a woodsman."

91. ST II-II, q. 23, a. 2. Sanctifying grace modifies the soul as a non-predicamental accident which makes its powers of mind and will capable of exercising the infused virtues of faith and charity. In addition, God prepares the soul for this reception of grace. The analogy given is of a person turning their eyes towards the sunlight, as a preparation for seeing the light. See ST I-II, q. 109, a. 6.

92. Cf. *De caritate* 1c.

93. *De caritate* 1, ad 14.

94. ST I-II, q. 110, a. 2.

95. *In 1 Sent.* d. 17, q. 1, a. 2. On the preparation of the soul by the Spirit, see ST III, q. 112, a. 2.

96. ST I-II, q. 110, a. 2.

and secondary causes signals that God "disposes all things sweetly"[97] precisely because He gives us forms and powers by which we tend to Him freely, pleasantly, and meritoriously.

V. Conclusion

Aristotle's fourfold causal analysis can be applied fruitfully to a trio of ecclesial themes in Maritain, which serve as final causes in the soul's advance in charity. They also undergird the interplay of formal, material, and efficient causes at work in Aquinas's mystical theology. Taken together, these themes provide elements of both the deductive and inductive approaches recommended by Garrigou in the study of mystical theology, and affirm the ecclesial dimension of Thomistic spirituality in our contemporary landscape of forgotten signposts: namely, the Church as a transcendent, eternal Person, the Church triumphant as the life of the blessed, and the Church as the spotless Bride of Christ. They also provide a sometimes lyrical foundation for more systematic renderings of the paradox of a holy yet sinful Church.

Aquinas's Aristotelian commitments saturate his own mystical theology in his views on contemplation, sanctifying grace and charity in the soul, the sacraments, and the relation of the Church to the Trinity. In arguing against the Lombard's identification of the Holy Ghost and charity in the soul, Aquinas deploys an Aristotelian theory of causal order and intrinsic principles to further his interpretation of the efficient causes of spiritual growth. Doing so avoids both pantheism and occasionalism, errors which sideline the virtues and merit by denying free will. For both Maritain and Aquinas, then, Aristotle's metaphysics, often derided for its static ahistorical quality, proves to be a surprisingly versatile and rich foundation for discussions of our supernatural life.

97. *De caritate* 1c.

ALICE RAMOS

Ratzinger on Faith, Philosophy, and Trust

I. Introduction

PERHAPS NOT AS WELL-KNOWN as his other works, *Faith and the Future* provides us with important insights not only into Joseph Cardinal Ratzinger's thought but also, for our purposes here, perhaps with a "new" way of considering the meaning of faith in contemporary human life—a way which I think coincides with what faith meant in the lives of Jacques and Raïssa Maritain. While this particular book consists of relatively brief chapters first presented as radio addresses in 1969 and 1970, Ratzinger's reflections on what he calls "the problem of faith and the future" are as vital today as they were forty-five years ago.

In this paper I will focus first on what faith means for Ratzinger. According to him, faith is not a system of knowledge, but rather an existential attitude of trust—trust in a Person who is truth itself. His description of faith is, in my opinion, powerful, harmonizing as it does with who the human person really is—that is, a spirit-endowed being—even if the dominant culture in which we live does not present the person in this light. When we say that we believe in God, or that we believe God, we are actually saying that we trust and rely on God, and this reliance gives us a certainty which, although different from the certainty of science, is nonetheless comparable to it. For Ratzinger, "Faith is a disclosure of reality that is granted only to him who trusts, loves, and acts as a human being."[1] Although faith is like knowledge, it is even more basic and essential to our authentically human

1. Joseph Cardinal Ratzinger, *Faith and the Future* (San Francisco: Ignatius Press, 2009), 29–30. Throughout this essay, I will be referring to Ratzinger rather than to Benedict XVI, as all the works cited here are prior to his papacy.

nature than the knowledge of an array of supernatural facts is.[2] And this is so because faith, even if enigmatic and impracticable, entails the loving and trusting relationship of a child to his mother. In referring specifically to the assent given to God by the Christian, Ratzinger says:

> Christian faith lives on the discovery that not only is there such a thing as objective meaning but that this meaning knows me and loves me, that I can entrust myself to it like a child who knows that everything he may be wondering about is safe in the "you" of his mother. Thus in the last analysis believing, trusting, and loving are one, and all the theses around which belief revolves are only concrete expressions ... of the discovery of God in the countenance of the man Jesus of Nazareth.[3]

Christian faith, then, is an encounter with a Person who upholds and loves each individual human person, and fulfills all the hopes of the person, guaranteeing that persistent longing for a life that will not end.[4] As Ratzinger sees it, faith in the Person of the risen Christ assures life beyond death, but also creates responsibility for the present, giving it substance, since the present then falls under the measure of eternity: a measure that refers not only to the judgment of God in man's conscience but also to the transforming power of grace and to divine forgiveness.[5]

Given Ratzinger's definition and description of faith, I will briefly bring to bear here what Thomas Aquinas says about the trust of faith and hope and how he explains the act of belief and also unbelief. Because both intellect and will are involved in belief, we will see why there is unbelief according to Ratzinger, and why faith today finds itself in a state of intellectual void or, as he puts it, in a state of "philosophical homelessness."[6] We are not, however, left without hope, for there seem to be indications of a renaissance at work in philosophy, made possible by those who live their faith as "a decision for a meaningful structure."[7] As an example we will refer to the life and work of Jacques and Raïssa Maritain.

2. Ibid., 30.

3. Ratzinger, *Introduction to Christianity*, translated by J. R. Foster (San Francisco: Ignatius Press; Communio Books, 1990), 48, quoted in *Faith and the Future*, 33–34.

4. Ibid.

5. Ratzinger, *Faith and the Future*, 55 and 58–59. See also Ratzinger, *Verdad, Valores, Poder*, translated by José Luis Del Barco (Madrid: Rialp, 2000), 76–77, where Ratzinger beautifully notes that the truth of Christianity is not only demanding, judging us in our very conscience, but more importantly transforming forgiveness.

6. Ibid., 83.

7. Ibid., 84.

II. The Adventure of Faith and the Mystical Capacity of the Human Mind

From the perspective of faith, Ratzinger presents us with an understanding of human existence and of the person that is rarely attended to in our culture and that attests to the grandeur of the human person. It is both a challenging and ecstatic understanding of the person precisely because it takes us out of the realm of the comfortable and engages us in an arduous adventure, the very severity of which, according to Ratzinger, makes it beautiful.[8] That Ratzinger should juxtapose the beauty and the severity of an adventure almost sounds paradoxical by present-day standards, but it seems warranted when he speaks of commitment to the adventure in terms of a mountain ascent,[9] entering "into the cloud of the incognito of God,"[10] so as to ultimately become a seer;[11] or when Ratzinger describes the adventure according to the image of a journey—a journey which requires detachment from the person's immediate environment or accustomed world—in order to embark on a nomadic existence that will enable the person to explore the whole of creation until the ultimate foundation of the whole is discovered.[12] What is implicit in this understanding of the adventure of faith toward vision and the discovery of the whole and its foundation, or what seems to make it possible, is, according to Ratzinger and as we shall see, the expansiveness of the human soul—which has been called a potency unto the infinite or a spiritual substance, which is in a sense "all in all," being able to comprehend all there is.[13]

8. Ibid., 85.

9. Ibid., 36.

10. Ratzinger, *What It Means to Be a Christian*, translated by Henry Taylor (San Francisco: Ignatius Press, 2006), 37.

11. Ratzinger, *Truth and Tolerance*, translated by Henry Taylor (San Francisco: Ignatius Press, 2004), 161.

12. Ratzinger, *Faith and the Future*, 41.

13. Thomas Aquinas, *Summa Contra Gentiles* III, chap. 112. The human mind, according to Thomas, is ordered to the totality of all that is. As he says in this text, "Spirit endowed beings possess a higher affinity to the whole of reality than other beings. Every spiritual substance namely, in a certain sense, is all in all, insofar as it is able, through its cognitive power, to comprehend all there is. Any other substance, in contrast, enjoys but an incomplete participation in the realm of being." In *De Veritate*, q. 2, a. 2, resp., Thomas says something similar about the human soul and its end: "It has been said that the soul is in a certain sense all in all; for its nature is directed toward universal knowledge. In this manner is it possible for the perfection of the entire world to be present in one single being. Consequently, the highest perfection attainable for the soul would be reached when the soul comprehends the entire order of the universe and

The model of faith that Ratzinger holds out to us in *Faith and the Future* is that of Abraham, who met God, responded to his word, and placed his future in God's hands, even if this future was enveloped in darkness. In hearing God's call, Abraham underwent a mystical experience which indicated the way he should take. Ratzinger describes Abraham as having "something of the seer about him, a sensitivity to being, which enlarged his perception beyond the bounds of what is accessible to our normal senses. He had a faculty for perceiving the divine."[14] This faculty may be compared to the mystical capacity that the human mind has when the inner life of man is strengthened.[15]

While making use of the images of the mountain ascent and of the journey, Ratzinger cites as a concrete example of the inner strength and mystical capacity of the human mind an incident toward the end of St. Benedict's life. This incident is recounted by St. Gregory the Great in his *Dialogues* and gives us the following depiction of Benedict: The founder of the monastic order was sleeping in the upper story of a tower reached from below by a vertical ladder. He awakened to keep a night vigil, standing at the window and praying to God. As he looked out in the darkness of the night, "he suddenly saw a light pouring from above and driving all the darkness of the night away. ... Something quite marvelous happened in this vision, as he himself later recounted: the whole world was held before his eyes, as if brought together in a single ray of sunshine."[16] The fact that Benedict would have seen the whole world in a single ray of light seems unfathomable, and yet Gregory the Great explains how this happened: "If he ... saw the whole world as one before him, then it was not that heaven and

---

its principles, according to the philosophers. They therefore see precisely in this the ultimate end of man, which—as we believe—will be realized in the beatific vision; for as Gregory says, 'what would those not see who see him who sees all?'" These texts are cited in Josef Pieper, *Living the Truth* (San Francisco: Ignatius Press, 1989), 84–85. As Thomas sees it, "beings endowed with cognitive ability somehow resemble God himself in whom all things preexist, as Dionysius says," (*De Div. Nom.*, 5, 1, also quoted in ST I, q. 80, a. 1, resp.).

14. Ibid., 43. According to Ratzinger, Abraham's enlarged perception is also characteristic of "all the great religious geniuses." This capacity is not meant solely for the good of the individual person, but rather is meant to be used so as introduce others to God. For this reason Ratzinger says, "A relationship with God is not the private affair of each individual, something into which no one else can or may enter; rather, it is something at once wholly interior and yet wholly public." See ibid., 43–44.

15. Ratzinger, *Truth and Tolerance*, 159.

16. Ibid., 159–60.

earth became narrower but [that] the visionary's soul became so wide."[17]

Ratzinger goes on to further explain this incident: Benedict had begun a difficult and long journey in a cave near Subiaco; he had interiorly struggled up the mountain of his life and had reached the tower—the symbolic look-out point from which he could gaze upon the world—by means of ascending, step by step up the vertical ladder, by means of undergoing repeated purifications throughout his life which would enable him to mature inwardly and to grasp truth more clearly. As Ratzinger puts it, "It is not the world that is narrowed down but the soul that is broadened out, being no longer absorbed in the particular, no longer looking at the trees and unable to see the world, but now able to view the whole. Even better, he can see the whole because he is looking at it from on high, and he is able to gain this vantage point because he has grown inwardly great."[18] Such an arduous process of interior transformation—the journey and climb of faith—which leads to the maturity and greatness of the inner man and to his becoming a seer, is little understood in today's world because of the emphasis on the outer man to the real detriment of his inner life and the cultivation of his inner strength.[19] Ratzinger reminds us that the mystical capacity of the human mind, which was at work in Abraham and in Benedict, needs to be strengthened once again. As Christians who are, according to St. Paul, the children of Abraham, we too are on the road of faith traveling to God; we too are *in statu viatoris*. One of our priorities, given the all-absorbing technological age in which we live, should be according to Ratzinger the cultivation of this mystical capacity of our mind, with its capacity for self-renunciation and the discipline to focus our attention on what truly matters.[20]

In faith, then, man's authentic destination appears: he is freed from the realm of the calculable and from the hold of material goods so as to enter into a new and limitless horizon, that is, the "horizon toward the Eternal, toward the Creator."[21] The man of faith places his trust in the God who alone can guarantee his future and ultimate life—the God who is not a local god, but rather the maker of the whole universe, and as such knows man personally and accompanies man wherever he goes. Faith for Ratzin-

17. Gregory the Great, *Dialogi* 2:35:5 and 7, quoted in *Truth and Tolerance*, 160.
18. Ratzinger, *Truth and Tolerance*, 161.
19. Ibid., 159.
20. Ibid.
21. Ratzinger, *Faith and the Future*, 41.

ger, then, cannot be described as an inscrutable system of knowledge, but rather must be "an existential attitude, a fundamental decision about the direction of life," which he calls trust.[22] Faith at its core is trust.

While the details of faith may remain obscure, the assent of faith according to Ratzinger regards the whole and only secondarily the part.[23] The man of faith lives his life in a spirit of trust, realizing not only that a theoretical grasp of particular dogma may forever exceed him in this life, but also and perhaps more importantly in practice that the details and parts of his life, which often remain incomprehensible to him and cause him to suffer, fit into a greater whole that God sees and comprehends and provides for. In this way, the man of faith realizes that his life is not confined to his immediate surroundings, that he is more than a material being, that he naturally desires and is interested in lasting things and in the Eternal, and that there is within him a natural desire and interest which enables him to break out of the visible and calculable realm and to make contact with the Eternal.[24] Faith thus conceived takes man beyond his smallness and petty attachments, which deprive him of his true greatness; faith makes him boldly realize that he can have dealings with the Eternal.[25] According to Ratzinger faith signifies a change in the accustomed, contemporary understanding of values, a change which is more in keeping with what and who the human person is. As he puts it, "Not what is useful for the moment, but what is conformed to eternity, is appropriate to man. What is conformed to eternity: that is what is worthy of lasting."[26] It is evident from what Ratzinger says that faith in no way diminishes man but on the contrary ennobles and dignifies him.

III. Unbelief and the Lack of Trust

Given this lofty, even if arduous, understanding of the faith—which precisely because of its arduousness is attractive and, as Ratzinger says, beautiful—one might wonder why so many men and women live lives of unbelief. The answer, of course, lies in what Ratzinger would call their lack of trust, since for him faith is not simply adherence to a set of dogma, as we have

22. Ibid., 35.
23. Ibid., 32.
24. Ibid., 42.
25. Ibid.
26. Ibid., 53.

seen, but more importantly an existential attitude of trust—that is, trust in a Person. According to Aquinas, trust is an integral part of both faith and hope, referring to their formal objects. The material object of the virtue of faith is truth and as such this virtue lies in the intellect; on the other hand, since the material object of hope is the arduous good, this virtue lies in the will. When Aquinas considers the formal objects of these two virtues, what is singled out is the reliance on someone: in faith we rely on God himself, on his word; and in hope, we expect help from another. The trust of faith and hope can thus be defined in terms of "an assured reliance on someone"—for knowledge in the case of faith, and for help in the case of hope.[27]

In a culture characterized by the hermeneutics of suspicion, trust is not easily cultivated, nor is the virtue of humility, so essential for trust. Because philosophy today is ever suspicious that truth can be attained, then the possibility of the mind's reaching the fullness of truth in faith and the recognition of the faith's enhancing the person's rational powers, as Edith Stein saw it,[28] are of little or no concern to many a contemporary philosopher. As Ratzinger puts it, the real obstacle to faith is the attitude that closes itself to questioning because it considers that truth cannot be reached or that it is not worth aiming for.[29] Given our present day predicament of cognitive and ethical relativism, with its banishment of absolute truths, and the stress in our culture on the autonomous individual whose freedom seems to be limitless and bound to no norm or truth, it is no wonder that trust in God's word and that reliance on God for his help are in such a precarious state. But here we can also stress, as we mentioned above, that trust requires humility, that is, the humility to entrust ourselves to someone who knows and sees more clearly than we do and thus to let ourselves be helped.

Now in considering the act of faith as an internal act of belief, Aquinas will say that it is "an act of the intellect determined by the will's command" and that therefore the act of faith is related to the good and the end—that is, to the object of the will, and to the true, which is the object of the intellect,[30] the true being the good of the intellect. For Aquinas, then, the act of believ-

27. Marie I. George, "Aquinas on the Nature of Trust," *The Thomist* 70 (2006): 103–105.

28. Alasdair MacIntyre, *Edith Stein. A Philosophical Prologue, 1913–1922* (Lanham, Maryland: Rowman and Littlefield, 2006), 143–44.

29. Ratzinger, *Faith and the Future*, 29; see also 73.

30. *Summa Theologiae* (ST) II-II, q. 4, a. 1, resp. All quoted passages from the *Summa* are taken from *Summa Theologica*, translated by the Fathers of the English Dominican Province (New York: Benziger Brothers, 1948).

ing requires that the will move the intellect to assent.[31] We may therefore choose not to believe, although it would seem from what Aquinas says that unbelief is contrary to the nature of the human mind, as the mind naturally desires to know. As Aquinas says, "To have the faith is not part of human nature, but it is part of human nature that man's mind should not go against its inner instinct, and the outward preaching of the truth. Hence, in this way, unbelief is contrary to nature."[32] Of interest and relevance here, I think, is Alasdair MacIntyre's claim in his Carus lectures that intellectual errors are often, although not always, rooted in moral error.[33] For in referring to heresy as a species of unbelief, Aquinas not only refers to the proximate end of heresy as adherence to one's own opinion but also addresses its remote end or cause which lies in pride or covetousness, or in some illusion of imagination.[34] Given the pride that can then cause the mind to dissent from the truth, and given the covetousness that can lead to amassing more than is necessary in the disordered tendency toward self-sufficiency such that one would hope only in oneself, it is not surprising that trust as an integral part of faith and hope would be lacking to many a contemporary man.

IV. The Maritains' Quest for Truth and the Faith Made Visible

If we consider here the lives of Jacques and Raïssa Maritain, we will see the relevance of Ratzinger's understanding of faith as trust in a Person who is truth itself. As is only too well known, the Maritains were convinced that without truth life was not worth living; they were in search of the meaning of life to which they could give their full allegiance.[35] The lectures of Bergson at the Sorbonne and in particular his course on Plotinus prompted in them a sort of intellectual conversion, because they were being put into contact with a philosophical tradition that was both sapiential and in

31. ST II-II, q. 2. a. 1, ad 3. In response to the question whether to believe is to think with assent, Aquinas says, "The intellect of the believer is determined to one object, not by reason, but by the will, and so assent is taken here for an act of the intellect as determined to one object by the will."

32. ST II-II, q. 10, a. 1, ad 1.

33. Alasdair MacIntyre, *Dependent Rational Animals: Why Human Beings Need the Virtues* (Chicago: Open Court, 1999), 96.

34. ST II-II, q. 11, a. 1, ad 2–3.

35. Ralph McInerny, *The Very Rich Hours of Jacques Maritain: A Spiritual Life* (Notre Dame, Indiana: University of Notre Dame Press, 2003), 16.

the last analysis theological, a tradition in which truth could be known, in which the human mind was capable of knowing reality with certainty and truth. Despite the relativism of the scientists and the skepticism of the philosophers they had encountered, they were being convinced that life did have a meaning after all and that it could be lived according to the truth.[36]

Bergson's lectures not only made them realize that the truth could be attained by the human mind but also opened their minds to a reality beyond the physical realm.[37] Their sincere quest for the truth predisposed them to the fullness of truth in the faith and to the realization that their life was to be lived in conformity with the Person who is truth.[38] We might say that the Maritains' search for meaning favorably inclined them to the faith, which they would later live as "a decision for a meaningful structure," to use Ratzinger's words from *Faith and the Future.*[39] While it is the case that faith is a gift from God, a supernatural virtue infused in the soul by God, and that the person's mind and heart need to be prepared by God's grace in order to believe,[40] it is also the case that there can be in the person a sort of preparation or disposition—even if this, too, is said to be the work of divine grace—for turning toward God in faith, and this seems evident in the Maritains' quest for truth.

Their introduction to the Christian faith through Léon Bloy did not, interestingly, dispel their intellectual doubts, for Bloy did not present arguments to them to counter their doubts, but on the contrary suggested that they read the Bible, the Word of God, that they visit the cathedral of Chartres where they would have a glimpse into sacred history in and through the cathedral's architecture, sculpture, and windows, and that they read the lives of the saints.[41] All of this, in addition to the living witness of believers such as Bloy himself and Rouault, would "ignite" their imaginations and also their minds.[42] Bloy's advice to them was meant, I think, to cultivate that mystical capacity of the mind that Ratzinger speaks about—the faculty for perceiving the divine, such that one's vision and understanding is ef-

36. Ibid., 17–19.

37. Ibid., 20.

38. As they would learn through Léon Bloy, "Il n'y a qu'une tristesse, c'est de n'être pas des saints."

39. See note 7 above.

40. See ST II-II, q. 6, a. 1, ad 3.

41. McInerny, *The Very Rich Hours of Jacques Maritain*, 33–34.

42. Ibid., 26.

fectively enlarged—and so that the soul and its powers become broadened. Bloy had them in fact reading the texts of visionaries and mystics, and in their discussions of these texts with him what became especially evident was his profound faith—a faith that spoke to them perhaps more eloquently than the texts themselves.

From their readings, discussions, and experience of seeing the faith and its demands lived by Bloy, the Maritains were becoming steeped in Catholicism, in its history, theology, literature, and mysticism. Their view of the Church was also transformed when they realized the way in which all believers are bound together in the Communion of the Saints, the Mystical Body of Christ, which is forever animated by the Holy Spirit; with this new understanding of the Church, they no longer viewed the Church as "a gathering of the smug and comfortable."[43] The Maritains were clearly drawn to the accounts of mystical experiences, and could see the beauty of a life of faith even if the move toward conversion seemed to go against the grain of their environment and upbringing, and thus was no easy step to take.[44] They needed, therefore, to trust and to respond to the truth and goodness which was also calling them from within, realizing that God, too, was waiting.[45]

Bloy's advice to the Maritains, that they immerse themselves in the experience of Chartres and in the writings of holy men and women, also coincides in great part with what Ratzinger considers to be the most effective apologia for Christianity, namely, "the saints that the Church has produced and the art that has grown in her womb."[46] As Ratzinger puts it, "Better witness is borne to the Lord by the splendor of holiness and art which have arisen in the community of believers than by the clever excuses which apologetics has come up with to justify the dark sides which, sadly, are so frequent in the Church's human history."[47] For Ratzinger abstract repre-

43. Ibid., 25.

44. Ibid., 26.

45. Raïssa Maritain, *We Have Been Friends Together,* translated by Julie Kernan (New York: Longmans, Green and Co., 1942), 174. Their preparation and disposition toward the faith was such that Raïssa speaks as though the seeds of faith had been implanted in the depths of their souls; this was revealed to them upon the reception of the sacrament of Baptism. See ibid., 178.

46. Ratzinger, *The Ratzinger Report,* quoted in John Saward, *The Beauty of Holiness and the Holiness of Beauty* (San Francisco: Ignatius Press, 1997), 8.

47. Ibid. Ratzinger goes on to speak in this passage of the special place which beauty has in the Church and stresses the importance of beauty in the liturgy as he had done in his book *The Spirit of the Liturgy,* translated by John Saward (San Francisco: Ignatius Press, 2000): "If the

sentations cannot explain to us the real meaning of faith. On the contrary, faith is made visible to us through the lives of men and women who have lived the attitude of trust, committing themselves to the arduous journey or mountain ascent, and who have thus demonstrated through their lives that this faith can be lived in a coherent and consistent way.[48] Ratzinger cites numerous examples of such men and women who trusted because they also loved. Faith, then, also involves "a particular kind of passion," as Ratzinger says, "a kind of love that seizes a man and points the way he must go, even if that way is wearisome. That way may turn out to be a mountain ascent that seems folly to the comfortable and narrow-minded middle-class citizen but, to the one who has committed himself to the adventure, the one and only way, which he would not wish to exchange for all the comfort in the world."[49]

And so revolted by the anti-metaphysical materialism of their time, the

---

Church is to continue to transform and humanize the world, how can she dispense with beauty in her liturgies, that beauty which is so closely linked with love and with the radiance of the Resurrection? No. Christians must not be too easily satisfied. They must make their Church into a place where beauty—and hence truth—is at home. Without this the world will become the first circle of Hell."

48. I think it is important to emphasize that the faith about which Ratzinger speaks is the Christian faith—the faith transmitted by Christ to his apostles. The truth of this faith is upheld and defended by the Catholic Church, although in *Faith and the Future* Ratzinger simply refers to the Church as the Church of Jesus Christ. In giving his reasons for being in the Catholic Church, Ratzinger says, "I am in the Church for the same reasons that I am Christian: because one cannot believe on one's own.... One can only be Christian in the Church, not beside her," quoted by Silvano Zucal in "The Intellectual Relationship between Joseph Ratzinger and Romano Guardini," *L'Osservatore Romano* (December 10, 2008): 3. Elsewhere, in his essay "Vérité du Christianisme," ms., 13, Ratzinger speaks of the *Logos*, the Word that not only accounts for the intelligibility of the universe, but also as creative love takes on human nature to redeem mankind. Jesus Christ is the *Logos*, the Word through whom all things were made, and thus Christianity, the Church of Jesus Christ, is the religion of the *Logos*. The Person of Christ is the fullness of truth that the human person reaches in the Christian faith, and to whom the person must entrust himself or herself if he or she is truly to believe. While believers of other religions may be exemplary in the living out of their faith as they know it, they are still lacking the fullness of truth as it is communicated to us through Christ in and through his Church.

49. Ratzinger, *Faith and the Future*, 36. Elsewhere, in *Truth and Tolerance*, while not speaking of saints, the notion of sanctity is implied in those whom Ratzinger calls seers and pathfinders. Ratzinger says, "The essential point is this: man has to learn to climb up; he has to grow and broaden out. He has to stand at the window. He must gaze out. And then the light of God can touch him; he can recognize it and can gain from it the true overview. Our being planted on earth should never become so exclusive that we become incapable of ascending, of standing upright. Those great men who, by patient climbing and by the repeated purification they have received in their lives, have become seers and, therefore, pathfinders for the centuries are also relevant to us today. They show us how light may be found even in the night and how we can meet the threats that rise up from the abysses of human existence and can meet the future as men of hope" (161).

Maritains were willing to take on the demands of the faith and to obey the voice of their consciences which indicated insertion in the Church as alone promising them the light of truth—truth for which they were in fact willing to turn forever away from philosophy, at least so Jacques thought.[50] The truth of faith was not, however, going to ask this of them; on the contrary, Jacques was to serve this same Truth by devoting himself to the task of philosophy. According to Raïssa, his vocation was to "reinsert [Thomism] into the existential reality of the movement of culture and philosophy," and while he did philosophize in faith and theology, his work was not theological but properly philosophical.[51]

The reasons for the dilemma in which the Christian faith finds itself today are, I think, similar to those of the time in which the Maritains lived. As Ratzinger sees it, the faith is for the most part in a state of "philosophical homelessness," thus finding itself in an intellectual vacuum. This was not, however, always the case, for as Ratzinger says, "In ancient times and in the Middle Ages, one of the things that helped men to find faith was that philosophy provided them with a picture of the world in which faith could find a meaningful place."[52] As we have seen, while Bergson and Plotinus were influential in producing in the Maritains an intellectual conversion, it was not until their encounter with Léon Bloy that they found the meaning that they needed and could make a decision for this meaning, a decision which led Jacques to dedicate himself to a philosophy where faith could in effect find a home. In finding "a new philosophy of the world and of man,"[53] we will need to take more seriously both the wisdom of Aquinas and the apologetics that Ratzinger calls for—an apologetics based on the beauty of the arduous lives of the saints and on the splendor of Christian art, both of which played a role in the Maritains' decision for the truth of the faith and for their life's work. Such an apologetics will no doubt help to cultivate the mystical capacity of the human mind and enlarge the soul of the person. Philosophers have been called recently to explore the realm of the beautiful as a way to the truth and to goodness, for the beautiful is not only intelligible and loveable, but also "in specifying our knowledge,

50. McInerny, *The Very Rich Hours of Jacques Maritain*, 26. See also Raïssa Maritain, *We Have Been Friends Together*, 174–75.

51. Raïssa Maritain, *Adventures in Grace*, translated by Julie Kernan (New York: Longmans, Green, and Co., 1945), 214–15.

52. Ratzinger, *Faith and the Future*, 61.

53. Ibid., 83.

it attracts us, or captures us with a ray capable of igniting marvel,"[54] and marvel is precisely what leads philosophers to seek the ultimate principles and causes of all of reality, and thus to attain to the beauty of truth.

54. "The *Via Pulchritudinis*, Beauty as a Way for Evangelization and Dialogue," post-plenary document of the Pontifical Council of Culture, *Cultures and Faith* 14, no. 2 (Vatican City, 2006): 120.

JOHN J. CONLEY, S.J.

Canticle

Maritain, John Paul II, Benedict XVI

IN HIS BOOK *Twentieth-Century Catholic Theologians,* the Scottish Dominican theologian Fergus Kerr argues that one of the oddest traits of Catholic theology in the latter part of the twentieth century was the growing influence of the biblical book, the *Song of Songs.*[1] Although the brief text has long been savored by mystics and artists, this collection of love songs has had little influence on Jewish or Christian doctrine. In fact, its presence in the biblical canon has long been considered somewhat of an embarrassment. It is the only biblical book which makes no explicit mention of God. Its detailed and sensual descriptions of the human body and erotic desire have led some to find it scandalous.[2] The purpose of this paper is to explore the contrasting uses of the *Song of Songs* in the writings of Jacques Maritain, John Paul II, and Benedict XVI.

1. See Fergus Kerr, *Twentieth-Century Catholic Theologians* (London: Wiley-Blackwell, 2006).

2. The history of the composition of the *Song of Songs* (or *Canticle of Canticles*) remains a matter of dispute. Biblical exegetes claim that the oldest sections of the book may date as far back as the ninth century BC and that the most recent could have been composed as late as the third century BC. Jewish and Christian authorities have long associated the book with King Solomon, but the language indicates that some of it must have been written well before the existence of the court of Solomon. The process of recognizing the book as canonical in Judaism was a long and controversial one. In the first century BC rabbis disputed whether the book should be considered divinely inspired or not. Only in the second century AD did the book become part of the universally accepted canon. Christians have always included the book as part of their biblical canon and treated the book as part of the Old Testament's wisdom literature.

I. Maritain

In *Approches sans entraves* (1973) Maritain interprets the book in an ecclesiastical fashion. The Bride in the nuptial songs is identified as the Church and the Bridegroom as Christ. This is not an unusual identification. Early in Judaism, rabbinical commentators had identified the nameless bride or fiancée as Israel, citing the explicit parallels made between the bride and Israel in the prophets Hosea and Isaiah. Later Christian commentators easily transformed this nuptial union between the bridegroom and the bride into the mystical union between the new Israel (the Church) and her spouse (Christ). Medieval commentators began to interpret the bride as the human soul, called to mystical communion with God, and to identify the bride with the Blessed Virgin Mary, an identification which survives in the liturgical use of the appropriate passages from the *Song of Songs* in various Marian feasts.

Even if Maritain's identification of the spouse with the Church is entirely traditional, his treatment of the moral character of the spouse is very much his own. He insists that the spouse is sinless—that is, morally perfect. This is so because the Church, Christ's spouse, is sinless, despite the obvious sins and failings of her members:

> The person of the Church is indefectibly holy but her personnel is not, no more so than her other members. When the personnel speak and act as an instrumental agent of the Church (extraordinary and ordinary magisterium and the entire sacramental order), we are certain that it is the person of the Church who is speaking and acting by it, with her holiness and her infallibility. When it speaks and acts as its own proper cause, the personnel represents the Church to the degree to which it is faithful to grace and to the assistance of the Holy Spirit. But it can be mistaken and badly mistaken. We have no lack of examples of this down through history.[3]

Although the biblical text itself makes no such reference to the bride's moral composition, Maritain develops such a reading to defend the holiness, infallibility, and indefectibility of the Church herself. Ecclesiological concerns are clearly driving the biblical exegesis.

To reinforce this ecclesial reading of the text, Maritain denies that the original or primary meaning of the text is a celebration of physical love. The references to natural love are simply symbolic expressions for the

3. Jacques Maritain, *Approches sans entraves* (Paris: Fayard, 1973), 549. All translations from the French are my own.

purely spiritual covenant of love between Christ and His Church. He takes great pains to defend the supernatural nature of the Church in this ecclesial interpretation: "The Canticle sees in the pure ecstasy of love a supernatural ecstasy. To chant it, it places all the power and beauty of carnal love at its service. This is purely a sign and method for expressing [the supernatural love]."[4] The natural here is completely subordinated to the supernatural. The proper interpretation of the spouse's love, like the proper understanding of the origin of the Church, must avoid any effort to eliminate or diminish their squarely supernatural natures.

This unusual ecclesiological interpretation of the *Song of Songs* raises an obvious question: Why did Maritain take such pains to argue that the bride in the poem is without moral blemish and that the love depicted in the poem is strictly supernatural? Maritain himself provides the answer when he informs the reader that his commentary on and his related translation of the *Canticle of Canticles* is tied to his work on an earlier book, *L'Église du Christ* (1970).[5] In this work Maritain staunchly defended the impeccability and the infallibility of the Catholic Church against post-conciliar theologians who had denied, diluted, or ignored these ecclesiological truths. He also defended the supernatural nature of the Church against those who saw the Church as a purely natural, social institution and who had dangerously misunderstood the essence of the Church's magisterium and sacraments. Maritain's unusual interpretation of the *Canticle of Canticles* is part of a broader campaign to refute errors in ecclesiology which were vitiating Catholic belief and practice during the post-conciliar crisis.

In fact, Maritain had employed an ecclesiastical interpretation of the *Song of Songs* even earlier in the *Paysan de la Garonne* (1966). Here, the impeccability of the Church is his focus: "The Church is without stain or wrinkle.... The Church is *sine macula, sine muga*. She is immaculate. There is no one dearer to the One who loves her [Christ, her spouse] who says: '*Veni columba mea*, come my dove, my perfectly beautiful one, without stain or wrinkle, holy and immaculate. ... Christ would have more gladly pardoned the spit on his face than He would pardon the least doubt concerning the sanctity of His Bride."[6] In the post-conciliar period, the incapacity of Church members, especially theologians, to recognize the impeccability

4. Ibid., 535.

5. See Jacques Maritain, *L'Église du Christ* (Paris: Desclée de Brouwer, 1970).

6. Jacques Maritain, *Paysan de la Garonne* (Paris: Desclée de Brouwer, 1966), 78.

of the Church—and, concomitantly, the impeccability of the bride who serves as a literary figure of the Church in the *Canticles*—is a symptom of the anti-supernatural "kneeling before the world" which Maritain believed was devastating Catholicism in its efforts at renewal.

Maritain's ecclesiological interpretation of the *Song of Songs* represents an unusual use of the book in the service of specific Catholic doctrine. While most Catholic interpretations of the work extend its passages in the direction of mysticism, with the sulfurous lyricism such mystical literature prizes, Maritain places the aesthetic description of the bride's appearance into a precise doctrinal key. The poetic features of the elusive bride are marshaled into a doctrinal argument on behalf of the Church's infallibility and impeccability. Doctrinal polemic on the traits of the true church has been placed at the center of the *Canticles*'s romance.

II. John Paul II

In a celebrated series of general audiences in 1984, John Paul II uses the *Song of Songs* in a different way. Constructing his "theology of the body," the pope uses the biblical book to explore legitimate and illegitimate expressions of sexual desire. The erotic desire between man and woman is perfectly legitimate, indeed necessary, for the covenant of marriage. But this powerful desire must always be accompanied by the exercise of the virtues of modesty, temperance, and chastity. Continence must be esteemed if erotic excess is to be avoided. It is only in the covenant of marriage—an exclusive, life-long commitment between one man and one woman—that the erotic desire expressed in the poetry of the *Song of Songs* can be properly grasped. Unsurprisingly, the philosopher-pope's analysis of this desire, as expressed by the spouses in the *Song of Songs*, reflects his philosophical allegiances to phenomenological method and to personalism.

In a phenomenological vein, reminiscent of the work of Max Scheler,[7] John Paul II analyzes the moral sentiments unveiled by the interaction between bride and groom. Rooted in sexual alterity, wonder and admiration characterize their first and enduring sentiments:

7. Max Ferdinand Scheler (1874–1928) applied the phenomenological method to the field of ethics and value theory. Karol Wojtyla devoted his second doctoral dissertation to Scheler's moral philosophy: "An Evaluation of the Possibility of Constructing a Christian Ethics on the Basis of the System of Max Scheler," (1954).

The point of departure as well as the point of arrival for this fascination—mutual wonder and admiration—are in fact the bride's femininity and the groom's masculinity, in the direct experience of their visibility. The words of love uttered by both of them are therefore concentrated on the body, not because in itself it constitutes the source of this mutual fascination. But it is also and above all, because the body there lingers directly and immediately, that attraction toward the other person, toward the other "I"—female or male—which in the interior impulse of the heart generates love.[8]

As the marital relationship matures in the establishment of a common household, other sentiments, such as the sense of mutual belonging, complement the originating sentiments of wonder and admiration.

In a personalist vein, John Paul II argues that the romantic odyssey of the Song's couple indicates the dignity of the human person. The way in which the bride and groom esteem and respect each other in their gestures and words of love indicate that the "possession" essential to erotic love is never one of domination or objectification:

In this interior necessity, in this dynamics of love, there is indirectly revealed the near impossibility of one person's being appropriated and mastered by the other. The person is someone who surpasses appropriation and domination, of possession and gratification, which emerge from the same language of the body. If the groom and the bride reread this language in the full truth about the person and about love, they arrive at the ever deeper conviction that the fullness of their belonging constitutes that mutual gift in which love is rendered as 'stern as death.'[9]

Transcendent, the amatory human person can never be reduced to an object of sexual conquest. Moreover, even in the most loving marital covenant, the other can never be fully possessed. Something remains elusive and ungraspable in the relationship. As the loving union deepens, the mysterious alterity of the other partner becomes more, and not less, palpable.

The customary recourse to allegory is strikingly absent in John Paul II's interpretation of the *Song of Songs*. He explicitly endorses the consensus opinion of most contemporary exegetes that originally this biblical book was a collection of romantic poems sung or recited at ceremonies surrounding marriage and betrothal. Their object was a celebration of purely human love. John Paul II acknowledges this original sense of the

8. Pope John Paul II, "General Audience of 23 May 1984": no. 3, https://www.ewtn.com/library/ PAPALDOC/jp2tb108.htm.

9. Pope John Paul II, "General Audience of 6 June 1984": no. 3, https://www.ewtn.com/library/ PAPALDOC/jp2tb110.htm.

book, but his analysis differs from those offered by strict adherents of the historical-critical method. His is a phenomenological analysis, unveiling the various moral sentiments of the couple, and it is a personalist analysis, using the love depicted in the text to demonstrate the dignity of the human person in the sexual arena. Clearly, a philosopher is at work.

John Paul II's exegesis of the *Canticles* is also the work of a social critic. Behind his exegesis, indeed behind the entire cycle of addresses limning the theology of the body, lies the empirical fact of the sexual revolution. His personalist reading of the biblical book attempts to show how the only morally proper way to express the type of sexual desire evoked by the *Song of Songs* lies in a lifelong, exclusive, marital covenant between partners of the opposite sex. The powerful increase in the practice of divorce, concubinage, and adultery in recent times is a grave distortion of amatory desire and the implicit object of the exegesis's critique.

III. Benedict XVI

In the encyclical *Deus caritas est* (1995) Benedict XVI uses the *Song of Songs* to legitimize erotic union as an analogue to the union of the believer with God. He combats a longstanding tendency in modern Christianity to claim that Christian love is a purely disinterested one. The *agape* and *philia* of the Christian is allegedly a disinterested love of God and neighbor; as such, it is opposed to *eros*, a possessive love which treats the other as a romantic object. The pope insists that such a distinction is not grounded in Scripture. Among other biblical books, the *Song of Songs* demonstrates the parallel between the erotic desire between the two sexes and the desire of the believing soul for union with God. The mystical writings of the saints have long vindicated the truth of this parallel. In this interpretation, the *Song of Songs* discloses the erotic edge of faith itself as well as the proper role of chaste eroticism in Jewish and Christian life.

Benedict argues that in God *eros* and *agape* are united. Divine love is erotic inasmuch as it seeks union with the human person; it is apagistic inasmuch as it is gratuitous and forgiving. Benedict uses the traditional mystical interpretation of the *Song of Songs* to show how the relationship between God and humanity is reciprocally erotic:

> *Eros* is supremely ennobled, yet at the same time it is so purified as to become one with *agape*. We can thus see how the reception of the Song of Songs in the

> canon of Sacred Scripture was soon explained by the idea that these love songs ultimately describe God's relation to humanity and humanity's relation to God. Thus, the Song of Songs became, both in Christian and Jewish literature, a source of mystical knowledge and experience, an expression of the essence of biblical faith: that humanity can indeed enter into union with God—its primordial aspiration.[10]

The act of faith, centered in the loving covenant between God and the believing person, can be understood analogously in terms of the romantic relationship between the lovers in the *Song of Songs*. The sacred text illuminates the mutual, loving commitment at the heart of biblical faith.

The *Song of Songs* clarifies what sort of mystical union is proper to the biblical believer. The divine-human union proper to the Jewish and Christian believer is neither an annihilation of the human self nor a descent into the purely unknowable; it is covenant where the specific attributes of both the divine and human persons are strongly affirmed: "This union is no mere fusion, a sinking into the nameless ocean of the Divine; it is a unity which creates love, a unity in which both God and humanity remain themselves and yet become fully one."[11] While the love between the spouses in the *Song of Songs* can rightly receive a mystical interpretation, not all such interpretations are legitimate. A purely apophatic interpretation, where the human self disappears and the divinity becomes utterly opaque, is unfaithful to the biblical text and to a proper theology of the covenant. Benedict thus introduces a personalist reservation into the mystical interpretation of the *Canticle* as he uses the romance between the spouses as an analogue for the Christian act of faith.

Benedict's interpretation of the *Song of Songs* in terms of faith confirms a longstanding project of Ratzinger the theologian: to transcend the neo-scholastic concept of faith as an intellectual assent to a set of religious propositions. In his *Introduction to Christianity* Ratzinger claims that the act of faith is always an act of conversion of the entire person, the will as well as the intellect. It involves a total trust in God and a radical re-orientation of one's relationship with the world: "Faith is located in the act of conversion, in the turning of one's being from worship of the visible and the practicable to trust in the invisible."[12] In *Deus caritas est* Benedict argues that even

10. Pope Benedict XVI, *Deus caritas est* (1995): no. 10.

11. Ibid..

12. Joseph Cardinal Ratzinger, *Introduction to Christianity* (San Francisco: Ignatius Press, 1990), 88.

erotic love has its proper and necessary place in this robust and life-altering act of faith.

IV. Conclusion

As Fergus Kerr has suggested, one of the surprises in recent Catholic thought is the emergence of the heretofore obscure *Song of Songs* as a central reference in philosophical and theological debates. Perhaps even more surprising is the wide diversity of interpretations and applications of the book in the current revival, clearly evident in the divergent glosses on the *Canticle* in the writings of the three authors we have examined. Each author to some degree exercises eisegesis since he projects his own particular concerns and the preoccupations of his own time and society into the reading of the book he develops. There is nothing arbitrary in this eisegesis. Every biblical exegete inevitably brings his or her own questions into the treatment of the text. By its very genre, the *Song of Songs* might well facilitate this freewheeling, more personal style of biblical interpretation. It is brief, anonymous, elusive—Just who are these shifting personages?—disjointed (clearly a collation of disparate poems), and theologically minimalist. After all, it is the only biblical book to have no explicit reference to God.

In their quite different interpretations of the *Song of Songs*, three masters of Catholic thought—Maritain, Wojtyla, and Ratzinger—have shown how Scripture can be plumbed to address a crisis in the Church at a particular moment. What unites these divergent interpretations is precisely this ecclesial hermeneutical perspective. For Maritain, the *Canticle* is used to defend the infallibility and impeccability of the church in the immediate post-conciliar confusion. Against the all-conquering sexual revolution, John Paul II uses the book to highlight the moral sentiments of a loving couple within the proper bounds of sacramental marriage. In counterpoint to conceptualist reductions of the act of faith, Benedict XVI employs the text to show the erotic dimension inherent in the act of faith itself.

On the surface the text of the biblical book itself has nothing to do with ecclesiology, phenomenological ethics, or the nature of Christian faith. But from the perspective of a *sensus plenior* of Scripture, this trio of Catholic commentators demonstrates that the *Song of Songs* has everything to do with such apparently distant issues. Their ecclesiological tract, phenomenological ethics treatise, and exposition on faith indicate why and how insightful and prophetic exegesis involves far more than good philology.

VI

POLITICS AND SOCIETY

WALTER SCHULTZ

Toward a Grammar of Liberation

Exploring the Contours of Salvation in the Twenty-First Century

> When the Church hears the cry of the oppressed it cannot but denounce the social structures that give rise to and perpetuate the misery from which the cry arises.
>
> —Saint Oscar Romero[1]

> There can be no rest for the Christian as long as justice and love do not hold sway over the lives of men. And since their requirements will never be completely fulfilled within history, the Christian will therefore never have rest within history—and that's perfectly proper to his condition.
>
> —Jacques Maritain[2]

I. Introduction

No more than a modest proposal for future research and further clarification, this paper seeks to delineate what may prove to be a prescient observation by Jacques Maritain concerning historical process and the emerging temporal ideal for Christian commitment and action in the twenty-first century. This historical ideal would function as the lamp post guiding the construction of a framework for temporal lib-

1. Saint Oscar Romero, "The Son of Man, Light of Pilgrims on Earth," homily given August 6, 1978.

2. Jacques Maritain, *On the Philosophy of History*, edited by Joseph W. Evans (New York: Charles Scribner's Sons, 1957), 155.

eration, a grammar of liberation, while indicating the path to be taken by Christians thematically concerned with salvation.

In *On the Philosophy of History,* Maritain tells us that "We will never have the Kingdom of God within temporal history"; however, he adamantly asserts that "This is all the more reason why we should strive toward it."[3] Furthermore, one can argue that for Maritain this striving toward the Kingdom of God in the twenty-first century, as in every historical period, amounts to actualizing the contours of salvation for a given time. Such Christianity is a restless Christianity, adhering within history to the means made available through which salvation is offered.

This proposal for developing a grammar of liberation derives from consideration of Maritain's notion of the concrete historical ideal, its explication in relation to temporal process and salvation, its current embodiment, and what appear to be Maritain's suggestions concerning the emergence of a new historical ideal.

II. The Concrete Historical Ideal and Salvation

In his seminal text, *A Theology of Liberation,* Gustavo Gutiérrez (the acclaimed Peruvian progenitor of Liberation Theology) stated that "Salvation is not something otherworldly, in regard to which the present life is merely a test. Salvation—the communion of human beings with God and among themselves—is something which embraces all human reality, transforms it, and leads it to its fullness in Christ."[4] The corollary of this appreciation of salvation is clear: "Therefore, sin is not only an impediment to salvation in the afterlife. Insofar as it constitutes a break with God, sin is a historical reality, it is a breach of the communion of persons with each other, it is a turning in of individuals on themselves which manifests itself in a multifaceted withdrawal from others."[5] Quite simply, "The history of salvation is the very heart of human history."[6] Yet heeding the prophetic tradition of the Jews culminating in the New Testament writings, Gutiérrez is careful

3. Ibid.

4. Gustavo Gutiérrez, *A Theology of Liberation: History, Politics, and Liberation,* translated and edited by Sister Caridad Inda and John Eagleson (Maryknoll, New York: Orbis Books, 1988), 85. The relationship between Maritain and Gutiérrez has been partially explored previously in Walter Schultz, "Liberation, Postmodernism and Jacques Maritain: Confronting Individualism and Collectivism in the Twenty-First Century," *Toronto Journal of Theology* 33, no. 2 (Fall 2017): 247–58.

5. Ibid.

6. Ibid., 86.

to acknowledge the eschatological fulfillment: "The eschatological promises are being fulfilled throughout history, but this does not mean that they can be identified clearly and completely with one or another social reality; their liberating effect goes far beyond the foreseeable and opens up new and unexpected possibilities. The complete encounter with the Lord will mark an end to history, but it will take place in history."[7]

Maritain is more traditional than Gutiérrez in his approach to the eschatological fulfillment; quite simply, for Maritain it involves the supernatural which places it beyond the temporal pale of history, definitively stated in his *On the Philosophy of History*: "The absolutely ultimate end, the final end of history is beyond history. For Christian eschatology, there will be a discontinuity between history, which is in time, and the final state of mankind, which will take place in a world transfigured."[8] Sin will plague us continuously until the Parousia, and Maritain even suggests a two-fold contrasting progress in good and evil within history; he acknowledges the ambivalence of history and the fructifications of good and evil.[9]

Although criticized by Gutiérrez for thereby retaining a "two planes model,"[10] Maritain is not prevented from as forthright a denial of the mythical state of "pure nature" as Gutiérrez. Maritain argues adamantly that not only is nature elevated within its own order through grace, but it is superelevated to the supernatural Kingdom of God: "I would insist that, given the actual condition of the world—that is, the fact that the world is not in a state of pure nature but is vitally and organically related to the Kingdom of God—the *actual* natural end of the world is this natural end superelevated."[11]

Furthermore, confronting eschatology from within Maritain's more traditional framework has the advantage of clearly avoiding either Marxist or Fukuyamaesque pronouncements concerning the end of history. Quite simply, Maritain respects the mystery and contends that Christians must never allow complacency—standing in vigilance, they always must be prepared to detect injustice in the world and struggle against it.[12]

For Maritain, grace completes nature and superelevates it to the supernatural Kingdom of God, and history becomes a salvific process through the Church, a Church which may be invisibly present within the world. For

7. Ibid., 97.
8. Maritain, *On the Philosophy of History*, 138.
9. See ibid., 43–62.
10. See Gutiérrez, *A Theology of Liberation*, 27–46.
11. Maritain, *On the Philosophy of History*, 131; emphasis in original. For the full context see 119–63.
12. See ibid., 155.

Christians there can be only one Savior of the world, and for Maritain there is only one visible manifestation of the body of those united in Christ for the salvation of the world. Maritain acknowledges the apex of the Church's visibility and efficacy in the mystery of the Eucharistic celebration,[13] and he never wavers from maintaining that it is what he calls the person of the Church herself speaking through the magisterial authority of the Roman Catholic Church (he maintains that this is so even though the personnel of the Church remain sinful and fallible).[14] However, Maritain proposes that the visible Church is invisibly present and active in those committed to other belief structures, although only the Christian denominations contain elements of the Church in the proper sense as organized bodies.[15] Writing after the Second Vatican Council, in *On the Church of Christ: The Person of the Church and Her Personnel,* Maritain summarizes his bottom line for membership in the Church of Christ:

> It is an absolutely fundamental and universal element of Church which we must discover. Where to seek it? In my opinion, in *man himself such as he comes into the world*. I think that the primitive and fundamental element of Church, and one which exists everywhere on earth,—it is each human person who bears it in him, according as by nature he aspires to know the Cause of being, as also to a state of happy expansion of his being, and according as, wounded in his nature by the sin of Adam,—to such a degree that in his first act of freedom he cannot choose the good (and therefore love naturally above everything the subsisting Good) without grace *naturam sanans,*—he has at the same stroke, if he does not slip away from the grace initially given, a thirst for God which is at one and the same time of nature and of grace (of grace, in other words "exceeding all created nature").[16]

Here Maritain reiterates prior treatment of "the first act of freedom" expressed by every human agent, wherein he argues that faith in God as the Savior Who is none other than Jesus Christ can be present *in confuso* and remain in a pre-conscious or barely conscious apprehension without any conceptual framework, leading to salvation.[17]

13. See Jacques Maritain, *The Peasant of the Garonne: An Old Layman Questions Himself about the Present Time,* translated by Michael Cuddihy and Elizabeth Hughes (New York: Holt, Rinehart and Winston, 1968), 214–20; and Jacques and Raïssa Maritain, *Liturgy and Contemplation* (New York: P. J. Kennedy and Sons, 1960).

14. See Jacques Maritain, *On the Church of Christ: The Person of the Church and Her Personnel,* translated by Joseph W. Evans (Notre Dame, Indiana: University of Notre Dame Press, 1973), 24–30, and 135–51.

15. See ibid., 93–134.

16. Ibid., 129; emphasis in original.

17. See Jacques Maritain, *The Range of Reason* (London: Geoffrey Bles, 1953), 66–85.

All of this coincides nicely with the universal offer of salvation espoused by a founding liberationist like Gustavo Gutiérrez.[18] What is more, as Gutiérrez teases out of certain pronouncements from the Second Vatican Council and the Gospel of Matthew as presented in a quotation from the Conference of Latin American Bishops (CELAM) at Medellin, Columbia in 1968, the fundamental implication of this approach to nature and grace is that

> Human existence, in the last instance, is nothing but a yes or a no to the Lord: "Persons already partly accept union with God, although they do not explicitly confess Christ as their Lord, in so far as they are moved by grace (*Lumen gentium*, no. 16), sometimes secretly (*Gaudium et spes*, nos. 3, 22), renounce their selfishness, and seek to create an authentic fellowship among human beings. They reject union with God in so far as they turn away from the building up of this world, do not open themselves to others, and culpably withdraw into themselves (Mt. 25:31–46)."[19]

As the parable of the sheep and the goats in Mt. 25:31–46 clearly states, at the Parousia all people, not only those who "explicitly confess Christ as their Lord," will be held accountable for their yes or no to the Lord indicated by their action within the world, i.e., within history.[20]

Now for Maritain, as for Gutiérrez, history makes available certain specifications whereby salvific action is indicated; these specifications may be called the contours of salvation for a given locus in the varied tapestry of history. Gutiérrez focuses on the experience in Latin America during the latter half of the twentieth century,[21] and Maritain attends primarily to vast historical epochs through his notion of the concrete historical ideal. As professed Christians, both address the responsibilities of professed Christians within the Church of Christ visibly present. Giving food to the

18. See Gutiérrez, *A Theology of Liberation*, 83–86.

19. Ibid., 84–85, and 85n8.

20. It is true that explicit confession of Christ as Lord, the recognition of Who Jesus is, enables a consciously profound compliance with the will of God in history. Mary chose the better part sitting at the feet of the Lord while Martha worked (Lk. 10:38–42), and the glory of Transfiguration on the mountain (Mt. 17:1–8; Mk 9:2–8; Lk 9:28–36), like partaking in the Eucharist, is a taste of the triumph and beatitude to come. However, in Mt. 25:31–46 Jesus reminds us that whatever we do for the least we do for Him. When Jesus accepts the adulation of the woman bathing His feet with expensive oil, and admonishes those who would feed the poor instead, precisely by noting the fact that the poor will always be with us (M.t 26:6–13; Mk. 14:3–9), He reminds us of our continual struggle against injustice in history (the restless Christianity espoused by Maritain) and the necessity of His sustaining presence enabling the struggle for justice in the world while we await the Parousia to come. The parable of the sheep and the goats received due recognition at Medellin in 1968.

21. Gutiérrez makes this evident throughout his foundational text, *A Theology of Liberation*.

hungry, clothing the naked, and welcoming the stranger, as the parable suggests, certainly defines the human condition to be remedied throughout history. Doing such, the will of the Father, bearing fruit by responding to every other as the Image of God in Christ in mundane affairs—thereby fulfilling the directive initiated by signs and wonders and authentic praise of the Lord (Mt. 7:15–23)—constitutes the praxis through which salvation occurs in obedience to grace. Different times and places present different opportunities for salvific action in the world.

As an example of the way in which the concrete and ideal work together within a given historical context, Maritain argues that mediaeval society was motivated by the ideal of the holy empire. This ideal was "realizable not as something made, but as something on the way to being made, an essence capable of existence and calling for existence in a given historical climate."[22] What made this ideal an authentic possibility, something which was "capable of existence," was its adherence to a particular event of epoch making proportions. For this reason it was a *concrete* historical ideal, "a *prospective image* signifying the particular type, the specific type of civilization to which a certain historical age tends."[23] The event which made the historical ideal of mediaeval Christendom concrete was the empire of Charlemagne.[24]

According to Maritain, mediaeval society strived to maintain a distinction between the spiritual and temporal powers, without allowing their radical separation. For this reason, mediaeval society sought to maintain an organic whole, a living dynamism with a common transcendent goal and temporal task. There was a certain amount of diversity—a pluralism of functions and interests. Nevertheless, maximal unity was the prime directive of mediaeval society. Although the empire sought to unify the temporal sphere, while the Church sought to unify the spiritual, ideally all things were placed under the reign of Christ. According to Maritain, this transcendent orientation respected the human person, who remained the focal point of salvation upon whom the vestments of spiritual and temporal order were bestowed:

22. Jacques Maritain, *Integral Humanism: Temporal and Spiritual Problems of a New Christendom*, translated by Joseph W. Evans (Notre Dame, Indiana: University of Notre Dame Press, 1973), 128.

23. Ibid., 127; emphasis in original.

24. See ibid., 143–44.

> Whether it is a question of each Christian notion or of Christendom in its higher unity, the temporal unity aimed at by the Middle Ages was a *maximal* unity, a unity of the most exacting and the most completely monarchical sort. The center of its formation and consistency was set very high in the life of the person, above the temporal, in that spiritual order itself to which the temporal order and the temporal common good are subordinated; its source was thus in men's hearts, and the unity of national or imperial political structures only manifested this primordial unity.[25]

Maritain does not wish to present as perfect what was decidedly not perfect, as we read in this statement concerning the function of the concrete and ideal during the mediaeval period: "The idea of the *Sacrum Imperium* was preceded by an event: the empire of Charlemagne, the aims of which, it seems, were not exempt from Caesaropapism; and the idea, arising after this event, was capable of only precarious, partial, and contradictory realizations."[26]

Mediaeval society had what Maritain calls "a *Christian sacral conception of the temporal*."[27] Because of this, the role of the temporal sphere was not only subordinate to the spiritual, but tended to become the instrument or merely the means of the spiritual.[28] Temporal institutions were used for spiritual ends. The execution of heretics by temporal authority is an example of this.[29] The ideal of the holy empire, although establishing the contours of salvation for the mediaeval period, gave way to secularism and a more holistic appreciation of the human person through the emergence of new concrete historical ideals: one clearly defined by Maritain as the goal of Christian action in accord with the salvific opportunities bestowed upon us by the events of the European Enlightenment, and the American and French Revolutions; the other, decidedly less Euro-centric, hinted at in the writings of the elderly Maritain.

III. From Holy Freedom to Holy Community

The two concrete historical ideals explicated here—one fully explored by Maritain within the context of his social and political thought; the other stemming from observations in his later writings—involve the coming of

25. Ibid., 147.
26. Ibid., 143–44.
27. Ibid., 146; emphasis in original.
28. See ibid., 148–49.
29. See ibid., 149–50.

age of temporal society and a more profound appreciation of the human person, who is the subject of salvation, than was operative in the maximal unity fostered by mediaeval Christendom.

Considering the complexity of thought patterns, events, and diverse legacy of the European Enlightenment and the French Revolution, while appreciating the unique contribution to modernity of the American Revolution, Maritain detects a new concrete historical ideal emerging: "the idea of the *holy freedom* of the creature whom grace unites to God."[30] This ideal is exemplified in Maritain's listing of natural rights, beginning with the right to existence and freedom of conscience before God, and in his involvement with drafting the United Nation's Universal Declaration of Rights in 1948.[31] Positive and negative rights are acknowledged; along with the rights of assembly and speech, we have rights to health care, education, and a living wage.[32]

Succeeding the collapse of the mediaeval concrete historical ideal, the new ideal of holy freedom does not imply a form of divine imperialism, which seems to have been the case with the ideal of the holy empire. The ideal of the human being's freedom is even more transcendent than the mediaeval ideal, because it distinctly acknowledges the rational and spiritual status of each person before God. In this new historical climate, Maritain condemns any attempt to return to the mediaeval ideal, as was the case with Franco in Spain, as a corruption of the mediaeval ideal of holy empire into the mere empire of the totalitarian state.[33] For Maritain, democracy, pluralism, and securing rights of self-expression—along with rights insuring the health, education, and material conditions necessary for participation—depict a package indicative of natural human development inspired by Christianity.[34]

30. Ibid., 163; emphasis in original.

31. See Jacques Maritain, *The Rights of Man and Natural Law*, translated by Doris C. Anson (London: Geoffrey Bles, 1944), especially 60–62. For an informative treatment of Maritain's influence on the United Nation's Universal Declaration of Rights, see Andrew Woodcock, "Jacques Maritain, Natural Law and the Universal Declaration of Rights," *Journal of the History of International Law/Revue d'histoire du droit international* 8, no. 2 (2006): 245–66. See also Jacques Maritain, *Man and the State*, Charles R. Walgreen Foundation Lectures, Phoenix Books (Chicago: The University of Chicago Press, 1966), 76–80.

32. See ibid., 103–107.

33. See Maritain's introduction to Alfred Mendizabal, *The Martyrdom of Spain: Origins of a Civil War*, translated by Charles Hope Lumley (London: Geoffrey Bles; The Centenary Press, 1938), 1–48; and Maritain, *Integral Humanism*, 277.

34. See Jacques Maritain, *Christianity and Democracy*, translated by Doris C. Anson (London: Geoffrey Bles, 1945); *The Rights of Man*; and *Man and State*, 76–107.

The spiritual unity fostered by the mediaeval period, never fully attained, shattered into what Maritain chastises as a fundamentally anthropocentric humanism amidst the seeds of a theocentric, integral humanism advancing awareness of the historical development of the person. For Maritain, the anthropocentric canvas of modernity depicts an ever-greater concentration on the individual alone, as a truncated image of the human being—such is the portrait of humanity which emerges from the time of the Renaissance and Protestant Reformation, through the enlightened age of liberalism, coming to completion in the various modes of totalitarianism covering the latter half of the twentieth century and highlighted in the Nazi racial state.

Simply stated, the individual denotes the material pole of a human being, the biological organization housing our instinctual drives and spatio-temporal orientation; the human being is a person by virtue of a spiritual pole—the seat of intellect and will. Each human being is a unique composite of the two, and orientation toward one to the diminishment or exclusion of the other is perceived by Maritain as pathology: materialism and atomism when focusing on the individual; rationalism and what Maritain calls "angelism" when attempting to define *human* intellect and will in a way which denies the body with its location, attributes, and operations.[35] The human composite (body and soul—instinct, intellect, and will operative as a unique presence in the world), is a person by virtue of intellect and will issuing from a center capable of understanding, choosing, and acting in the world: "As an individual, each of us is a fragment of a species, a part of the universe, a unique point in the immense web of cosmic, ethnical, historical forces and influences—and bound by their laws. Each of us is subject to the determinism of the physical world. Nonetheless, each of us is also a person and, as such, is not controlled by the stars. Our whole being subsists in virtue of the subsistence of the spiritual soul which is in us a principle of creative unity, independence and liberty."[36]

It is precisely the intellectual nature of the human composite which separates it and elevates it in the most formidable way: "In intellectual creatures alone, Aquinas teaches further, is found the image of God. In no other creature, not even in the universe as a whole, is this found."[37] As the estab-

35. See Maritain's early treatment of "angelism" in relation to Descartes in his *Three Reformers: Luther – Descartes – Rousseau* (London: Sheed and Ward, 1928), 54–81.

36. Jacques Maritain, *The Person and the Common Good,* translated By John J. Fitzgerald (Notre Dame, Indiana: University of Notre Dame Press, 1972), 38.

37. Ibid., 18–19.

lishment of our unique personhood constitutes an opportunity for choosing to struggle toward our temporal liberation and accept the gift of eternal salvation, the selfish aspirations of the truncated individual constitutes our sin as alienation from God, self, and others, including the natural world in which we find ourselves; thereby, fostering the technical control and manipulation of nature—a travesty of the dominion proclaimed in Genesis. For Maritain, what he perceives as the "angelism" and consequent rationalism engendered by the Cartesian reform in a multifaceted way throughout modernity, issues in voluntarism, pragmatism, and allegiance to technique alone for the satisfaction of the individual alone:

> An appropriate technique should permit us to rationalize human life, i.e., to satisfy our desires with the least possible inconvenience, without any interior reform of ourselves. What such a morality subjects to reason are material forces and agents exterior to man, instruments of human life; it is not man, nor human life as such. It does not free man, it weakens him, it disarms him, it renders him a slave to all the atoms of the universe, and especially to his own misery and egoism. What remains of man? A consumer crowned by science. This is the final gift, the twentieth century gift of the Cartesian reform.[38]

And for Maritain, the individual consumer eagerly anticipating the newest gadget or fashion is but a step behind the individual giving allegiance to the totalitarian state with its false promise of what is infinitely more.

For Maritain, freedom is much more than the ability to choose while floundering in the jungle of consumerism, hounded by debt and/or the ubiquitous lure of more. Neither is freedom found in submission to some variant of the General Will *a la* Rousseau, which opens history to the totalitarian plague.[39] As seen in the collective rights of the family, and rights of assembly and organization, our freedom and fulfillment as human beings necessarily involves our bonding with others as well as attaining the essentials of physical well-being for ourselves.[40]

For Maritain, love and its fruition through intimacy in the family, and its extension into the broader community through what he calls civic love or friendship, secures the self and others within community.[41] The development of personality is intimately connected with love, which is the central

38. Jacques Maritain, *The Dream of Descartes together with some other Essays*, translated by Mabelle L. Andison, The Philosophical Library (New York: F. Hubner and Co., 1944), 182–83.

39. See Jacques Maritain, *Three Reformers*, 93–164; *Scholasticism and Politics*, translated by Mortimer J. Adler (London: Geoffrey Bles, 1954), 74–75; and *Man and the State*, 43–49.

40. See Maritain, *The Rights of Man*.

41. See Jacques Maritain, *Freedom in the Modern World*, translated by Richard O'Sullivan,

tenet in Christianity. Love is not connected with qualities (as Pascal said), but with the substantial or truly existential dimension of the beloved.[42] Love is connected with that which is capable of giving itself and receiving another self. Moreover, "to bestow oneself, one must first exist; not, indeed, as a sound, which passes through the air, or an idea, which crosses the mind, but as a thing, which subsists and exercises existence for itself."[43] A loving being must first be master of itself, or self-possessed: "Personality, therefore, signifies interiority to self."[44] Love implies the existence of the subject.

It is crucial to recognize that Maritain's focus on uniqueness points the way toward a truly human community and society acknowledging the inalienable rights of all, wherein each is for all and all is for each. As Maritain would have it, "Man finds himself by subordinating himself to the group, and the group attains its goal only by serving man and by realizing that man has secrets which escape the group and a vocation which the group does not encompass."[45] The common good of human society, because it consists of persons, is what is good for both whole and parts: "The common good of the city is neither the mere collection of private goods, nor the proper good of a whole which, like the species with respect to its individuals or the hive with respect to its bees, relates the parts to itself alone and sacrifices them to itself. It is the good *human* life of the multitude, of a multitude of persons; it is their communion in good living. It is therefore common to both *the whole and the parts* into which it flows back and which, in turn, must benefit from it."[46]

Having accentuated the unique human being as the irreplaceable image of God fostering and constituting authentic human community, it was after World War II that Maritain clearly addressed the emerging global dimension of human community in the search for a lasting peace. In a speech delivered at a meeting of UNESCO on April 21, 1966 (published in *Untrammeled Approaches*),[47] Maritain reiterates and augments by way of

---

K.C. (New York: Gordian Press, 1971), 51–52; *The Person and the Common Good*, 59, and 79–81; *Man and the State*, 206 and 209.

42. See Maritain, *The Person and the Common Good*, 38–39.

43. Ibid., 39–40.

44. Ibid., 41. For a treatment of Maritain's appreciation of the subject and love as a critique of postmodernism, see Schultz, "Liberation, Postmodernism and Jacques Maritain."

45. Maritain, *The Rights of Man*, 13.

46. Maritain, *The Person and the Common Good*, 50–51; emphasis in original.

47. See Jacques Maritain, *Untrammeled Approaches*, translated by Bernard Doering (Notre Dame, Indiana: University of Notre Dame Press, 1997), 199–204.

structuring certain concerns he expressed during lectures he gave under the auspices of the Charles R. Walgreen Foundation for the Study of American Institutions, at the University of Chicago in December, 1949 (subsequently published as *Man and the State*). Addressing UNESCO, Maritain reiterates his concern for "supranational political authority," and "a real *political organization of the world,* based on the free consent and the free cooperation of nations and peoples."[48] In *Untrammeled Approaches,* and more fully in *Man and the State,* Maritain presents the ideal fullypolitical world society, freely formed, encompassing multifarious institutions and communities within the global body politic, avoiding the merely governmental solution of World Empire.[49] In 1966 as in 1949, Maritain cautions that "the problem for our time is not to bring into actual existence a world-wide political society, it is rather to work at the *distant preparations* for this society, by putting into motion the long effort of reason and good will thanks to which this utopia will end up becoming a realizable ideal. The hope of men in a temporal ideal, a dynamic ideal of peace on earth, must be preserved at any cost, even though it may seem utopian at the outset."[50]

What Maritain proposes in *Man and the State,* and again in *Untrammeled Approaches,* appears to be prescient concerning the evolution in awareness of the human person at the close of the twentieth century and into the first decades of the twenty-first century. It remains to delineate in a brief outline how events seem to herald a new concrete historical ideal—acknowledging that we may still be awaiting a crucial event, like the crowning of Charlemagne or the American and French Revolutions. As the ideal of "the holy freedom of the creature whom grace unites to God" replaces the ideal of "holy empire," by way of acknowledging a more profound appreciation of the human person, what might be called the ideal of "the holy community united in peace through the grace of God" may replace the ideal of "holy freedom," albeit a less dramatic rupture than the emergence of "holy freedom" in the wake of "holy empire," by acknowledging a more profound appreciation of the communal and global implications of personhood.

48. Maritain, *Untrammeled Approaches,* 202; emphasis in original.
49. See ibid. and Maritain, *Man and the State,* 188–216.
50. Maritain, *Untrammeled Approaches,* 202; emphasis in original.

IV. Toward a Grammar of Liberation

Less than perfect, the concrete historical ideal of "holy empire" involved contradictions; likewise, the ideals of "holy freedom" and "holy community" are not without their contradictions. For undermining the positive advantage of secularism and our temporal coming of age, Maritain denigrates what he labels "bourgeois democracy," "bourgeois individualism," or simply "bourgeois liberalism."[51] For Maritain, echoing Nietzsche, "bourgeois liberalism" extols the self-seeking comfort of the "last men," given to cleanliness, order, the polite smile, and complacency in temporal comforts attained. In *The Person and the Common Good*, Maritain distinguishes the attitudes of three political philosophies toward Christianity which plague modernity: "bourgeois individualism, communistic anti-individualism, and totalitarian or dictatorial anti-communism and anti-individualism."[52] Maritain unabashedly states in a vitriolic passage:

> Of the three, the most irreligious is bourgeois liberalism. Christian in appearance, it has been atheistic in fact. Too skeptical to persecute, except for a tangible profit, rather than defy religion, which it deemed an invention of the priesthood and gradually dispossessed by reason, it used it as a police force to watch over property, or as a bank where anyone could be insured while making money here below, against the undiscovered risks of the hereafter—after all, one never knows![53]

Indicative of the consistency of Maritain's vehemence, as well as of his sympathies during his later years, is his contention that the hippies of the 1960s "are the victims of this bourgeois world which they are right in detesting."[54] Maritain perceives this first global wave of refusal after World War II as "a worldwide phenomenon of great significance: according as it appears as a sentence of condemnation—merited, besides—brought against a culture proud of its idolatry of science and of money, and which is rotting from within."[55] The only problem with the hippies is that their refusal is not sufficiently radical: "The saints, when they decide to change their life, posit also from the outset an act of refusal: but because they have discovered a

51. Such terminology appears throughout Maritain's extensive critique of modern economics, society and politics. See especially, Maritain, *Integral Humanism* and *The Person and the Common Good.*

52. Maritain, *The Person and the Common Good*, 91

53. Ibid., 97.

54. Maritain, *On the Church of Christ*, 126.

55. Ibid., 125.

truth infinitely superior to the world, and to which they give themselves."[56]

It is "bourgeois liberalism" which taxes the ideal of "holy freedom"; and it taxes the ideal of "holy community" as well, by fostering the global neoliberal agenda which seeks to establish as normative what Maritain disparages as "the old disguised anarchistic conception of individualistic materialism in which the whole function of the city is to safeguard the liberty of each; thus giving to the strong full freedom to oppress the weak."[57] What comes under attack here in the economic order is what Franz Hinkelammert outlines as "savage capitalism," with its aggressive anti-stateism, exclusion of major portions of the global population from any meaningful participation in the economic process, and the maximization of profit over development.[58]

At the outset of the twenty-first century, a considerable collection of voices, ideas, and events appears to be coalescing within a framework suggesting Maritain's targeting "bourgeois liberalism" while pursuing global personalist community. Dialogue toward a grammar of liberation should engage all of these elements. Only a few notable voices, ideas, and events can be indicated here, suggesting directives for activism in line with the historical ideal of "holy community."

Consistent with Maritain's targeting individualism and "bourgeois liberalism" while promoting global community, the new economic developments, social justice movements, democratic organizations, and environmental initiatives catalogued and analyzed by innovative economists David C. Korten and Gar Alperovitz offer a viable foundation for promoting dialogue engaging small, integral communities on a global basis—seeking to address global economic sustainability, environmental integrity, and the fostering of human rights and democracy beyond the boundaries of state sovereignty.[59]

Michael Hardt and Antonio Negri, two revolutionary thinkers often working together, would like to establish the surprising success of protests

56. Ibid., 125–26.

57. Maritain, *The Person and the Common Good*, 50.

58. See Daniel M. Bell Jr., *Liberation Theology After the End of History: The Refusal to Cease Suffering*, Radical Orthodoxy Series, edited by John Milbank, Catherine Pickstock, and Graham Ward (London and New York: Routledge, 2001), 9–12. References to Bell in this essay have previously appeared in Schultz, "Liberation, Postmodernism and Jacques Maritain."

59. See David C. Korten, *Agenda for a New Economy: From Phantom Wealth to Real Wealth*, A publication of the New Economy Working Group (San Francisco: Berrett-Koehler Publishers, 2010); and Gar Alperovitz, *America beyond Capitalism: Reclaiming our Wealth, Our Liberty, and Our Democracy* (Takoma Park, Maryland: Democracy Collaborative Press; Boston: Dollars and Sense, 2011).

which prevented the continuation of the WTO conference in Seattle, Washington in 1999 as the concrete ideal of an emerging global revolution.[60] This one event may or may not be the crucial event establishing a new concrete historical ideal *a la* Maritain, but it contains all the features of the global, pluralistic, consensual hope for unification and peace indicated by Maritain in *Man and the State* and again in *Untrammeled Approaches.*

Since the battle of Seattle a plethora of actions have occurred, similarly comprised of diverse voices seeking justice in response to oppressive and exclusionary measures. Here the confluence of voices at least in the early stages of the Arab Spring, and throughout the occupy movement, various anti-austerity movements around the world, operations against corporate economic and environmental transgressions, and against state and police suppression of all such endeavors merits exploration.[61] We see research and education emerging from a North-South dialogue addressing economic sustainability, environmental integrity, and issues related to human rights and social justice in organizations like the International Forum on Globalization (IFG) and in meetings like the World Social Forum (WS-F).[62] Before the Internet, Maritain knew that the task of preparing a world society "will obviously develop first of all as a deep and continuing task of education and enlightenment, discussion and study."[63]

Maritain would agree with the avant-garde Argentine liberationist Ivan Petrella when he criticizes liberation theologies for allowing themselves to be trapped within a specific identity consciousness: e.g., black, Latin American, African, feminist, gay.[64] Certainly Maritain would also agree with Petrella's presenting life itself and human reproduction (not exclusion, marginalization, and eventual extermination) as the common ground, the foundation, the *sine qua non* of all our goals—this is forthrightly exemplified in Maritain's insistence on the right to existence as the primary human right.[65]

60. See Michael Hardt and Antonio Negri, *Multitude: War and Democracy in the Age of Empire* (New York: The Penguin Press, 2004), 215, 217–18, and 268–88.

61. The tendency toward cohesion in all such action on a global level is strikingly apparent in the participatory and inclusive methodology of Occupy Wall Street in 2011 and developed further through *Indignados* and *Nuit debout* in Europe.

62. See the International Forum on Globalization (IFG) website: http://ifg.org/about/about-us/; and the World Social Forum website: https://fsm2016.org/en/

63. Maritain, *Man and the State,* 213.

64. See Ivan Petrella, *Beyond Liberation Theology: A Polemic* (London: SCM Press, 2008), especially chapter 3, 78–112.

65. See ibid., chapter 1, 5–44; and Maritain, *The Rights of Man,* 60.

In this vein, Maritain—no doubt glancing at the universal activity of the Holy Spirit in history—appeals to a common secular faith, embracing all those of good will from whatever creed or philosophical stance, when pursuing common human goals establishing and securing human life.[66] Liberation is about establishing community; it is not about identifying and isolating minorities, whether in pursuit of their flourishing or demise. Exploring the contours of salvation in the twenty-first century, seeking to construct a grammar of liberation, necessarily involves a serious study, appreciation, and application of contributions from global and local movements engaged in a pluralistic effort to challenge the neoliberal agenda with its exclusion of the vast majority of humanity through the idol of the market, wherein truncated human beings, the detached individuals so clearly described by Maritain, attempt to exercise their hegemony.

Aspects of liberation theology demand attention in any serious exploration of God's design for temporal liberation and salvation in the twenty-first century. However, Maritain's supernatural eschatology, what Gutiérrez criticizes as the retention of an anachronistic "two planes model," would not allow Maritain to agree fully with Petrella's or any liberationist's insistence on class struggle as central.[67] Daniel M. Bell, Jr., a radical orthodox theologian developing insights gleaned from Gilles Deleuze and Michel Foucault, appears to be more perceptive when he asserts that "Capitalism extends its reign by far more than merely fostering a particular mode of production and division of labor; it is best understood as an ensemble of technologies that disciplines the constitutive human power, desire."[68] Securing the idolatry of the market, this discipline morphs into societies of control, which construct the subjectivities of all adhering to the *status quo*—the oppressed as well as the oppressors.[69] Simply stated, we are all victims of the system through the entrapment of our instinctual drives and imagination.

For Deleuze, the way out of such entrapment is through ever-greater "deterritorialization," beyond global market hegemony and the allure of consumerism, intensifying the madness-producing mechanisms of control until desire is free of all order, thereby attaining "genuine freedom: the anarchic, creative, experimental movement that Deleuze labels 'schizo-

66. See Maritain, *Man and the State*, 111.

67. See Petrella, *Beyond Liberation Theology*, 70–77, and 81–84.

68. Bell, *Liberation Theology After the End of History*, 3.

69. See ibid., 9–41.

phrenia.'"[70] Reflecting on such a solution, Bell parts company with postmodernity, revealing his orthodox allegiance. Given Maritain's Thomistic orientation, it is worth noting that Bell criticizes this "madness beyond madness" as a perverse denial of transcendence, placing politics before being and proclaiming the univocity of being in opposition to the Thomistic *analogia entis*.[71] Bell raises penetrating questions for the postmodern thinker: "Is madness the way beyond madness? Or does madness intensified finally collapse in the black hole of nihilism, where life becomes death and an absolute violence is unleashed? Perhaps madness is simply madness, schizoid desire nothing but the far side of the madness that is savage capitalism, which makes it that much more savage."[72]

Systemic control of desire enslaving members of every class would not diminish the importance of Paulo Freire's "conscientization," whereby the oppressed become aware of their oppressors and the extent of their oppression, allowing for the necessary social and political movements against those wielding power in such a situation.[73] However, for professing Christians, as exemplified in the activism and martyrdom of anointed leaders like Dr. Martin Luther King, Jr. and Saint Oscar Romero, it must become eminently clear that love alone should control all action (1 Cor. 13; Jn. 13:14, 15, and 35).[74] Even a seasoned radical like Michael Hardt appreciates the political importance and implications of the Biblical view of love.[75] Furthermore, in an interview, Hardt speculates that any meaningful revolution must be able to liberate the oppressors as well as the oppressed.[76] Perhaps Hardt would agree with Jean Vanier's admonition that we should acknowledge all of our suffering sisters and brothers, not only those who suffer in the impoverished dwellings of the world but also those suffering "in the luxurious apartments of Toronto."[77]

70. Ibid., 33.

71. See ibid.

72. Ibid.

73. For a brief overview of the concept, "conscientization," as employed by Freire, see Paulo Freire, "Cultural Action and Conscientization," *Harvard Educational Review* 68, no. 4 (Winter, 1998): 499–521; and *The Politics of Education: Culture, Power and Liberation*, introduction by Henry A. Giroux, translated by Donald Macedo (Westport, Connecticut: Bergin and Garvey Publishers; Greenwood Publishing Group, 1985).

74. Jn. 13:14, 15, and 35 was suggested from a banner of *Followers Mission*, 129A Sherbourne Street, Toronto, Ontario, Canada.

75. See Hardt and Negri, *Multitude*, 51–352.

76. See Michel Hardt, in *Examined Life: Philosophy is in the Streets*, DVD (Montréal, Québec: National Film Board of Canada, 2008).

77. Jean Vanier, *Eruption to Hope* (Toronto: Griffin Press Limited, 1971), 102.

Bell may be helpful here as well, with his suggestion of a crucified forgiveness which no longer seeks redress, even though he develops this while challenging the language of rights and criticizing Gutiérrez as well as Maritain for retaining a "two planes model."[78] Assessing the contributions of Saint Oscar Romero, Ignacio Ellacuría, and Jon Sobrino, who compare the Church of the suffering poor with the crucified Christ,[79] Bell contends that "The crucified people who are gathered as the Church of the poor are enacting God's forgiveness, not demanding what is due, in an effort to liberate desire from capitalist discipline."[80] The solution to the entrapment of desire by savage capitalism lies in technologies fostered by grace, mobilizing desire away from death:

> Specifically, we focus on three technologies—confession, repentance, and penance or reparations—that the liberationists testify are at the heart of the therapy of forgiveness as enacted by the Church of the poor. It is the presence of these technologies that establishes the therapy of forgiveness as a form of resistance to capitalist discipline. . . . Through them, the Church of the poor is extending God's gift of forgiveness and redirecting desire toward its true end: the shared love that is friendship in God.[81]

In this vein, we may have something to learn from the various attempts at restorative justice.[82] Evolution in awareness concerning the human person may require buttressing and nurturing a proper appreciation and allocation of rights through community involvement in a radical forgiveness emanating from eternity. Such a community would be a poor Church, a crucified Church comprised of impoverished sinners, speaking and acting in the world as the witness and offering of divine forgiveness, evangelizing by way of attraction as exemplified in the words and deeds of Pope Francis.[83] The remarkable community cohesion and refusal to become violent in the face of brutal opposition, so evident in the early stages of the Arab Spring, the occupy movement, various anti-austerity actions around the world, actions

78. See Bell, *Liberation Theology After the End of History*, 51–65 and 144–203.

79. See ibid., 170.

80. Ibid., 171.

81. Ibid.

82. For especially profound examples of successful outcomes of restorative justice see the interviews in *Rwanda: Living Forgiveness*, DVD (Worcester, Pennsylvania: Vision Video, 2006).

83. The direction and zeal indicative of the pontificate of Pope Francis in relation to social concerns is especially evident in his early Apostolic Exhortation, *Evangeli Gaudium* (November 24, 2013).

against global corporate economic and environmental transgressions, and actions against police brutality itself, suggest the operation of grace and the Church invisibly present, often in unison with voices from the visible Church who bear the brunt of the biblical admonition: "From everyone to whom much has been given, much will be required; and from the one to whom much has been entrusted, even more will be demanded" (Lk 12:48). It is the elder Maritain who suggests that the Church may become the final refuge of the person.[84]

It appears that through the originary activism of the Incarnation there is a supra-temporal healing balm at work throughout history, which Maritain refuses to ignore and which must become evident in any grammar of liberation. That such pervasive love can be appreciated from within the specific confines established by history is indicated by Julian Asange while participating in a conference by video from exile in the Ecuadorian embassy in London, England. Speaking with no less seasoned radicals than Yanis Varoufakis and Slavoj Žižek, Assange speculates on ways to alleviate the immediate sorry condition of world affairs (for Assange exemplified not only in the controlling societies of savage capitalism but perhaps even more so in societal organizations like ISIS). Assange concludes that some form of Christianity, opposing the desire for death and the will to power with the desire for life and the will to love, may be the only chance we have for combating injustice effectively and continuing our journey through time.[85]

84. See Maritain, *The Peasant of the Garonne*, 51.

85. See "Europe is Kaput. Long live Europe!" Southbank Centre, Nov. 23, 2015. https://www.youtube.com/watch?v=yjxAArOkoAo.

MICHAEL D. BREIDENBACH

Jacques Maritain and Leo XIII on the Problem of Church-State Relations

I. The Problem of Church-State Relations

Jacques Maritain wrote in *Man and the State* (1951) that the "complete differentiation and full autonomy" of the temporal sphere found in the modern, secular age fulfilled the "very distinction between God's and Caesar's domains" found in the Gospel.[1] English philosopher Thomas Pink has argued that such a view is incompatible with what he calls the "Leonine model" of soul-body union articulated by Pope Leo XIII in *Immortale Dei* (1885).[2] Pink's claim that Maritain opposed the ideal model of Church-state relations, however, does not succeed for two reasons. Firstly, his conclusion overlooks critical qualifications in *Man and the State* that saves Maritain's theory from advancing a strict separationist view of Church-state relations. Secondly, Pink ignores one of Maritain's early works, *The Things that are Not Caesar's* (1931), which reveals his full support of Leonine teaching in the tradition of St. Thomas Aquinas and St. Robert Bellarmine.

Nevertheless, Pink's critique of Maritain's view offers important reflections on the relationship between principles and practicalities in the debates over Church and state. Maritain's theory of a "new Christendom" attempts to present a practically attainable ideal whereby lay Christians are

1. Jacques Maritain, *Man and the State* (Washington, D.C.: The Catholic University of America Press, 1998), 159.

2. Thomas Pink, "Jacques Maritain and the Problem of Church and State," *The Thomist* 79, no. 1 (2015): 1–42, esp. 1–13, 32–42.

free to influence society through their moral conscience and faith witness despite living under a secular state. While this theory conforms to the ideal Church-state union as much as the circumstances of a modern, secular state allows, the merit of a practically attainable theory is also measured by whether the theory is, in fact, practically attainable. Recent threats to religious freedom have created renewed urgency for returning to Maritain's project and to the immutable principles of Church-state relations that inspired it.

II. Interpreting Leo XIII on Church and State

In his 1885 encyclical *Immortale Dei*, Pope Leo XIII maintained that the Church and the state possess distinct powers and ends. The ecclesiastical power, which governs "divine" things, is ordered to the spiritual good of the community, while the civil power, which governs "human" things, is ordered to their temporal good. While these two divinely ordained powers are sovereign with respect to their distinct ends, Leo XIII taught that, since the spiritual good of the community is higher than its temporal good, the Church's end is higher than the state's end. In order to achieve these ends, Leo concluded, "There must … exist … a certain orderly connection" between Church and state, "which may be compared to the union of the soul and body in man."[3]

Several implications follow from these absolute principles. Firstly, the ideal harmony between Church and state is a confessional state that publicly professes the Catholic faith and conforms its laws to Catholic teaching. Secondly, the Church may call upon a Catholic confessional state to serve as the Church's secular actor or "body" in moral and spiritual matters—even by employing the state's coercive power through civil law and punishment—for the sake of spiritual ends. Thirdly, since the Church serves a higher good, the ecclesiastical power can act in temporal affairs through counseling, teaching, and, most controversially, overseeing civil rulers. Because the stated reasons for acting in temporal affairs are spiritual—the avoidance of sin and the salvation of souls—the Church's actions in this sphere are considered "indirect." Such indirect temporal power does have direct political consequences, however, including annulling civil laws, im-

3. Pope Leo XIII, *Immortale Dei* (1885): nos. 13–14. By "the Church" in Church-state relations, Leo XIII emphasized the juridical, hierarchical nature of the Catholic Church.

prisoning heretics, excommunicating and deposing civil rulers, and abjuring Catholics' civil oaths. Such a claim ultimately prevented early modern Jesuit Scholastics such as Francisco Suárez and Bellarmine from endorsing the full independence of temporal jurisdictions.[4]

Since at least the fourteenth century, theologians, canonists, and historians within the conciliarist tradition have opposed the kind of Church-state unity that Leo XIII, following many other theologians and popes, articulated. Conciliarist canonists and theologians denied that the pope has any power in the temporal affairs of other nations. Instead, they advocated a juridical view of the ecclesiastical and temporal powers in which each power remains separate, without one being subordinated to or directed by the other in their respective realms.[5] As the fourteenth-century jurist John of Paris wrote in his *Tractatus de potestate regia et papali*, "The secular power is greater than the spiritual in some things, namely in temporal affairs, and in such affairs it is not subject to the spiritual power in any way."[6] Conciliarists have provided significant intellectual contributions to the transition from the hierocratic, Church-over-state arrangements of the Middle Ages to modern theories on the juridical, strict separation of Church and state, whose influence on the Second Vatican Council's declaration, *Dignitatis Humanae*, continues to be disputed.

A recent critique of Maritain's theory of Church and state has located him in the juridical, strict separationist school of thought and therefore in contradiction with the Leonine model and Magisterial teaching. This claim is surprising, not least because scholars have traditionally understood Maritain as a faithful follower of Leo XIII's social and political thought.[7] The

4. Harro Höpfl, *Jesuit Political Thought: The Society of Jesus and the State, c. 1540–1630* (New York: Cambridge University Press, 2004), 357–60.

5. Antipapalist thinkers such as Jean Gerson, John Mair, and Jacques Almain, as well as the decrees of the Council of Constance (1415), denied papal claims to authority in temporal affairs. See Norman P. Tanner, editor, *Decrees of the Ecumenical Councils*, vol. 1, *Nicaea I to Lateran V* (Washington, D.C.: Georgetown University Press, 1990), 403–51. For an overview of this juridical view and its rivals since the eleventh century, see Brian Tierney, *The Crisis of Church and State, 1050–1300, with Selected Documents* (Toronto: University of Toronto Press, 1988); Francis Oakley, *The Conciliarist Tradition: Constitutionalism in the Catholic Church, 1300–1870* (New York: Oxford University Press, 2003); and *Conciliarism and Papalism*, edited by J. H. Burns and Thomas M. Izbicki (Cambridge: Cambridge University Press, 1997).

6. John of Paris, *Tractatus de Potestate Regia et Papali*, 1302–1303, in *Jean de Paris et l'ecclésiologie du XIIIe siècle*, edited by Jaques Leclercq (Paris: Librairie Philosophique, J. Vrin, 1942), 184. Quoted and translated in Tierney, *The Crisis of Church and State*, 209.

7. John P. Hittinger, "The Cooperation of Church and State: Maritain's Argument from the

recent criticism leveled against his work underscores the importance of careful metaphysical and juridical distinctions within Church-state theories and the difficulties in applying absolute principles in contingent political realities.

III. A Critique of Maritain's Church-State Theory

The contention that Maritain's Church-state theory opposes the Leonine model rests on a certain interpretation of his 1951 book, *Man and the State.* In the chapter "Church and State," Maritain explained, "The order of terrestrial civilization and of temporal society has gained complete differentiation and full autonomy, which is something normal in itself, required by the Gospel's very distinction between God's and Caesar's domains."[8] This statement, when shorn of context and qualification, presents an absolute claim on the sovereignty of the temporal power that conciliarist John of Paris had supported. If the temporal society has achieved full autonomy *simpliciter*, then the Church does not have any power to interfere in temporal affairs or direct the civil ruler in any way. Maritain's theory, as well as his exegesis of Matthew 22:21, appears to assert not only the distinction between Church and state, but also the strict separation between the two powers.

To claim that the Gospel requires the eventual severing of any "orderly connection" of Church and state would be to judge the medieval arrangement as an error. Yet, in the same work, Maritain noted that the medieval *respublica Christiana* reflected a soul-body union of Church and state, in which the state acted as the Church's secular arm, and the Church possessed the right to intervene in temporal affairs when the matter concerned faith or morals.[9] For Maritain, however, instantiating this medieval arrangement in a secular age was no longer practical, for "the modern age is not a sacral, but a secular age." Since the state is no longer confessional, and because citizenship does not require baptism, Maritain reasoned that

Unity of the Person," in *Reassessing the Liberal State: Reading Maritain's "Man and the State,"* edited by Timothy Fuller and John P. Hittinger (Washington, D.C.: American Maritain Association, distributed by The Catholic University of America, 2001), 179–201. See also John P. Hittinger, *Liberty, Wisdom, and Grace: Thomism and Democratic Political Theory* (Lanham, Maryland: Lexington, 2002), 5; Pope Leo XIII, *Aeterni Patris* (1879).

8. Maritain, *Man and the State,* 159.

9. Ibid., 157–58.

the state cannot privilege one religion over another, even if it is the true religion.[10]

To avoid historicizing medieval Church-state relations while accounting for historical context, Maritain enumerated several immutable principles on Church and state: firstly, the distinction yet essential cooperation between the Church and the state; secondly, the hierarchy between spiritual powers and their goods over temporal powers and their goods; and thirdly, the liberty of the Church to fulfill these spiritual goods. He saw Magisterial teaching from the Middle Ages to the modern era as continuous in the proclamation of these absolute principles, even though the application of them differed in history. In a secular state, these immutable principles could no longer be applied fully as the Leonine analogy of soul-body union. Instead, the Church should focus on the primacy of its spiritual and moral teaching authority to inform the faithful within the political society.[11]

Since Maritain argued that the soul-body union is an inappropriate Church-state model in a secular age, a recent critic, Thomas Pink, has inferred that Maritain rejected the Leonine model as an "error." According to Pink, Leo XIII's teaching was an "embarrassment" for Maritain's claim that the Church-state union is "a dead letter in our age," since Leo XIII supported the ideal in the modern, secular age. Furthermore, Maritain's theory allegedly implies that Leo XIII's teaching is a "damaging error," since it inhibits the final truth about the Church-state distinction: "a fully secular state" that does not "juridically … privilege the Church." If this criticism has juxtaposed Maritain's and Leo XIII's view properly, the conclusion would certainly follow, and scholars of Maritain and modern Church-state relations would need to reassess the validity of Maritain's theory in light of Magisterial teaching.[12]

IV. Rehabilitating Maritain's View on Church and State

Did Maritain hold contradictory views from those of Leo XIII on Church-state relations? Maritain cited Leo XIII's *Immortale Dei* favorably in *Man and the State* and certainly saw himself as working within the

10. Ibid., 159.
11. Ibid., 152–54, 159–61.
12. Pink, "Jacques Maritain and the Problem of Church and State," 8–10.

Thomistic tradition, of which Leo XIII was a famous expositor and proponent.[13] A reasonable case may be made that Maritain and Leo XIII's views on Church and state are, in fact, reconcilable if one considers an essential footnote to the critical passage in *Man and the State* cited above and if one takes into account one of Maritain's earlier works, both of which Maritain's critic has ignored.

The recent misinterpretation of Maritain's theory stems, in part, from overlooking a footnote affixed to the critical passage in question. As quoted above, Maritain wrote that, in the modern age, "the order of terrestrial civilization and of temporal society has gained complete differentiation and full autonomy," which he called "normal" and in accord with the Gospel.[14] However, Maritain included an important footnote after the phrase "full autonomy": "I mean, in its own sphere and dominion."[15] Maritain's full text therefore reads that the modern temporal society has gained complete differentiation and full autonomy within its own temporal sphere and dominion.

It is tempting to construe this passage as support for severing the necessary "cooperation" of Church and state and for judging the union of Church and state as an "error," especially since Maritain quoted John Courtney Murray, who believed that the soul-body union was never an ideal.[16] Like Charles Journet and Murray, Maritain showed how the medieval *respublica Christiana* was a sacral state that assumed "many functions and responsibilities pertaining ... to political society."[17] But, unlike Murray, Maritain did not argue that the soul-body ideal was an error.[18] As Maritain's recent crit-

13. See also Pope Leo XIII, *Sapientiae Christianae*, quoted in Jacques Maritain, *The Things that are not Caesar's*, translated by J. F. Scanlan (London: Sheed and Ward, 1939), 140.

14. Maritain, *Man and the State*, 159.

15. Ibid., 159n14.

16. Maritain did not agree with Murray's account that the medieval Church's soul-body union was an error, even though Maritain was aware of Murray's thought. A year before Maritain gave the Walgreen lectures out of which *Man and the State* came, Murray critiqued the soul-body union that directly contradicted Maritain's earlier work, *The Things that are Not Caesar's*. See John Courtney Murray, "St. Robert Bellarmine on the Indirect Power," *Theological Studies* 9 (1948): 499–500.

17. Maritain, *Man and the State*, 158, citing Charles Journet, *L'Église du Verbe Incarné* (Paris: Desclée de Brouwer, 1952), 253–96. See also Murray, "St. Robert Bellarmine on the Indirect Power," 530–31.

18. On Murray's judgment on Leo XIII's teaching, see Michael J. Schuck, *That They be One: The Social Teaching of the Papal Encyclicals, 1740–1989* (Washington, D.C.: Georgetown University Press, 1991), 107n79 and 108n83.

ic acknowledges, Maritain "admire[d]" the medieval Church-state union.[19] Maritain merely argued that such a union was no longer feasible since in the modern era the Church no longer performs the ordinary functions of the political order. In that discrete sense, Maritain argued, the state has achieved complete differentiation and full autonomy in the temporal sphere, that is, in its own jurisdiction. Maritain's statement appears no different than what Leo XIII wrote in *Immortale Dei*: "Each [power, ecclesiastical and civil] *in its kind* is supreme."[20] In fact, Maritain's footnote in which he qualified "full autonomy" with "its own sphere and dominion" referenced his earlier citation of *Immortale Dei*.[21] With this reference, Maritain clearly intended for the passage on the Church-state distinction to align with Leo XIII's teaching.

In addition to their agreement in principle, Maritain and Leo XIII agreed that Church-state unity was no longer feasible. Maritain argued that the "immutable principle" of the primacy of the spiritual remains operative in a secular age, even if it is no longer effective by the Church's "expelling heretics" or "using ... the spiritual sword to seize upon temporal affairs for the sake of some spiritual necessity."[22] Leo XIII also came to the same prudential conclusion. In his 1892 encyclical *Au milieu des sollicitudes*, promulgated less than a decade after *Immortale Dei*, Leo XIII argued that while the strict separation of Church and state is "absurd" and "false," the practical separation of Church and state—in which the Church is "reduced to the liberty of living according to the law common to all citizens"—may be tolerated in light of the worse alternatives.[23] While Maritain might have expressed more optimism about the good spiritual effects of a practical separation but cooperation of Church and state, neither Maritain nor Leo XIII thought that a soul-body union is practical in a secular society or that anything less is outside of Magisterial toleration.

19. Pink, "Jacques Maritain and the Problem of Church and State," 7, quoting Maritain, *Man and the State*, 163.

20. Leo XIII, *Immortale Dei*: no. 13; emphasis added: "Utraque est in suo genere maxima: habet utraque certos, quibus contineatur, terminos, eosque sua cuiusque natura causaque proxima definitos; unde aliquis velut orbis circumscribitur, in quo sua cuiusque actio iure proprio versetur."

21. Maritain, *Man and the State*, 159n14 citing *Immortale Dei*: no. 152–53.

22. Ibid., 162–63.

23. Pope Leo XIII, *Au Milieu des Sollicitudes* (1892): no. 28.

V. *The Things that are Not Caesar's*

Maritain and Leo XIII's agreement on Church-state relations is even more apparent in one of Maritain's early works, *Primauté du spirituel*, published in 1927 and translated into English as *The Things that are not Caesar's* in 1931.[24] Maritain in *Man and the State* referenced his earlier work on the primacy of the spiritual, yet most other scholars do not mention the work at all.[25] He wrote *Things that are not Caesar's* after the 1926 condemnation of Action Française, a French movement that opposed modernity and sought to restore the French monarchy. Its newspaper, *L'Action Française*, favorably cited and reviewed Maritain's works, even though Maritain did not have a formal role in the movement. Maritain critically engaged with the opinions of its intellectual leader, Charles Maurras, and while he disagreed with much of Maurras's work, he suggested various proposals to reconcile, if possible, the movement's tenants with the Catholic Church.[26] Maritain's overtures did not persuade Pope Pius XI, who prohibited Maurras's books and excommunicated those who remained in the group. Since some Catholic members of Action Française viewed their organization as purely political and outside the jurisdiction of the Church, they viewed the pope's action as a usurpation of his power and rebuffed the papal judgment. In response, Maritain sought to rehabilitate the principle of papal power in temporal affairs when spiritual goods are at stake.[27] The result, his *Primauté du spirituel*, presented both a specific historical intervention in French society, as well as a theoretical defense of Leonine teaching on the ideal application of Church-state principles.[28]

24. Jacques Maritain, *Primauté du spirituel* (Paris: Plon, 1927).

25. Maritain, *Man and the State*, 150n2. For passing references to *Things that are not Caesar's*, see, for example, Hittinger, "Cooperation of Church and State," 180, 183n11, 193; Thaddeus J. Kozinski, *The Political Problem of Religious Pluralism: And Why Philosophers Can't Solve It* (Lanham, Maryland: Lexington, 2010), 49–80.

26. Jacques Maritain, *Une Opinion sur Charles Maurras et le Devoir des Catholiques* (Paris: Plon, 1926).

27. On the view of Action Française members, see Peter J. Bernardi, *Maurice Blondel, Social Catholicism, and Action Française: The Clash over the Church's Role in Society during the Modernist Era* (Washington, D.C.: The Catholic University of America Press, 2009), 210–11.

28. For Maritain and Action Française, see Bernard E. Doering, *Jacques Maritain and the French Catholic Intellectuals* (Notre Dame, Indiana: University of Notre Dame Press, 1983), 6–36; Michael J. Kerlin, "Anti-Modernism and the Elective Affinity between Politics and Philosophy," in *Catholicism Contending with Modernity: Roman Catholic Modernism and Anti-Modernism in Historical Context*, edited by Darrell Jodock (New York: Cambridge University Press, 2000),

Like Leo XIII, Maritain maintained that the Church holds a right to exercise indirect power in temporal affairs for the sake of moral or spiritual interests. The Church has power over the temporal within the spiritual order of salvation, including the denunciation or avoidance of sin, the preservation of the good of souls, and the maintenance of the liberty of the Church. Maritain expressed this relationship in the language of Thomistic philosophy: The Church intervenes in the temporal with a view not to the temporal itself, which is the "subject matter," but to the spiritual, which is the "formal object."[29] He emphasized that the subject matter of the spiritual power was extensive: any sort of temporal act—public decree, legislation, taxation, declaration of war and peace, or political activities—may be connected with the good of souls or liberty of Church, and the Church alone should decide in which temporal affairs, if any, the Church should intervene.[30]

As in later works, Maritain acknowledged that the difficulty of sustaining and applying this extensive right to intervene in temporal affairs *ratione peccati* led the Church to abstain prudentially from exercising indirect power in most political affairs and to direct such power to teaching on faith and morals only. But the Church retained the principle of indirect power, even in a secular age, to teach, counsel, and, if necessary, order civil rulers, which included the right to annul civil laws, depose civil rulers, and absolve civil oaths. In Christian states whose rulers adhered to the Church's teachings, the Church's indirect power would be used merely to counsel civil rulers and teach moral and spiritual truths to the faithful. Since states often fall short of this ideal, the Church's indirect power extends as far as the primacy of the spiritual requires and as far as prudence allows.[31]

Nevertheless, the fundamental principles concerning Church and state do not change, whether in the Middle Ages or in the secular age. Maritain argued that the Church's teachings present continuous agreement from Boniface VIII's *Unam Sanctam* in the fourteenth century to Leo XIII's *Im-*

319–26; and Phillipe Bénéton, "Jacques Maritain et L'Action Française," *Revue Française de Science Politique* 23, no. 6 (1973): 1202–38. Francesca Aran Murphy seems to suggest that the Vatican influenced Maritain's writing or publishing of *Primauté du spirituel*. Francesca Aran Murphy, *Art and Intellect in the Philosophy of Étienne Gilson* (Columbia, Missouri: University of Missouri Press, 2004), 100.

29. Maritain, *The Things that are not Caesar's*, 9–10, 21.

30. Ibid., 22–24.

31. Ibid., 15.

mortale Dei in the nineteenth century.[32] Maritain endorsed Leo XIII's teaching that the civil and ecclesiastical powers are supreme in their respective jurisdictions, but that while the state is sovereign in its own domain, it is subordinate to the Church in matters of faith and morals, and therefore cannot be sovereign in an absolute sense. Because the Church's right over the temporal sphere does not dominate or oppress the temporal power, but instead controls and orients it to spiritual ends, the civil ruler remains free to govern civil affairs without ecclesiastical interference, so long as the temporal power's actions affect the good of souls, to the extent that the civil authority can serve that good.[33]

Maritain's analysis derived principally from Leo XIII and the Thomistic tradition. As Maritain noted, Aquinas argued that, since humans are ordered to their final end, the civil society must pursue the common temporal end so far as it enables humans to obtain eternal life. Since the end of temporal power is subordinate to the end of spiritual power, the latter can direct the former by counsels and, if the interests of the soul require it, control the temporal power through orders.[34] Robert Bellarmine, in whose tradition Maritain found compatibility, also grounded the Church's indirect power on the subordination of ends. For Bellarmine, as for Maritain, the importance of this indirect power is metaphysically significant for *libertas ecclesiae*. Refusing the right of the spiritual power to intervene in temporal affairs denies the existence of an independent spiritual power. Such a rejection implies that moral values affecting political acts depend upon the temporal power alone, and effectively transfers jurisdiction over spiritual things to the temporal power. The primacy of the spiritual, therefore, depends on the doctrine of indirect power.[35]

In both *Things that are not Caesar's* and *Man and the State*, Maritain countenanced practical considerations without contradicting immutable principles. It is highly implausible that Maritain contradicted his early

32. Ibid., xii, xvi, 13.

33. Ibid., 4–7, 12, 14.

34. Ibid., 11–12. See Thomas Aquinas, *De Regno*, bk. 1, chap. 15; Michael D. Breidenbach and William McCormick, "Aquinas on Tyranny, Resistance, and the End of Politics," *Perspectives on Political Science* 44, no. 1 (2015): 10–17. Maritain also saw this principle in Aquinas's *Sentences Commentary*, which stated that the spiritual sword is not only for spiritual ends, but also can order and direct the temporal sword. Thomas Aquinas, *In IV Sent.*, d. 37, expoitio textus, cited in Maritain, *The Things that are Not Caesar's*, 129.

35. Maritain, *The Things that are Not Caesar's*, 18, citing Robert Bellarmine, *De Potestati Papae in Rebus Temporalibus*, chap. 2.

work, for he cited from it in his later work and did not advertise any repudiation. Instead, from his early writings on Church and state to his mature political theory, Maritain defended Leo XIII's principle of a "certain orderly connection" of Church and state, including the soul-body analogy, which Maritain saw as continuous from Aquinas and Bellarmine to Leo XIII. This connection recognized the distinction between Church and state, affirmed the primacy of the spiritual, and admitted the right of ecclesiastical intervention in temporal affairs for the sake of higher spiritual goods. These principles, however, also came with the implicit provision that the Church is free to judge prudentially *not* to intervene.[36] The Church's indirect power extends as far as the primacy of the spiritual requires, but it should be applied as carefully as prudence demands. While Maritain argued that it would be imprudent for the Church to intervene in secular states in the way that popes did in medieval Christian states, his conclusion is not a contradiction of Leo XIII's teachings but a prudential application of them.

VI. Ideals and Practicalities in Church and State

While Leo XIII's and Maritain's absolute principles on Church-state cooperation are congruent, it may be argued that Maritain's positive account of how Christianity can operate in modern society contradicted these principles. How can one reconcile, on the one hand, Maritain's clear affirmation of the Leonine soul-body union analogy, and, on the other hand, his political theory of a secular state in which Christians leaven modern democratic society, but where the Church holds no juridical privilege in the state?

An "integral Maritainism" would suggest that these seemingly opposing views are reconcilable if the former is read, as it should be, as a more perfect realization of the immutable principles of Church and state, while the latter is understood, as it reasonably can be, as an attempt to apply these principles to the difficult reality of a modern democratic regime. The latter practical theory should not be confused as being the same as the immutable principles, for every application of these principles—including attempts in the medieval era—are somehow imperfect with respect to the principles. Employing Aristotle's distinction between the "most ideal" political theory and the practically attainable ideal provides a helpful hermeneutic for understanding Maritain's approach. The former type of theory

36. See, for example, Maritain, *Man and the State*, 180n30.

assumes no external impediments to implementing the ideal, while the latter theory considers the given circumstances of and the appropriateness for the society in which it will be implemented. Aristotle taught that both the "unqualifiedly best" and the "best in the circumstances" are necessary considerations in political theory.[37] One does not supplant the other; they are both required for a proper understanding of Church-state relations.

Likewise, Maritain maintained that any "thesis" about how the immutable principles ought to be applied should not be confused with the "absolute ideal" itself, for that would fall into contradiction: "the very notion of an absolute ideal" is "supra-temporal," while the application of an ideal is necessarily temporal.[38] Equally damaging, according to Maritain, is to consider these absolute principles as not absolute at all, but instead as statements whose meanings change, even to the point of contradiction, depending on the historical circumstances. On the contrary, Maritain argued that these "absolute and immutable and supra-temporal" principles are "analogically realized" through "particular, concrete applications." The application of the immutable principles of Church-state cooperation should take "various typical forms in reference to the *historical climates* or *historical constellations* through which the development of mankind is passing."[39] It is impossible for the immutable principles themselves to be strictly identical ("univocal") with an application of them in historical circumstances.[40] All applications, therefore, are "analogical" in the sense that the immutable principles and an application of them have aspects of similarity and dissimilarity. Since analogical argumentation is inductive in form, the success of the conclusion—in this case, the success of the application of the immutable principles—is not guaranteed. More relevant similarities between the immutable principles and their application entail a better analogical application. But to expect a mirror image of the immutable principles in history is, Maritain argued, chimerical: not even the medieval era enjoyed such a result.

Maritain stressed that the immutable principles of Church-state relations remain in this new era but need to be applied differently now because of religious diversity and the existence of the secular state. The first change from the Middle Ages to modern society was religious pluralism.

37. Aristotle, *Politics*, 4.1, 1288b21–38.
38. Maritain, *Man and the State*, 154–55.
39. Ibid., 156–57; emphasis in original.
40. See Hittinger, "Cooperation of Church and State," 183–84.

Maritain did not believe that religious pluralism is a new good that offers Church-state harmony, but rather believed it to be a dis-grace: religious diversity signals a privation of the grace of true faith. All the same, Maritain took the fact of religious pluralism as dispositive, both for the state to abstain from coercing theological conformity and for the Church to refrain from intervening in the political affairs of nations. He did not count these conclusions as perfect instantiations of the Church-state ideal—neither, for that matter, did the medieval era represent a perfect application—but rather as the best of what is politically possible.[41]

Maritain departed from Leo XIII, however, by viewing religious pluralism as not something simply to be tolerated, but as a phenomenon that should be integrated with an authentic Christian spirit as much as possible. One of the advantages of evaluating proposals for the practically attainable ideal, such as Maritain's political theory, is that the inability to implement the "most ideal" theory can reveal goods that would otherwise have been overlooked. While Maritain was reluctant to declare unambiguous progress between the medieval and modern eras—for neither, he insisted, should be "absolutely condemned or absolutely approved"—he did detect in the modern period a good development: a more complete recognition of *dignitatis humanae personae*, which his friend Pope Paul VI would explicitly declare in the Second Vatican Council.[42] The belief in the dignity of the person entails the equal right to religious freedom, by virtue of which the state affirms and protects the primacy of a person's spiritual duties to God and to pursue religious truth (even if, during that pursuit, one might believe falsehood) and likewise refrains from any action that deliberately undermines his or her moral and spiritual mission. The reliance on laypeople as constitutive members of the Church, who are also citizens of the state, to represent the Christian faith to the larger body politic through their conscience and moral witness signaled for Maritain a new, positive development that reflected the evangelical spirit of the Gospel.[43]

The second, not unrelated, development since the Middle Ages was the

41. Maritain, *Man and the State*, 154–57; Kozinski, *Political Problem of Religious Pluralism*, 55–56.

42. Jacques Maritain, *On the Philosophy of History* (New York: Charles Scribner's Sons, 1957), 56; Vatican Council II, *Dignitatis Humanae* [Declaration on Religious Freedom], (1965); and Catherine M. A. McCauliff, "Jacques Maritain's Embrace of Religious Pluralism and the Declaration of Religious Freedom," *Seton Hall Law Review* 41, no. 2 (2011): 593–624.

43. Maritain, *Integral Humanism*, 174–76, 192–94.

shift from a sacral to a secular state. To be sure, any account of Church-state relations that leaves out the juridical status of the Church in the state and sidelines the notion of the state as a "secular arm" of the Church, is a privation of Leo XIII's soul-body union analogy. However, Maritain's account does so not in order to repudiate or contradict the Church's ideal status, but in recognition of its infeasibility in the modern age. What prevents the soul-body union analogy in the modern age is not necessarily religious pluralism, but modern democracy, for even if each member of the body politic were Christian, Maritain argued, a confessional state "could not be conceivable" due to modern democratic principles.[44] In such a state, the application of the immutable principles of Church and state would be very difficult, if not impossible, to implement as an analogous soul-body union. The historical reformulation of the state has rendered this impractical.

However, Maritain also innovated from Leo XIII by arguing that relying on baptized citizens to fulfill the Church's mission "manifests in a clearer manner the freedom and purity of the spiritual," and therefore better ensures the "primacy of the spiritual" compared with the state's use of the coercive power.[45] Maritain's statement does not contradict Leo XIII's teaching, as Pink has argued, since Maritain did not repudiate, in principle, the soul-body union analogy, nor did Leo XIII argue that state coercion is a spiritually superior method for fulfilling the Church's mission. To be sure, the efficacy of relying on baptized citizens may be questioned, just as Maritain doubted the effectiveness of state coercion in religious matters. But Maritain's claim—that a society in which all baptized citizens followed Church teaching without the use of state coercion would more clearly manifest the superiority of the spiritual—is consistent with Leo's ideal of Church-state union, since even under a regime of state coercion, a society in which that coercion proved unnecessary would surely be a spiritual advancement.

Maritain emphasized that nothing in his "Church and State" chapter in *Man and the State* should be construed as contradicting the "thesis" that the Church's "privileged juridical situation" should be "sought, by virtue of the rights she possesses as a messenger of divine truth." But, he explained, "the conditions of realization (what is called the 'hypothesis') for such an ideal situation suppose a people in whom division in religious matters has

44. Maritain, *Man and the State*, 181.
45. Ibid., 164.

disappeared, and in whom the Catholic faith is accepted by all." This "religious unanimity" is required by the "factual circumstances" of modern democratic society: namely, "the principle of the quality of all before the law" and the non-coercive power of the state in religious matters. Even if unanimity could be achieved, Maritain noted, these "factual circumstances" would prevent the state from being the "secular arm of the Church." While that kind of application of the soul-body analogical union would not be possible in modern democratic society, Maritain believed that the only way the Church's "privileged juridical situation" could be achieved would be by a different kind of soul-body union: the religious unity of the body politic.[46]

Maritain again assured that "the principles which were applied in a given way by the sacral civilization of the Middle Ages always hold true, but they are to be applied in another way in modern secular civilization."[47] Just as holding a right, such as personal freedom, is distinct from the exercise of that right, the Church does not surrender its right—for instance, to annul civil laws for the sake of a spiritual good—simply because the Church refrains from exercising that right for a superintending reason.[48] It is "intrinsically erroneous" to propose, Maritain charged, that the "principles which had been applied in the Middle Ages" are "perishable principles" simply because they are "inapplicable today."[49]

What John Hittinger has called "Maritain's unique breakthrough on the topic of Church and State," Thomas Pink has instead viewed as Maritain's break from Magisterial teaching.[50] However, there is a difference between contradicting the absolute ideal as found in Magisterial teaching on the one hand, and refraining from its full implementation for prudential reasons on the other. Maritain did not contradict Leonine teaching on the need for an "orderly connection" between Church and state or on the condemnation of the "false" principle of Church-state separation. Instead, Maritain applied the immutable principles, which both he and Leo XIII shared, differently in a new political theory. Unlike Maritain, Leo XIII never articulated a "best in the circumstances" political theory for modern Church-state relations. Leo XIII's encyclicals presented the absolute principles of Church and state,

46. Ibid., 173n27.
47. Ibid., 180.
48. Ibid., 180n30.
49. Ibid., 180.
50. Ibid., 183.

as well as ideal application of those principles, which he compared to a soul-body hylomorphism. For Leo XIII, the soul-body union was an analogy, an application of the "orderly connection" principle between Church and state, and he recognized that such an analogy might not be possible to implement in the modern age.

One should not infer, therefore, that Leo XIII believed the absolute principles of Church and state contained in themselves the ideal of how they should be applied in every circumstance. Just because Leo XIII offered in the modern age only one analogy for Church-state relations, it is not necessarily entailed that this application must be realized in the modern age, or that any practically attainable ideal would contradict Magisterial principles. Pink has assumed that, since Leo XIII articulated both immutable principles of Church and state and offered the ideal application of them—a soul-body union—that both the immutable principles and their ideal application are of a piece: that, without the latter, one has necessarily and utterly failed in applying the former. Leo XIII's own writing betrays this binary standard.

Leo XIII himself declared that in this modern age—when the state does not profess the Catholic religion, does not enjoy Christian rulers who rule over a Christian community, and does not function as the "secular arm" of the Church—the Church does not censure certain Church-state arrangements that do not meet the ideal. In a passage from *Immortale Dei* not cited by Pink but equally part of Leonine teaching, Leo XIII conceded that "custom or usage" of a political community could be "a kind of sanction" for multiple religions to have their "place in the State." The Church, he assured, "does not … condemn those rulers who, for the sake of securing some great good or of hindering some great evil," allow for religious pluralism in the State. While the "Church, indeed, deems it unlawful to place the various forms of divine worship on the same footing as the true religion," this in itself does not necessarily entail that the soul-body model should be applied in circumstances where multiple religions are practiced. Other considerations are required, including the state's recognition of individual religious liberty, for Leo XIII stressed that "no one shall be forced to embrace the Catholic faith against his will."[51] With this recognition of religious pluralism, Leo XIII granted that a soul-body analogical union of

51. Pope Leo XIII, *Immortale Dei*: no. 36.

Church and state—in which the state enforces doctrines and punishments according to Church teachings—would not be possible.

It was in light of Leo XIII's qualifications, which also constitute Magisterial teaching, that Maritain worked to develop a practically best theory. Maritain did not take *de facto* or *de jure* Church-state separation as a normative principle, but as a particular, historical fact around which any practically attainable ideal needed to be built. To achieve "a certain orderly connection" in these circumstances, Maritain focused on the human person, whose union of soul and body held out the promise of integration between the Church's mission and the duties of citizenship. In *Integral Humanism*, Maritain maintained that in the "new Christendom" the Christian faith operates in modern society primarily through persons rather than through the state's juridical recognition of the Church as the authority on faith and morals.[52] In this new Church-state arrangement, the Church—more fully understood as not only juridical and institutional but also secular and lay—could continue to cooperate with the state and to leaven society with the Christian spirit. The state, for example, should call for "the public acknowledgement of the existence of God" and "guarantee" the Church's "full freedom" to exercise its spiritual mission, while the Church should help the "body politic" with "all the activities which aim at enlightening human minds and life," including "religious, social, and educational work."[53] Maritain had in mind not the strict separation found in Europe, which formed the context of Leo XIII's and other popes' condemnations of Church-state separation, but the "sharp distinction *and* actual cooperation" between Church and state as practiced in the United States.[54]

In criticizing Maritain, however, Thomas Pink has raised important questions about whether this new Christendom is ultimately tenable and, more generally, about how to reconcile ideals with practicalities. Even as a supporter of the Leonine ideal application, Pink acknowledges that such an ideal "is certainly not now realizable." Nevertheless, he argues that this union remains the sole available ideal even in modernity, for "the credibility of an ideal does not depend on its continued practicability."[55] This is a powerful statement, especially since so many "practical ideals" have proved not only impractica-

52. Jacques Maritain, *Integral Humanism: Temporal and Spiritual Problems of a New Christendom*, translated by Joseph W. Evans (New York: Charles Scribner's Sons, 1968).

53. Maritain, *Man and the State*, 178. For the terms of such cooperation, see ibid., 171–79.

54. Ibid., 183.

55. Pink, "Jacques Maritain," 11.

ble but also not truly ideal. It is therefore important to emphasize that, even if the "best" ideal can never be attained, it still needs to be recognized, since it is the standard for judging whether the practically attainable ideal is ideal at all. Maritain's own work, from *The Things that are Not Caesar's* to *Man and the State,* attempted this bifocal political theory: the ideal theory continued to be a source of inspiration and renewal for the best practically attainable theory.

The argument of this paper has not been that Leo XIII's and Maritain's views on Church and state are the same, or that they do not differ in important ways, but that they do not contradict at the level of unchanging Magisterial doctrine. However, it is fair to question whether Maritain's argument for a more secular and lay cooperation between Church and state—a project that he generally shared with John Courtney Murray—is the Church's most effective public posture in a secular age, or whether it now can genuinely be called an "orderly connection."[56] To rely on the state's recognition of the dignity of the human person and the protection of religious freedom—two requirements for the baptized laity to advance the Church's mission—might turn out to be, if it has not already been, an inadequate substitute for the special juridical status of the Church. It appears implausible that modern secular states will recognize the transcendence of religion and the Church's authority in faith and morals without the recognition of the Church's privileged jurisdiction. Church-state harmony seems equally implausible with the rise of secularism in society, which places increasing doubt as to whether Maritain's practically attainable ideal is still, in fact, practically attainable. At the same time, however, insisting on that favored status in our age will likely result in practical paralysis. After all, simply appealing to the Church's liberty in the face of an increasingly aggressive secular state has proved to have mixed results.[57] While the prophetic witness of teaching the immutable Church-state principles and their "most ideal" application, as both Leo XIII and Maritain did, remains pressing in every era, the full fruits of the practical accommodation that Maritain proposed remain to be seen.[58]

56. In addition to the argument in *Man and the State,* see also Jacques Maritain, *Freedom in the Modern World,* translated by Richard O'Sullivan (London: Sheed and Ward, 1935); Jacques Maritain, *The Rights of Man and Natural Law,* translated by Doris C. Anson (New York: Charles Scribner's Sons, 1943); and Jacques Maritain, *Christianity and Democracy,* translated by Doris C. Anson (New York: Charles Scribner's Sons, 1944).

57. See, for example, *Zubik v. Burwell,* 578 U.S. ____ (2016).

58. I would like to thank Janice Chik Breidenbach, John Conley, S.J., William McCormick, S.J., Michael Pakaluk, Thomas Pink, and Joseph Trabbic for their helpful comments, and Chadwick Medel for his research assistance. Any remaining faults are my own.

WILLIAM MCCORMICK, S.J.

"All the Articulations of the Real"

Jacques Maritain on Catholic Social Teaching

THE YEAR 2016 MARKED the 125th anniversary of *Rerum novarum*, and thus the 125th anniversary of modern Catholic Social Teaching (CST).[1] As scholars assess the *status quaestionis* of CST in the 21st century, a vital question is the relationship between CST as taught by the Magisterium and as studied in academic scholarship.

Scholarly reflection on CST has grown alongside the Magisterium from the beginning. *Rerum novarum* itself was born out of conversations among scholars, mostly Italian clerics, who inspired and aided in the Thomistic renaissance of *Aeterni Patris*, and who were not afraid to bring Thomism to bear upon economic, social, and political concerns.[2] But CST scholarship is no longer primarily "in-house," as CST scholarship has burgeoned in many non-ecclesial institutions. Further, as CST has attracted an ever-wider audience, much scholarly analysis of it depends upon disciplines beyond theology, especially the social sciences. Further, the Church itself has had little to say thematically to scholars working in this endeavor. Thus, just because CST has become an increasingly popular object of scholarship, it risks losing its ecclesial and theological foundations.

1. For an account of *Rerum novarum* and the beginnings of Catholic Social Teaching, see J. Brian Benestad, *Church, State, and Society: An Introduction to Catholic Social Doctrine* (Washington, D.C.: The Catholic University of America Press, 2011), 58–64; and Charles Curran, *Catholic Social Teaching, 1891–Present: A Historical, Theological, and Ethical Analysis* (Washington, D.C.: Georgetown University Press, 2002), 8–9.

2. See Russell Hittinger, "Introduction," in *The Teachings of Modern Roman Catholicism on Law, Politics, and Human Nature*, edited by John Witte Jr. and Frank S. Alexander (New York: Columbia University Press, 2007), 11–18.

And so I think it helpful to ask: What kind of goals, questions, and assumptions ought to guide scholarly reflection on CST? As CST pursues the human person's good in the temporal sphere, how can the spiritual guide that search? In this paper I turn to Jacques Maritain's "The Spiritual Conditions for Progress and Peace" to sketch out an answer to that question. This text, a speech he gave to UNESCO in 1966, is one of his more thematic treatments of how the Church can influence society, one with significant allusions to *Gaudium et spes* and Pope Paul VI's 1965 address to the United Nations General Assembly. I hope for this study to clarify what kind of "renewal" Maritain hopes the Church to bring about in the political order. A more robust sense of "renewal," I hope, will provide fruitful challenges and guidance for CST as it continues to develop in academic strains.

While Maritain is not often turned to in CST circles beyond as a historical note, his reflections on politics and society without doubt have considerable bearing upon CST.[3] We can thus hope that this inquiry will shed light on Maritain's broader political commitments.

I. Maritain's Preliminary Remark

Maritain begins his lecture by noting a change to the title of the paper. Originally titled "The Spiritual Conditions for Progress and Peace," Maritain amended it to "The Role of the Spiritual with Regard to Progress and Peace."

As Maritain proceeds, the significance of this change becomes clear. "Peace and progress," he writes, "are things *of this world* or of *the temporal order*." The "spiritual can furnish inspiration, light and encouragement ... and in this way it can *help* ... resolve the problems of this world and of the temporal order." However, he notes, "The spiritual cannot *take upon itself the responsibility* of resolving these problems, and it can make no claim to do so." The role that the spiritual exercises in politics is not easy to synthesize, for it is at once a small and indirect role, and yet also one of great inspiration and influence. As Maritain has it, it would thus be misleading to speak of "the spiritual conditions for progress and peace" as though the

3. As should be clear, my project is in substantial sympathy with Joseph M. de Torre, "Maritain's 'Integral Humanism' and Catholic Social Teaching," in *Reassessing the Liberal State: Reading Maritain's "Man and the State,"* edited by Timothy Fuller and John P. Hittinger (Washington, D.C.: American Maritain Association, distributed by The Catholic University of America Press, 2001), 202–208.

spiritual founded politics. But it would also be a mistake to deny the spiritual a role in politics.[4]

This complex dynamic is perhaps not surprising coming from Maritain, but it is a crucial point. He cites Paul VI's 1965 speech to the United Nations as an important example of this approach.[5] In that speech, the pope notes that the Holy See has been purged of any temporal power and comes before the U.N. only as a benevolent spiritual authority. While the pope thus comes as "the least" among sovereign nations, he comes with "unique greatness" insofar as he comes in the name of all "Christian brethren" for the benefit of all mankind. Notably, Paul VI does not come with political initiatives of his own but with "support and approval" to encourage them in their task of peace.

Yet the role of the spiritual in politics is not simply irenic. As Maritain continues, he notes that "men need in a very particular way" the help of the spiritual, "subject as they are to the temptation of despair." The spiritual can "offer … serious warnings, which men need just as sorely." Paul VI himself notes that pride and the lust for power are pervasive difficulties in political life and that humility and solidarity are very much God-given and needed in politics. Paul strikes an Augustinian note in arguing that "For it is pride, as inevitable as it may seem, that provokes the tensions and struggles over prestige, over domination, over colonialism, over selfishness. It is pride that shatters brotherhood." Having made these preliminary claims about the role of the spiritual in politics, Maritain then notes the context in which the spiritual exercises that role. It is history.

The ambiguity of history is a crucial notion for Maritain. In *Integral Humanism,* he notes that "the world and the temporal city" are "the kingdom *at once* of man, of God, and of the devil. Thus appears the essential ambiguity of the world and of its history."[6] This is Maritain at his most Augustinian: the world is saved in hope, he says, "but it is not *holy,* it is the Church which is *holy.*"[7] Thus man must "dispute with the devil." The essential dif-

4. Jacques Maritain, "The Spiritual Conditions for Progress and Peace," in *Untrammeled Approaches,* translated by Bernard Doering (Notre Dame, Indiana: University of Notre Dame Press, 1997), 199; emphasis in original.

5. Paul VI, "Address of the Holy Father Paul VI to the United Nations Organization," 4 October 1965.

6. Jacques Maritain, *Integral Humanism,* in volume 11, *The Collected Works of Jacques Maritain,* edited Otto Bird (Notre Dame, Indiana: University of Notre Dame Press, 1996), 220.

7. Ibid.

ficulty is discerning what is of God and what is of Satan—with man caught between them in the ebb and flow of history.

In this speech, Maritain emphasizes the sheer length of time it takes for the spiritual to work itself out in history:

> Of course, all this needs time, in some cases many long years. This is precisely why the action of the spiritual on men and on history is more vast and powerful by far than even the most violent and stormy temporal action, which exerts all its force at a moment in time and whose effects are then just as quickly borne away in the flux and fluctuations of time – and in addition, all of this, especially if it is of considerable scope, is radically dependent on what took place over time in the spiritual order.[8]

Maritain brings out what he has in mind here with the examples of "Marxism and the Communist revolution." Such phenomena would never have occurred without Hegel, and never "without a Descartes and a Luther." The implication seems to be that temporal activity comes and goes, quickly subsumed by change. It is, moreover, radically dependent upon its antecedents. Maritain thus wants to say that temporal activity connects across time but also that any one moment passes. This is crucial to any account of modernity: what has been set in motion perdures but does not take long in radically changing. This temporal activity also has a spiritual origin, for Descartes and Luther would never have come about "without the spiritual *élan* imprinted one day on the history of mankind, whatever deviations and falls from its potential it may have undergone *en route* since that day, by the preaching of a few Galilean fishermen."[9] Maritain's references to "deviations and falls" makes it clear that the relationship between the temporal and spiritual is not always a happy one: much of modern thought and practice is a falling away from Christianity.[10]

In his address to the U.N., Paul VI underscores the necessity of acting through and in spite of the ambiguity of history. "It is hard to foresee the future," he says, "but easy to assert that the world has to set out resolutely on the path toward a new history." This new history must be "peaceful … truly and fully human, the one that God promised to men of good will." Paul highlights the hopes that many had after World War II, hopes perhaps

8. Maritain, "The Spiritual Conditions for Progress and Peace," in *Untrammeled Approaches*, 199–200.

9. Ibid., 200.

10. This theme runs throughout Maritain's works, not least in *Three Reformers*.

best reflected in *Gaudium et spes.* Those hopes were not without foundation, and they were largely Christian hopes. Christianity, after all, played a leading role in reviving Europe after World War II.[11] As Europe lay in ruins, it was Christian statesmen like Robert Schumann, Jean Monnet and Konrad Adenauer who turned Europe's thoughts toward renewal. Only with Christian hope could they imagine fruitful peace in the aftermath of such violence and carnage.

And yet, for all the great hopes for a post-war future, by 1968 it was clear that something had gone horribly wrong, as Ratzinger notes in the preface to *Introduction to Christianity.*[12] But what exactly went wrong? Were the historical forces at work not of God? Did Christians not fully or wisely cooperate with them? How ought the Church to have engaged in such historical forces? Academic reflection on CST needs to inquire into such successes and failings of Christian-inspired politics. For, as aware of the ambiguities of history as Maritain and Paul VI were, it seems probable that they put too much faith in movements of democracy and peace in the post-war period.[13]

I noted above that the temporal role of the spiritual is not only irenic. The pride and *libido dominandi* to which Maritain and Paul refer play out in history, of course. Thus, while the spiritual should console and encourage, it ought also to amplify the pinpricks of conscience that are rarely felt under the sway of sin and vice. Indeed, the Magisterium, Donal Dorr notes, often speaks as though "people need only to be encouraged and animated to cooperate more fruitfully."[14] In fact, serious disagreements exist even among people of good faith, and the disordered will looms large as a source of conflict in our world. Such considerations might add a sober tempering to conversations about just war theory, for instance, and the need for a broader theology of peace.

These words and examples point to the need to attend to what theology of history we bring to our political analysis. For CST must guard against

11. On Adenauer, see Robert Kraynak, *Christian Faith and Modern Democracy* (Notre Dame, Indiana: University of Notre Dame Press, 2001), 144–46.

12. Joseph Ratzinger, *Introduction to Christianity,* translated by Michael J. Miller (San Francisco: Ignatius Press, 2004), 11–14.

13. On Maritain's theology of history, see Thaddeus Kozinski, *The Political Problem of Religious Pluralism: And Why Philosophers Can't Solve It* (Lanham, Maryland: Lexington Books, 2010), 47–126. See also Maritain's *Peasant of the Garonne* for Maritain's own misgivings.

14. See Donal Dorr, *Option for the Poor and for the Earth: Catholic Social Teaching* (Maryknoll, New York: Orbis Books, 2012), 92.

both the influence of Hegelian views of history that are fundamentally too hopeful and post-modern views of history that deny the agency of the Spirit. The *Magnificat* of Mary, Maritain urges, reminds us that we must remain in but not of our worldly circumstances: "We are not co-operators with history; we are co-operators with God."[15]

II. Inspiration

Let us turn now to what Maritain considers the first role of the spiritual in politics: inspiration. We said that Maritain begins with this statement: "Peace and progress are things *of this world* or of *the temporal order*." It was upon the basis of this claim that Maritain modified the title of his talk. It is also with this statement that Maritain puts forth a fundamental theme of his political philosophy: the relative autonomy of the temporal or political vis-à-vis the spiritual. This motif is most famously expressed in his *Man and the State* with the "democratic charter."[16] Maritain was constantly at pains to emphasize the relative autonomy of the political so as to take its task seriously. He was therefore also at pains to emphasize the relative autonomy of moral philosophy, or what one can know about the human person in his practical life through unaided reason, from theology.

In Maritain's *Essay on Christian Philosophy*, he lays out the relationship between moral philosophy and theology.[17] Moral philosophy differs from speculative philosophy, Maritain argues, in having a state as well as a nature. For the person is the object of such moral or practical investigations: "an object which is *natural* by virtue of its essence, but whose *state* is not purely natural, and depends on the supernatural order."[18] Philosophy could not uncover by itself, but must learn from revelation through theology, that man "is not in a state of pure nature, he is fallen and redeemed."[19] Maritain goes on to explain that such a philosophy must be a "Christian philosophy": one that must make "use of principles received from faith and

15. Jacques Maritain, *Freedom in the Modern World,* in volume 11, *The Collected Works of Jacques Maritain,* edited by Otto Bird (Notre Dame, Indiana: University of Notre Dame Press, 1996), 3–118, at 48.

16. Jacques Maritain, *Man and the State* (Washington, D.C.: The Catholic University Press, 1998) 108–46.

17. Jacques Maritain, *An Essay on Christian Philosophy,* translated by Edward H. Flannery (New York: Philosophical Library, 1955), 38–43 and 61–108.

18. Maritain, *An Essay on Christian Philosophy,* 38–39.

19. Ibid., 39.

theology," yet "remains a philosophy and proceeds according to the proper mode of philosophy."[20]

For our purposes, we note that Maritain thinks that moral philosophy, including in matters of politics, society, and economics, must take cognizance of man's fallen yet redeemed state: "It is one thing to possess a speculative knowledge of human nature, to know the essence of the human being ... it is quite another thing to have the practical science *of the conduct of man* in the state of pure nature," and even more so to have such a science that makes sense of man's decidedly "unpure" nature.[21] It is thus appropriate that Paul VI speaks frankly to the United Nations of both man's elevated dignity and his lowly state, what is "loftiest in human wisdom" and the "real danger" that comes from man's pride and his bellicosity, as particularly evidenced by his military technology when divorced from any moral considerations about their use.

Again, however, Maritain and Paul VI both speak such teachings in the name of promoting a flourishing politics, one that has its proper autonomy. While what Maritain means exactly by this continues to be controversial, let me draw some tentative conclusions from it based upon this statement and what we have already noted.

First, the spiritual has a role of inspiration for the temporal precisely because the spiritual cannot take the place of the temporal. Taking this broadly, it means that spiritual governance, notably the Church, cannot replace temporal governance as found in the state and civic institutions, and that spiritual reflection, most notably theology, cannot replace temporal reflection, or the secular sciences like economics, political science, and philosophy. Most crucially for politics, the state must be the state. The common good served by the state is a real good, and when we say that the modern state ought to be "instrumental," we refer to the character of the state's service in procuring the good, not the character of the good so procured.[22] Maritain's political philosophy attempts—in a way perhaps only matched by Yves Simon, Charles McCoy, and John Courtney Murray—to navigate between individualism and collectivism, to see political community as essential to, but only a part of, the person's perfection.[23]

20. Ibid., 40. On "Christian philosophy," see Thomas D'Andrea, "Rethinking the Christian Philosophy Debate: An Old Puzzle and Some New Points of Orientation," *Acta Philosophica* 1 (1992): 191–214.

21. Maritain, *An Essay on Christian Philosophy,* 63.

22. Russell Hittinger, "Reasons for a Civil Society," in *Reassessing the Liberal State,* 11–12.

23. On Murray, see Douglas Kries, "Defending Robert Bellarmine," in *Jerusalem, Athens, and*

Thus a fundamental task of CST—both the Magisterium and scholarly reflection upon it—must be to clarify the distinction between the spiritual and temporal. This distinction is a uniquely Christian innovation, and in every age powerful alternatives arise to challenge it.[24] Indeed, one can understand Western political history—from Eusebius on the providence of the *pax Romana* to the controversies over the Affordable Care Act contraception mandate—as a series of attempts to negotiate this distinction. How this distinction is to be sorted out in each aeon will be something the Church must take the lead on, for the state will not always have incentives to do so.[25]

While CST must respect the autonomy of the state, man's fallen condition makes it likely that he will not know or will ignore important facts about himself that he in principle should know. Thus this Christian distinction arises against the background of basic facts about humans crucial to politics, all that CST must find ways to emphasize: humans are persons, they are naturally social and political, immanent life is not the *summum bonum*, death is not the *summum malum*, politics is not the whole of reality, the state is founded on reason and not will, neither the state nor the people are sovereign, and other such things. Such truths cannot simply be quoted from ancient texts, however: they must be taught dialectically with a view toward the contemporary person's self-understanding.[26] As Maritain writes, "to understand and reinterpret in the light of a wisdom that is passionately faithful to reality and capable of growing endlessly because it lasts for all time ... renewed from age to age in that mysterious fountain of youth which is truth."[27]

Second, if the state must be the state, then the Church must be the Church. The Church in its various ways must inspire, educate and renew, as Maritain has it herein, and so leaven the temporal with the spiritual. CST

Rome: Essays in Honor of James V. Schall, S.J., edited by Marc D. Guerra (South Bend, Indiana: St. Augustine's Press, 2013), 120–138.

24. Cf. Eric Voegelin, "The Political Religions," in *Modernity Without Restraint: The Collected Works of Eric Voegelin*, vol. 5 (Columbia: University of Missouri Press, 2000), 47–50; and Eric Peterson, "Monotheism as a Political Problem: A Contribution to the History of Political Theology in the Roman Empire," in *Theological Tractates*, edited and translated by Michael J. Hollerich (Stanford, California: Stanford University Press, 2011), 68–105.

25. Kraynak, *Christian Faith and Modern Democracy*, 223–24.

26. Robert Sokolowski is a brilliant example of this challenge. Consider, for example, his "What is Natural Law? Human Purposes and Natural Ends," *The Thomist* 68 (2004): 507–29.

27. Maritain, "The Spiritual Conditions for Progress and Peace," in *Untrammeled Approaches*, 201.

of course is a leading voice in this effort. But the Church in its promotion of CST cannot be simply another NGO, nor can it be a "third way" or an ideology on par with other political beliefs.[28] When we see CST doctrines adopted as slogans of ideological parties, we must worry. "Social justice" on the left is an obvious example, but the right suffers such temptations with "subsidiarity."

Third, if the Magisterium and the scholarly community are to speak on such fraught matters of politics, they need prudence to distinguish when, where, and how to do so. Scholars working on CST can grant the Church an invaluable service by thinking reflectively on this point. When should the Church "weigh in" on politics, and how can it do so in ways that are likely to be effective? When, in other words, is the Church's voice likely to be genuinely inspirational, accepting of course that on the Church's own self-understanding her voice will often fail to be heard in this life?

When Maritain speaks of "inspiration," then, we have to understand it in a deep and broad sense, akin to the "leavening" of the Gospels. The spiritual at times must virtually *found* politics in calling it back to its *telos* but not overstepping its own bounds. This may well be all that CST can do in "barbarous societies," as Maritain says in *Man and the State*.[29] Indeed, much of CST scholarship occurs in the economically advanced nations of the West, and so often concerns itself with culturally sophisticated questions of political and ethics, e.g. bioethics. But such studies will not be fruitful if they do not begin with a principled basic account of the person, the state, and history. Such studies will not be helpful, moreover, if they make assumptions about the fundamentals of society that are not tenable in developing nations.

Thus CST needs to get back to the basics of political philosophy, both in the Magisterium and in academia. We cannot be unreflective about the relationship of the spiritual and temporal, for the sake of both.

III. Education

A question that could seem to be left open by Maritain's emphasis on inspiration, however, is inspiration toward what? To what end? Maritain

28. On the Church vis-a-vis NGOs, see Benedict XVI's *Deus caritas est*; on ideology, see John Paul II in *Sollicitudo rei socialis* (1987): no. 41.

29. Maritain, *Man and the State*, 71–75.

emphasizes that this inspiration must be conjoined with an education in what it is to be man. The "inspiration and the spiritual impulse ... necessarily entail and require a *vast work of reason* renewing its perspective and grasping in greater depths all the articulations of the real."[30]

This striking phrase—"all the articulations of the real"—points to what makes Maritain's project of inspiration distinctively human. This spiritual inspiration must "be completed by a theology and a philosophy because man is man," because "no inspiration truly inspires man if it does not come down to the point where the intellect and the senses wrestle with what is, and with the multiplicity posed by existence." To paraphrase Aristotle, we must concern ourselves with politics because man is not a beast or a god, but firmly in between. In fact, Maritain adds, "the deepening and the renewal of that theological and philosophical knowledge" is "a basic need of man."[31]

The role of the spiritual in temporal affairs must thus be supremely anthropological. Maritain's own work was often called "personalist," and whatever else the term may mean, it is clear that Maritain attached central significance to the character of the person in his political philosophy and particularly in his defense of democracy and natural rights.[32] One can find a similar message in Paul VI's U.N. address, and it indeed rings throughout the Magisterium. Consider John Paul II's words in *Redemptor hominis*: "Man is the primary route that the Church must travel in fulfilling her mission: he is the primary and fundamental way for the Church, the way traced out by Christ himself, the way that leads invariably through the mystery of the Incarnation and the Redemption."[33] The truth about the person, Benestad argues, is central to CST's teaching on what it means for humans to live in domestic and political community, to seek peace, justice and the truth, and to fulfill their nature as made in the image of God.[34] This dignity is both a "permanent endowment and an ongoing achievement": we must respect the dignity of others, and we must strive to act in accord with our own.[35]

30. Maritain, "The Spiritual Conditions for Progress and Peace," in *Untrammeled Approaches*, 200; emphasis in original.

31. Ibid.

32. See Mary Keys, "Personal Dignity and the Common Good: A Twentieth Century Thomistic Dialogue," in *Catholicism, Liberalism, and Communitarianism: The Catholic Intellectual Tradition and the Moral Foundations of Democracy*, edited by Kenneth L. Grasso, Gerard V. Bradley, and Robert P. Hunt (Lanham, Maryland: Rowman and Littlefield, 1995), 173–195.

33. John Paul II, *Redemptor hominis* (1979): no. 14.

34. Benestad, *Church, State, and Society*, 35–80.

35. Ibid., 80.

A line of the magisterial CST emphasizes "integral human development": namely, that the human person's full realization is not simply in the economic order, but also encompasses his rational and spiritual nature. Development initiatives and scholarship that treat humans as *homo oeconomicus,* then, are missing something vital to the human person. To take but one example of this danger, John Paul II warned in *Centesimus annus* that capitalism as much as socialism must guard against treating humans as an instrument in an economic system, for "the human inadequacies of capitalism and the resulting domination of things over people are far from disappearing."[36] Thus the pope's distinction between capitalism *qua* "economic system which recognizes the fundamental and positive role of business, the market, private property and the resulting responsibilities for the means of production, as well as free human creativity" and as "a system" that exalts "freedom" that "is not circumscribed within a strong juridical framework," and is indeed a freedom that knows no bounds on its means proportionate to its ends.[37]

These claims about human nature, and the very assertion that there is a human nature, push back against modern interpretations of the person as material or historical.[38] It is thus appropriate that Maritain continues by emphasizing that this education cannot comprise "pseudo-renewals in philosophy which betray reason in their effort to grasp being, nor pseudo-renewals in theology which claims to change those truths which came forth from the mouth of God."[39] This thought can be found all over Maritain's writings, but it has a special and practical significance in this context. As we noted with regard to inspiration, the Church must remind politics of its task. In other words, as we noted earlier, faith must recall to reason what reason *in se* could and should know but *in fact* does not.[40] Perhaps most obscure of these data is not this or that opinion about policy, but what reason is itself, what man is and how he is rational, and how reason relates to faith.

But to raise such questions is to move into the heart of modernity.[41] If

36. Pope John Paul II, *Centesimus annus* (1991): no. 33.

37. Ibid., no. 42; cf. John Paul II, *Laborem exercens* (1981): no. 7.

38. It also pushes back against a certain critique of CST as "anthropocentric," one that takes *Laudato Si'* as a charter (cf. Dorr, *Option for the Poor and for the Earth,* 422).

39. Maritain, "The Spiritual Conditions for Progress and Peace," in *Untrammeled Approaches,* 201.

40. Aquinas of course speaks of *revelabilia* in similarly broad terms; cf. *Summa Theologiae* I, q. 1, a. 1.

41. For differing accounts, see Charles Taylor, *A Secular Age* (Cambridge, Massachussetts:

one wishes to hazard sweeping generalizations about modern philosophy in the wake of the "Radical Enlightenment," we can say that it has regarded a certain reaction against the Church and the faith as a necessary propaedeutic to its work, and with considerable implications for theology.[42] Theology and philosophy are not always seen to have complementary goals, and at times philosophies taken up by theologians are inimical to the task of theology as traditionally understood by the Church. How, then, is the Church to grapple with the sheer quantity of "pseudo-renewals" in philosophy and theology that characterize vast swathes of modernity? This problem is no less pressing for political philosophy, as Maritain points out with regard to Machiavelli and his "technical rationalization" of politics in *Man and the State*.[43]

In the face of such intellectual and cultural obstacles, how can scholarship on CST maintain the truth about man and thus educate the temporal in a matter of central importance? There are no easy answers to this question, but it does require us to revisit the relationship between philosophy and theology, and particularly what sort of philosophy needs to undergird our theological ethics or moral theology. We can compare this to the task set out in *Fides et Ratio*.

Such questions will also require a concrete exploration of CST scholarship as it is practiced. For while it is not necessarily bad that scholarship on CST has come under the influence of many modern and post-modern philosophies, one must wonder how such scholarship will remain true to its ecclesial roots, which are profoundly "pre-modern," if one must speak in such historicist terms, in their emphasis on reason, substance, and *telos*. This of course has been a leading question with regard to liberation theology, but it is no less of concern with a host of other investigations founded on the presuppositions of postmodern and critical theory. And the task must not simply be negative. As Maritain was open to innovating in his understand-

Belknap Press, 2007); and Michael Gillespie *The Theological Origins of Modernity* (Chicago: University of Chicago Press, 2008).

42. Robert Sokolowski, *Introduction to Phenomenology* (Cambridge: Cambridge University Press, 2000), 198–200.

43. *Man and the State*, 54–75. Slade and Sokolowski also make a great deal of Machiavelli's role in founding modern political philosophy, including in Francis Slade, "Teleology and the Genesis of the Modern State," in *Natural Law in Contemporary Society*, edited by Holger Zaborowski (Washington, D.C.: The Catholic University Press, 2010), 235–63, and Robert Sokolowski, "Recovering Classical Philosophy in the Modern Context: The Work of Francis Slade," *Perspectives on Political Science* 45, no. 1 (2016): 4–8.

ing and application of St. Thomas Aquinas's theology and philosophy, so those invested in CST must question how the perennial tradition can grow in its comprehension of modern realities.

These questions issue in a series of concerns about the nature of CST, both the Magisterium and its scholarly commentary. First, as we have said, is the issue of the kinds of philosophy that undergird and intersect with theology in CST. A second vital task of CST scholarship must be to grapple with the unity of its message in the human person. In this context, we might consider how often we present CST as a series of bullet points. What keeps them from being appropriated piece-meal so that one comes to find, for instance, solidarity and subsidiarity or human rights and the common good in conflict with one another? What distinguishes the Church's teaching on the person, in other words, as a doctrine that is at once widely accessible to a host of other doctrines, most notably liberalism, but also challenging to understandings of humanity that undercut human dignity?

Then there is the universalism of CST. Is it visible to non-believers? Should it be? How ought we balance the dual concerns of maintaining the universal appeal of reason to all men while also proclaiming the revealed data known by faith in a particular God?[44] This is a tension at the core of proclaiming the Gospel to the world, of course. It is thus an area where CST can benefit from dialogue with its roots in the tradition of Catholic theology.[45] That reflection, in turn, can then be directed toward what John XXII called us toward, "a spirituality of engagement that asked Christians to be creatively engaged in the world as a chief characteristic of their spiritual journey."[46]

If one thinks our exploration of Maritain has led us far afield, consider further how we must also consider the problem of *Rerum novarum* as a starting point of CST. *Rerum novarum* may inaugurate a new era in the Church's teachings on politics. But the Church's teachings on politics did not begin with modernity, because the Church's teaching on man did not begin with modernity. CST, to be sure, has taken its lead from *Rerum novarum* as seeing

44. It is significant that scholars of CST since Vatican II, taking their cue from *Gaudium et spes*, have placed a renewed emphasis on Scripture in academic CST and in natural law scholarship. See John R. Donahue, S.J., "The Bible and Catholic Social Teaching," in *Modern Catholic Social Teaching: Commentaries and Interpretations*, edited by Kenneth R. Himes, O.F.M. (Washington, D.C.: Georgetown University Press, 2004), 9–40.

45. See David Hollenbach, S.J., on "dialogical universalism" in "Commentary on *Gaudium et spes*," in Himes, *Modern Catholic Social Teaching*, 278.

46. Dorr, *Option for the Poor*, 91.

questions of workers and labor as key to the social question, and the social question in turn as of fundamental concern for the Church. But this focus cannot ignore more fundamental political questions which frame economic ones.[47] Moreover, if it is true that CST needs to return to the fundamental questions of political life, then CST needs to move beyond modern answers to those questions, which are so often reactions against the ancient ways of formulating those questions. In other words, CST needs to compass the entirety of Church teaching on politics, and the pre-Christian horizon against which it understood itself. For it is that tradition against which modernity defined itself without freeing itself, and it is that tradition that shaped and continues to shape the life of the West as a community of empire, Church and nation-state.[48]

To conclude this section, we can see that the spiritual seeks to inspire in the temporal an awareness of the dignity and primacy of the human. That inspiration amounts to an education toward a more perfect realization of human communal life. What does that renewal of communal life look like?

IV. Cultural Renewal

The latter half of "Spiritual Conditions" slips somewhat ambiguously from the three-fold temporal task of the spiritual—inspiration, education, and cultural renewal—into a historical and spiritual excursus, and so identifying the meaning of "cultural renewal" for Maritain is somewhat tricky in this essay. But the phrase seems to mean at once the integration of the afore-mentioned inspiration and education—the "*vast work of reason* renewing its perspectives and grasping in greater depths all the articulations of the real"—and their application in temporal life, an application that depends very much upon prayer: "And when we speak of the *application* of the teachings of the Council, we should think first and foremost of how necessary it is for us to *bring these teachings to life within our souls,* in such a way that it truly recasts our entire way of thinking."[49] Before the Church

47. In *Laborem exercens* John Paul II takes work to be "the essential key to the whole question" and urges that "As a *person, man is therefore the subject of work*" (no. 6). Yet it is a broad notion of work that takes in many of man's more elevated activities, including politics.

48. See Pierre Manent, *Metamorphoses of the City,* translated by Marc LePain (Cambridge, Massachussetts: Harvard University Press, 2013), 318–27.

49. Maritain, "The Spiritual Conditions for Progress and Peace," in *Untrammeled Approaches,* 201.

can propose this or that policy, she has to bring people to see reality more fully and to will the good for others. The inspiration and education that the Church can give to the world has to work in the will as well as the intellect. This problem, of course, looms no less in our time than in that of Maritain: certainly many if not most U.S. Catholics cherry-pick the parts of CST to which they subscribe, and their selective adherence to it often seems to depend upon their political preferences and ideologies. More likely, however, many Catholics have simply never heard of CST.[50]

How does such change of heart come about? For Maritain, it is clear that the Church's influence on the world must be one of conversion. Ultimately, we have to learn to engage in CST prayerfully, to assay the world prayerfully, to do the hard work prayerfully. Our witness must be spiritual, grounded in *caritas*. Here, too, much work must be done if we are to move beyond the superficialities that inform so much of Western culture. Rather, we must learn to think and desire with the Church. Here I cannot help but think of the spirituality of St. Ignatius of Loyola.[51] CST needs to be an agent of faith in the midst of the world, which means CST scholars must see themselves not as proud, accomplished academics, but as servants and children of God. They must also see the world not as a tableau for their success and enjoyment, but as a vineyard which God calls us to harvest. They must, in short, see themselves as possessed of a vocation. As Massingale eloquently puts it: "Vocation means living in response to something that is beyond and deeper than myself. … Vocation, then, is more than simply a career; it is more than an endeavor pursued for notoriety, fame, self-satisfaction, or material comfort. To speak from a faith perspective, vocation is a loving response to the Mystery that has taken hold of and possesses us."[52] We can sum up these considerations with the "primacy of the spiritual," a phrase dear to Maritain's heart. Just as CST scholarship must approach human persons as being supremely spiritual, so they must also see their own work as finally spiritual. Paul VI made this very clear in his United Nations address:

50. See Michael J. Naughton, "Preface to the Series," in James P. Bailey, *Rethinking Poverty: Incomes, Assets, and the Catholic Social Justice Tradition* (Notre Dame, Indiana: University of Notre Dame Press, 2010), ii.

51. E.g., "Rules for Thinking with the Church [*Sentire cum Ecclesia*]," in St. Ignatius of Loyola, *Draw Me into Your Friendship: The Spiritual Exercises,* edited by David L. Fleming, S.J. (St. Louis: The Institute of Jesuit Sources, 1996), 280–90.

52. Bryan Massingale, *Racial Justice and the Catholic Church* (Maryknoll, New York: Orbis Books, 2010), 153.

> The edifice you are building does not rest on purely material and terrestrial foundations, for in that case it would be a house built on sand. It rests most of all upon consciences. Yes, the time has come for "conversion," for personal transformation, for interior renewal. We have to get used to a new way of thinking about man, a new way of thinking about man's community life, and, last of all, a new way of thinking about the pathways of history and the destines of the world. As St. Paul says, we must "put on the new man, which has been created according to God in justice and holiness of truth" (Eph. 4:23).

The pontiff goes on to assert that human development depends not upon "progress" or "science," but upon "the moral conscience of man." That conscience must be developed to make the best use of technological and scientific progress, the pope urges, and also to draw together men in peace and cooperation. Maritain would agree with Paul's statement that this "new way" of envisioning man and his communal life depends upon a change in attitude, a new moral orientation that cannot be assumed or replaced by material progress, but must rather arise out of attention to what humans are and a movement of the will to pursue their ends "in justice and holiness of truth." The quotation from Ephesians underlines that scholarship on CST can never but be prayerful, for it rests upon contemplation of the human person as "created according to God."

As we have said, then, Maritain would encourage CST scholars to approach their work with an attentiveness to its spiritual depth, both in the objects of their study, and as a dimension of their own practice. A CST scholar who does not understand his work as rooted in the spiritual, and as something about which to pray, is missing something. It is perhaps no surprise, then, that Maritain ends the talk by marking out "an awakening of that life of contemplative prayer and union with God" as a great sign of hope for the world today.[53] Noting that Paul VI closed Vatican II with remarks on the dignity of contemplation as "the most perfect form of human activity," Maritain closes his own discourses by urging that an "invisible constellation of souls devoted to the contemplative life, I mean *in the world itself, in the very midst of the world,* this in the final analysis is our ultimate reason for keeping hope alive."[54]

This consideration should also alert us to the context of CST scholar-

53. Maritain, "The Spiritual Conditions for Progress and Peace," in *Untrammeled Approaches,* 204.

54. Ibid.

ship. Much of CST scholarship occurs in secular universities and in disciplines other than theology as well as in Catholic universities where the question of mission is a debated one. Scholars of CST are in a unique position to help their colleagues and students think through what it means to make sense of man's communal life in the light of revelation, even if they themselves are not theologians. How can CST scholars, wherever and whoever they are, respond to Massingale's challenge to live out what they teach?

Maritain's excursus on *Gaudium et spes* helps draw out what he has in mind by cultural renewal and serves as a cipher for the entire speech. Maritain identifies II.IV and II.V of *Gaudium et spes* as exemplars of the great work of the Spirit at the Second Vatican Council in bringing about the inspiration, education, and cultural renewal that Maritain has in mind throughout this talk. These chapters touch upon two issues: political education and world government. The first consideration touches upon much that we have already considered: the Church's teaching on politics and society calls us to move beyond paradigms of politics that "since the time of the Renaissance" sees politics "as no more than a simple matter of intelligent cynicism, something essentially amoral, delivered up to the laws of deception and violence."[55] For Maritain, the great danger of this notion of politics is the "illusion of *immediate success*" with which it cloaks human affairs, that has no patience for the resignation with which pre-modern thinkers accepted so many of the limitations of human existence, for these "limitations" in modernity have become technical problems to be solved.[56]

We can see where CST's role of inspiration and education could lead to renewal vis-à-vis such concerns. CST cannot fall prey, Maritain would argue, to "technocratic paradigms" that obscure politics' fundamentally moral character, and it must help secular institutions similarly guard against such error. On the one hand, CST could not be said to be at risk of such temptation given its focus on the "integral development" of the human person, a development that certainly extends far beyond the economic. It can, moreover, render a great service to humanity in continuing to emphasize such a conception of development. On the other hand, modernity has brought with it a massive shift toward the improvement of the "human condition," a new emphasis that risks assuming that such improvement is

55. Ibid., 202; cf. Jacques Maritain, "The End of Machiavellianism," *Review of Politics* 4 (1942): 1–33.

56. Maritain, *Man and the State*, 57–58.

limitless and open-ended, to the point of denying human nature, and further that nothing beyond that terrestrial condition is of concern for human community. CST in its emphasis on economic development may find itself called upon to point out the inherent limitations of resolving man's terrestrial difficulties.

Maritain approaches more cautiously the second issue, world government, indicating that "I prefer to say a supranational political authority consisting, not of a world-wide empire or a world super-State, but of a real *political organization of the world,* based on the free consent and the free cooperation of nations and peoples." Maritain recognizes that "in the present state of the world such an idea appears utopian." The task at hand must then be "not to bring into actual existence a world-wide political society," but rather to "work at the *distant preparations* for this society."[57] Notably preparation involves both "reason and good will," not simply technological innovation or better economics or communications capacities. Maritain is thus far soberer in his advocacy of international governance than are many, and thereby sets for a model for CST: we cannot advance policies without a clear awareness both spiritual and material of the situations upon which CST would speak.

The secular push for world governance, however, has often moved far more quickly than Maritain is here advocating, and the "free consent and the free cooperation of nations and peoples" has become a fraught issue.[58] Resistance to European integration, for example, has been strong from the beginning, and this resistance has only mounted since the rocky history of the European Union. Maritain might never have used the phrase "democracy deficit," but he would have sympathized with the concerns behind the phrase's invocation. It is thus perhaps not surprising that the promotion of international authority, most notably by Benedict XVI, has met with muted response in the West.[59]

Maritain's sobriety on this matter arises in part from his awareness of the need for "reason and good will" to prepare for international government, which in turn are paralleled by the "two primordial considerations" he singles out within that preparation. The first is "the decisive renuncia-

57. Maritain, "The Spiritual Conditions for Progress and Peace," in *Untrammeled Approaches,* 202.

58. Pierre Manent, *A World Beyond Politics? A Defense of the Nation-State,* translated by Marc LePain (Princeton, New Jersey: Princeton University Press, 2006).

59. See Benedict XVI's *Caritas in veritate* and *Deus caritas est.*

tion of the idea or of the idol of the sovereignty of the State, of the very idea of that moral God," and about which Maritain devoted many pages in *Man and the State*.[60] Maritain does not have much to say about this issue here, but one could imagine at least two counts of its relevance: first, to clarify that the authority of the state does not preclude the existence of a higher authority, and second, that the "sovereignty" of the states ceded to the international governing body does not render the super-national authority a "mortal God" with no conditions and limits on its power.

> The second "primordial" condition is simple: love. Or, to be more precise: the awakening among all thinking me, governing and governed, of a very real concern, ever present and active in the depths of the heart, for the common good of humanity and for the good itself, the intrinsic good of each national community, and of the very nations with which, on the level of political and economic interests, a given national community finds itself in competitions.[61]

Maritain argues that supra-national authority, like any authority, can only work when motivated by a genuine movement of the will for the good of others. He rejects claims, in other words, that such authority can arise out of grudging necessity, out of self-interest, out of a desire to control others for material gain, or even out of a patronizing desire to improve the lot of the less fortunate. For this reason, Maritain continues, "Nothing will be accomplished, even with the most ardent work of social renovation, even with the most generous effects of apostolic action, absolutely nothing will be accomplished without charity, without … *agape*."[62] As remarkable as this challenge was in 1966, it strikes us as even more audacious in our time time: how can a country like the United States, for example, manifest genuine concern for the common good of other communities, or even for "humanity" and "the good itself," when the people of the U.S. struggle to manifest such concern for their own neighbors, never mind their ideological opponents in national political affairs?[63]

It is fitting that this theme of *caritas* and mercy has become a prominent

60. Hittinger, "Reasons for a Civil Society," in *Reassessing the Liberal State*, 11–23.

61. Maritain, "The Spiritual Conditions for Progress and Peace," in *Untrammeled Approaches*, 203.

62. Ibid.

63. Cf. *Political Polarization in American Politics*, edited by Daniel J. Hopkins and John Sides (New York: Bloomsbury, 2015); or Morris Fiorina and Samuel J. Abrams, *Disconnect: The Breakdown of Representation in American Politics* (Norman, Oklahoma: University of Oklahoma Press, 2011).

part of the Magisterium, especially in completing justice. This emerged particularly with Popes John Paul II and Benedict XVI, and continues with Pope Francis' reflections on mercy.[64] With the phrase "civilization of love," moreover, John Paul II not only indicates the basis of human community in love, but that this "civilization" is a community beyond the juridical state in its scope and end.[65] CST proponents may find that an emphasis on charity properly understood will ground CST more deeply theologically and also serve to distinguish it from those who debate over highly ideological interpretations of justice. As the Church promotes its social teaching in a given context, it can employ themes like the person and *caritas* to cut across ideological positions.

Maritain's comments on a love that transcend national particularities also raises the issue of solidarity, a virtue John Paul II defined as "a firm and persevering determination to commit oneself to the common good; that is to say to the good of all and of each individual."[66] A solidarity that can indeed overcome such particularities, and not least the conflicts and differences that often distinguish such communities, is no easy feat.[67] Maritain's urging here should remind us that love alone is capable of such a feat, and that we should not be satisfied with "thin" or "humanist" accounts of solidarity that do not do justice not only to the deep divisions in the world, but also the transformative power of God's love to alone heal those conflicts and reconcile persons.

Maritain can be accused of an excessive optimism in *Man and the State*, although that claim certainly cannot apply to a great number of his claims therein.[68] As we noted above, the hopes of many Christians for the post-war order were dashed, and it is important that we consider if and how they went awry in their analysis. On the other hand, we can distinguish between

64. For instance, in *Dives in misericordia, Deus caritas est,* and *Evangelii gaudium.* None of these are typically thought of as CST documents, but the need to anchor CST in trans-ideological truths may lead us to integrate the CST tradition more thoroughly in the Church's broader range of teachings.

65. Torre, "Maritain's 'Integral Humanism' and Catholic Social Teaching," in *Reassessing the Liberal State,* 203.

66. John Paul II, *Sollicitudo rei socialis,* no. 38

67. Reinhold Niebuhr may be a companion with Maritain in this vein. Cf. C. Firer Hinze, "The Drama of Social Sin and the (Im)Possibility of Solidarity: Reinhold Niebuhr and Modern Catholic Social Teaching," *Studies in Christian Ethics* 22 (2009): 442–60.

68. See John Hittinger, *Liberty, Wisdom, and Grace* (Lanham, Maryland: Lexington Books, 2002), 35–60 regarding Jacques Maritain and Yves Simon on Aquinas's teaching on democracy.

the conditions Maritain sets for earthly progress from his prognosis of their likelihood: we might disagree with the measure of hope that Maritain put in prospects for post-war global integration but still agree with his formulation of the criteria according to which such integration ought to be judged. And Maritain would urge more conservative strains of Catholic thought to guard against a hyper-Augustinianism that would itself obscure the moral character of politics. As Maritain argues, "The hope of men in a temporal ideal, a dynamic ideal of peace on earth, must be preserved at any cost, even though it may seem utopian at the outset"[69]

In other words, even if much of the function of CST must be negative, to educate secular thought and practice away from deleterious conceptions of the person and human community, it must also not fail to inspire men to greater things. For failures in the secular order arise not only from ambition, but from the fears of pain, suffering and death that have animated so much of modern political thought. CST must be on hand to direct man's sights upon something higher, and thereby inspire true renewal in the temporal order.[70] To repeat, that renewal requires love, and "a great change of heart, by virtue of which primacy, even in such matters as politics and relations between peoples, where up till now cynicism held sway, true primacy will be accorded to an authentic and efficacious friendship – and, as regards Christians in particular, that love which sees in every single man ... exactly what he in intrinsically: a member of the Mystical Body of Christ, at least potentially."[71] Such an emphasis is not one that will lead to any immediate practical changes, nor will it issue in an implementable program of action. Indeed, perhaps such things cannot be the great focus of CST. But CST can assist the temporal order with an education in man's essential nature and orientation to the good beyond the temporal, and thereby inspire men to seek authentic renewal despite the considerable obstacles. And if CST must also reveal these obstacles to be rooted in the pride of sin, and thus intractably beyond the reach of technology and consultant-developed five-year plans, CST can also reveal a deeper source of resistance to such

69. Maritain, "The Spiritual Conditions for Progress and Peace," in *Untrammeled Approaches*, 202.

70. Judith Shklar insightfully raised this dimension of modernity in "The Liberalism of Fear," in *Liberalism and the Moral Life*, edited by Nancy L. Rosenblum (Cambridge, Massachusetts: Harvard University Press, 1989), 21–37.

71. Maritain, "The Spiritual Conditions for Progress and Peace," in *Untrammeled Approaches*, 203–4.

sin: the love that leads the human person to seek friendship, truth, and justice in any setting in which he finds himself.

V. Conclusions for CST

To recapitulate our analysis, for Maritain the temporal role of the spiritual is three-fold: inspiration, education, and renewal. In all three functions, the primacy of the spiritual leads to a tension that between calling politics back to the fundamental needs of man and also reminding man of his heavenly destination. In living out this tension, man comes to know himself and God's creation in "all the articulations of the real."

If in his works Maritain over-emphasizes the autonomy of the temporal, it is out of a concern that the temporal be done right. It is out of a concern to emphasize the importance of politics in perfecting man as a rational and social animal, out of a concern for man to embrace his full liberty and rational agency *sub Deo*. Maritain wants man to become political again.[72] Even if a 21st-century reader must wrestle with the neo-Kantian dimensions of Maritain's work, and thereby recover a "Two Cities" doctrine for CST, one would not wish to lose sight of Maritain's desire that man be man.[73]

For to be political is to be rational, a characteristic by which man is open to being spiritual. It is to relate what is most knowable to us, namely ourselves, to what is most knowable as such, namely God. And so we owe to Maritain thanks for his ceaseless effort to disclose "all the articulations of the real" for an age that has lost confidence in attaining an even passing familiarity with the real.

72. Maritain shares this concern with Pierre Manent, even if Manent could hardly be called a "neo-Thomist progressive," as Fuller has it of Maritain (Timothy Fuller, "Jacques Maritain and Michael Oakeshott on the Modern State," in *Reassessing the Liberal State*, 24–33, at 25).

73. Kraynak, *Christian Faith and Modern Democracy*, 45–106.

VII

THE BIG PICTURE

MARIO O. D'SOUZA, C.S.B.

The Unity of the Thought of Jacques Maritain

I. Introduction

THE UNITY OF Maritain's thought is evident across his philosophical corpus; however, it is a corpus that is not easily replicated today. The kind of philosophical edifice that he built is historic for many reasons, not least of which is that in our day such an expansive philosophical undertaking would be unimaginable, even within the limited framework of a single area of philosophy. Given the diversity and specialization of knowledge today, it would be an impossibly herculean task for a philosopher to master the many specializations of that field in a way that Maritain was able to accomplish. But the unity of Maritain's thought goes much deeper than the mastery of his field and his philosophic command of that discipline. He understood *philosophy* in its original meaning as the quest for *wisdom*, and what unifies his thought, ultimately, I believe, is the human person. Such unity depends upon the inspiration of the philosopher, one who *philosophizes* and who searches for *wisdom*:[1] "Maritain's philosophical corpus is as much a sustained commentary on the history of philosophy as it is a commentary on the integral life of the person in interaction with the wealth of the created and the uncreated orders."[2]

1. "Philosophy is in strictest truth *wisdom*, for it is the province of wisdom to study the highest causes: *sapientis est altissimas causas considerare.* It thus grasps the entire universe in a small number of principles and enriches the intellect without burdening it." Jacques Maritain, *An Introduction to Philosophy* (London: Sheed and Ward, 1981), 80.

2. *Being in the World: A Quotable Maritain Reader*, edited by Mario O. D'Souza, C.S.B. (Notre Dame, Indiana: University of Notre Dame Press, 2014), 1.

Maritain also looked to culture, society, and to nations to provide the necessary scaffolding for the personal and ontological unity of the person. He paid special tribute to the United States of America in devoting one of his works to that nation. In his book, *Reflections on America*, Jacques Maritain speaks movingly about the reasons for this particular tribute: "There were in America great reserves and possibilities for contemplation; the activism which is to the fore appears … in many cases a remedy against despair, and masks a hidden aspiration to contemplation."[3] Secondly, he states, "What the world expects from America is that she keep alive, in human history, a fraternal recognition of the dignity of man—in other words, the terrestrial hope of men in the Gospel."[4] Our age is marked by a relentless activism that needs the calming stillness of contemplation, and our world also increasingly loses sight of human dignity. Both contemplation and human dignity presuppose human unity, and the unity of Maritain's thought in promoting contemplation and human unity is a shining beacon for our age.

II. The Unity of Maritain's Thought

I remember my philosophical studies at University College, Dublin, when our professor of general metaphysics, Fr. Desmond Connell, later the Cardinal Archbishop of Dublin, said that he was sure that Maritain was a saint. The saintliness of Maritain is evident in his writings. Amidst some complex philosophical point, Maritain brings you into an oasis—a garden of joy, beauty, hope, and peace—whose foliage is nourished by the Christian message, by the consolation and comfort of the Gospel, and the unimaginable joy of the freedom that the Risen Lord offers us in saving us from sin and death. These convictions are not introduced for the sake of piety, or as a means to construct an artificial edifice of apologetics for his Christian philosophy. Maritain's Christian inspiration is one that is integrated into the very fiber of his being. This is movingly displayed in the memorable work of late Ralph McInerny: *The Very Rich Hours of Jacques Maritain: A Spiritual Life*.[5]

Let me frame my position in this way. Recently, I organized a conference

3. Jacques Maritain, *Reflections on America* (New York: Charles Scribner's Sons, 1958), 41.

4. Ibid., 199.

5. Ralph McInerny, *The Very Rich Hours of Jacques Maritain: A Spiritual Life* (Notre Dame, Indiana: University of Notre Dame Press, 2003).

sponsored by my religious congregation (the Congregation of St. Basil—the Basilian fathers) on Catholic education. I was speaking about the intellectual dimension of Catholic education, something that Maritain repeatedly emphasizes in his philosophy of education. I was also eager to emphasize that Catholic education cannot be limited to a class in religious education or the occasional celebration of Mass at that school, so crisply encapsulated in Edward Leen's work, *What is Education?*[6]

At that conference, I was anxious to emphasize Maritain's position regarding an integral and humanistic education and that the unity of the student is dependent upon everything that happens during the school day and not just in the classroom through a narrow conception of intellectual knowledge, one that Maritain identifies as the error of intellectualism.[7] I concluded by saying that Jesus did not come to establish Catholic schools, Catholic universities, or Catholic hospitals. He came, rather, to save us and free us from the pernicious and imprisoning cycle of sin and death. But once that salvation is won for us, and once the message of that salvation is preached to each generation, then everything changes. And because everything changes, and because the message of the Gospel has implications for all dimensions of human living, Catholics must establish Catholic schools, Catholic universities, and Catholic hospitals, among other agencies.

This implication I learned from Maritain, who is devoted to exploring how the Christian message imbues and inspires so many areas of life: from poetry to painting, from science to politics, from education to the common good, from history to nature, from metaphysics to human fellowship, and from society to contemplation. Maritain's vision of the world is, in his words, "quickened and inspired" by the saving message of Christ because this message—given its implications in the diverse modes of living and human expression—and one which unifies the individual human person, their personal, ontological unity. He outlines in careful detail—and not just restricted to his educational texts, what the education of the whole person entails: both the utter simplicity and sophistication of that invitation.

6. "It is but reasonable to expect that a Catholic school should give a Christian formation. It would be a great mistake to think that it does this because it is staffed with Catholic teachers, offers facilities for the frequentation of the Sacraments, and has each day half-an-hour's doctrinal instruction sandwiched between the other subjects in the scholastic programme." Edward Leen, *What is Education?* (New York: Sheed and Ward, 1945), 79–80.

7. See Jacques Maritain, *Education at the Crossroads* (New Haven, Connecticut: Yale University Press, 1943), 18–20.

In my experience, Catholic educators are too quick to confirm that they are dedicated to the education of the whole person, but often this conviction sounds like a platitude—just the right thing to say, and usually unaccompanied by any significant explanation of what the education of the whole person means and entails. Educators often don't seem to recognize that the education of the whole person is hardly completed at the end of school or university education, and so it can never be limited to the confines of institutional education alone. Educational institutions can only educate the whole person in an ongoing way, and as one among other agencies and influences, such as the family, the Church, governments, the public square, and culture. But, of course, history has a very checkered record in this regard, and were it not so, Maritain would not have spent time emphasizing the urgency of the redemption of history, the necessity of redeeming time, the urgency of the purification of means and ends, or elaborating on an integral humanism and on what the common good means and entails in every age.

I have been reading and studying Maritain's thought for a long time, and like other inspirational and holy Christian thinkers through the ages, one reads them with a new level of intensity and self-awareness during the different seasons of one's own life, especially as the shadows of life lengthen, as one continues to grow in the awareness of one's own sinfulness and the precariousness of the spiritual and moral life—after all, all our dance cards seem to include that inevitable hesitation waltz with sin—and as one encounters sadness over the loss of loved ones. All these horizons shape and reshape how one reads and rereads the masters of the Christian spiritual and intellectual life, and Maritain is no exception. Our Christian pilgrimage through time lies somewhere between Holy Thursday and Easter Sunday, but our diminishment through sin and our frailty find Good Friday overwhelming; we want to rush to Easter Sunday, but Maritain, like other saintly Christian thinkers, suggests resisting that temptation. He says, "The hour at which Christ is nailed to the Cross is not a convenient time at which to ask Him to change water into wine or to multiply loaves and fishes. In that hour something is being enacted that is greater than miracles. The Resurrection will take place; but after the expiration of three days."[8]

But the stark beauty of this truth is tempered by another powerful conviction from his work, *The Range of Reason*: "The perfection of life does

8. Jacques Maritain, *Freedom in the Modern World,* translated by Richard O'Sullivan, K.C. (New York: Gordian Press, 1971), 146.

not consist in a stoic athleticism of virtue or in a humanly calculated application of holy recipes, but rather in a ceaselessly increasing love, despite our mistakes and weaknesses, between the Uncreated Self and the created Self."[9] One can see why Maritain spends so much time, from his political philosophy to his aesthetics, and from his philosophy of education to his metaphysics, on the distinction and relationship between the person and the individual, and given the centrality of this distinction and relationship, there is astonishing depth to his seemingly simple claim that "as individuals, we are subject to the stars. As persons we rule them."[10]

The unity of Maritain's thought grounds his understanding of personal unity. The depth and variety of his works attests to his command not just in the philosophical field but in other areas as well: politics, law, theology, culture, mysticism, education, contemplation, society and the common good. In my study, which has been more particularly focused on his philosophy of education, I realized earlier on that in order to fully understand what Maritain says on any one topic, one must read as many of his works as possible, and not simply in order to get his wider philosophical outlook. Rather, more importantly, because his worldview is unified: and so, for example, while reading his work on metaphysics one may come across an implication for the common good; a work on his aesthetics may reveal a beautiful passage on the nature of the person; or his moral philosophy will uncover the relation between beauty and the resurrection of the dead. After all, his *magnum opus, The Degrees of Knowledge*, is really its subtitle. Its full title of course is *Distinguish to Unite or The Degrees of Knowledge.*

He tells us repeatedly that personality requires unity, that "personality presupposes oneness; there is no personality without complete oneness of being and of life."[11] The pivotal relationship between individuality and personality is subtle and sophisticated; it is neither angelistic nor Manichean, nor is it overwhelmed by action or reaction. It is futile to turn introspectively into oneself seeking the essence of our being. We know our spiritual natures only by analogy, and we know ourselves not through knowledge of our essence, but "only by our acts and operations"; thus, "psychological ob-

9. Jacques Maritain, *The Range of Reason* (New York: Charles Scribner's Sons, 1953), 101–102.

10. Jacques Maritain, *Three Reformers: Luther—Descartes—Rousseau* (London: Sheed and Ward, 1950), 21.

11. Jacques Maritain, *The Peasant of the Garonne: An Old Layman Questions Himself about the Present Time,* translated by Michael Cuddihy and Elizabeth Hughes (New York: Holt, Rinehart and Winston, 1968), 176.

servations, artificially separated from intelligence" only reveal "a stream of consciousness," not our essence but only a "phenomenal manifestation."[12]

Maritain's understanding of human unity and the growth in self-awareness is at once psychological, philosophical, theological, and ethical, with implications for all dimensions of living, particularly the intellectual, moral, religious, and social. The mystery of human unity lies within and outside of the self; it is personal and communal. Neither a flight from the self (or rejection of material individuality), nor a flight into activism (or the frenzied reduction of human living to a stream of consciousness and duration that confine human living to respond to phenomena)—one of Maritain's main disagreements with Bergson—will result in an integral knowledge of the self. We see dangers of both extremes in the course of history, and our age shows a worrying escalation in both directions. In *Art and Poetry,* he says, "man does not know himself through his own essence. His substance is hidden from him, he perceives himself as refracted by the world of his own acts which itself refracts the world of things: if he does not fill himself with the universe he remains empty to himself."[13] This is a truth that should surely jolt our therapeutic culture.

What then is the source of our individual unity? And how is this perennial growth fostered? Persons reveal themselves through their principal characteristics: intelligence and will; they transcend the physicality of space and time through a "spiritual superexistence" in "knowledge and love."[14] We hear echoes of Christ's injunction, prominent in St. John's Gospel, of being in the world but not of it. Recall St. Paul's exhortation in *The Letter to the Romans* of not being conformed to the world but renewing our living by renewing our minds according to the teachings of Christ. Maritain offers his own spiritual commentary:

> *Man does not find his unity in himself: he finds it outside himself, above himself.* It was in willing to be self-sufficient that he lost himself.... Nothing is more illusory than to ask immanentism to reconcile man with himself. Man becomes reconciled with himself on the cross, which is hard and exterior to him: that cross to which he is nailed. Objectivity is the first condition of unity.[15]

12. Jacques Maritain, *Bergsonian Philosophy and Thomism,* translated by Mabelle L. Andison (New York: Philosophical Library 1955), 115–16.

13. Jacques Maritain, *Art and Poetry,* translated by E. de P. Matthews (New York: Philosophical Library, 1943), 89.

14. Maritain, *Education at the Crossroads,* 7–8.

15. Jacques Maritain, *St. Thomas Aquinas* (New York: Meridian Books, 1958), 61; emphasis in original.

Human perfection lies in perfecting something else; hence "by knowing and loving an agent capable of immanent action receives a perfection which it confers on itself by its own activity."[16] Activity and activism are not the same, and while action and interiority to self are indispensable in response to Christ's invitation to follow Him, the Christian life flourishes when love for one's neighbor and perennially striving for the common good are realized precisely by forgetting oneself in Christ, so beautifully encapsulated in the Letter to the Colossians: "For you have died, and your life is hid with Christ in God. When Christ who is our life appears, then you will also appear with Him in glory" (Colossians 3:3–4). Thus, while Maritain, like philosophers of old, recognizes the centrality of the Socratic call to *know oneself*, he warns that in the imprisoning quest of seeking to know our essence, of plunging into the psyche amidst the dangerous swirls of the maelstrom of the unconscious, that in such instances the Socratic call to know oneself is better replaced by the Christian call to "forget thyself." However, for the Christian philosopher, the knowledge of reality and the forgetting of self are not attained in a "simple look, innocently receptive, stupidly with no question whatever, as the bull sees a daisy or a poppy in the pasture. But this knowledge is not philosophy. Philosophy demands of the philosopher that he lose himself in the object."[17]

Personality requires unity, and nature does not bring the human person into the world unified. The unity of personality depends upon the unity of the virtuous and the moral life, and the life of faith and prayer: "The truly and fully natural man is not nature's man, the uncultivated soil, but the virtuous man, the human soil cultivated by undeviating reason, man formed by the inner culture of the intellectual and moral virtues. He alone has a consistency, a personality."[18] Human development and the quest for the happy life have necessary material dimensions, but ultimately it is mainly moral and religious. For the Christian it is mainly religious and moral, because a state of pure nature where God abandons us to the "resources of the activities" of our minds and wills has never existed. Hence the beauty of this conviction: "From the earliest times God willed to bring to the knowledge of men things far in excess of the requirements of any nature

16. Jacques Maritain, *A Preface to Metaphysics: Seven Lectures on Being* (London: Sheed and Ward, 1943), 123.

17. Jacques Maritain, *Moral Philosophy* (London: Geoffrey Bles, 1964), 354–55.

18. Jacques Maritain, *Religion and Culture*, vol. 1 of *Essays in Order*, translated by F. F. Scanlon, edited by Christopher Dawson and T. F. Burns (New York: Sheed and Ward, 1940), 7.

that ever was or could be created. He revealed to them the depths of His divine life, the secret of His eternity. ... He spread over the world, like a tablecloth, grace which was capable of divinizing our knowledge and our love."[19] The good life, a term infinitely bandied about in every age, with an equal infinitude of facile responses, is, for Maritain, "a life conformable to the essential exigencies and the essential dignity of human nature, a life both morally straight and happy."[20]

The unity of personality, therefore, culminates in happiness—happiness that aims at an end and is guided by reason and intelligence. Happiness without an end or finality, however, becomes a relentless movement toward an ever-elusive goal, "at once limitless and increasingly lower, more and more stagnant."[21] Personality includes interiority to self,[22] and in spite of Descartes's dream, human persons master themselves not through self-doubt in search of an antiseptic empirical objectivity, but by mastering and transcending themselves through "reason aided by grace," and "pruning" their lives through "love and mortification."[23] For we complete through our will the sketches of life that nature has bestowed upon us, but our will as liberated by the transcending freedom of love and grace. The unity of the Christian is the unity found in Christ, not simply of the perceived sense of his existence, but through his "absolute impeccability," his "faultless wisdom," and his "ineffable memory," and that "he had consciousness of the fact that he transcended the human condition, and that there was in Him something divine."[24] We participate in Christ's divine consciousness through our call in baptism, where the meaning of our lives lies beyond concepts. That meaning, ultimately, is mysterious, and is hidden below the life-giving waters of baptism. Our redemption is ultimately never open to concepts; it is a matter of faith:

> There have always been Christians for whom to know that Christ redeemed the sins of the world is a piece of purely intellectual information of the same caliber as

19. Ibid., 10.

20. Maritain, *The Range of Reason*, 142.

21. Ibid., 188.

22. See Jacques Maritain, *The Person and the Common Good*, translated by John J. Fitzgerald (Notre Dame, Indiana: University of Notre Dame Press, 1966), 41.

23. Jacques Maritain, *The Dream of Descartes*, translated by Mabelle L. Andison (New York: Philosophical Library, 1944), 82.

24. Jacques Maritain, *On the Grace and Humanity of Jesus*, translated by Joseph W. Evans (New York: Herder and Herder, 1969), 16.

the information that the temperature this morning was 54 degrees Fahrenheit. For them, stating the fact is enough, just as the reading of the thermometer is enough. They have every intention of using the information to get to heaven; but they have never been face to face with the reality of the mystery of the Redemption, with the reality of the sufferings of the Savior.[25]

III. Wisdom and Unity

In his work, *Untrammeled Approaches,* Maritain repeatedly explores the place of wisdom. In Chapter XII of that work, subtitled, "The Substitute for Theology Among the Simple," he explores an issue of pressing concern for us today: the theological and intellectual education of the laity. The vast number of Catholics will not acquire "the habits of mind called the intellectual virtues ... particularly the *theological habitus.*" He goes on, "This simplification of theological truths for the general public will never go very far and will never engender in the minds of this audience what can properly be called *knowledge* or *science.*"[26] Because of this, he emphasizes prayer and mysticism, not as a condescending second prize for the theologically unsophisticated, but precisely because of the unity and order that wisdom, prayer, and contemplation instill in human life. All three are concerned with our final end, and all three put that end in relation to this life and this world as the theatre of our salvation. It is in *Education at the Crossroads* that we see this unifying and integrating role of wisdom:

> That knowledge we call wisdom, which penetrates and embraces things with the deepest, most universal, and most unified insights. Such a knowledge, which lives not only by supreme science, but also by human and spiritual experience, is over and above the field of specialization, for it has to do with realities that permeate each and every being and with aspirations which call to the very nature and freedom of man. It is in itself the highest value of the human mind.[27]

The means and ends of the world and the means and ends of wisdom do not always intersect, for the means of wisdom are not the influential, powerful and material means of the world.[28] The confusion between means

25. Maritain, *The Range of Reason,* 208.

26. Jacques Maritain, *Untrammeled Approaches,* translated by Bernard Doering (Notre Dame, Indiana: University of Notre Dame Press, 1997), 272.

27. Maritain, *Crossroads,* 48.

28. See Jacques Maritain, *On the Philosophy of History,* edited by Joseph W. Evans (New York: Charles Scribner's Sons, 1957), 70–71.

and ends is really a confusion between individuality and personality. The individual is swayed by so much: by the state, money, power, opinion, which strike at the very root of the mystery of personhood, for after all, the word "*person* is reserved for substances which, choosing their end, are capable of themselves deciding on the means, and of introducing series of new events into the universe by their liberty. . . . And what makes their dignity, what makes their personality, is just exactly the subsistence of the spiritual and immortal soul and its supreme independence in regard to all fleeting imagery and all the machinery of sensible phenomena."[29]

Philosophy has been defined as the quest for wisdom, and the "knowing" of philosophy is not "a wisdom of conduct or practical life that consists in acting well. It is a wisdom whose nature consists essentially in *knowing*."[30] Nonetheless, while the wisdom of philosophy depends upon knowing, the fruit and the implications of that wisdom lie in virtuous and moral action. But all this is in relation to order and unity, and not just of human knowing but the order and unity of the individual person. With implications for the school and university curricula, Maritain says that the various bodies of knowledge exert their independence by being faithful to their own method of investigation and pursuing the truth. It is because of the hierarchies of knowledge and values that the diversity of the curriculum can be brought into philosophical unity, and it is because wisdom "creates order in knowledge" that human persons can attain the "peace of intelligence." In this search for unity, Maritain says, "human knowledge is not endowed with essential and perfect unity."[31] The unity of knowledge is only incremental, and depends upon that distinction between natural intelligence and the intellectual virtues, and it is the failure of modern education with its premature emphasis on specialization, during the early stages of education, that handicaps the unifying nature of natural intelligence. Failure to realize this leads to what Maritain would undoubtedly have added to his list of seven as the *eighth misconception of education*: that only those who go on to the university are truly educated.

The history of philosophy recounts its own periods of imperialism that have added to this challenge in the unity of knowledge and the unity of persons: the philosophical and metaphysical imperialism of Plato and Aris-

29. Maritain, *Three Reformers*, 20.
30. Maritain, *An Introduction to Philosophy*, 76.
31. Maritain, *The Range of Reason*, 10.

totle; the theological imperialism of the Middle Ages, prior to St. Thomas; and the increasing scientific imperialism of Descartes, Kant, and Comte.[32] Our age has contributed its own imperialisms that strike at the unity of knowledge and the person. The act of existing is itself mysterious, and goes beyond concepts and ideas. But the mystery is grounded in all that makes up the totality of human existence from eating and thinking to discerning and contemplation. Limiting self-knowledge to the psychological, to "phenomena" and to "images and memories" is to render it "incomplete." It is only when knowledge "become ontological, then knowledge of the Self is transfigured.... Subjectivity, this essentially dynamic, living and open center, both receives and gives. It receives through the intellect, by superexisting in knowledge. It gives through the will, by superexisting in love."[33]

We turn to Maritain's social and political philosophy to appreciate the role of wisdom, reason, and the intellect in unifying the person. It is in the political and public squares within human community that the unity of knowledge and truth and human living must be manifested. He asks what living together means, saying that it is more than "being subjected to the same physical or external conditions or pressures or the same patterns of life. ... Living together means sharing ... a common task." That task is housed within society and political community. And what is that common task? It is "the conquest of freedom."[34]

Donald and Idella Gallagher, who introduced and edited Maritain's collection of essays, *The Education of Man: The Educational Philosophy of Jacques Maritain,* refer to his chapter "The Conquest of Freedom," as "Maritain's most comprehensive treatment of this theme and one of the most original statements of the Thomistic philosophy of freedom."[35] We see today how the freedom of the person has shrunk to free will, with no appreciation of how free will is simply a stepping stone and the handmaid in service of what Maritain refers to as freedom of expansion, autonomy and independence.[36] Concentrating exclusively on the freedom of the will—which often seems

32. Ibid., 11.

33. Ibid., 91.

34. Jacques Maritain, *Man and the State* (Chicago: The University of Chicago Press, 1951), 207.

35. Donald and Idella Gallagher, "Introduction," in *The Education of Man: The Educational Philosophy of Jacques Maritain,* edited by Donald and Idella Gallagher (Westport, Connecticut: Greenwood Press, 1976), 10.

36. Maritain, "The Conquest of Freedom," chapter 8 in *The Education of Man,* 159–79.

the case today and which in itself must transcend the world of creation[37]—deteriorates into a "bourgeois-individualistic type of society [where] there is no common work to do, nor is there any form of communion. Each one asks only that the State protect his individual freedom of profit against the possible encroachment of other men's freedom."[38]

That is exactly where we are today, and have gone further—where, as Pope Emeritus Benedict XVI says, we are now not just being torn apart by religious violence and intolerance and political ideologies, but by nations and peoples who live according to a philosophy of history and those who do not. Today the materiality of the world and our materiality have been so exaggerated that the essential knowledge that we gain through our senses and its transformation through the intelligibility of the mind seem frighteningly out of sync. The question, "Why is there something rather than nothing?" is bogged down by what the Pope Emeritus refers to as "mere-materiality"[39] devoid of reflection and choice born from more than the freedom of the will. Today, he says, there are "no longer any values except the goals of progress."[40] Not only have we moved away from a religious and collective understanding of sin, we have now arrived where freedom—manifested through intention, choice, decision, judgment and action—is only seen in relation to the material order and to the individual. It is the tyranny of a solipsistic free will. For Maritain, apart from providing for the material dimensions of life, persons primarily seek to live in society because society enables persons to realize their call to perfection through "communications of knowledge and love which require relationship with other persons."[41]

IV. Education and Human Unity

Human unity is realized through the stages of life and through the different personal and communal expressions of human living, and I have presented a few snapshots as to how Maritain addresses the theme of uni-

37. See Jacques Maritain, *The Sin of the Angel*, translated by William L. Rossner S.J. (Westminster, Maryland: The Newman Press, 1959), 33.

38. Jacques Maritain, *The Rights of Man and Natural Law*, translated by Doris C. Anson (New York: Charles Scribner's Sons, 1947), 39.

39. Joseph Cardinal Ratzinger, *A Turning Point for Europe? The Church in the Modern World—Assessment and Forecast*, translated by Brain McNeil (San Francisco: Ignatius Press, 1994), 227.

40. Joseph Cardinal Ratzinger, *Europe Today and Tomorrow: Addressing the Fundamental Issues*, translated by Michael J. Miller (San Francisco: Ignatius Press, 2004), 29.

41. Maritain, *The Person and the Common Good*, 47.

ty. Education is only one means, albeit an important one, in the quest for human unity. However, the tyranny of some schools of education, and the perennial oscillation between one educational excess and another, reminds me of the wisdom of Maritain's advice, neither caustic nor dismissive, that "educators … must not expect too much from education."[42] Ultimately what shapes human persons is wisdom, which cannot be taught, and for life and living there is nothing greater than "intuition and love," and neither are a "matter of training and learning, they are gift and freedom. In spite of all that, education should be primarily concerned with them."[43]

Maritain's educational philosophy has been accused of being intellectual, speculative, heady, and removed from the living of life, distant from the practicalities of the school day. Certainly his two educational texts in English, *Education at the Crossroads* and the *Education of Man: The Educational Philosophy of Jacques Maritain* unsettle many of today's educational first principles and ideologies. While written with flair and a passionate voice, they are demanding texts. Further, given the way Maritain's works all flow into each other, it is hard to imagine giving a graduate student Maritain's educational works on their own and expecting students to profit from them.

In addition, and I say this as one who has long taught Catholic teachers and administrators pursuing graduate degrees in theology, the intellectual landscape of those preparing to teach in Catholic schools, at least in Canada, is arid and parched. We seem to think that graduating from a Catholic high school, going to a secular university for an undergraduate degree and for a degree in teacher-education, magically transforms one to be qualified to teach in Catholic schools, particularly religious education. It may be referred to it as the "any-Catholic-can-teach-religion syndrome." Suddenly the mysterious waters of baptism, that are beyond the infiltration of concepts and speculative ideas, seems to transform one to teach the Catholic faith in a school; given this newfound unifying power of baptism, surely it should also transform one to be able to teach physics, history, and calculus as well. The documents from the Congregation for Catholic Education have much to say on the role of the Catholic teacher, and chief among them is that the curriculum is secondary compared to who the teacher is, and the defense of the Catholic faith through the witness of the teacher's life. It is

42. Maritain, *The Education of Man*, 43.
43. Maritain, *Education at the Crossroads*, 23.

alarming when students graduating from Catholic high schools know more about the teacher's dissent from the Catholic faith than what the Church actually teaches and why.

I have found that chief among the criticisms of Maritain's philosophy of education is that it is outdated, too European and elitist, and not abreast with where the educational world is today. These objections cannot be fully and adequately responded to here, except to say that the unity of his thought should answer his critics. He acknowledges that since education is not an autonomous discipline, it must keep up with all forms of genuine progress—based on the nature of the person as person. Since it is dependent upon philosophy and ultimately upon theology, education today is vastly incomplete because it concentrates upon far too little. Analogously, I am reminded of Pope St. John Paul II's at first shocking and then brilliant insight that the problem with pornography is not that it shows too much of the person, but that it shows far too little. Maritain's critics dwell on the practicalities of education and curricular methodologies and matters of educational and social psychology, and again he would be the first to admit that educational philosophy must learn from the progress of every age. What they miss is the revolutionary nature of his philosophy of education; again they concentrate on too little, and that little that they do concentrate on and criticize is anyway subject to change in every age. Before I conclude, let me make some brief remarks on two areas: the teacher and unity and teaching, and education. As with the Church, Maritain confirms the important formative role that teachers play. While students are the primary agents of their learning, the teacher is the secondary and "dynamic and ministerial agent" in the student's learning.[44] Though the teacher teaches many things and in different ways, as truth is the domain of teaching, teaching is necessarily more speculative than practical.[45] While institutional education is concerned with the intellect, and through the intellect, indirectly with the will and moral and religious education, the social dimension of education can never be forgotten because it is in the midst of community and society, through communal and social relations, that personhood grows and flourishes. Education is fundamentally human formation, the gradual conquest and realization of internal and spiritual freedom, and such formation naturally flows from and is realized in community and

44. Ibid., 31.
45. See ibid., 26.

society. The primary aim is to form the pupils to attain their full formation as persons.[46] The difficulty is that methodologies and techniques dominate the educational landscape, but what the teacher lacks in using techniques and methodologies effectively is a failure in understanding who the student is and is meant to become as a person.

Among Maritain's seven misconceptions of education, the fourth is *sociologism* and concerns social conditioning and its failure in understanding the nature and purpose of society.[47] Today we see an overemphasis on citizenship and social behavior at the expense of integrated knowledge; it is such knowledge that enlightens social behavior and citizenship, and not the other way around.[48] Accordingly, the real task of teaching and the responsibilities of the teacher emerge: as education is an ethical art, teaching is an act of liberation enabling students to grow in their internal and spiritual freedom.[49] If teaching is primarily an act of liberation, how is the personal liberation of the teacher to be understood? How have knowledge and learning unified their lives, for otherwise, "it is preposterous to ask people who lead an enslaved life to perform a task of liberation, which the educational task is by essence."[50]

Repeatedly Maritain refers to the mysterious nature of education, teaching, and learning.[51] It is because education is in one way an immanent activity,[52] and while education and teaching begin with experience but are to be completed in reason,[53] the unity of the student grows through the mastery of things learned. He states in his third rule, under the fundamental norms of education, that "the whole work of education and teaching must unify not to spread out; it must strive to foster the internal unity of man."[54]

In distinguishing between knowledge value and training value, and knowledge of least worth and knowledge of most worth, Maritain is not proposing some elitist distinctions or preference of intellectual and speculative work over practical work, but rather pointing to those forms of knowledge and learning that contribute to one's internal and spiritual freedom. Hence,

46. See Maritain, *Education of Man*, 50.

47. See Maritain, *Education at the Crossroads*, 15–18.

48. See ibid., 104.

49. See ibid., 2 and 11.

50. Maritain, *Education of Man*, 60.

51. See Maritain, *Education at the Crossroads*, 4 and 9.

52. See Maritain, *Education of Man*, 43.

53. See ibid., 46.

54. Ibid., 45.

Maritain is at pains to emphasize that liberal education and the humanities are not the prized possession of an elite class, those who can sit back and engage in ideas and knowledge disengaged from life and working for the common good. Early specialization violates human unity in diverting the mind to a single field, thus compromising liberation that grows incrementally in relationship with all dimensions of knowledge and knowing. Animals are specialists; all their "knowing-power" is fixed upon "a single task." Premature specialization results in the inability to judge beyond one's field leading to a "progressive animalization of the human mind and work."[55] It is the ordered and systematic knowledge of a diverse curriculum that sows the seeds of wisdom.[56]

One of the looming backdrops to our educational challenges today is summed up in Maritain's seventh misconception of education: "Everything can be learned."[57] An outcomes-based education suggests that what has not been confirmed in learning goals and outcomes has not been learned. Outcomes-based educators would find it inexplicable that education should be ultimately concerned with intuition, love, wisdom, and discernment. Doubly inexplicable would be the confirmation that while the primary task of education is intellectual, and not moral or social, it has enormous implications for the social and moral life of the person, for there it is that internal and spiritual unity and freedom are realized.

The final word goes to Maritain, and from a text other than on the philosophy of education:

> Nothing is more necessary to man than to *discern*, and nothing does he find more difficult. Ordinarily we work with intellectual instruments that we have not taken the trouble to sharpen, we use steam hammers to crush a fly, and telegraph poles to mount a butterfly; and we bring the paws of bears to the task of following out and drawing apart the threads of a spider's web.[58]

55. Ibid., 19.
56. See ibid., 47–48.
57. Ibid., 22.
58. Jacques Maritain, *Theonas: Conversations of a Sage*, translated by F. J. Sheed (London: Sheed and Ward, 1933), 173–74.

MICHAEL NOVAK

The Crucial Role of Léon Bloy in the Maritains' Catholicism[1]

THE WORLD IN which Raïssa Oumançoff and Jacques Maritain began life at the university was a spiritual desert. In a horrifying pact, they swore together to give themselves one more year to find some meaning in life. If that search failed, they promised to commit suicide together. The Maritains seem to have argued themselves into this decision much as Albert Camus was later to argue in *The Myth of Sisyphus*. If human life is absurd, then the only way to give it meaning is to give at least one act in it one's own meaning. One could at least choose the time and the mode by which to exit from it. Suicide would not make life any more meaningless than it already was. But it could put at least one moment of purpose into it.

As things stood, science seemed to them full of power but empty of meaning. Science fostered intellectual skepticism and moral relativism. As Matthew Arnold put it in "Dover Beach":

> Ah, love, let us be true / To one another! for the world, which seems / To lie before us like a land of dreams, / So various, so beautiful, so new, / Hath really neither joy, nor love, nor light, / Nor certitude, nor peace, nor help for pain; / And we are here as on a darkling plain / Swept with confused alarums of struggle and flight, / Where ignorant armies clash by night.[2]

1. Originally given at the 39th Annual International Meeting of The American Maritain Association, on Saturday, February 27, 2016, at Fordham University, this essay was first published as "Léon Bloy's Role in the Catholicism of Jacques and Raissa Maritain," *Crisis Magazine* (March 24, 2016), online at https://www.crisismagazine.com/2016/leon-bloys-role-in-the-catholicism-of-jacques-and-raissa-maritain. Reprinted by kind permission of the publisher.

2. Matthew Arnold, "Dover Beach," in *New Poems* (London: Macmillan and Company, 1867).

Religion seemed to the Maritains to offer nothing better. The French bourgeoisie had turned religion into a kind of bookkeeping. So many penances and so many prayers produced small gains on the plus side. It remained only to avoid a certain list of sins to keep one's balance sheet in order. Religion had become—as Flannery O'Connor put it—"the poor man's insurance company," quoting from *The Habit of Being*.[3] Jacques and Raïssa were repulsed by such a religion. But many believers, alas, were quite proud of their own supposed virtue. French artists—Bloy, Mauriac, Marcel, Bernanos, Péguy—took delight in unmasking such pharisaism, and mocking it.

More and more of the Maritains' friends were reporting that they found Bloy one of the strangest yet most compelling persons in France, and kept urging the Maritains to meet him. Eventually, in 1905, they did.[4] They were immediately enthralled by Bloy's threadbare mode of life and his inner spiritual fire. This meeting with Bloy occurred not long after Henri Bergson had given a set of lectures mapping a route out of materialism. Bergson emphasized the role of *the human spirit* in all human inquiries, sciences, and ethical paths. Now Léon Bloy appeared to the young Maritains as the embodiment of one of the most intense human spirits they had ever met. He was obsessed by a palpable hunger for the Infinite. Meeting Bloy was for the Maritains an abrasive shock. In a world that had settled for materialism, Bloy was the experience of so intense and pure a spirit that it ruptured all previous categories. The Maritains could never erase from their minds their first encounter with pure spirit.

One other thing about Bloy: his language was contemptuous and rough regarding the ordinary, safe, boring materialism of extant French culture. He particularly loathed bourgeois religion, with its petty calculations of merit and demerit. In his lightning bursts of anger, Bloy sharply distinguished between the smugness of false religion and true religion's passionate pursuit of the Absolute. His powerful novel *The Woman Who Was Poor* opens with the words, "This place stinks of God."[5] Bloy hated the bourgeois, because the

3. Quoted in Erasmo Leiva-Merikakis, "Léon Bloy and Jacques Maritain: Fratres in Eremo," in *Understanding Maritain: Philosopher and Friend*, edited by Deal W. Hudson and Matthew J. Mancini (Macon, Georgia: Mercer University Press, 1987), 73.

4. See Ralph McInerny, "Matins (1881–1906)," in *The Very Rich Hours of Jacques Maritain* (Notre Dame, Indiana: University of Notre Dame Press, 2003), available at: http://maritain.nd.edu/jmc/etext/RichHours2.html.

5. Léon Bloy, *The Woman Who Was Poor*, translated by I. J. Collins (New York: Sheed and Ward, 1947), 3.

bourgeois trivialized the mystery of Christianity. His language was unalterably crude, his contempt for false religion matchless. His very being seemed to flash out the message: "If you are going to talk about religion, you must talk about the real thing. Do not dim the real fire of the Absolute with the dust found in so many French churches."

If Bergson's recognition of the role of the spirited subject cleared the way for the Maritains' confidence in their own inquiring spirits, Léon Bloy's sharp distinction between true religion and false, between the cardboard-holy-card calculations of a major part of French Christianity and the passionate search for the Infinite, cleared away one crucial objection that blocked Raïssa and Jacques from considering the Catholic faith.

Like many young Frenchmen who stumbled from materialism as if out of a dark cave and into the bright quest for the true, the good, the beautiful, and for infinite Love, they saw only one path. Remaining rationalists would doom them to relativism and by that route to the abandonment of reason. At the heart of the universe, there had to be impulsion toward the most real of all realities, from which all that exists had sprung. In short, only Christianity answered all the longings of the human spirit. For those awakened by Bloy, tutored to the rigors of the whole kingdom of the Absolute, only Catholicism was Christianity full and straight; Protestantism seemed a kind of "Christianity light."

But Raïssa and Jacques, like hundreds of others who shared similar experiences, could not possibly see in the Catholic Church a plausible home. Its historical sins and its nineteenth-century bourgeois face made it appear to them as "that dunghill."[6] Léon Bloy's very crude expressions of loathing for this false form of Catholicism blasted Raïssa and Jacques past this blockage. They were freed from being misled by false religion and opened to the far more demanding Real.

Léon Bloy taught the Maritains that God is to be addressed as the Absolute, the total Creator and Lover who demands of his children everything. Everything. Look at the crucifix on the wall: this is what God demanded of his own Son. How could he demand less of the rest of us? In fact, God warns us that each of us will have to pick up his own cross, follow the stones on the way up to Calvary, and die to ourselves. The Good Lord does not give Christians false promises. He tells us the straight and demanding truth:

6. Leiva-Merikakis, "Léon Bloy and Jacques Maritain," in *Understanding Maritain*, 118.

we will suffer. We might well become martyrs. Of each of us is asked everything. The Maritains saw how Bloy had endured bitter poverty for many years, even the pain of watching his own children barely survive. His living was at one with his speaking.

Léon Bloy brought to birth two great goods in the souls of the Maritains. First, he himself embodied for them the inflamed human spirit alive in every act of questioning, seeking, and braving the unknown future. Bloy taught them how to live by and through their own spirits. He showed them how to leap over the defensive wall of materialism. Second, Bloy wiped out the great scandal of middle-class smugness they experienced in the Church. In his own person, Bloy brought them into contact with an altogether different inner sort of Catholic faith. Bloy's spirit now enflamed, inspired, and guided the Maritains. Neither for Bloy nor for them was it possible to desire merely to sit in the pews. Bloy taught them to give everything, to aspire ever higher. This is precisely what Jacques and Raïssa desired and demanded. Nothing less satisfied them. They made Bloy's saying their own, and Jacques repeated it more than once. It is the last sentence of *The Woman Who Was Poor*: "There is only one misery . . . and that is not to be saints."[7]

Consider this passage by Erasmo Leiva-Merikakis from Deal Hudson and Matthew Mancini's excellent collection, *Understanding Maritain: Philosopher and Friend*:

> Jacques, Raïssa, and her sister, Vera Oumançoff, were baptized, with Léon Bloy as their common godfather, less than a year after having met with him. Obviously the speed of the conversions may be attributed to the superior power of lived witness over argumentation. Before they discovered Henri Bergson, Jacques and Raïssa had been nothing if not argumentative and rationalistic, and this path of sheer logical demonstration had led them to despair. But what Jacques and Raïssa could not find even in Bergon's intuitionism, and did find in Bloy's Christian faith, was the living Logos, with all the resonances this word carries for an Origen of Alexandria. Bloy mediated to them not primarily a philosophical principle of spiritual order but a living utterance continually so taken into men's hearts by the Lover of Mankind.[8]

It is also really profitable to go back through the second chapter of *Untrammeled Approaches*, "In Homage to Our Dear Godfather, Léon Bloy."[9]

7. Bloy, *The Woman Who Was Poor*, 356.

8. Leiva-Merikakis, "Léon Bloy and Jacques Maritain," in *Understanding Maritain*, 82.

9. Jacques Maritain, *Untrammeled Approaches*, translated by Bernard Doering (Notre Dame, Indiana: University of Notre Dame Press, 1997), 27–45.

Here, Maritain himself states in eight words what Léon Bloy meant to him and Raïssa: "Without him, we would not have become Christians."[10] Maritain describes Bloy as:

> a sort of bedazzled prophet, of extraordinary intuitive genius, in a kind of wild primitive state, possessed by the Holy Spirit. He was filled with supernatural gifts of extraordinary power joined to the sensitivity of a pure poet in which the ways and tools of reason played almost no role at all—"I understand only what I divine," he liked to say so that it was not very surprising to find in him sometimes, along with the prodigiously penetrating intuitions of a visionary which enabled him to touch the ineffable and to reveal the most profound truths, an enormous naïveté as well concerning matters of secondary importance. We must note also, and he did so himself, that he experienced immense impulses of a love obsessed by the desire for God which overflowed its banks and because of which, due to his affectionate loving nature, his life was filled with lapses, with remorse, with confessions, and with relapses, that left him tortured by moral anguish in the midst of material destitution.[11]

But Maritain's is not the only account of this debt.[12] Leiva-Merikakis complements Maritain's recollection of Bloy by adding additional materials from both Maritain and such friends of his as Georges Bernanos. Bernanos himself says, "I owe him everything."[13] Pierre Termier testifies further of Bloy:

> He is at one and the same time ... judge in the service of divine justice, promulgator of the Absolute, a beggar praying on the church steps; and yet he is an artist, because he cannot imagine that God is not beauty itself, and because he wants to put into his work as brilliant a reflection as possible of the glorious vision which

10. Ibid., 27.

11. Ibid., 29.

12. Raïssa also gives a touching account of her exchange with Bloy on his deathbed, quoted in *Untrammeled Approaches*, 34: "He died on Saturday the 3rd of November, 1917, 'towards the evening at the hour of the Angelus, without a death-rattle and without agony.'" "On October 31st," Raïssa writes in *Les Grandes Amitiés*, "While I was at his bedside he confessed to me that he was in great suffering. 'You are suffering for your godchildren,' I said in my great desire to help him in some way. But he went on: 'The baseness of my nature is expiated by ...' His voice was scarcely audible and I did not hear the last words. 'I wish I could do something for you,' he said a moment later with great tenderness. And I replied, my heart breaking with pity: 'You have done everything for me, since you brought me to know God.' I added: 'I wish I could take your suffering upon me.' 'Don't say that!' he said with a certain vivacity, and then looking at me solemnly, 'You don't know what you are asking.' If [he] spoke this way to his godchild, it was because he remembered the day when, impelled by his living faith in the mystery of the Communion of Saints, he had asked to suffer 'all that a man can suffer, in order that his friends, his brothers and souls unknown to him who were living in darkness might receive help,' and it was also because he remembered the terrible manner in which his prayer had been heard."

13. Ibid., 30.

is in Him. Nothing is beautiful enough for the monument he is erecting; nothing is beautiful enough for the Truth and for Love. "I wanted," he says somewhere, "to be the sculptor of the Word": a sculptor never satisfied, who dreamed perpetually of undiscoverable marbles and of a bronze whose secret is lost. Neither the frightful harshness of his life, nor the constant injustice of men, nor the all too prolonged silence of God are capable of curbing his ardor.[14]

And then the words of Leiva-Merikakis: "I propose, then, that Jacques Maritain owed the shape of his religious destiny to the 'phenomenon Léon Bloy' just as he owed the shape of his intellectual destiny to Saint Thomas. Indeed, Jacques found Thomas' love of objective truth anticipated in the very unphilosophical Bloy."[15]

For Bernanos, for Jacques and Raïssa Maritain, and for many others, Bloy pulled back the veils of bourgeois Christianity. By his life, he revealed the burning Word of God. In the words of Leiva-Merikakis, "It is no exaggeration to say that Bloy stands quite alone as the undisputed turning point in modern Catholic literature and piety—as the decisive catalyst in that religious and cultural renewal which abandoned many patterns of nineteenth-century bourgeois Catholicism and shattered the canonical forms and conventions that had long imprisoned the fire of God's Word."[16]

Now, all of us in the Maritain Association are heirs of Léon Bloy. It is a frightening thought. It gives us much to correct in ourselves—and to teach our students.

14. Ibid., 27–28.
15. Leiva-Merikakis, "Léon Bloy and Jacques Maritain," in *Understanding Maritain*, 72.
16. Ibid., 75.

MICHAEL D. TORRE

'Un Bras d'Athlète et Une Haute Voix de Lamentateur'

Why I Love Jacques Maritain

I. Introduction: A Presidential Address

Our last president, John G. Trapani Jr., regularly gave a presidential address at some time during the conferences he organized. His last one had the same subtitle as this paper: "Why I Love Jacques Maritain."[1] While I have not given a presidential address at the previous two conferences, I follow John in ending my term as president, both by giving one and by following in the path he laid down, in the hope of establishing an AMA tradition: it seems right and good to me that an AMA president have his last word to you be a tribute to Jacques and to the love he has inspired.

Such an account cannot but be more personal than a usual presentation. There seems to me at least some justification, for this comes from the office. It is a matter of some general interest to know what has caused others to follow in a tradition or to be guided by an intellectual when they have represented an association such as ours. Despite my being a "nobody" and Maritain the single most important witness to Thomism in the 20th century, I have nevertheless convinced myself that tracing the lines of how

1. See John G. Trapani Jr., "'Things Are Not Only What They Are'—Why I Love Jacques Maritain," his presidential address to the 36th Annual International Meeting of The American Maritain Association, given on Saturday, October 13, 2012, at La Salle University, Philadelphia.

a tradition or a person's influence is passed on is not without some merit here. I will first attempt this tracing, then, by telling some of my own story.

II. Journeying Towards the Church

In late January of 1973, when Jacques made his last trip to Paris where the memorable final photo of him there was taken in Le Jardin des Plantes,[2] I, too, was in Paris—a young man just graduated from college. Perhaps I was even walking in that very garden. Not that I would have recognized Jacques. At that time, he meant nothing to me (much less his earlier pact with Raïssa).

Like Ernest Psichari, my "introduction to religion [had] stopped short with … [my] baptism."[3] I grew up without any religious formation whatsoever and entered college a self-described "card-carrying agnostic." While I had no animus against Christianity, I was not very well-disposed towards the Catholic Church. As a freshman four years earlier, I had risen during the question period following a history lecture on the Medieval Church to ask "what possible good can we now expect from an institution that has given us the Inquisition, the Bartholomew Day Massacre, and the condemnation of Galileo?" I was not as violently opposed to the Church as the young Jacques had been, but something in me resonated to his youthful animosity.[4]

The late 19th century *zeitgeist* that magic had given way to religion, which, in its turn, had been surpassed by science, certainly had influenced my own grandparents and was still at work in my parents. I roughly shared their "Enlightenment" perspective. Upon entering college, my view was that there was no good reason to think God existed and little to nothing to expect from "organized religion." I may not have been as haughty or as confident in the power of reason as to declare with Laplace that "je n'ai pas besoin de cette hypothèse la!" (i.e., he had no need to posit God to explain the universe), but my *Weltanschauung* was uncomplicatedly secular.

2. The photo can be found in Julie Kernan's *Our Friend Jacques Maritain: A Personal Memoir* (Garden City, New York: Doubleday, 1975), before page 97.

3. Raïssa Maritain, *We Have Been Friends Together* (New York: Longman, Green and Co., 1942), 50.

4. Jacques wrote Ernest Psichari on September 26, 1899 that "to establish the new Religion, to suppress all the evil in Catholicism, to destroy the pope, one must attack, one must destroy all of Catholicism, with what it has of good and what it has of evil." Jean-Luc Barré, *Jacques et Raïssa Maritain: Les Mendiants du Ciel* (Paris: Stock, 1995), 61; my translation.

Yet I also had come of age in the 1960s. This was less than two decades since the end of the Holocaust, which by then was well known and dramatized. The quagmire of Vietnam placed in front of many, including myself, the question of whether or not to serve in an undeclared war in which we did not believe and that seemed unjust. The Civil Rights Movement was still exploding around us: the ghettos of the northern cities were on fire and civil rights leaders such as Medgar Evers and Martin Luther King Jr. were being gunned down. I did not come of age in the optimistic era of John F. Kennedy's Peace Corps or the calling of the second Vatican Council, but in an age marked by Kennedy's assassination and that of his brother Bobby, as well as of those civil rights leaders. Ours was a generation marked by a strong "anti-establishment" attitude, one to which the Watergate scandal—just unfolding while I was in Paris—provided the punctuation mark.

We came of age in a time of national war and conflict, and we were dramatically confronted with the issue of *justice*. It would have been hard to resist the conviction—and I not only did not resist it, but consciously embraced it—that certain acts were plainly, objectively, and absolutely unjust and were worth standing against and, if necessary, dying to oppose (while others were *not*). To my mind, there was no "possible universe" in which the Holocaust could be anything other than an unmitigated horror and a completely unjustified offense against human life and human rights. Likewise, it seemed plain to me that the cause for which black Americans were marching in Selma and elsewhere was manifestly just, as was their chosen tactic of non-violent civil disobedience. And while the Vietnam War seemed to me a somewhat more complicated case, this was offset by its touching me and my generation more personally, since the possibility of *dying* in it was all too real. To me, it seemed an unjustified war and one of which I wished to have no part.

Yet, what account could I give myself that would justify my conviction that certain acts were objectively just and others objectively unjust? Did not science show that the universe evolved, and all action in it continued to be caused, by inexorable physical laws? And was it not more "sophisticated" to think that all moral truth was *relative* to the culture, society, or context out of which the goods it defended had come? What right, then, did any youthful idealism or a zealous moral stand have, in a world whose tale was "told by an idiot, full of sound and fury, signifying nothing"? Even entering college, I knew that a dissonance existed between my heart and my head.

Maritain once wrote this: "A man is bound to die for justice. That means that he stakes *his all* on the moral order of justice. To stake all, to give my life, I need to know [that] the intrinsic value of justice and the obligation of justice are unconditional or absolute ... a thing which no mere statement of fact, as are all statements of phenomena, and no possible consideration born out of Empiricism, can ever establish."[5] I think, when he wrote that, he must have been thinking of his own youthful ardor and moral certainty as well as his consequent spiritual struggles.[6] It certainly well describes my own difficulty as I felt it then. It placed me on an intellectual search.

Several of the courses I took in college proved decisive. In a course on Plato from a great expert on (and proponent of) Socrates,[7] I rather abruptly (and somewhat ruefully) discovered that the moral relativism I had thought so sophisticated was in truth merely sophistical and had been examined and intelligently opposed by Plato. In a course that included Augustine, I recognized my own attraction to the virtues of hope and especially love he passionately affirmed. I felt that, should I ever come to any faith, it would surely be that of Christianity, whose ethic still lived within me. But especially I discovered Aquinas. I was not able to rise to the level of his metaphysical thinking and thus was not entirely persuaded by his arguments, but I was impressed and indeed captivated by the fact that he had *made* such arguments. I recognized that the existence of God might not just be the idle fancy of some naïve faith but might accord with our native reason. With him, I first began to take seriously that theism and the Christian faith might be intellectually defensible.

Maritain gives his qualified approval to Bergson's claim that thinkers spend all their lives developing one single intuition.[8] If so, this occurred

5. Jacques Maritain, "The Cultural Impact of Empiricism," in *From an Abundant Spring: The Walter Farrell Volume of the Thomist* (New York: Kenedy and Sons, 1952), 465.

6. Six months before writing Psichari about the need to destroy the pope, he had already written this to him (on March 19, 1899): "Like you, I have a sort of religion of human progress. But ... I claim to build my faith on reason and ... I know that reason is wavering and that Science does not yet give me sufficient certitudes." Barré, *Les Mendiants*, 57; my translation.

7. His name was Laszlo Versényi. His book, *Socratic Humanism* (New Haven, Connecticut: Yale University Press, 1963), was one of the first scholarly attempts to describe Socrates' philosophy. For an appreciation of Versényi, see Gregory Vlastos's passing comment in *Socrates: Ironist and Moral Philosopher* (Ithaca, New York: Cornell University Press, 1991), 19.

8. See Henri Bergson, *L'Intuition Philosophique, Revue de Métaphysique et de Morale* 19 (1911): 809–27, and then published separately (Paris: Helleu and Sargent, 1928). Quoted by Maritain in *Bergsonian Philosophy and Thomism,* translated by Mabelle L. Andison in collaboration with J. Gordon Andison (New York: Glenwood Press, 1968), 158 and n. 1.

for me as I used my passable French to read a thesis on the principles of Aquinas's moral thought.[9] As if lightning struck, I was shocked into seeing what his theism affirmed: that *everything* was a *gift*; that I was "part of the show" by a sheer act of, and overflow of, generosity; that I was the product of Love and was called back to it, to the *Commedia*'s culminating words, to "l'amor che move il sol e l'altre stelle."[10] *There* was a God worth believing in! I remember walking across the Williams College campus from its library in the deep cold of a New England winter night feeling the warmth within from that deep intuition.

After college, I took the opportunity to continue my intellectual quest by spending a year in Europe, primarily in Paris. I left Paris after Easter to journey to Rome. After bicycling through the Dordogne, I passed through Toulouse. I had no idea that Jacques had died there but a few days before. I carried a paperback in my knapsack that I had run across in the window of La Procure bookstore. Its author was unfamiliar to me. Its title was *La grâce et l'humanité de Jesus.* I remember putting it down when getting to the sentence "the joy of Easter ... is a dazzling crown of pure silver on the bloody gold of good Friday,"[11] thinking then "this is too rich for my blood!" This was my first encounter with Jacques Maritain.

I was headed to Rome in more than one sense. "Roma non basta una vita." I fell in love with the city and its heritage even more than I had with Paris. I formally entered the Church just one year later. My intellectual search and struggles had been decisive in freeing me from some intellectual prejudices and ideas that had stood as obstacles to any faith (for I knew I could not embrace one were it opposed to what I rationally held to be true). The reading of some books,[12] and a continued and closer struggle with Aquinas in the months prior to my formal entrance,[13] helped achieve

9. Its title was *Caritas et Ratio: Étude sur le double principe de la vie morale chrétienne d'après S. Thomas d'Aquin* (Nijmegan: Drukkerij Gebroeders Janssen, 1956), originally a thesis written at the Angelicum. Its author was Conrad A. J. van Ouwerkerk, then a Redemptorist priest. I owe him a great debt. He was really the first Catholic intellectual I had ever encountered.

10. I had also read much Shakespeare and Chaucer and all of Dante while in college. A good liberal arts education cannot but put before the inquiring student many expressions of Catholic culture, signposts of its faith.

11. Jacques Maritian, *On the Grace and Humanity of Jesus,* translated by Joseph W. Evans (New York: Herder and Herder, 1969), 15.

12. I had two other paperbacks in my knapsack: *La nuit privée d'etoiles* (a French translation of Thomas Merton's *Seven Storey Mountain*) and *L'amour seul est digne de foi* (a French translation of Hans Urs von Balthasar's *Glaubhaft ist nur Liebe*).

13. I must here also pay tribute to the teacher with whom I read Aquinas then, Kevin Wall,

that freedom. But I was not led into the Church through my head. Rather, I am confident I was just as, if not more, moved to enter the Church by the flickering candles lit by pious women in the dim light of Notre Dame, by the pervasive sense of mystery and beauty felt there and in Chartres, and in the liturgy celebrated within.[14] (Indeed, my faith was to be centered on the Eucharist, as seems true of all Catholics and Orthodox.) It was above all the witness of charity in the hearts of two Irish Catholic women who had helped raise me in the summers of my youth spent at my grandmother's house that was truly decisive. I wanted to drink from the source of the goodness that I had seen in them and that they had so abundantly showered upon me throughout my youth. Aquinas teaches that the greatest sign of the Church's credibility lies in the heroic lives of its "ordinary" saints.[15] So it was for me.

As I said, it was clear to me that *my* conversion must be to the *Christian* faith. That the God who had loved us into being should have loved us enough to die for us was too much in my blood. The carols I sang at Christmas, of the Lord who "did come for to die,"[16] had left their imprint. Yet, especially given my earlier negative sentiments towards the Church, it is a reasonable question why I should have ended a *Catholic*. Gabriel Marcel, another Cath-

O.P., who later directed my thesis on Francisco Marín-Sola, O.P. He had studied at the Angelicum under the likes of Garrigou-Lagrange and Francisco Muñiz and obtained his doctorate (with a thesis on relation in Hegel) under I. M. Bocheński, at Fribourg. He possessed quite an independent mind and underlined the pivotal category of real relation in understanding Thomas.

14. "I have often affirmed my conviction that the true apology of Christian faith, the most convincing demonstration of its truth … are the saints and the beauty that the faith has generated." Joseph Ratzinger, "The Feeling of Things, the Contemplation of Beauty" (Congregation of the Doctrine of the Faith, August 24, 2002). "Yet, the beauty of Christian life is even more effective than art and imagery in the communication of the Gospel message. In the end, love alone is worthy of faith, and proves credible. The lives of the saints and martyrs demonstrate a singular beauty which fascinates and attracts, because a Christian life lived in fullness speaks without words. We need men and women whose lives are eloquent, and who know how to proclaim the Gospel with clarity and courage, with transparency of action, and with the joyful passion of charity." Benedict XVI, *Address to the Participants to the Plenary Assembly of the Pontifical Council for Culture* (November 13, 2010).

15. "It would be truly more wonderful than all the [other] signs [of Christianity's truth] if the world had been led by simple and humble men [as it was] to believe such lofty truths, to accomplish such difficult actions, and to have such high hopes." Thomas Aquinas, *Summa Contra Gentiles*, translated by Anton C. Pegis (Notre Dame, Indiana: University of Notre Dame Press, 1955), I, chap. 6, no. 3, p. 73. For Thomas's view here, see my "Aquinas and the Credibility of God," *Logos* 3, no. 2 (Spring, 2000): 107–17.

16. "I wonder as I wander": "I wonder as I wander out under the sky / How Jesus the Savior did come for to die." The idea is expressed by many another carol (e.g., "O Holy Night!").

olic convert who had apparent reasons to be attracted to a form of Protestant faith,[17] pondered the same question. I could have given his own answer: "It clearly seemed to me that to choose Protestantism was to remain in an ambiguous position which I definitely intended to leave.... Did not Catholicism alone concentrate in itself the fullness of the Christian message? Was there another way for me to commit myself to it other than by explicitly embracing the Catholic faith?"[18] That was my sense as well: there I would find the *fullness* of truth and grace. I knew the "Roman obedience" could be demanding, perplexing, and even a trial. Nevertheless, this seemed right to me. Was the Church not, after all, a "Jewish mother," one who "hovered" over her children, always wanting what was truly best for them, which could be nothing less than the perfect love their heavenly Father desired?

Yet when all is said and done, it was the flame of charity in the women who touched my childhood that was truly the key influence.[19] I believe that, had I been raised in an Orthodox household, and truly celebrated an Orthodox Easter, I should never have wanted to part from that celebration.[20] Had I gone to a church in which Mahalia Jackson was singing "Lord

17. I had myself been exposed to much Protestant theology when in college: the latest issues of exegesis and the "search for the historical Jesus," Bultmann, Tillich, and Barth, as well as the work of the redoubtable Max Weber. By the time I went to graduate school, these names were being replaced by Moltmann, Pannenberg, and Whitehead. Hermeneutics was all the rage, Gadamer's *Truth and Method* "essential reading," and Karl Rahner's star in its ascendency.

18. Gabriel Marcel, *Awakenings*, a translation of Marcel's autobiography *En chemin ver quel éveil?* by Peter S. Rogers (Milwaukee, Wisconsin: Marquette University Press, 2002), 124. I had run across Marcel in college and his recent autobiography in Paris. He was then more important to me than Maritain.

19. As Baron Friedrich von Hügel taught his niece, the "great tradition" is that "one torch lights another torch." *Letters From Baron Friedrich Von Hügel to a Niece*, edited with an introduction by Gwendolen Greene (London: J. M. Dent and Sons, 1928), xv. Maritain rendered homage to von Hügel directly after Bloy and Péguy as one to whom he owed a real debt and for whom he had a special admiration. See his "Contemporary Renewals in Religious Thought," in *Religion and the Modern World* (Philadelphia: The University of Pennsylvania Press, 1940), 1–20. Von Hügel says that he "learnt all that I know from Huvelin" (*Letters*, xv). Abbé Henri Huvelin (1830–1910) was the one who converted Charles de Foucauld and was a confessor in the line of the Curé d'Ars. Like Bloy, von Hügel would say, "To sanctify is the biggest thing out" (*Letters*, viii), something he learned from Huvelin. Here is a quotation from him (*Quelque Directeurs d'Ames*), on the frontispiece of *Letters*: "The world sees in itself passions, interest, ambition; it sees the bitter water that fills things; and we [spiritual directors], we seek under these bitter waters that small Artesian well that continues on its way, that little spring of grace, deeper, more hidden, but that nevertheless exists" (my translation). It is curious that Maritain seems not to know of Huvelin: his name appears in none of the indices of his complete works.

20. My view of the Orthodox Church is one with that of Louis Bouyer, C.O.: "The Orthodox Church and the Catholic Church, though dreadfully tempted by the spirit of division,

don't let me fail, I want to be in your pride" or was wishing she "could only hear my mother pray again," I would have always wanted to return to hear her sing out that "shining gospel way."[21] But I am glad that instead it was the candles in Notre Dame and the faith of the Irish, dyed into them through their long suffering, which was decisive for me. How could I not want to be in communion with the successor of Peter, that wonderfully head-strong and loving man? Among other things, one thus did not need to spend spiritual energy on having always to justify why one was *not* with him!

I am conscious, in sketching this account, that I have left out what is no doubt essential. Being a convert, one is often asked about one's conversion and I never really try to tell the story fully. Like the character Tom Hanks played in "Saving Private Ryan," some of the memories in it are "just for me." But no doubt the true reason a convert is reticent is that we do not know our depths very well, and we certainly cannot see all the mysterious action of the Holy Spirit at work in our heart. As Baron von Hügel told his niece, "Before all greatness, be silent—in art, in music, in religion: silence."[22] As abbreviated and inadequate, then, this is the account I can offer you.[23]

III. A Guide in our Intellectual World

I have given this account principally in order to explain why I might consequently have found myself so attracted to Jacques Maritain, to which

remain one Church, in fact and by right, despite contrary appearance." *The Church of God: Body of Christ and Temple of the Holy Spirit*, translated by Charles Underhill Quinn (Chicago: Franciscan Herald Press, 1982), 512.

21. There will always be souls of deep faith and sanctity who feel they must in conscience protest against the Church's teaching and thus be parted from her "sacramental way." Since this protest has almost become "institutionalized" within Reformation churches, it seems there is less likelihood of a reunion between them and the Catholic Church. As Schleiermacher wrote, Protestantism "makes the individual's relation to the Church dependent on his relation to Christ." *On the Christian Faith*, vol. 1, § 24 (Philadelphia: Fortress Press, 1978), 103; whereas the principle of both Orthodox and Catholic faith is "in the Spirit, through the Son, to the Father": Christ is found first in His Church and her sacraments.

22. Friedrich von Hügel, *Letters*, x.

23. I find that in this account I have referred to a truly catholic group of influences on my conversion: Irish (caregivers of my youth, Wall), Dutch (van Ouwerkerk), French (Marcel, Maritain, Notre Dame, Chartres, Garrigou-Lagrange, indirectly), English (Chaucer, Shakespeare), Italian (Aquinas, Dante, Rome), North African (Augustine), Swiss (von Balthasar), German and English (von Hügel), German and Austrian (Rahner), Spanish (Marín-Sola and Muniz, indirectly), Polish (Bochenski, indirectly), Hungarian (Versényi), American (Merton). My confirmation sponsor was of Croatian descent and a disciple of Marcel. Not all of these people or their ideas were equally important to me, but the "catholic symphony" of influences is striking.

attraction I now turn. In the first place, it seems to me this was because I had taken a very similar journey to his own. My father, like his, came from a Catholic family and had a Catholic youth, but he, too, had lapsed from his faith; my mother came from a liberal Protestant family and herself had no religious affiliation. I grew up outside any religious observance, opposed the Church's claim to authority, and saw no special good in her. I had the zealous righteousness of youth regarding moral issues (and opposed the vile treatment of Jews), and yet I felt a conflict between my commitments and any theoretical account I could give that would justify them. This led to an intellectual search and to philosophers who helped free me from a scientism before which I had felt rather defeated. Yet it was not philosophy but the lived experience of charity that was decisive in bringing me into the Church—my Irish caretakers being for me what Bloy was to Jacques and Raïssa. Both he and I were married laymen who entered the Church near the time we were married. Both of us entered at a "time of crisis" in the Church, provoked by Modernism and by Vatican II. (Indeed, it was much the same turmoil and confusion.) We both found in the philosophy of Aquinas what we felt was "the right way through" that confusion and crisis. I was ready to be quite attracted to Jacques's thought, then, because I came from the same place, the same intellectual background and struggle and the same desire to find my way back to a faith tradition not compromised by modernity, while nevertheless accepting much from it that continued to mark me. It seems to me that I have ever understood Jacques "from within," our journeys having been so similar.

Reflecting on this, it has occurred to me that the "pattern" of our search had already been described by the one who first detailed his own conversion in a way never to be surpassed. I refer, of course, to Augustine in his *Confessions*. He, too, came from a "mixed" religious background (Catholic mother and pagan father) and a childhood marked by the Catholic faith from which he was increasingly alienated as a youth. He, too, was placed on an intellectual search, by Cicero. He, too, found himself with intellectual obstacles to a Catholic faith (the problem of evil), from which philosophers (Plotinus and Porphyry) had then freed him. Yet this was not enough to bring him within the Church; rather, what was needed was above all the ever-present heart and prayers of his mother, Monica, the witness of the Egyptian monks and their Roman followers, and the words of Scripture. The story he tells is deliberately crafted to support his view that only by the grace of God reaching down to touch his inner being, his viscera, and heart, was he finally enabled to enter the Church. So it was also with Jacques. So it was also with me.

We are led to the Father, who is the Abyss of all reality, and who is not sent into the world, by the Persons who are: the Word of Truth and the Spirit of Love. One can also catch a glimpse of this with the youthful Aquinas. His reported question was not "*who* is God?"—the Creed had already told him that: the Father, Son, and Holy Spirit—but "*what* is God?": just *what* are we speaking of when we speak of "God"? (His adult answer is clear: in this life, we cannot answer the urgent question posed, for we do not know *what* God is, and thus we do not know *what* we are talking about when we rightly use our halting language to speak of God, nor do we know the *way* God is all that we rightly attribute to Him.) This is clearly an intellectual's question (and answer), and of the first order. Yet we also glimpse that other and more hidden side of Aquinas in his slamming the red-hot poker against the door he shuts behind the startled and retreating courtesan introduced into his room to seduce him from his vocation. It was not *her* love he sought but a greater and more fiercely jealous Love. He brings to his vocation all his mind and heart.

Upon entering the Church, Jacques had an immediate and crucial influence upon *my* own mind and heart through a fellow student who was a "devout Maritainista."[24] Like Augustine, I was exercised by the problem of evil. For example, that God could have been even the indirect cause of the Holocaust I found grotesque, not to say repellant. Yet, if God is the fount of all being and action (including our own free choices), how do we avoid this conclusion? My friend pointed me to Maritain's account in *God and the Permission of Evil* and his vindication there of the holiness and absolute innocence of God (just in relation to our sin). He set me on the path to my doctoral thesis.[25] I have defended the line of Maritain's thought to us before.[26] What was above all important for me was that he saw and de-

24. His name was Terrence Miller. His "interventions" in my life then (unknown to him) were significant. One need not have a degree or publish to be a deep Thomist and Maritainista!

25. This was published years later as *God's Permission of Sin: Negative or Conditioned Decree?* (Fribourg, Switzerland: Academic Press Fribourg/Editions Saint-Paul Fribourg Suisse, 2009).

26. See my "The Grace of God and the Sin of Man: The Drama of Man Before God," *Aquinas and Maritain On Evil: Mystery and Metaphysics*, edited by James G. Hanink (Washington, D.C.: American Maritain Association, distributed by The Catholic University of America Press, 2013), 170–203.

fended what Francisco Marín-Sola, O.P., had seen so well and defended so brilliantly before him:[27] that Aquinas clearly and rightly affirmed that the *cause* and *explanation* of sin *began* with the *creature's* will—the *first* cause of sin—*not* God's will, even permissive.

Perhaps even more important, and certainly more "personal," was my friend's effect upon my will. I came into the Church just at the time when many Catholics were up in arms against the teaching of *Humane Vitae*, released but five years previously. It is hard now to recall accurately the anger and deep confusion of that time. Directly following Vatican II, many read it as though its final (and most optimistic) document—*Gaudium et Spes*—was but the harbinger of a spirit that would continue into some imagined Vatican III, and that the Church was about to be transformed from an ugly, crawling caterpillar into a beautiful, soaring butterfly. The Counter-Reformation was thankfully behind us—as indeed it was!—and the world was about to see a renewed, joyful, and reunited Church: a lovely dream, perhaps, but an absurdly simplistic one and at root irrational. The pope's encyclical was as a bucket of cold ice-water thrown into the face of such dreams, thereby breaking the image of a new "age of Aquarius." Surely, Paul VI must have been mistaken! This was a fallible magisterial document and did not deal with a doctrine of faith. Surely it would soon be "reformed" (a conviction that was only "laid to rest" or "forced underground" by the pontificate of John Paul the Great). After all, its teaching had not been accepted or "received" by the faithful (whose "*sensus fidei*" it seems was to be discovered by opinion-polls of self-described Catholics). Was not the "magisterium of the theologians" also against the encyclical? Was it not right, then, that it only be accorded one's "respect," treated as a "prudential counsel" from which one could justifiably dissent?[28] Such was the miasma in which I found myself when I entered the Church.

At that time, I understood the many good reasons that might motivate couples to postpone children; I myself had no strong feelings against oral contraceptives, and I doubted the strength of the arguments that distinguished Natural Family Planning from contraception. (I could see the dif-

27. For Maritain's connection to Marín-Sola, see my "Francisco Marín-Sola, O.P., and the Origin of Jacques Maritain's Doctrine on God's Permission of Evil," *Nova et Vetera* 4, no. 1 (2006): 55–94.

28. It is not a caricature of the view of many then that all Catholics had a right to do as Henry Higgins claims women do: "listen very nicely and then go out and do precisely what they want."

ference between it and NFP, but I could not see well the importance of that difference.[29]) On the other hand, I had a knowledge of the Catholic theological tradition, and I could read. I knew that the teaching might not be *de fide* but *was* a matter of Catholic doctrine, and that the Church traditionally had held—and *Lumen Gentium* had just unequivocally reaffirmed—that Catholics owed magisterial teaching the religious *assent* of their mind and will.[30] And here my friend's "intervention" proved decisive. He did not insist on some *argument* being clear and right. He simply asked me whether I did not think Catholics owed the pope their loyalty on this matter. Did we not, as Catholics, believe we should be guided here by the Church's *magisterium*? That simple question seemed to me to have but one honest answer: yes. So I have ever believed since then. For many years thereafter I sought to adhere to the teaching just out of obedience, before I finally came to see Paul VI's wisdom in prophetically reaffirming that God had united the marital embrace with its order to life and that what God had joined together we should not seek to put asunder.[31]

29. It is easy to sympathize with reasons people have for wanting to use contraceptives, but what gets missed is how deeply important it is to maintain the unity between the marital embrace and the life that flows from it. If this is not clear in itself, it becomes so by its later effects.

30. "Bishops who teach in communion with the Roman Pontiff are to be *revered* by all as witnesses of divine and Catholic truth; the faithful, for their part, are *obliged* to *submit* to their bishops' decision, made in the name of Christ, in matters of faith and morals, and to *adhere* to it with a ready and respectful *allegiance* of mind. This loyal *submission* of the *will* and intellect must be given, in a *special* way, to the authentic teaching authority of the Roman Pontiff, even when he does not speak *ex cathedra,* in such wise indeed that his supreme teaching authority be acknowledged with respect, and sincere *assent* be given to decisions made by him." Vatican Council II, "*Lumen Gentium,*" Chapter III, no. 25, in *The Documents of Vatican II,* edited by Austin P. Flannery, O.P. (New York: Costello Publishing Company, 1975), 379; emphasis added.

31. Good arguments *are* available against the use of contraceptives. First (as Rowan Williams famously argued before becoming the Anglican Archbishop of Canterbury), "if it is legitimate to sterilize a heterosexual union, it is hard to see what is so wrong with an intrinsically sterile same-sex union. In fact, of course, in a church which accepts the legitimacy of contraception, the absolute condemnation of same-sex relations of intimacy must rely either on an abstract fundamentalist deployment of a number of very ambiguous texts, or on a problematic and non-scriptural theory about natural complementarity." *The Body's Grace* (London: Lesbian and Gay Christian Movement, 1989), 320. If sex is about "me and you, kid" (and not about "me and you and the kid"), then it is hard to see why Jack can sterilize sex with Jill but Bob cannot have sterile sex with Bill. Yet both the divine command to be fruitful and multiply and the constant tradition of both Orthodox Judaism and Christianity see homosexual acts as disordered (even if both the culture and the Anglican Church, following its logic in the other direction, deny this). If legitimizing contraceptive sex leads to denying this truth, then something is amiss with that legitimation. Second, and just as telling, is how the sexual act will be viewed when separated from its natural order to life. Surely this separation chiefly accounts for the "downward spiral"

I say this was an influence that *Maritain* had upon me—indirectly through my friend, a devout Maritainista—for I think that his attitude exactly represented the mind of Maritain. He, too, had been led to wonder about the permissibility of oral contraceptives,[32] or at least about the advisability of making a negative declaration at the time it was made. That he wondered about this *when* he did was clearly permissible: it was then a "debated," if delicate, question, and his concern of "advisability" was simply one possible prudential consideration. Maritain, however, was above everything else a faithful Catholic and he was ready to give his loyal assent to Paul VI, who was of course also his friend. I think *my* friend's view was *Maritain's*: obedience settled the matter.

I am coming here to the main theme of my present section: Maritain as a guide through the perplexing issues of our time. But, before speaking to it, allow me to pause for a moment, for I feel I should at times go beyond the personal to offer a few *arguments* we can discuss. It seems to me that Maritain's attitude of "careful public reserve" on this matter is entirely in keeping with something Aquinas teaches but that is less averted to than it should be. It is well-known that Aquinas thinks the precepts of the Decalogue reiterate natural law precepts evident to almost all;[33] and it is equally well-known that he thinks these precepts can be *specified* variously by human law—in which case they lack the full force of natural law—or they can serve as principles from which other precepts can be *derived*, in which case *these* have the full binding force of that law.[34] Again, it is well-rehearsed that he thinks these more or less remote derivations from the precepts of the Decalogue are *not* known to all, but only to "the wise."[35] Thus, he notes that these "cor-

of contemporary Western society regarding our sexuality and the immodest and tawdry sexual practices that increasingly inform it (e.g., the widespread viewing of pornography).

32. For Maritain's struggles over contraception, see Bernard Doering's summary of his correspondence with Charles Cardinal Journet: "Maritain, Journet, and *Humanae Vitae*," in *Redeeming Philosophy: From Metaphysics to Aesthetics*, edited by John J. Conley, S.J. (Washington, D.C.: American Maritain Association, distributed by The Catholic University of America Press, 2014), 15–62.

33. Aquinas holds that the most basic moral precepts are unexceptionally known by all (ST I-II, q. 94, a. 2). The Decalogue is immediately derived from these most general precepts and is evident after "very little consideration" (ST I-II, q. 100, a. 1) and so is known to all, save exceptionally. (Thus Aquinas allows that the ancient German tribes did not recognize that robbery was wrong [ST I-II, q. 94, a. 4].) For the Decalogue reiterating the natural law (save regarding certain specifications, such as the day to honor God), see ST I-II, q. 100, a. 3, ad 2.

34. ST I-II, q. 95, a. 2.

35. ST I-II, q. 100, a. 1.

ollaries" had to be taught to the Jewish people by Moses and Aaron,[36] since, given our fallen moral state, they would *not* be clear to most people, absent such instruction.

What is less adverted to is just *what* acts will *not be seen as wrong* by those who *lack* the religious instruction of Moses and Aaron, the inspired teaching of religious leaders (whom Catholics believe were continued in the apostles, and their successors, the bishops): precepts against idol worship; blasphemy; hatred and violence towards our neighbor; homosexual acts, prostitution, and bestiality; fraud; lying; or the positive precepts to treat elders with reverence and dependents with kindness.[37] We should pause to consider Aquinas's list well; for it details what secular reason, uninstructed by the wisdom of a true religious tradition, will be unable to see or affirm. (We should not forget that abortion and infanticide were commonly practiced in pagan society and that not even its wisest men—i.e., Plato and Aristotle—felt any reason to object to such practice.)

Now, clearly if—absent God's instruction—most save the wise will not see that bestiality and prostitution are wrong, they are hardly going to find anything amiss with contraception! After all, even Catholic theologians deeply trained in the Church's moral tradition had disagreed about this matter. Here, as with many another moral truth, what is *in principle* accessible to reason, and derivable from a known and accepted moral precept, will not *in fact* be seen, nor will its derivation be clear—save to a few, after considerable time, and with an admixture of error (to use Aquinas's words from another context).[38] In thinking about how to advocate for some moral truths of their tradition, Catholics need to face this fact. They need to be clear that their commitment to these truths does not repose in the first instance upon *reason* but upon the wisdom of their *holy tradition*. This brings with it a two-fold implication. First, in relation to the Catholic community, bishops should stress its conviction that the Holy Spirit continues to guide its chosen teachers in the holy way of the apostles, martyrs, and saints. For those not in the Catholic community, they should emphasize that what is being offered for their consideration are truths anchored first

36. ST I-II, q. 100, a. 11.

37. It is striking (but not surprising), how many of these truths are just those now being contested in Western society.

38. See the SCG I chap. 4, nos. 3–5, 66–68. While Aquinas there speaks of metaphysical truths about God that may be *per se* more difficult than the moral truths referred to, there is no obstacle in our will to affirming them (as to moral truths), and both are accessible only to "the wise."

in a holy tradition. Knowing that others may not share their tradition (or not fully share it), Catholics should begin by emphasizing their solidarity with them in truths seen and shared (in this case, all the ends that lead people to choose contraception as a means to them), and acknowledge that it may be hard for others to see the truth of *their* tradition (and even harder to follow it), absent the graces God offers to make that possible. What neither Catholics nor their leaders should do is just what so many did: present this teaching as though its *main basis* was natural law argument. Maritain had just cause to be unhappy with the way the Church's teaching on this point was often handled.[39]

By embracing the civil right to religious freedom, in the context of our present pluralistic democracy, the Church has returned us to the time just prior to Constantine, when the Church had a definite but contested influence in an empire of many different faiths. But it has now eschewed the development that then followed: the promulgation of the Church's faith, and its being favored, by the State. For Catholic faith and morals to shape our own day, we must rely on the witness that had proved so winning: the path of holiness and the inner beauty of the saints and martyrs. When it comes to a moral truth such as contraception, what the Church should *chiefly* be about is not arguing with secular Western society and law but getting its own house in order. If its own faith community cannot willingly embrace its own wisdom, the rest of society hardly will! The original conversion of Western society and culture was effected by means of the Church's holiness, and its "re-conversion" will only occur through the renewed inner beauty of her ordinary members.

This issue of course is but one in our ongoing "culture war." Maritain having influenced me on *this* issue, I naturally looked to him in relation to others. Indeed, the culture I came from and that had in part formed me was studded with those whose "hermeneutic of suspicion" stood against my new-found faith: men such as Marx, Nietzsche, and Freud.[40] Thus, I found myself repairing often to Maritain to see how he saw these figures and the ideas that marked our age.[41]

39. For a fuller defense of the argument of this paragraph, see my "Murray After Fifty Years: Reflecting On America and its Proposition," in *The Renewal of Civilization: Essays in Honor of Jacques Maritain*, edited by Gavin T. Colvert (Washington, D.C.: American Maritain Association, distributed by The Catholic University of America Press, 2010), 59–81.

40. See Paul Ricoeur, *Freud and Philosophy*, translated by Denis Savage (New Haven, Connecticut: Yale University Press, 1970), 32–36.

41. Maritain treats Marx at some length in *Integral Humanism* and references Nietzsche

As one coming from a pluralistic and democratic society, I was naturally interested in how a Thomist should think about the issue of equality and human rights.[42] As one from a family that practiced no religion, it was important for me to have a better sense of the implicit way God might still be at work in non-believers.[43] As someone familiar from college courses with the *Upanishads, Bhagavad Gita, Dhammapada, Tao Te Ching,* and *Analects,* I wanted help in how to think about Eastern religious thought, practice, and mystical experience.[44] As one who had some familiarity with Jewish practice, who had celebrated Passover with Orthodox Jewish cousins, and who loved Buber's Hassidic rabbis, I wanted better to understand Jewish-Christian dialogue.[45] I also wanted to know what a Catholic ought to make of those "skeletons in the closet" I had averted to when in college.[46] Maritain would disappoint me on *none* of these matters! I wanted to see how a Thomist could appropriate and respond to my contemporary world and this was above all Maritain's self-appointed mission: to show forth the possible contemporaneity and vitality of Thomism.

I was also seeking to understand many issues within Thomism. How could I not be excited to see that it contained principles for a rich aesthetic,[47] and that it could offer a sound critique on the moral dimension of art without confusing its end with that of morality?[48] I was concerned to think about how to philosophize in faith while recognizing the legitimate autonomy of rational inquiry and was helped by his use of the distinction between the *nature* of philosophy and the *state* in which it was practiced. I, too, want-

---

throughout his works; for Freud, one can particularly consult "Freudianism and Psychoanalysis" in *Scholasticism and Politics.*

42. As but two examples among many of his other discussions, one can consult "Human Equality" in *Ransoming the Time* and *The Rights of Man and Natural Law.*

43. See "The Immanent Dialectic of the First Act of Freedom," in *The Range of Reason,* or "Who is My Neighbor?" in *Ransoming the Time,* or comments in *Approaches to God* or *On the Church of Christ.*

44. As one example, see "The Natural Mystical Experience and the Void," in *Ransoming the Time.*

45. See, as but one example, "The Mystery of Israel," in *Ransoming the Time.*

46. Maritain expressly treats at length of those and other Catholic "skeletons in the closet" in *On the Church of Christ: The Person of the Church and Her Personnel,* translated by Joseph W. Evans (Notre Dame, Indiana: University of Notre Dame Press, 1973), 152–231.

47. For a succinct yet complete account of Maritain's aesthetics, see John G. Trapani Jr.'s *Poetry, Beauty and Contemplation: The Complete Aesthetics of Jacques Maritain* (Washington, D.C.: The Catholic University of America Press, 2011).

48. See *The Responsibility of the Artist* (New York: Charles Scribner's Sons, 1960/Gordian Press, 1972).

ed to affirm that, whatever might be the subjective conditions of a philosopher, any *philosophical* truth reposed entirely on truths arrived at and defensible from rational premises and insights. I was especially concerned to come to terms with contemporary empirical science and understand how one could effect a true synthesis between its methods and discoveries and those rooted in a sound and defensible philosophy of nature.[49] *Over and over again,* when I repaired to the work of Jacques Maritain I received aid and light.

Indeed, when one stops and reflects on his work, it truly is remarkable, the range of his own reason breathtaking, the richness of his thought almost inexhaustible! That a man in his eighties should have been responsible for the diverse and significant essays collected in the volume that this conference has celebrated is nothing short of astonishing! Maritain's thought has provided the basis for over more than three dozen conferences and two dozen books of our Association and there is no end in sight to what the fecundity of his work may continue to evoke from us.

As most educated persons of our contemporary world, I accepted the evolutionary account of the cosmos, Earth, and man. Maritain did not disappoint me here, either, giving us "Toward a Thomist idea of Evolution."[50] In order to offer some connection to the chosen book of our conference, allow me again to offer some *arguments* for our consideration, now from this essay.

Maritain had the courage to challenge many contemporary Catholic opponents of abortion, defending the reasonableness of Aquinas's position, and I think he was right to do so (even though one could rightly quarrel with some of his presentation). I have often heard it argued that, at conception, an unborn being possessing DNA from its human parents is a unique human individual. It is often rhetorically asked, "How could a human individual not be a human person?"[51] Excuse me, but this won't do. From when this issue was first raised in philosophy, by Aristotle in his *Gen-*

49. See *The Philosophy of Nature, Science and Wisdom,* and of course *The Degrees of Knowledge.*

50. Jacques Maritain, "Toward a Thomist Idea of Evolution," in *Untrammeled Approaches,* translated by Bernard Doering (Notre Dame, Indiana: University of Notre Dame Press, 1997), 85–131.

51. Congregation for the Doctrine of the Faith, "*Donum Vitae*" [Instruction on Respect for Human Life in Its Origin and on the Dignity of Procreation] (1987): no. 5.1.1. This question is carefully nuanced in *this* document. It is directly preceded by the statement that "no experimental datum can be itself sufficient to bring us to the *recognition* of a spiritual soul." Many are less careful than this document in the claims they make.

eration of Animals, it has rightly been affirmed that our intellectual soul—a spiritual or *immaterial* entity—"comes from without."[52] Furthermore, it is and has long been Catholic teaching that this soul is created immediately by God.[53] The one thing we can be sure our biological DNA does *not* include is the intellectual soul; but just this is what *defines* a "human being" or "human person" in the *formal* sense of that word. The answer, then, to the rhetorical question posed is that "human" is here plainly being used *equivocally*, just as to speak of a "human corpse" is to use "human" equivocally: for, supposing the intellectual soul is *absent*, what would exist would be *neither* a "human person" *nor* a "human individual" in the *formal* sense of that word. What then, no doubt it may plaintively be asked, might it be? As Maritain pointed out, we should be as careful in answering this question as we are in answering the *analogous* question of what the progenitors of our species were in our evolutionary past: prior to our species (*homo sapiens*), there were others leading up to it that were not properly or formally "human beings" but only "hominids."[54] Just as these were virtually human, so any biological individual with human DNA but absent the intellective soul would be a "human" being only *virtually*.[55]

Maritain was also right to argue that several relevant distinctions ought

52. Regarding the nutritive, sensitive, and rational souls, Aristotle had written "Plainly those principles whose activity is bodily cannot exist without a body.... For the same reason also they cannot enter from outside.... It remains then for the reason alone so to enter and also to be divine, for no bodily activity has any connection with the activity of reason." *Generation of Animals* 2.3, 736b23–28, translated by A. Platt, from *The Complete Works of Aristotle*, vol. 1, edited by Jonathan Barnes (Princeton, New Jersey: Princeton University Press, 1984), 1143. See ST I, q. 118, a. 2, ad 2.

53. "The Church teaches that every spiritual soul is created immediately by God—it is not 'produced' by the parents." *The Catechism of the Catholic Church*, 2nd edition (Vatican City: Libreria Editrice Vaticano, 1994), English edition by the United States Catholic Conference, Inc., no. 366, 93.

54. I here suppose that the biological definition of *homo sapiens* at least roughly coincides with the philosophical definition of man as a "rational animal." The artifacts of Cro-Magnon man certainly suggest he was one. The first human beings could possess an intimate awareness of God in the world they beheld, and be ready to live off the fruits of the good earth, to befriend animals, and to be good stewards of creation. Nothing we know of our earliest forbearers makes such traits impossible and remnants of each of them can still be found in various ways amongst human beings now: in practice or in aspiration.

55. Thomas Aquinas, *In II Sent.*, d. 31, q. 1, a. 1, ad 2: "In semini *non* est natura humana *nisi in virtute* ... quia per virtutem quae est in semini, generatio *ad* natura humanam *terminatur*" ("the human semen [i.e., all active bodily power at work in human generation] is *not* a human being *save virtually* ... because, by the power that is in semen [or, today, our genes or DNA], generation *terminates in* human nature" [my translation and emphasis]).

to be made of the unborn. Thus, it is plainly absurd—and nothing short of outrageous—not to recognize the full humanity of a *viable* human child when we recognize this and grant the child full protection of the law when it is no longer in the womb. (And it is all the more outrageous given that, in but a few minutes and with ordinary surgery, it can be removed from that place.)[56] Being attached to the mother by an umbilical tube, or to a machine by plastic tubes, is plainly *accidental* to *what* it is. Indeed, once the unborn being is *sensitive* and is formally an animal, there is no adequate reason for supposing that it could not possess the radical power of reason that is constitutive of our species—whether we hold the Catholic teaching that this is due to the spiritual (i.e., immaterial) soul given by God or whether we are materialists who regard reason as an "emergent property" educed from the biological matter. The burden of proof in either case—in relation to a sensitive individual with DNA from its human parents—is to demonstrate that this rational power is *not radically present* in it, and this plainly is a burden of proof that its potential killer cannot meet.

However, the matter is not the same with the unborn being *prior* to sensation. Aquinas thought that God prepared the body to receive the human soul, and, since the human intellect can only *function* on the basis of sensory images, he thought it *reasonable* to conclude that God infused the rational soul when it could function. One of the incongruous consequences of arguing for its infusion *earlier* is that the separated soul of one who dies before being sensitive will be a *tabula rasa*, a blank slate with no content. He thought it reasonable to suppose that God avoided such an incongruity by doing with us as God does with the rest of nature: causing forms to exist in a matter ultimately disposed for them. Nothing we have learned about human biology makes this argument in the least bit *untenable*. It only shows us that the biological blueprint for all of a person's *bodily* characteristics is present at conception, not that the *defining* intellectual soul is then present.

What these considerations should alert us to is that the dispute regarding this period of our development will turn on who has the burden of proof. For, while it certainly is possible that the intellectual soul is not infused until we are sensitive, it is also *possible* that it is infused even from

56. The *only* possible difference is that a cesarean section would kill the mother: a likelihood for all practical purposes non-existent and an exception the law could recognize, as a necessary price to end the outrage of not according the child the legal standing to which it is obviously entitled.

conception. In that case, each of our human powers would become *active* at the proper time, but they would *exist* prior to becoming active, rooted in the one *properly* human soul. No Catholic is prepared to tell the Almighty when He *must* create the rational human soul! And a materialist has even less reason to claim that what constitutes our humanity is *not present* in our genetic make-up from conception. Given that the matter is uncertain, then, the key issue will lie in the burden of proof: must a "pro-lifer" show it likely must be present or a "pro-choicer" show it likely is not?

The Catholic Church, with its deep respect for the image and likeness of God, has always *rightly argued* that human life from conception to natural death should be respected and protected[57] (and thus it is ready to argue that the one who would kill *cannot meet the needed burden of proof*). Yet I think Maritain is prescient here too, in stressing the respect due *even* a *virtual* human being. This accords not only with what the Church has held in the past (when most theologians favored delayed ensoulment), but it also points to the argument most likely to move many today. All know that, by waiting but a few short months, the mother and father will be cradling in their arms their daughter or son, and all know that this child is unique and unrepeatable. How could one not want to nourish the growing unborn child-to-be so that its unique and magnificent promise comes to fruition? It seems to me this is likely the best way to *move* our democratic society to protect all of its unborn.[58]

Personally, I hope that Thomas's reasonable opinion is the true one and that our society has not systematically murdered the unborn who are not yet sensitive and separated their immortal souls from their mortal bodies.

57. And thus, Pope John Paul II, in *Evangelium Vitae* (1995), after quoting *Donum Vitae*, reaffirms that "the Magisterium *has not expressly committed itself*" to "scientific debates . . . and philosophical affirmations" [regarding the time of ensoulment], but nevertheless rightly rejects all abortion from conception on, since "the mere *probablility* that a human person is involved [from conception on] would suffice to justify an absolutely clear prohibition of any intervention aimed at killing a human embryo" (no. 60, para. 2); emphasis added.

58. The reason democratic society has difficulty seeing its need to protect the unborn at all stages of their development derives from the fact that, in the first instance, the burden of proof lies with the government when it seeks to restrict personal freedom. If that burden is to shift, grounds must be provided. Those grounds are forthcoming when one is speaking of the unborn when sensitive or an animal; at that point, one naturally wants to know why it cannot be a rational animal: that is, why the *radical* power of reason is *not* present in it. However, prior to sensation, the burden once again shifts back to the government limiting freedom. While a person might concede that the *moral* burden of proof *can be* met, he might still dispute that the *legal* one is. The best way to get the *law* to see that it *is* met will be to get the *people* to feel that the one "*on the way*" is sufficiently "*one of our own*" that it would be wrong to deprive it of legal protection.

Nevertheless, our society *is* presently *willing to kill* a human being; or, at a minimum, it is willing to countenance involuntary manslaughter.[59] *This must stop.*

It is very hard, in the anguish generated by the present bloodbath we are witnessing, not to want to make "slam dunk" arguments that decisively show that a human being *formally* is present from conception. This, however, is to attempt what is not possible, and it will only end by driving people to the opposing position. Maritain's remarks call us away from such a precipitous course. He remains, on this point as on many another, someone to whom we can repair for wise counsel.

I deliberately chose to treat of Maritain's views on contraception and abortion because I thought it likely that these might rub even some of the assembled Maritainistas here the wrong way. As much as we may all wish to avoid the "Sheep of Panurge" and the "Ruminators of the Holy Alliance," we each have our own tendencies, towards one side or another, on the difficult issues that confront us today. To "hold to the center" is a precarious business, and one that may well escape us. Yet, if his remarks on one or another of these matters manage to rub even some of *us* the wrong way, I take this to be a likely sign of just how deeply anchored Maritain was in his faith. He mostly, and beautifully, manages to "stay the course"—his "touch" is sure.

IV. Conclusion: The Strong Arm of a Bewailer

I have just spoken of Maritain's faith and it is with this that I wish to conclude my thoughts today. Lest I be accused of being unduly "hagiographic" in my final remarks, I will begin by noting the way my own appropriation of Aquinas differed somewhat from his.

Maritain became a Catholic at the time of the ascendancy of Aquinas, following Leo XIII's call to revive his philosophy. At issue was not *that* Catholics should seek to follow the Angel of the Schools but *how* they should best

59. Involuntary manslaughter is the unintentional killing of another, usually through recklessness or "criminal negligence," a standard higher than that used in civil law. Many who abort do not believe they are killing a human being and do not intend to do so. Nevertheless, societies that permit abortion are willing for their citizens to kill what they cannot deny *could* be another human being, one with DNA from its human parents that all recognize possesses unique individual characteristics. These societies countenance a *recklessness* in relation to their unborn, a *negligence* they do not permit in relation to their other members.

do so. Disputes raged between "pure" or "rigorous" Thomists and Suarezians, between Dominican advocates of the 24 Theses and Jesuits desirous of a more ample and freer approach to appropriating his thought. Thinkers could be sharply divided over whether they were proponents of a "Neo-Scholastic" or "Existential" brand of Thomism, whether they were "realist" or "transcendental" Thomists, whether they favored the markedly Aristotelian stripe of "River Forest" or "Laval" Thomism, or whether instead they were perhaps attracted to a "Lublin" Thomism more open to contemporary phenomenology. Disputes could become heated, even bitter. By contrast, I came upon Aquinas as a non-Catholic in a non-Catholic college, and I pursued graduate studies on him when Catholics were doing anything *but* study him, fleeing as they did any tradition they associated with a "pre-Vatican II mentality." In such a climate, the degree of animosity between Thomists was bound to seem to me to be a bit recherché and the issue of whose Thomism was the "true" one somewhat "academic." Clearly, by comparison to what was then being proffered me, all of the schools in question were more united than divided!

Thus, I was happy to learn from fine Thomists wherever I found them: whether from a Jew like Adler or an Anglican like Mascall, whether from Maritain and Simon or from Gilson or Pieper, from an Ashley, Clarke, or Wippel.[60] Aquinas is too great a mountain, too titanic a philosophical genius, not ever to have fine thinkers for disciples, and they are likely to come to him in various ways (as one can see just by looking at how this occurred for laymen such as Maritain and Gilson, Simon and Pieper). It seemed obvious to me that Aquinas was a realist in the tradition of all Neo-Platonic Aristotelians. It also seemed obvious to me that, as all doctors of his age, Aquinas was an Augustinian theologian, albeit one who—having access to all of Aristotle, as Augustine did not—could see that Aristotle stood on the huge shoulders of *his* teacher to clarify and improve his thinking on a number of crucial points. Finally, it seemed obvious to me that the Dominican commentators had a greater "filial" devotion to his thought than Jesu-

60. I do not mean here to exclude what can be learned from a so-called "transcendental" Thomist such as Lonergan, or a Lublin Thomist such as Wotyła, nor even from those of a "more Augustinian bent" such as a von Hildebrand or a Marcel. (Obviously, I myself am inclined towards "Thomistic realists.") For the amplitude of vision proper to one of Catholic *faith* (which is wider than any philosophy), see Christopher Dawson's assessment of the Catholic intellectual revival in his remarkably informed General Introduction to Maritain's *Religion and Culture*, translated by J. F. Scanlan (London: Sheed and Ward, 1931), vii–xxvii.

its did, but that this could be a double-edged sword: commentators who are closer to a thinker are just those whose differences from him may be hardest to perceive and whose mistaken developments may be hardest to correct. Getting Thomas himself right, and the reward for doing so, mostly was enough for me![61] Given these general dispositions, however, I was ever ready to learn from Thomists of various stripes. Thus, I wanted to follow Maritain in advocating a living, contemporary Thomism, but I was alert (à la Gilson) to keeping key positions anchored in Thomas himself, and even (à la Pieper) to recognizing that some of these positions ultimately stood on the broad shoulders of Plato.[62]

The point of all of the above is just to say that, if I found one fault in Jacques it was that he took himself a little too seriously. He has been accused of many things, but never, I believe, of having a robust sense of humor! (I must confess my own partiality for the "hillybilly Thomism" of Flannery O'Connor!) Especially in his early years, he was a bit too ready—in a way I found unnecessarily narrow—to insist on a certain line of "Thomistic orthodoxy." A number of French Catholic thinkers found this "streak" in him somewhat hard to take.[63] I understood their difficulty.

61. By the time I had completed my doctorate, my view of Aquinas was at one with Marín-Sola's: "the habitual reading of the works of Saint Thomas has led us to form such a concept of the truly amazing amplitude, profundity, and exactitude of the Holy Doctor" that he was ready to follow his clear teaching on any philosophical or theological point. See Francisco Marín-Sola, O.P., *Do Not Resist the Spirit's Call* (Washington, D.C.: The Catholic University of America Press, 2013), 6. I would qualify this on only three matters. First, Aquinas hardly has an aesthetic, only a few sound principles. Second, the application of his political principles supposed the relation of Church and State then current, and no contemporary Catholic could possibly apply them just as he had. Third, his cosmology is outdated and his philosophy of nature needs to be harmonized with the new findings of empirical science. It was just in these three areas that Maritain was most helpful to me (in works such as *Art and Scholasticism, Integral Humanism,* and *The Degrees of Knowledge*). When it came, however, to basic philosophical principles, I rarely found anything to equal Aquinas's own words and arguments.

62. From my very first paper to an AMA conference, I also have been willing to disagree with Jacques. Thus, in that first paper—"Maritain's Notion of Christian Politics" (given in 1986, just before we began our publication series and never published)—I argued against his distinction of practical philosophy "adequately considered"; and I also disagreed later with his views on the relation between our natural desire to see God and God's grace: see "Maritain On The Natural Desire To See God: Reflections Appreciative and Critical," in *Distinctions of Being*, 128–44.

63. Marcel describes Meudon as an "ultra-Catholic milieu" *(Awakenings*, 137). Henri Cardinal de Lubac, who clearly preferred Gilson to Maritain, after quoting Gilson to the effect that no one could resist Maritain's presence, somewhat ruefully comments "except he did not favor all philosophies with his presence": *Letters of Étienne Gilson to Henri de Lubac, Annotated by Father De Lubac*, translated by Mary Emily Hamilton (San Francisco: Ignatius, 1988). Fr. Louis Bouyer, C.O., whom I had the great good fortune to come to know personally, told me he felt Maritain

Nevertheless, even here I find myself wanting to come to his defense. I, too, am a convert. I, too, know what it is like to have oneself "turned inside out like a glove."[64] I, too, have "come in from the cold." The Church has always had Jews and Gentiles, "cradle Catholics" and converts. I have observed that the first have an instinctive "feel" that, no matter how black their sins, a place will always be made for them at their mother's good table. Converts bring something else to that table: an awareness of just how cold it can be outside the warm hearth of the Church, how desperate our heart can become, and how easily—absent our Good Shepherd—the Prince of this world will eat us for his lunch. We are aware of how precious is the gift of the faith we have been given and how much it is worth defending. We also know how skeptical are those who remain in the cold and how they will not accept false coin: how ready they will be to submit any philosophical argument to rigorous examination and to doubt the credibility of the Church.[65] We fail to appreciate Jacques unless we realize how much, coming in from the cold, he then honored and loved the Church.[66]

I remain attracted to an idea that John Hittinger was beginning to work out at our meeting in Providence: the "Trinitarian" dimension of Maritain's spirituality.[67] Unquestionably, his *mind* was shaped by *Dominican* Thomists, chiefly Frs. Dehau and Clérissac. But his *heart* was nourished first and *only* on the saints and mystics, whose lives he devoured in his formative years. His favored contemplatives were the Spanish *Carmelites* John of the Cross and Teresa of Avila, their radical love summed up in her three words

---

arrogated too much importance to his own person. Bernanos castigated him at one point for the same, for the "mantle of authority" he seemed to be assuming in defending Rome's condemnation of L'Action Française. Marcel regretted following his request not to publish a critical review of *The Degrees of Knowledge* (even while acknowledging his own failure at working as hard as he should have to understand scholastic philosophy: see *Awakenings*, 127).

64. See Jacques Maritain, *Art and Faith* (New York: Philosophical Library, 1948), 73.

65. As I have argued before, I think Jacques was as much a lay apologist as he was a philosopher. See my "To Philosophize *For* the Faith: Jacques Maritain's Intellectual Vocation," in *The Vocation of the Catholic Philosopher*, edited by John P. Hittinger (Washington, D.C.: American Maritain Association, distributed by The Catholic University of America Press, 2010), 110–31. In any case, no other layman in the history of the Church has ever authored for her an official creed! For the way his authorship of Paul VI's *Credo of the People of God* came about, see George Cottier, O.P.'s explanation of this in Gianni Valiente's interview of him for *30 Giorni* (2008), no. 4.

66. Here is Raïssa's testimony: "Jacques has not feared her [the Church], he has loved her and given himself to her with complete trust." Raïssa Maritain, *Adventures in Grace* (New York: Longman, Green, and Co, 1945), 215.

67. His paper was "La Salette, Solesmes, and the Root of Maritain's Spirituality" and was given on March 1, 2014.

"Solo Dios basta!" Finally, his *soul* was that of a *Benedictine* oblate. His daily life was centered on the liturgy, his own home favored with the reserved host. His soul was formed early through the *lectio divina* daily practiced with Raïssa and Vera. To understand Jacques, we must appreciate the way his spirit was formed in the first years following his conversion, before he had ever written a single word in defense of Thomism.

What I "hear," beneath and through his many words, is the "high voice" that his godfather heard: the cry that "Love is not loved!" His godfather was never far from his heart and he had learned from him—and both he and Raïssa were fond of quoting—the words the Lord spoke to Angela of Foligno: "it was not to laugh that I have loved you."[68] His God is the One who loved us unto death, the tears behind his own words those of a sinner with an inkling of the cost of his redemption. He had consecrated himself to Mary and had a fervent devotion to our Lady of La Salette: she who had revealed herself in heaven still weeping for her children. When he takes up the arm of his intellect, it is in defense of our Lord's love for us sinners. So I do not begrudge him some possible narrowness that sometimes may be there as this "athlete of faith" does battle.[69] If he repairs to the "technical" or "scholastic" positions of Aquinas, it is because he knows that the Church today stands in need of his precision and the brilliance of his mind and that philosophy (and also theology!) requires hard thought and exactitude. He fought not just for those *within* the Church, to protect them from the bitter acid of the world's skepticism, but for those *without*, who would settle for nothing less than sound argument and who would not be fobbed off with false coin. Like Thérèse of Lisieux, Jacques "chose all," his "fight" was for all whom Christ's blood had redeemed. It is his *love* of Christ our Savior that I ever sense, in and behind the distinctions of his arguments. What I find so much in his work is what I can only describe as his "nobility of soul." And it was above all because of that nobility of soul that I came to love Jacques Maritain.

68. Jacques quotes this line in "Quelque Pages sur Léon Bloy," in *God and the Permission of Evil*, and in *The Peasant of the Garonne*; Raïssa quotes it in *We Have Been Friends Together* and in *Raïssa's Journal*.

69. Not that I have failed to be sharply critical of him at times for this "narrowness"! For an example of this, see my "The 'Annex' to Maritain's 1914 Lectures on 'The Spirit of Modern Philosophy': The Role of Germany in Modern Philosophy," in *The Wisdom of Youth: Essays Inspired by the Early Work of Jacques and Raïssa Maritain*, edited by Travis Dumsday (Washington, D.C.: American Maritain Association, distributed by The Catholic University of America Press, 2016), 78–98, especially 88.

About the Authors

MICHAEL BREIDENBACH is Assistant Professor of History at Ave Maria University. His research concerns the history of political, religious, and legal thought, particularly concerning religious liberty and church-state relations. His articles have been published in the *William and Mary Quarterly* and *Perspectives on Political Science,* and he is co-editor of the forthcoming *Cambridge Companion to the First Amendment and Religious Liberty.* He has held fellowships at Princeton, Oxford, and Cambridge, where he received his Ph.D.

ROMANUS CESSARIO, O.P., is a fellow of the Pontifical Academy of Saint Thomas Aquinas and a professor of theology at St. John's Seminary in Brighton, Massachusetts. He is the author of numerous books, including *Christian Faith and the Theological Life* (1996), *A Short History of Thomism* (2005), *Introduction to Moral Theology* (2013), *Theology and Sanctity* (2014), and *Thomas and the Thomists: The Achievement of Thomas Aquinas and His Interpreters* (2017).

JOHN J. CONLEY, S.J., holds the Francis J. Knott Chair in Philosophy and Theology at Loyola University Maryland in Baltimore. His research interests focus on ethics, aesthetics, and early modern philosophy. Among his publications are *The Suspicion of Virtue: Women Philosophers in Neoclassical France* (Cornell University Press, 2002), *Jacqueline Pascal: A Rule for Children* (University of Chicago Press, 2003), *Adoration and Annihilation: The Convent Philosophy of Port-Royal* (University of Notre Dame Press, 2009), and *Angélique de Saint-Jean Arnauld d'Andilly: Writings of Resistance* (Toronto/Iter, 2015).

MARIO O. D'SOUZA, C.S.B., was a member of the Congregation of St. Basil. He held the Basilian Fathers Chair in Religion and Education, at the Faculty of Theology, the University of St. Michael's College, Toronto, where he served as Dean of Theology. His research interests included Catholic Education and the philosophy of education, concentrating on the thought of Jacques Maritain, Bernard Lonergan, and Josef Pieper. In 2016, he published *A Catholic Philosophy of Education: The Church and Two Philosophers*, with McGill-Queens University Press. He died on September 26, 2017.

TRAVIS DUMSDAY is an assistant professor at Concordia University of Edmonton, where he holds the Canada Research Chair in Theology and the Philosophy of Science. He has published in a number of areas, including analytic metaphysics, Scholastic philosophy of nature, criminal justice ethics, and Eastern Orthodox theology. His long-term life plan is to design a line of T-shirts containing the 24 Thomistic Theses (12 on the chest, 12 on the back) and retire a wealthy, wealthy man.

HEATHER M. ERB teaches the Great Books in the Ignatius-Angelicum Liberal Studies Program, is an Associate Professor of Philosophy at Our Lady Seat of Wisdom College, as well as teaching philosophy at Lock Haven University. Her publications focus on the nexus of metaphysics and mystical theology in Aquinas and his interpreters, as well as on issues in Catholicism and culture. Her recent book, *The Path of Spiritual Happiness*, examines the philosophy of happiness as developed by Aristotle, St. Thomas, and Josef Pieper, and as applied through Pope John Paul II's encyclicals.

LAWRENCE FEINGOLD is Associate Professor of Theology and Philosophy at Kenrick-Glennon Seminary in St. Louis. He is the author of *The Natural Desire to See God According to St. Thomas Aquinas and His Interpreters* (The Catholic University of America Press, 2010), *Faith Comes from What Is Heard: An Introduction to Fundamental Theology* (Emmaus Academic, 2016), and *The Eucharist: Mystery of Presence, Sacrifice, and Communion* (Emmaus Academic, 2018). His scholarly interests center on St. Thomas Aquinas and the Thomistic tradition, the relationship between nature and grace, Christology, fundamental theology, the sacraments, the Jewish roots of the Catholic faith, and the relationship between art and Christian faith.

MEGAN FURMAN is a Ph.D. student in Philosophy at the University of Dallas. A graduate of the University of Notre Dame (B.A. English), Oxford

University (M.St. English), and The Dominican School of Philosophy and Theology in Berkeley (M.A. Philosophy and M.A. Theology), Furman's work has focused on the philosophy of beauty, aesthetics, moral philosophy, and the philosophy of language. She has worked for ten years in international and foreign affairs authoring three books, editing three academic volumes, and contributing to three documentary films, including two for *National Geographic.*

MARIE I. GEORGE received her Ph.D. in philosophy from Laval University, and is currently Professor of Philosophy at St. John's University, New York. An Aristotelian-Thomist, her interests lie primarily in the areas of natural philosophy and philosophy of science. She has received several awards from the John Templeton foundation for her work in science and religion, and in 2007 was co-recipient of a grant from the Center for Theology and the Natural Sciences (CTNS) for an interdisciplinary project entitled, "The Evolution of Sympathy and Morality." Professor George has authored over 60 peer-reviewed articles and two books: *Christianity and Extraterrestrials? A Catholic Perspective* (2005) and *Stewardship of Creation* (2009). She is currently working on Augustine and Aquinas's views on forgiveness, and also on a variety of questions concerning living things (self-motion, consciousness, empathy, evolution, etc.).

JAMES G. HANINK is a Los Angeles-based independent scholar. He is editor of *Aquinas and Maritain on Evil: Mystery and Metaphysics* (American Maritain Association, 2013). His research interests include metaphysics and social philosophy. Currently he serves as the President of the American Maritain Association. In addition, he is active in the American Solidarity Party.

GREGORY J. KERR is currently Associate Professor of Philosophy at DeSales University in Center Valley, Pennsylvania. He received his B.A. and M.A. in philosophy from Boston College and his Ph.D. from Fordham University, where he did his dissertation on *Maritain's Receptive Intuition and the Benefits of Art.* He is a former editor of the *Maritain Notebook,* the official newsletter of the American Maritain Association. He has published articles on Maritain's views on aesthetics, epistemology, ethics, love, and education in volumes in the AMA's series and elsewhere. He is currently finishing a volume that explores the very different and conflicting ways humans know. He is married to Cindy, and they have four sons and three grandchildren.

WILLIAM MCCORMICK, S.J., teaches at Saint Louis University in the departments of Political Science and Philosophy. He took his doctorate in government at the University of Texas at Austin under the direction of J. Budziszewski. He has published in the *Thomist*, the *History of Political Thought*, *European Journal of Political Theory* and *Perspectives on Political Science*, and is at present working on a book manuscript concerning Aquinas' *De Regno*.

MATTHEW K. MINERD, PH.D., is Professor of Philosophy and Moral Theology at the Byzantine Catholic Seminary in Pittsburgh, Pennsylvania. In addition to his scholarly articles, he is the translator of *The Sense of Mystery: Clarity and Obscurity in the Intellectual Life*, by Fr. Reginald Garrigou-Lagrange (Emmaus Academic, 2017), with a number of translations underway for publication in the near future..

MARK MOES completed an M.A. in philosophical theology at the Midwest Dominican House of Studies when it was located in Dubuque, Iowa, before it moved to Saint Louis. He received his doctorate in philosophy at the University of Notre Dame. He is currently Professor of Philosophy at Grand Valley State University in Michigan, specializing in Ancient Philosophy. He teaches the close reading of Plato, emphasizing the compositional structure and mimetic ironies of the dialogues. He is author of *Plato's Dialogue Form and the Care of the Soul* and articles on ancient philosophy and philosophy of medicine. He also teaches philosophy of religion courses, in which he contrasts the presuppositions of Thomistic-Aristotelian philosophical theology with those of the modern tradition of "philosophy of religion" since Hume. He is currently doing research on two connected projects: (1) a book on Plato's *Republic*, and (2) a book on the whole corpus of the published writings of Alasdair MacIntyre.

MICHAEL NOVAK, theologian, author, and former U.S. ambassador to the U.N. Human Rights Commission, held the George Frederick Jewett Chair in Religion and Public Policy at the American Enterprise Institute in Washington, D.C., for thirty years. He was the 1994 recipient of the Templeton Prize and wrote numerous influential books on economics, philosophy, and theology. His masterpiece, *The Spirit of Democratic Capitalism*, was published in 1982, and was subsequently republished underground in Poland in 1984, as well as in Czechoslovakia, Germany, China, Hungary,

Bangladesh, Korea, and many times in Latin America. For his work, he received many international awards. He died on February 17, 2017.

MICHAEL PAKALUK is Professor in the School of Philosophy and the Busch School of Business and Economics at The Catholic University of America. His main work as a researcher has been in ancient philosophy, as he has authored many papers and three books concerned with Aristotelian ethics; however, his interests span many areas of philosophy, including political philosophy, philosophy of psychology, and professional ethics. In 2011 he was appointed an Ordinarius of the Pontifical Academy of St. Thomas Aquinas.

ALICE RAMOS is Professor of Philosophy at St. John's University in Queens, New York. Her publications include a book titled *Dynamic Transcendentals: Truth, Goodness, and Beauty from a Thomistic Perspective* (The Catholic University of America Press, 2012), two edited books for the American Maritain Association: *Beauty, Art, and the Polis* (2000) and *Faith, Scholarship, and Culture in the 21st Century* (co-edited with Marie I. George, 2002), a book written in Spanish titled *Signum: De la semiótica universal a la metafísica del signo* (EUNSA, 1987), and over sixty articles in areas such as Thomistic metaphysics and ethics, aesthetics, and Christian anthropology. She is the recipient of grants for scholarly work both in the United States and in Europe. She is also a past president of the American Maritain Association (2002–2004) and has served several terms on the executive council of the American Catholic Philosophical Association.

WALTER SCHULTZ is Auxiliary Professor in the Faculty of Philosophy at the Dominican University College in Ottawa, Ontario, Canada, and he is currently President of the Canadian Jacques Maritain Association. He received his Ph.D. in Western Religious Thought from McMaster University, with his thesis entitled, *Jacques Maritain's Social Critique and His Personalism*. He has given courses in religious studies and philosophy in Canada and the United States, notably when he was with the departments of philosophy at King's College, University of Western Ontario, and the Franciscan University of Steubenville. For many years, he was a teacher and worked in Program Design for the Dufferin-Peel Roman Catholic Separate School Board, Mississauga, Ontario, developing and implementing throughout the board a senior level philosophy program based on the work of Jacques Maritain.

His publications are primarily concerned with education and the relevance of Maritain's thought for contemporary society and politics.

MICHAEL D. TORRE has been an associate professor of philosophy at the University of San Francisco for the last twenty-two years and recently completed a term as President of the American Maritain Association (2012–2016). He edited for it *Freedom in the Modern World: Jacques Maritain, Yves R. Simon, and Mortimer J. Adler*, (1989; second printing, 1990), which assembled the first collection of essays published on Yves R. Simon. As the General Editor of the AMA from 2009–2013, he oversaw the publication of eight of its volumes. He has published two books dealing with man's responsibility for sin: *God's Permission of Sin* (Fribourg University Press, 2009) and *Do Not Resist the Spirit's Call* (Catholic University of American Press, 2013). He has also published numerous articles in the AMA series of volumes, as well as further articles on Yves R. Simon.

NIKOLAJ ZUNIC is Associate Professor in the Department of Philosophy at St. Jerome's University in Waterloo, Ontario, Canada. His research and teaching focus on topics ranging from philosophical anthropology and ethics to phenomenology, metaphysics, and the philosophy of religion. However, of particular interest is the tradition of Christian personalism represented by figures such as Jacques Maritain, Gabriel Marcel, Max Scheler, and Saint John Paul II. He also teaches in the Human Sciences Program at St. Jerome's which introduces students to the core texts in Western civilization, such as Homer's *Odyssey*, St. Augustine's *Confessions*, and Dante's *Divine Comedy*. He lives in Kitchener, Ontario with his wife, Erin, and their six children.

Index

PUBLICATIONS OF THE AMERICAN MARITAIN ASSOCIATION

1. *Jacques Maritain: The Man and His Metaphysics*
Edited by John F. X. Knasas, 1988
ISBN 978-0-268-01205-2, (out of print)
Distributed by the University of Notre Dame Press

2. *Freedom in the Modern World: Jacques Maritain, Yves R. Simon, Mortimer J. Adler*
Edited by Michael D. Torre, 1989, Second Printing, 1990
ISBN 978-0-268-00978-6
Distributed by the University of Notre Dame Press

3. *From Twilight to Dawn: The Cultural Vision of Jacques Maritain*
Edited by Peter A. Redpath, 1990
ISBN 978-0-268-00979-3
Distributed by the University of Notre Dame Press

4. *The Future of Thomism*
Edited by Deal W. Hudson and Dennis Wm. Moran, 1992
ISBN 978-0-268-00986-1
Distributed by the University of Notre Dame Press

5. *Jacques Maritain and the Jews*
Edited by Robert Royal, 1994
ISBN 978-0-268-01193-2
Distributed by the University of Notre Dame Press

6. *Freedom, Virtue, and the Common Good*

Edited by Curtis L. Hancock and Anthony O. Simon, 1995

ISBN 978-0-268-00991-0

Distributed by the University of Notre Dame Press

7. *Postmodernism and Christian Philosophy*

Edited by Roman T. Ciapolo, 1997

ISBN 978-0-8132-0881-7

Distributed by The Catholic University of America Press

8. *The Common Things: Essays on Thomism and Education*

Edited by Daniel McInerny, 1999

ISBN 978-0-9669226-0-8

Distributed by The Catholic University of America Press

The Failure of Modernism:
9. *The Cartesian Legacy and Contemporary Pluralism*

Edited by Brendan Sweetman, 1999

ISBN 978-0-9669226-1-5

Distributed by The Catholic University of America Press

10. *Beauty, Art, and the Polis*

Edited by Alice Ramos, 2000

ISBN 978-0-9669226-2-2

Distributed by The Catholic University of America Press

11. *Reassessing the Liberal State: Reading Maritain's Man and the State*

Edited by Timothy Fuller and John P. Hittinger, 2001

ISBN 978-0-9669226-3-9

Distributed by The Catholic University of America Press

12. *Faith, Scholarship, and Culture in the 21st Century*

Edited by Alice Ramos and Marie I. George, 2002

ISBN 978-0-9669226-5-3

Distributed by The Catholic University of America Press

13. *Jacques Maritain and the Many Ways of Knowing*

Edited by Douglas A. Ollivant, 2002

ISBN 978-0-9669226-4-6

Distributed by The Catholic University of America Press

14. *Truth Matters: Essays in Honor of Jacques Maritain*
Edited by John G. Trapani, Jr., 2004
ISBN 978-0-9669226-6-0
Distributed by The Catholic University of America Press

15. *The Human Person and a Culture of Freedom*
Edited by Peter A. Pagan Aguiar and Terese Auer, OP, 2009
ISBN 978-0-9669226-7-7
Distributed by The Catholic University of America Press

16. *Maritain and America*
Edited by Christopher M. Cullen, SJ and Joseph Allan Clair, 2009
ISBN 978-0-9669226-8-4
Distributed by The Catholic University of America Press

17. *The Renewal of Civilization: Essays in Honor of Jacques Maritain*
Edited by Gavin T. Colvert, 2010
ISBN 978-0-9669226-9-1
Distributed by The Catholic University of America Press

18. *The Vocation of the Catholic Philosopher: From Maritain to John Paul II*
Edited by John P. Hittinger, 2010
ISBN 978-0-9827119-0-3
Distributed by The Catholic University of America Press

19. *Reading the Cosmos: Nature, Science, and Wisdom*
Edited by Giuseppe Butera, 2011
ISBN 978-0-9827119-1-0
Distributed by The Catholic University of America Press

20. *Distinctions of Being: Philosophical Approaches to Reality*
Edited by Nikolaj Zunic, 2013
ISBN 978-0-9827119-2-7
Distributed by The Catholic University of America Press

21. *Love and Friendship: Maritain and the Tradition*
Edited by Montague Brown, 2013
ISBN 978-0-9827119-3-4
Distributed by The Catholic University of America Press

22. *Aquinas and Maritain on Evil: Mystery and Metaphysics*
Edited by James G. Hanink, 2013
ISBN 978-0-9827119-4-1
Distributed by The Catholic University of America Press

23. *Human Nature, Contemplation, and the Political Order: Essays Inspired by Jacques Maritain's* Scholasticism and Politics
Edited by Peter Karl Koritansky, 2014
ISBN 978-0-9827119-5-8
Distributed by The Catholic University of America Press

24. *Redeeming Philosophy: From Metaphysics to Aesthetics*
Edited by John J. Conley, SJ, 2014
ISBN 978-0-9827119-6-5
Distributed by The Catholic University of America Press

25. *A Piercing Light: Beauty, Faith, and Human Transcendence*
Edited by James M. Jacobs, 2015
ISBN 978-0-9827-1197-2
Distributed by The Catholic University of America Press

26. *The Wisdom of Youth: Essays Inspired by the Early Work of Jacques and Raïssa Maritain*
Edited by Travis Dumsday, 2016
ISBN 978-0-9827119-8-9
Distributed by The Catholic University of America Press

27. *Engaging the Times: The Witness of Thomism*
Edited by Joshua Schulz, 2017
ISBN 978-0-9827119-9-6
Distributed by The Catholic University of America Press

The Things that Matter: Essays Inspired by the Later Work of Jacques Maritain
was designed in Arno and composed by Kachergis Book Design of Pittsboro,
North Carolina. It was printed on 60-pound Nature's Natural and
bound by Thomson-Shore of Dexter, Michigan.